Interfacing Microcomputers to the Real World

Interfacing Microcomputers to the Real World

Murray Sargent III and **Richard L. Shoemaker**

The University of Arizona

1981

Addison-Wesley Publishing Company
Advanced Book Program/World Science Division
Reading, Massachusetts

London • Amsterdam • Don Mills, Ontario • Sydney • Tokyo

This book was prepared in camera-ready form by one of the authors (Murray) on a Scroll Systems daisy-wheel printer, which consists of a Diablo HyType II printer equipped with the Scroll Systems Retroscroller text-output processor board. The authors wrote the text on their home computers, which are similar to computers discussed in this book. Your corrections and suggestions are welcome: please send them to the authors at the Optical Sciences Center, The University of Arizona, Tucson, AZ 85721.

First printing, 1981
Second printing, February 1982

Library of Congress Cataloging in Publication Data

Sargent, Murray
 Interfacing microcomputers to the real world

 Bibliography: p.
 Includes index.
 1. Microcomputers. 2. Computer interfaces.
I. Shoemaker, Richard L. II. Title.
QA76.5.S2177   001.64'04   81-705
ISBN 0-201-06879-6   AACR2

001.6404
S245i

Manufactured in the United States of America

ABCDEFGHIJ–AL–898765432

210253

To the next generation of computer addicts:

Nicole and Christine

David, Michael, and Jeffrey

Contents

Preface

Low-cost microcomputers can provide fast, accurate monitoring and control of virtually any device in your home, office, or laboratory. This book introduces you to microcomputers, and teaches you how to design and build interfaces between microcomputers and a wide variety of real-world devices. Since we believe that interfacing cannot be taught simply by reading about general principles, we use a specific microprocessor, the Zilog Z80, to illustrate the concepts, and provide a set of "hands-on" exercises to parallel the text. Although a number of today's microprocessors would be suitable for these purposes, we feel the Z80 represents the best combination of low cost, power and popularity. The Z80 can run almost all Intel 8080/8085 machine code unchanged and is itself the heart of more computers, big or little, than any other central processing unit, in large part due to the Radio Shack TRS-80 and the many S-100 bus computers. The exercises can be carried out using any of these computers, or with an inexpensive single-board computer, the SD Systems Z80 Starter System.

The book begins by discussing the important elementary building blocks of microelectronics, namely the diode, the transistor, and various useful TTL (Transistor-Transistor Logic) integrated circuits. The second chapter describes machine and assembly languages and explains how the Z80 is programmed to "think." A tiny operating system is also presented and explained.

The third chapter describes the Z80's Forty Pins, which give it "tendons and nerves," and then shows how to connect these pins up to input/output ports and to memory. The concept of the interrupt is discussed from both hardware and software points of view, and is used to make a real-time clock and an interrupt-driven keyboard that allows typed characters to be saved in a buffer, regardless of what the computer might otherwise be doing.

Direct-Memory-Access methods are described for use in high-speed input/output of data.

Chapter 4 shows how to connect the input/output ports to all kinds of real-world devices that provide the Z80 with muscle, sight, hearing, and a voice. These devices include lights, switches, relays, thermostats, photo-resistors, stepper motors, keyboards, solenoids, speakers, analog-to-digital and digital-to-analog subsystems. Experimental techniques are described that allow the computer to pull signals out of what appears to be pure noise. Generation of waveforms including music is explained. Vector, raster, and LED digital displays are described and illustrated.

Chapter 5 shows how to connect a microcomputer to computer terminals and to other computers using serial input/output. The very widely used RS232 and current-loop conventions are defined, and methods to talk to and transfer files to and from any interactive remote computer are described in detail. This kind of connection allows one to use a microcomputer to control an experiment and log the data, and to use a big computer for subsequent extensive data processing. The chapter concludes with the exotic serial communication media of fiber optics, power-line modulation, and radio frequency carriers. The latter two give you and your computer remote control of whatever turns you on, or whatever you want to turn on!

Chapter 6 progresses from memory circuits - RAM and EPROM, to secondary storage, namely disks, to computer controllers, and finally to larger systems based on standard computer busses. Chapter 7 describes the system software you need to have to program microcomputers efficiently. This software includes elegant screen editors, macroassemblers, debuggers, linkers, interpreters, compilers, and other marvelous programs people have dreamt up to simplify their lives and ours. The chapter concludes with a discussion of computer hierarchies, which shows how microcomputers fit into the overall scheme of digital computing.

Chapter 8 presents the hands-on exercises, which can translate the understanding you gain in reading the earlier chapters into practice. Having successfully carried out these exercises, you can design your own interfaces, fix other people's, and build computers directly using various IC's. We urge those of you who gain this ability to use it for constructive purposes only.

The appendices present ASCII, popular computer busses, and a number of useful software packages. These packages include TRSCOM, a computer-computer communications program; the DEMON, a small, but powerful DEbug MONitor; a tiny operating system; some useful keyboard routines; and a summary of the Z80 instructions.

The book should be valuable both to people who plan to use microcomputers and to people who want to have a fundamental feel for how computers work. It can be read on a self-study basis, or used as a textbook in a college or graduate-level course. More than enough material is included for a one-semester course. It is very helpful to have had either some prior programming experience, or some familiarity with electronic circuits. Three out of the fourteen hands-on exercises require an oscilloscope, and this device can be very helpful for the other exercises as well if something goes wrong. This book grew out of a course on microcomputer interfacing given at the University of Arizona, and draws on the authors' extensive experience in computerizing laboratory experiments, homes, and various devices. The book was written on our personal microcomputers and typeset by a Diablo daisy-wheel printer equipped with the Scroll Systems Retroscroller text-for-matting board, codesigned by one of us (Murray).

It's a pleasure to acknowlege help from many sources, including our draftsperson Elaine Hunter, Zilog and Intel Corporations for prototypes of numerous drawings and the inspiration of their inventions, and our home computers, without which (whom?) this book couldn't have been written. We'd also like to thank our students, who served as guinea pigs for the labo-ratory exercises, John Murray, Allen Shoemaker, Mike Simmons, Lee McDonald, Bob Murray, Jim Jonas, Chris Koliopoulos, Willis Lamb, George Seeley and Jack Gaskill. Finally, we thank our wives and children for their encouragement and patience in dealing with us incurable computerholics.

Murray Sargent III
Richard L. Shoemaker

So if into this book you should dip,
You will chance being caught in the grip
Of a practical craze
That does more than amaze -
It solves problems with elegant zip!

-Stanley Bashkin

Trademarks mentioned in this book are associated with their companies as follows: (see pp. 184-186 for company addresses)

Apple - Apple Computer
CAT-100 - Digital Graphic Systems
CP/M and MP/M - Digital Research
DEC-10 - Digital Equipment Corporation
Diablo, HyType - Diablo Systems
Eclipse - Data General Corporation
Electric Pencil - Michael Shrayer Software
ExpandoRAM, SBC-100, Versafloppy, Z80 Starter System - SD Systems
Intel, Multibus - Intel Corporation
KIM I, Pet - Commodore Business Machines
Magic Wand - Small Business Application
MATE - AOX Associates
Paper Tiger - Integral Data Systems
Qume - Qume Corporation
Retroscroller - Scroll Systems
Spinwriter - NEC Information Systems
SYM I - Synertek Systems Corporation
Tristate - National Semiconductor Corporation
TRS-80, TRSDOS - Tandy Corp.
UNIX - Bell Telephone Laboratories
WordStar - MicroPro International Corporation
Z80 and Zilog - Zilog

Chapter One

Introduction to Digital Logic

Evil is of such a fearful mien
That to be hated, needs but to be seen.
But seen too oft, familiar with her face,
We first endure, then pity, and finally embrace.*

-Pope, Essay on Man

*Microelectronics?

Before you begin reading this book, we are required by the Surgeon General to inform you that microelectronics may be dangerous to your mental stability, personal relationships, career, etc. The excitement, fascination, and quest for power that this pinacle of human creation can engender in the unwary or susceptible often proves to be close to uncontrollable. The resulting disease is called computeritis or computerholism and is currently only partly understood. The only complete cure seems to be to remove the addict from computers altogether. Unlike companion afflictions such as heroin addiction and alcoholism, nothing physiological is involved: it's purely mental, so you have nothing to blame but yourself. If, in spite of this warning, you still wish to continue, read on!

1-1. The Diode

What's a diode? Well it's one of the neatest inventions to come along and a beautiful example of effects in semiconductor physics. Most things in microelectronics are made up of diodes, if you include the back to back diode known as the transistor. This book treats it like everything else, namely as a black (or here maybe translucent) box with certain properties. The innards are covered elsewhere. A diode essentially passes current only in one direction (see Fig. 1-1). Its current-voltage characteristic is pic-

Murray Sargent III and Richard L. Shoemaker, Interfacing Microcomputers to the Real World, ISBN 0-201-06879-6

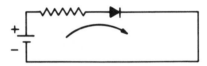

Fig. 1-1. Diode passes current from + to -. Current limiting resistor is needed.

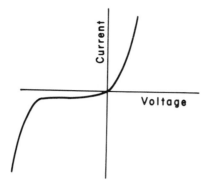

Fig. 1-2. Large current can flow when voltage difference across diode is positive, or when it is negative and exceeds the "breakdown voltage (check voltage rating).

tured in Fig. 1-2, where you see it's not at all linear in contrast to Ohm's law. In fact it's best to think of the forward-biased diode as being a conductor with a small voltage drop across it of about .7 volts. If you connect the diode between the terminals of a battery in the direction that current flows, you're likely to blow the thing apart. It needs the current limitation of a series resistor (Fig. 1-1). The typical diodes used for logic and display can handle 10-20 milliamperes (ma) easily, so for a 5-volt supply, a series 330 ohm series resistor is just fine [Ohm's law gives V/R=(5-.7)/330=13ma]. As a simple experiment, connect up a Light Emitting Diode (LED) in series with a 330 ohm resistor to a 5-volt supply and see how light is emitted for one orientation of the diode, and not emitted for the other. This little circuit makes a convenient probe for logic circuits. In addition to the LEDs, which come in red, yellow, amber, and green, there are logic diodes such as the 1N4148 or its equivalent the 1N914. (Reminds one of a Porsche!) Also, much heftier diodes are used in making the DC power supplies needed for computers and other electronic equipment.

1-2. TTL Gates - AND, NAND, OR, NOR, XOR

On to TTL (Transistor-Transistor Logic). Before going further, we note that Don Lancaster's TTL Cookbook is an excellent place to read about this subject (see especially Chaps. 1 and 2). If you're familiar with a high-level programming language's IF statement, you'll find it easy to get on board with TTL. This logic family (and others too) sticks into hardware what you often do in programming. TTL uses a 5-volt power supply regulated to within 5% (+ or - .25 volts). The gates (something with inputs and outputs that performs a logic function) and other functions are housed in DIP's (Dual Inline Package's) having 14, 16, 18, 20, 22, or 24 pins arranged in two parallel rows. The ground pin is usually the last in the first row (e.g., pin 7 of a 14 pin dip), and the 5-volt power pin is the highest numbered pin (pin 14 on the 14 pin dip). This is not always the case (e.g., the 7490), so beware! The inputs and outputs of most TTL are either high (about 3 - 5-volts) or low (0 - .7 volts), abbreviated by H and L respectively. The function of a TTL integrated circuit is typically given by a table called a truth table that enumerates what outputs (H's or L's) result for given inputs (H's or L's).

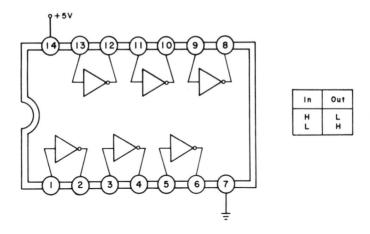

Fig. 1-3. 7404 TTL Hex inverter and function table.

The simplest gate is the inverter, which comes six to a package as pictured in Fig. 1-3. It converts an H into an L and an L into an H, as seen in the trivial truth table. The AND gate (four/package in a 7408) and its truth table are pictured in Fig. 1-4. If both inputs are H, its output is H. If either input or both are L, the output is L. The NAND gate (4 in a 7400) in Fig. 1-5 simply inverts the output of an AND gate; that is, if both inputs are H, the output is L, while if either or both inputs are L, the output is H.

The OR gate (4 in a 7432) is pictured in Fig. 1-6. If either input is H, its output is H, while if both inputs are L its output is L. Note that switch-

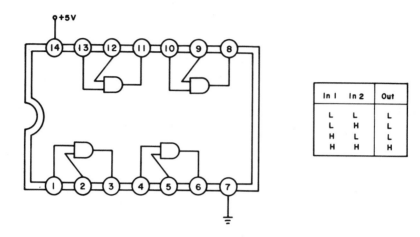

In 1	In 2	Out
L	L	L
L	H	L
H	L	L
H	H	H

Fig. 1-4. 7408 Quad 2-input AND gate with function table.

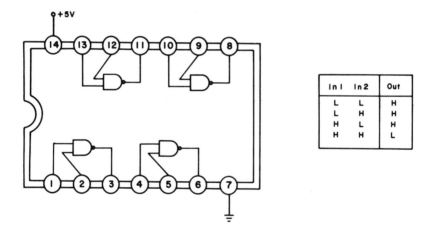

In 1	In 2	Out
L	L	H
L	H	H
H	L	H
H	H	L

Fig. 1-5. 7400 Quad 2-input NAND gate with function table.

ing H and L in the above descriptions exchanges the AND and the OR. Said another way, a positive logic AND is a negative logic OR. This fact is very useful in reducing the number of IC's required in a design, and typically the logic flow switches back and forth between negative and positive logic. This makes understanding the circuit a bit harder, but the result is more compact and cheaper.

The OR has a popular NOR version, the 7402 shown in Fig. 1-7. The final elementary logic gate is the XOR (7486). Its output is H if the inputs are different and L if they're the same. Note that the NAND, NOR, and

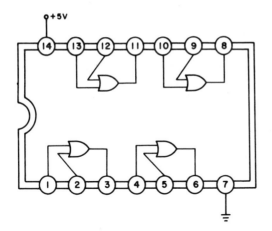

In I	In 2	Out
L	L	L
L	H	H
H	L	H
H	H	H

Fig. 1-6. 7432 Quad 2-input OR gate with function table.

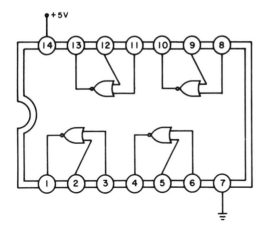

In I	In 2	Out
L	L	H
L	H	L
H	L	L
H	H	L

Fig. 1-7. 7402 Quad 2-input NOR gate with function table.

XOR gates can be used as inverters, e.g., by tying the NAND/NOR inputs together, which often allows one to reduce the IC count, as extra gates may be used in place of adding another 7404. A few extra gates left over in a design isn't all that bad, since they may be handy if custom modifications become called for. Finally Fig. 1-8 shows a WAS gate!

1-3. The Transistor as a Switch

To get a better understanding of how to hook up TTL, you need to know something about the famous building block, the transistor. This consists of a

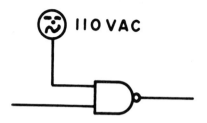

Fig. 1-8. WAS gate! Look out for faulty power supplies.

pair of diodes that share one end. More precisely, a diode has two parts, an N and a P part. When you connect + to the P and - to the N, current flows. A transistor is made up of three pieces, which can be N, P, and N; or P, N, and P. The first combination is called an NPN transistor and the second a

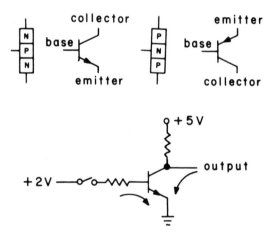

Fig. 1-9. Diagrams of NPN and PNP transistors. Closing switch causes current to flow from base to emitter pulling output low. Acts like a switch connecting output to ground.

PNP (see Fig. 1-9). Common examples are the 2N3904 and 2N3096, respectively. The incredible thing about transistors is that if you get a small amount of current to flow from the P of an NPN to the second N, a large amount of current can flow from the first to the second N. For small base-emitter (P to N) currents, the amount of current flowing from N to N is linearly proportional to the base-emitter current. But at larger values, the N to N current becomes limited by the resistance of the N-N circuit or by blowing the transistor up! In TTL logic circuits, many transistors are used and they operate in this current-limited fashion, which is known as satura-tion. It's really very simple: turn on some current from P to N and you turn on the N to N connection. The point is that a little current controls a lot. In short, for digital applications, the transistor is simply a current-con-trolled switch. The PNP transistor works in a similar way to the NPN in that a bit of current from the first P to the N turns on the P to P connection. There are basic principles of semiconductor physics behind all of this, but for our purposes, all you have to know about transistors is this switching behavior.

1-4. TTL Input/Output Characteristics

In Sec. 1-2, we considered the voltages corresponding to the high (H) and low (L) TTL states. In addition, one needs to know what currents are

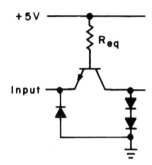

Fig. 1-10. Typical TTL input circuit. R_{eq} ranges from 1 to 4KΩ.

involved both for inputs and outputs. To convince a TTL input (Fig. 1-10) that it's L, you have to be able to sink 1.6 ma, that is, 1.6 ma may flow into you (you're another gate, of course!). So if you try to convince too many gates that you're low, you'll have to sink more than you can swallow. The spec is that a low TTL output can sink 10 TTL inputs. The highs are much less demanding. In fact an unterminated TTL input almost always acts like a high, but don't count on it. A high TTL output will attempt to source current, so if you connect H and L outputs, you'll have a fight. Typically a brief output short won't hurt anything, but your circuit won't do what you want it to do. For driving LED's, you should always sink current with standard TTL (point diode towards TTL output pin) and not source it (point diode away from pin). Summarizing, standard TTL is current sinking logic.

So what's nonstandard? Lots. In particular, many IC's in the 7400 series take higher input or output voltages for special purpose applications, and certain so-called bus driver IC's (which can drive signals over several feet of wire) can source as well as sink current. One famous example of the latter is the 74LS244 tristate buffer which can easily source current for several LED's. More about tristate circuits in a bit. Most TTL IC's have "totem pole" outputs (Fig. 1-11), meaning a PNP transistor connected to an NPN transistor such that the PNP tries to source current if the output is H and the NPN tries to sink current if the output is L. Another important kind of output is the open collector (Fig. 1-11b). This style has only the NPN

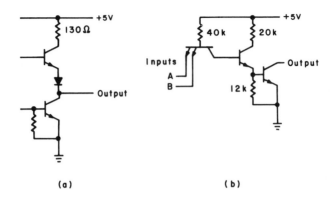

(a)   (b)

Fig. 1-11. (a) Totem pole output used in most TTL circuits. Egs., 7400, 7402, 7404, 7408, 7432, 7486. (b) Open-collector version of a 7400 NAND gate (comes in a 7401 package). Note that no current sourcing PNP transistor is connected to the output.

current sinking transistor in the output stage. The output doesn't attempt to source anything, so an external pull up resistor is required to yield a high output. The neat thing about this kind of output is that several of them can be connected together. If any one of them feels like sinking current, it can, i.e., you get a free n-gate negative logic OR. In the old days (or now too if you're using old backplanes such as on the Data General Eclipse and Nova computers, on the PDP 11 series, etc), the open collectors were used to drive the bus lines connecting the computer boards. Lines are all high until some selected board sticks some lows on the bus. The deal is that only one board drives the bus at a time, but that's a logical, rather than physical, restriction. New computer systems use tristate outputs as explained below. The open collector is also valuable for sinking currents through loads requiring higher voltages. For example the 7406 open collector inverter can withstand being pulled up to 30 volts.

Two other deviations from standard TTL are important: CMOS (74Cxxx series) and Low-power Schottky LS (74LSxxx series). CMOS (Complementary Metal Oxide Semiconductor) circuits require phenomenally low standby power by TTL standards and don't require accurate power supplies (typically, 3 - 15 volts will do). However, they switch substantially more slowly than TTL, are static sensitive and have considerably less drive power. The LS family is pin for pin compatible with the usual 74xxx series, requires one fifth the power, only .4 ma for a low input and is essentially as fast (switching times on the order of 20 nsec). An LS output can typically drive up to 5 standard TTL inputs. For the most complete summary of standard and LS TTL, see the latest edition of Texas Instruments' TTL Data book, which is a necessary part of any digital designer's book collection. In general, you're better off using LS where possible to reduce power consumption. Also unused inputs can be tied directly to the 5 volt supply, whereas there's a superstition that you may get into trouble with standard TTL (the military practice is to use a 1K pullup resistor).

In using either standard or LS TTL, an output can drive ten inputs of the same family. However, LS can typically only drive one standard TTL input, bus drivers like the 74LS244 excepted. When in doubt, consult the TI TTL Data Book.

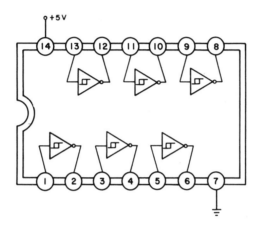

Fig. 1-12. Hex Schmidt trigger inverter 7414. The truth table is the same as that for the 7404 in Fig. 1-3. 7414 inverters incorporate hysteresis leading to increased noise immunity.

Special kinds of input circuits known as Schmidt triggers (Fig. 1-12) include hysteresis to cope better with noisy or slowly varying inputs. The 6 Schmidt trigger inverters in the 7414, for example, go high when the input goes less than .9 volts and go low when the input goes higher than 1.7 volts. The Schmidt trigger input is very useful in cleaning up signals such as making a nice 60 Hz square wave out of the power-line sine wave.

Finally, tristate outputs are superkeen! They have three states as their name implies: high, low and disconnected. TTL tristate buffer highs can often source a fair amount of current and the lows can sink an even larger amount of current. One or two lines on the package are used to enable or disable the outputs. This allows many outputs to be connected together as with open-collector systems, but substantially less power is involved. The logic signals have to decide which package talks, or there will be a fight. This style of output is very valuable for computer systems, which by their very natures have many devices wanting to talk to the microprocessor. A tristate output (Fig. 1-13) is "enabled" when the tristate line assumes an appropriate value. For the tristate buffers in Fig. 1-13, the outputs are enabled when the tristate lines $1\overline{G}$ and $2\overline{G}$ go low. Another useful tristate

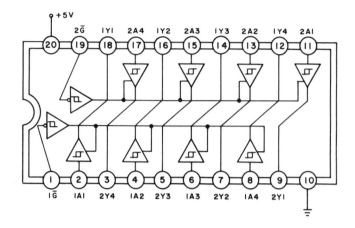

Fig. 1-13. Octal tristate buffer 74LS244 has Schmidt trigger inputs and can both source and sink considerble current. The Schmidt trigger hysteresis is about .4 volts, half that of the 7414.

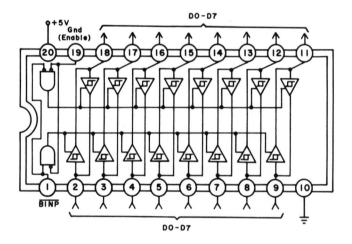

Fig. 1-14. 74LS245 octal bidirectional tristate buffer with Schmidt-trigger inputs (about .4 volts hysteresis). It is useful for driving microcomputer bidirectional data lines.

buffer is the bidirectional 74LS245 diagrammed in Fig. 1-14. This IC is particularly handy for interfacing microcomputer data lines to a bus.

A couple of remarks on power supplies are in order. First it's good practice to stick a .1 μfd capacitor between 5 volts and ground near every second TTL package. When a TTL gate switches, it draws a burst of current, which can wreak havoc with other IC's unless there's enough of these so-called decoupling or bypass capacitors distributed around the circuit. A related principle is that there should be a bypass cap connecting a path of no more than three inches between the power and ground pins of a given IC. If you find a board on which this principle is badly violated, connect a high-speed oscilloscope across the power pins and you'll observe peak-to-peak fluctuations of 1 volt or more! Amazingly enough, the circuit may work just great, which just goes to show theory isn't always necessary.

Another handy thing to know is that you can get up to a 1-ampere, 5-volt supply out of an unregulated 8 to 12 volt supply by using a 7805 three-

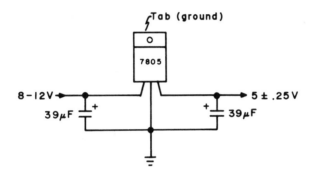

Fig. 1-15. 7805 IC makes a regulated 5 volt supply from an unre-gulated 8-12 volt supply.

terminal IC (Fig. 1-15). You should put 10 to 50 μf tantalum capacitors on each side of the circuit, being careful to get their polarity right, and mount the 7805 on a heat sink. A small package 78L05 exists for current demands under 100 ma. The 7805 is a member of positive-voltage regulators in the 78xx family. A corresponding negative voltage family is called 79xx.

Voltage regulators are based on special diodes, called Zener diodes, which have precise reverse-biased breakdown voltages (see Fig. 1-2 for illustration of breakdown voltage). These diodes can be used directly for small current requirements. Connect one in series with a current-limiting resistor against the current flow, i.e., opposite to the arrangement in Fig. 1-1. The Zener-diode-resistor combination then provides a precise voltage if the current drawn is sufficiently small.

1-5. Flip-flops

No, they're not to eat, but they are one of the most important building blocks in digital electronics. Some people think everything's black or white, no greys. Such attitudes are binary: on or off. A flip-flop is the way to store

store such a state of mind. It's a device with two states: on or off, high or

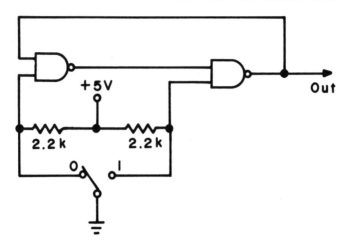

Fig. 1-16. Set-reset flip-flop made out of 7400 gates. This circuit debounces a switch and can also be flipped by TTL pulses
instead of a switch.

low. Figure 1-16 shows one way to make a flip-flop out of two 7400 NAND
gates. When you ground the left terminal, the output goes low since both
inputs to the right gate go high. Conversely grounding the right terminal
causes the output to go high. Leaving the switch in the middle, leaves the
output the way is was last. This interesting fact leads to what one calls a
"bounceless" switch. When you close a mechanical switch it bounces up and
down several times before settling down to stay. But one bounce of the
switch in Fig. 1-16 grounds an input and is sufficient to switch the output
regardless of further bounces on the contact. Note also that a TTL pulse
going from high to low and back can be used to flip the flip-flop as well as a
switch. So this circuit can be used by other electronic circuits as well as by
human beings.

   You may not have much use for people with binary opinions, but virtually everything in computers is built on binary information. By grouping
together the outputs of many flip-flops, we can make arbitrarily fine grada-
tions of grey. One important example is the way letters are represented by
these bits (binary digits) of information. Seven bits give $2^7 = 128$ possible
combinations, which is enough variation for upper and lower case letters, a
control case, numbers, and a fair amount of punctuation symbols. An A is
represented by 65, a B by 66, etc., in the ASCII code (see Appendix 1 for
the full code). This code shows up on the hardware level as information is
passed from keyboards to computers or from one computer to another over a
phone line. The flip-flop is also used extensively to indicate the status of a
device. When a keyboard wants to tell the computer it has a character, or
a 60Hz clock wants to signal the next tick, they set flip-flops that either
interrupt the computer (more in Secs. 3-4 and 3-5 on this super technique)

or are looked at (polled) by the computer periodically. Suffice it to say that flip-flops are indispensible to the whole arena of computer operation.

Although the circuit in Fig. 1-16 is very instructive and used occasionally in digital circuitry, a much more common and useful flip-flop is the

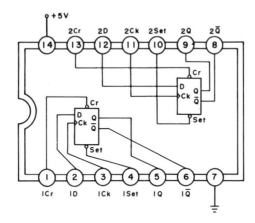

Fig. 1-17. 7474 positive-edge triggered flip-flop. Has a clocked mode as well as set reset capability.

edge-triggered D flip-flop shown in Fig. 1-17 and available in pairs in the 7474. This device has an input called D, two outputs Q and $\overline{Q}$ ($\overline{Q}$ is the inverted value of Q), two additional inputs, preset and clear, and a clock. If preset is low and clear high, Q is high, period. If clear is low and preset high, Q is low, period. These inputs are analogous to the switch positions in Fig. 1-16. Ground one input and the flip-flop is forced into one state. Ground the other and the flip-flop goes into the other state. The active, i.e., do something, level of these inputs is low, so they're called active-low inputs. In addition, we have the D input and the clock. The basic idea is this: with the clear and preset inputs high (not active), a transition of the clock input from low to high (called a positive edge) "clocks" the value of D into Q and the inverse into $\overline{Q}$. The clock transition is required; D can do anything it wants to, but nothing will happen to Q and $\overline{Q}$ unless the clock has a positive edge.

So how is such a device used? Several ways. One way is as a memory element. Q and $\overline{Q}$ tell whatever is connected to them what value was clocked in. If you want to turn on an LED from your computer to signal that an event has occurred, you output the bit to the D flip-flop. Addressing the flip-flop clocks in whatever data the computer presents to the D input. For such things, one usually uses more than two D flip-flops per package. The 74LS273 (Fig. 1-18), for example, houses eight in a 20-pin DIP, all clocked by the same clock line. This is very useful for outputting a status byte from your computer. What you do with the outputs is up to you. As we see later in the book, a low bit can easily turn on 20 amperes at 277

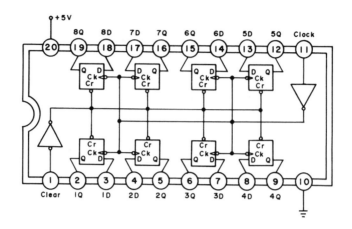

Fig. 1-18. 74LS273 clocked octal latch. A very useful IC for computer output. The 74LS374 has nearly the same pinouts with tristate output control and higher drive power.

volts! (Admittedly with the help of a relay or two.) Just sink a milliampere with a 74LS273 or 74LS74 in a computer running on 5 volts. Now maybe you start to see why this micro stuff can feed nascent drives for power! More generally, one of the two kinds of semiconductor computer memories consist of D flip-flops, the "static" kind. There's also a "dynamic" kind which is substantially cheaper and less power hungry (has only one transistor per bit instead of six), but has some disadvantages (see Sec. 6-1).

The 7474 style flip-flop is also used to signal the computer that something has happened. Suppose you want to have your computer read every character you type even if it's off thinking about some calculation and ignoring the keyboard. Section 3-4 shows how a keyboard ships a pulse down the line that clocks a high (D gets tied to 5 volts for this) into Q and a low into $\overline{Q}$. The $\overline{Q}$ is used to pull the computer's interrupt line low (see Fig. 3-12), causing the computer to save where it is and, assuming you've programmed correctly, branch to your special keyboard input routine which saves the character. Now to prevent getting interrupted again for the same character, the computer signal that reads the character in is also used to force the flip-flop's clear line low, causing $\overline{Q}$ to go high again. Since the keyboard's pulse has only one positive edge, all's done for that character. At first it seems like magic; it's really just plain logic!

Still another use for the D flip-flop is to divide the clock frequency (suppose it's a square wave) by two. You connect $\overline{Q}$ to D and watch it happen in Exercise 2. This procedure gets generalized in the form of counters such as the 74193, which we examine shortly in Sec. 1-7.

1-6. Clocks

Next let's look at what makes the whole show tick: the clock. If your computer seems dead, really dead (not just off in some inexplicable loop), either the power's off or the clock's stopped. Clocks, i.e., square waves, are used to run digital circuits just as a conductor's beat runs an orchestra. No clock, no music. The reason for clocks in complicated digital circuitry is to get rid of race conditions that occur when various gates fire at their own rates. With a clock, all gates do something and then settle down. The next tic causes the next step to happen. It's the settling down that's so important. In between, voltages fluctuate all over, and what ultimately (after 50 to 100 nanoseconds) becomes an H might have been an L for a few nanoseconds. So clocks are essential. Computer clocks typically tick 4 million times a second or faster and are derived from crystal oscillations as in Fig.

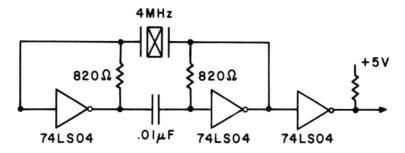

Fig. 1-19. Crystal oscillator circuit used in many microcomputers. The pullup resistor R=330 Ω gives the output the high value needed for Z80 systems

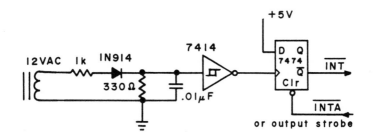

Fig. 1-20. 60 Hz clock derived from 110 v power line. Useful for giving computers a real time clock (i.e., the kind we live with rather than the submicrosecond kind).

1-19. Another clock that we use to tell the computer what time it is is shown in Fig. 1-20. This clock is derived from the power line frequency of 60 Hz. The diode and voltage divider network (two resistors) create a positive only periodic waveform something like a banged-in sine wave. The capacitor averages out any high frequency glitches and the Schmidt trigger inverter cleans it all up into a square wave with edges that rise in less than 40 nanoseconds.   Such a clock can be used to clock a D flip-flop that divides by two and interrupts your favorite computer 30 times a second. Since your computer undoubtedly has a low voltage AC output, and since this circuit costs about 90 cents in parts, you might wonder why manufacturers often charge $400 or more for their real-time clock hardware! Ask 'em.

A very popular clock is constructed using the CMOS 555 timer IC diag-

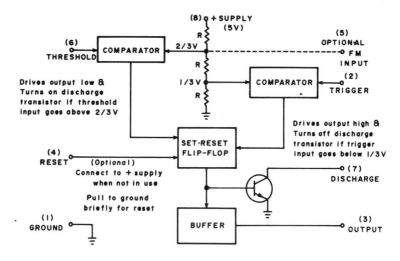

Fig. 1-21. Diagram explaining 555 timer IC. Appropriate choices of resistors and a capacitor can produce square waves (see Fig. 1-22) or one shots (see Sec. 1-8).

ramed in Fig. 1-21. This IC can run from a 4 to 15-volt power supply and its output can source or sink well over 100 ma. With a five-volt supply, the 555 uses only 3 ma and is TTL compatible. The output value is determined by the voltages on two comparator inputs called the trigger (pin 2) and the threshold (pin 6). When the voltage on the threshold goes above 2/3 the supply voltage V, the output goes low and an open-collector discharge transistor turns on shorting pin 7 to ground. When the voltage on the trigger is less than 1/3 V, the output goes high and the discharge transistor turns off. Appropriate choices of resistors and capacitors can give nonsymmetric square waves at the output (Fig. 1-22) or one shots (Sec. 1-8).

The square wave configuration of Fig. 1-22 charges the capacitor C through $R_1 + R_2$ until the threshold voltage exceeds 2/3 V. It then discharges C through R_2 alone until the trigger voltage is less than 1/3 V. While C is charging, the output is high; while discharging, the output is low. The charge time is $0.693(R_1 + R_2)C$. The discharge time is $0.693R_2C$. The oscillation period is the sum of these times, yielding a frequency of $1.44/[(R_1 + 2R_2)C]$. The recommended maximum total resistance is 3.3 megohms; the minimum is 1K. The minimum C is 500 pf, while the maximum

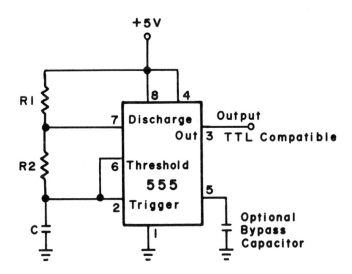

Fig. 1-22. The 555 timer IC wired as an asymmetric square wave generator.

is limited by the capacitor's leakage. For noncritical oscillation frequencies less than 200 kHz, the 555 makes an excellent choice. Lancaster's TTL Cookbook describes numerous interesting applications, ranging from temperature measurement to a music attack-decay generator.

1-7. Counters

As you saw in the flip-flop section, a D flip-flop can divide by 2. Since two D's are in a 7474, a 7474 can divide by 4. More generally if you combine 4 D's with appropriate preset and clear logic, you get the 74193 up/down counter pictured in Fig. 1-23. Now since computers are so good at calculating in general and counting in particular, you might ask, why should we be concerned with such an elaborate IC? Why not just input whatever is changing and count it with a program? Two situations come to mind. First computers are slower than counters. The 74193 can count 35 million times a second, while a typical microprocessor can count only about 100,000 times a second. So if you have a rapid count to record, you prescale the count using a TTL counter and then add up the result using the micro. Even if the count rate is within the computer's capability, you may not want to tie the computer up too much. Counting something thirty times a second is no big deal, but counting 10,000 times a second runs into a significant amount of execution time. In Sec. 3-5, we discuss a counter/timer circuit, the Z80 CTC, which has four counters (or timers) in one package, can count at about 1 MHz (2 MHz for CTCA) or slower and communicates with the micro without any intervening gates. For now, let's discuss the substantially faster, although less flexible, 74193.

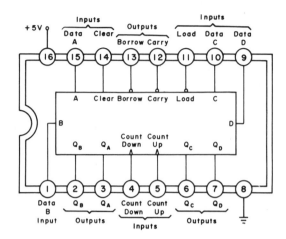

Fig. 1-23. 74193 synchronous up/down counter. Can be used to divide by any number from 2 to 16.

If you raise the clear input, all four outputs are cleared. If you lower the load input, the values on the A, B, C and D inputs are loaded into their respective flip-flops. If you toggle the up count input, the Q_A output divides by 2, the Q_B divides by 4, the Q_C by 8 and the Q_D by 16. This is a binary counting process such that 15 positive edges of the up counter leave all four outputs equal to 1, i.e., H, if they started with 0's. This is a divide by 16 counter. At any given time, the number of counts registered (modulo 16) is given by the binary number formed by the four outputs. By connecting various outputs to the load line and choosing various load values, you can divide by numbers smaller than 16. For example, if A=B=C=L and D=H, and you connect Q_D to the load line, you get a divide by 8, since everytime Q_D goes low, the binary number 1000 (=8) is loaded in as a starter. Can you make a divide by 2? By 3? By any number from 2 to 16? Yep! But they don't all have a symmetric square wave for outputs. If you can tolerate an additional divide by 2, a 7474 following the last stage yields a symmetric output. Figure 1-24 illustrates the behavior of a 74193 with the use of a timing diagram. This kind of a diagram is well worth understanding, since many sophisticated (Large Scale Integrated) circuits like the Z80 microprocessor only work if you pay attention to their timing diagrams (more in Sec 3-1). As shown in Fig. 1-24, the 74193 can count down as well as up, and can be cascaded using the carry output. This last characteristic means that the divide by 16 (or whatever) output can be connected to the count input of another IC to continue the division process. Two 74193's can thus divide by any number from 2 to 256. In computer applications, these counters are for high speed. For lower speed counting, you're better off with a programmable counter such as the Intel 8253 or the Z80 CTC (discussed in Sec. 3-5).

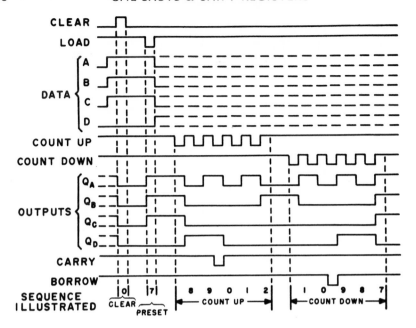

Fig. 1-24. Possible timing diagram for a 74193 up/down counter.

1-8. One Shots and Shift Registers

Two other common TTL IC's are one shots and shift registers. As the name implies, the one shot (the 74LS121 of Fig. 1-25 or two in a DIP in the

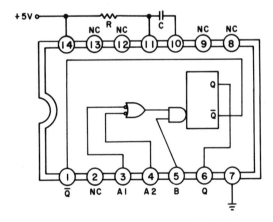

Fig. 1-25. 74121 one-shot IC. Unless a one shot is in progress, Q is low and $\overline{Q}$ is high. Whatever edge causes the $(\overline{A1}|\overline{A2})\&B$ logic value to be true starts the one shot (Q goes high).

74221) outputs a single pulse given an input pulse. The length of this pulse is linearly proportional to an RC time constant. The 74121 ignores all but the leading edge of the input pulse. When its output shot is over, it's ready to listen again to the input. The 74123 houses two <u>retriggerable</u> one shots. These have the property that so long as pulses arrive before the one shot is up, the one shot continues to be restarted. It's like keeping a balloon up in the air. If you keep hitting it upwards, it never falls to the ground. The retriggerability is handy for pulsed burglar alarm systems. The popular 555 IC discussed in Sec. 1-6 as an astable multivibrator can also be used as a one shot, by replacing R_2 in Fig. 1-22 by a wire. Unless fast response times or retriggerability is needed, the 555 is the best one-shot choice. We refer the reader to Lancaster's <u>TTL Cookbook</u> for a detailed discussion of one shots and multivibrators.

Shift registers come in many forms. A typical kind, the 74165, latches an 8-bit input word much as the 74LS273 does. But instead of having all bits available as outputs, the bits are shifted out a single output pin, one bit for each positive edge of the shift clock. This is called a parallel-to-serial conversion, and is used extensively in serial communications between computers and terminals or computers and other computers. A corresponding serial-to-parallel shift register, the 74164 also exists, and the two together are available in the form of LSI circuits known as UART's for serial communications (see Sec. 5-2). The shift register is also useful for generating precise clocked one-shots. Once again, we refer the interested reader to the <u>TTL Cookbook</u> for further discussion.

Problems

1-1. Construct an XOR gate out of simpler gates.

1-2. Derive a symmetric square wave with frequency 16x9600 = 153600 Hz from a 3.9935 MHz square wave using a 74LS193 counter and a 7474 flip-flop. (Useful for 9600 baud clock on Z80 Starter kit).

1-3. An electrically controlled set-reset flip-flop can be made by removing the switch in Fig. 1-16 and driving the 0 or 1 inputs with negative going pulses. Design a circuit which makes this into a D-type flip-flop. All you need to do to accomplish this it to add a few logic gates to the inputs.

1-4. Look up the truth table for a J-K flip-flop such as the 74109 and figure out how you could wire it up so that it becomes a D-type flip-flop.

1-5. Choose RC values to get a 31,300 Hz clock with a 11/10 duty cycle using a 555 timer IC.

1-6. Choose RC values to get a .1 msec one shot from a 74121.

1-7. Construct an accurate two-volt output given an accurate 5-volt supply and an appropriate Zener diode.

References

Don Lancaster, 1976, TTL Cookbook, Howard W. Sams & Co., New York.

The TTL Data Book for Design Engineers, 1976 (get the latest edition), Published by Texas Instruments, Inc., Dallas, Texas. Also see data books by Motorola, and National Semiconductor.

P. Horowitz and W. Hill, 1980, The Art of Electronics, Cambridge University Press, New York.

Chapter Two

Programming the Z80 Microprocessor

The trouble with computers is that they do what you tell them to, not what you want them to.

While you're digesting TTL, we switch horses to get moving on the programming end of things. A simple computer program can take the place of many integrated circuits, and where one stops adding hardware and uses software instead is quite flexible. Typically you use more hardware when the microprocessor is loaded down. But if your microprocessor is twiddling its thumbs, it might as well do more work and replace a bunch of IC's. We focus on the Zilog Z80 microprocessor in this book because it currently provides the best combination of price, power and software support. In fact more computers use the Z80 than any other CPU big or small, in large part thanks to the Radio Shack TRS-80 computers. Other processors such as the popular 6502 (used in Apple and Commodore Pet computers) and the very pretty Motorola 6809 can illustrate the principles equally well, but have smaller software support at the moment. We're sticking to 8-bit microprocessors for control applications because they require half as many data lines to worry about as the 16-bit varieties (unless they have an 8-bit mode like the INTEL 8088). We don't have space to tell you all you need to know about the Z80, but you will need to know all we tell you. The hope is that you can learn some of the Z80's spirit from our description and then firm up the details by writing programs yourself and reading the Z80 reference manuals as needed. This chapter deals with programming the Z80, while Chap. 3 shows you how the Z80 communicates through hardware with memory and input/output devices. First we describe machine and assembly languages, which suffice for much of the simple I/O interfacing developed in later chapters. We see how the Z80 moves and manipulates bits, bytes and 16-bit words, how and why conditional jumps and calls are done, how register contents can be shifted around, how the CPU inputs and outputs data, and how a very simple operating system works. The program illustrations deal with multiple-byte addition and subtraction, 16-bit multiplication, keyboard polling, and character manipulation. The hexadecimal and 2's complement notations are introduced and then used often.

2-1. Machine and Assembly Languages

Like all computers, the Z80 does what we want it to do by executing a list of instructions stored in memory. Each instruction is a binary number consisting of 8 to 32 bits (Binary digITS). These bits are grouped eight at a time into bytes. The list of instructions is called a program. In this section, we discuss two languages for writing programs, machine and assembly language. For much simple interfacing, these languages suffice. However, when you put an entire project together in a real-life application, you may want to use "higher-level" languages like Fortran and BASIC (see Sec. 7-3).

It would be very time consuming and error prone to enter a long list of 8-bit binary numbers manually using, for example, a set of switches. A somewhat better method is to enter the instructions from a keyboard as hexadecimal numbers while the computer runs a simple program translating these numbers into binary and storing them in memory. Hexadecimal numbers are base 16 and count like 0, 1, 2, 3, 4, 5, 6, 7, 8, 9, A, B, C, D, E, F, 10, 11, ... Since each hexadecimal digit specifies four bits, two of them specify a byte. We use hexadecimal (hex) numbers for the most part in this book because of their simple relationship to binary. To gain facility in translating between the two, compare the hex and binary columns in the ASCII chart of App. A. Learn hexadecimal; it's really useful. Too bad mankind didn't have eight fingers on a hand. Then we'd have a superior number system!

A program written in terms of binary or hexadecimal numbers is called "machine" language. A very simple example of such a program is

location	op code	description
0000	3E 03	Load the number 3 into register A
0002	06 02	Load the number 2 into register B
0004	80	Add the number in B to that in A
0005	76	Stop the computer

The left hand column shows the memory locations where the instructions are to be stored. The instructions themselves are called "op codes" (operation codes) and are listed in the second column. Note that the first two instructions are two bytes long, while the last two are only one byte long. The registers A and B are 8-bit storage locations inside the Z80 CPU (Central Processing Unit). To the programmer, the Z80 simply looks like a set of 20 such registers, some 8-bit, some 16-bit, some general purpose, some assigned to special functions. We discuss the registers in some detail later in this chapter.

The Z80 gets its next instruction from the memory address given by the 16-bit special-purpose register called the Program Counter (PC). In this capacity, the PC is said to hold a "pointer" into memory. The Z80 fetches the byte at this address, increments the PC to point at the next memory location, and interprets the fetched byte as an instruction (even if it's not!). You can set the PC to zero (along with a couple of other special purpose registers) by applying a TTL low to the Z80 reset pin. Assuming the program above is stored at zero as indicated, it would then be executed when you let the reset pin go high.

It's instructive to single-step through the program. After reset, the PC=0, so the Z80 fetches the contents of location 0, which is a 3E. This tells it to load the contents of the next byte in memory (at 0001) into the A register, and to increment the PC to point at location 0002. At this point the Z80 has finished executing the first instruction. The second is executed in the same way, and loads register B with the value in location 3, leaving the PC pointing at 0004. The instruction there tells the Z80 to add the contents of the 8-bit number in B to that in A, leaving the result in A. Finally it fetches the fourth instruction, which stops execution until the reset pin is pulled low and high again, or until an interrupt occurs (see Sec. 3-4).

While it is possible to write and execute programs directly in machine language as described above, it's hard to see what you've done. Although precise in meaning, the hexadecimal numbers don't suggest their meanings. For this reason and others, one almost always programs in "assembly language," at least, if a "low-level" language is desired. Instead of writing down the hexadecimal op codes, you write down mnemonics that describe the instructions. For example, the program above reads

```
label      operator   operand    comment
START:     LD         A,3        ;Set A=3
           LD         B,2        ;Set B=2
           ADD        A,B        ;A+B->A
END:       HALT                  ;Stop.
```

This program is easy to read even without the comments once you note two facts: first the operator is always just an abbreviation for the operaton that the computer is to perform, i.e., LD means LoaD, ADD means ADD, etc. Second, the operands specify the registers and/or data that the instruction operates on, and is written "backwards" in the form: destination, source. Thus the first instruction means LoaD 3 into A. Similarly, ADD A,B means add B to A and leave the result in A.

The first column (usually 8 characters wide) is reserved for labels. These are superfluous in the simple program above, but in general are very useful, since they are required to jump around and to refer to data locations, etc. The advantages of labels become apparent in later examples. The assembly language format shown in the example above is fairly standard. The labels are separated from the operators by a colon and comments are preceded by a semicolon. One or more blanks are used to separate operators and operands.

Assembly language programs are easier for a human being to read than machine language, but the computer cannot read them directly, since it only understands machine language. So we have to "assemble" the assembly-language program. You can do this manually (a process called "hand assembly") by looking up the op code corresponding to each mnemonic in the Z80 technical manuals. If the program is small, hand assembly is reasonably efficient. Otherwise, it's much easier and less prone to error to have the computer itself assemble the program by running a program called an assembler (see Sec. 7-2). For that method, you need a relatively large computer with disk drives, etc. The assembler can produce both a listing of the translation and a binary module that another program called a loader can load into memory for execution. The listing of the example program looks like

```
0000    3E 02    START:    LD     A,2      ;Set A=2
0002    06 03              LD     B,3      ;Set B=3
0004    80                 ADD    A,B      ;A+B->A
0005    76       END:      HALT            ;Stop
```

Only the assembly language is typed in; the computer generates the first two columns.

A word about documentation: in assembly language it's often difficult to "see the forest through the trees." The mnemonics identify the trees ok. In fact, you don't include comments such as those above, since the mnemonics really make those messages redundant, at least after you've programmed a bit. But you do need to include comments that explain why you're doing what you're doing. Otherwise, it's hard for other programmers to know what you've done, or even for you to know several months after writing the program. The Golden Rule says, "Document unto others as you would have them document unto you!" The remainder of this chapter is devoted to explaining many of the most useful Z80 instructions. We use assembly language for this purpose and include appropriate comments.

2-2. Moving Data in 8-bit Registers and Memory

The basic activity of a computer can be called data processing. Now that includes just about everything from business to burglar alarms, but the computer treats it all as combinations of bits organized 8 at a time into bytes. The data may exist in memory as part of a program calculating something, or it may be entered from the real world via keyboards, switch settings, voltage readings or various digital devices. The first thing the microprocessor has to be able to do is to move the data around, perhaps to store it more conveniently or to manipulate it more easily. The Z80 has a number of registers to facilitate such manipulations. In particular there are the A, B, C, D, E, H and L 8-bit registers. Inside the Z80, these registers are numbered 7, 0, 1, 2, 3, 4 and 5 respectively. We'll get to 6 in Sec. 2-4. We move data between these registers with the LD (for LoaD) command. Specifically LD r,r' loads the contents of register r with the contents of register r'. To illustrate this instruction let's interchange the contents of the B and C registers using A for temporary storage:

```
LD      A,B         ;Save contents of B
LD      B,C
LD      C,A         ;A and B are interchanged
```

The LD r,r' instruction has the binary machine language format 01dddsss, where ddd gives the binary encoding of the destination register r and sss gives the encoding of the source register r'. Hence 01 111 000 loads A (register $7=111_2$) with the contents of B. The grouping of bits into threes corresponds to the octal number system (0, 1, 2, 3, 4, 5, 6, 7, 10, ...) and allows a simple representation of many Z80 instructions. That's about the only advantage of grouping bits in threes, however. A byte has only eight bits, not nine, and the ASCII character code (American Standard Code for Information Interchange - see App. A) is grouped in fours. So we use the more efficient grouping by fours called hexadecimal instead, as discussed in Sec. 2-1.

In addition to the LD r,r' instruction, there's a LD r,n instruction that loads r with the byte n. This version of the LD instruction is used in Sec. 2-1. So if you want to set B to 1 you execute LD B,1. This instruction requires two bytes, one for the op code "LD B," and one for n.

2-3. Manipulating Data - INC, SET, ADD, AND

Registers can be incremented or decremented by 1 using the instructions INC r and DEC r respectively. Any bit can be set (to 1) or reset (to 0) by the instructions SET b,r and RES b,r respectively, where b = 0 to 7 is the bit number. Here bits are numbered according to the power of 2 that they represent. Hence the binary unit's place (2^0) is bit 0. This is the least significant bit. The binary ten's place (2^1) is bit 1, etc. Bit 7 is a byte's most significant bit and represents 2^7.

So far all the registers have been treated as being the same. But all registers are not created equal on the Z80. The A register has the name accumulator and has substantially more power than the others. For example, we can execute the instructions ADD A,r, SUB r, AND r, OR r, and XOR r, all of which do the indicated operation between A and r and leave the result in A. Note that we must specify the A register for the ADD instruction, since we can also add 16-bit numbers into the HL register pair (see Sec. 2-4). Admittedly, the notation is a bit clumsy here, but it's not too hard to get used to. So ADD A,B sets A to A+B; AND B ands A with B bit by bit and leaves the result in A. The r can be replaced by n in each of these instructions. For example, ADD A,5 adds 5 to the contents of the accumulator. The instruction sequence

```
LD      A,1B        ;Load A with 27₁₀
AND     0F          ;Kill the left hex digit
```

leaves A with the value 0B (hex numbers always start with a regular decimal digit, so that the number 0B isn't confused with the register B).

A very handy operation for complementing or "toggling" one or more bits is the exclusive or (XOR n). For example, to complement bit 0 in A, execute XOR 1. If it was a 1, it becomes a 0 and vice versa.

You can complement every bit in the accumulator with CPL. The following code subtracts 3 from B, leaving the result in A:

```
LD      A,3         ;Subtract 3 w/o using SUB
CPL
INR     A           ;Form "2's complement" of 3
ADD     A,B         ;Done.  Try it!
```

This example isn't as frivolous as it seems, since it demonstrates the way negative numbers and subtractions are done on most computers including the Z80. The SUB instruction takes the place of the CPL, INR and ADD instructions above. Try some examples to convince yourself that it really works.

The accumulator can be loaded with the contents of a memory location by the instruction LD A,(nn), where nn is a 16-bit memory address [the Z80 can directly address up to 2^{16} = 64 K (1K=1024) bytes of memory]. Similarly the nnth memory location can be loaded with the contents of the accumulator by the instruction LD (nn),A. Note that in Z80 assembly language, parentheses around a number nn means the operation is done on the <u>contents</u> of the location nn. Thus LD A,n means to put n into A, while LD A,(nn) means put the contents of location nn into A.

2-4. 16-bit Registers and Memory Pointers

The B, C, D, E, H and L registers can also be grouped in pairs forming the three 16-bit registers BC, DE and HL. These pairs can be loaded directly with 16-bit words by the LD dd,nn instruction. For example, LD

BC,0F123 loads B with 0F1 and C with 23. An important use for these register pairs is to load them with a memory address that can be used as a
"pointer" into memory. Thus the instruction LD A,(BC) can be used to load
the accumulator with the contents of the memory location pointed to by BC.

In this memory-pointer context, the HL pair has special power. For it,
we have the instruction LD r,(HL) which loads r with the contents of the
location specified by HL. Here r can be any register including H or L. Similarly, LD (HL),r stores r at the location given by HL. This (HL) is the missing "register" 6 left out of the register number sequence in Sec. 2-2. So
you can can also ADD A,(HL), which adds the contents of what HL is pointing at to the accumulator. In fact, all the commands that apply to the 8-bit
registers apply to (HL), so we'll just think of it as another register. This
means that any location in memory can be a register! Of course, you do tie
up HL (IX or IY can be used in the same way; check those 16-bit'ers out in
your leisure time).

The HL register pair also forms a 16-bit accumulator. ADD HL,DE puts
the 16-bit sum of DE and HL into HL. SBC HL,DE sets HL-DE-CY into HL,
where CY is the carry flag (a flip-flop equal to 0 or 1), which we come to
momentarily. So you have 16-bit addition and subtraction. There is no
direct multiplication or division, however. The various Z80 registers are
diagrammed in Fig. 2-1.

MAIN REG SET		ALTERNATE REG SET		
ACCUMULATOR A	FLAGS F	ACCUMULATOR A'	FLAGS F'	
B	C	B'	C'	GENERAL PURPOSE REGISTERS
D	E	D'	E'	
H	L	H'	L'	

INTERRUPT VECTOR I	MEMORY REFRESH R	SPECIAL PURPOSE REGISTERS
INDEX REGISTER IX		
INDEX REGISTER IY		
STACK POINTER SP		
PROGRAM COUNTER PC		

Fig. 2-1. Z80 registers. There are two sets of A, B, C, D, E, F, H,
and L registers, plus the 16-bit IX and IY registers (which are used
almost like HL). The Program Counter (PC) is discussed in Sec. 2-
1, the Stack Pointer (SP) in Sec. 2-8, the interrupt vector register
I in Sec. 3-5 and the memory refresh register R in Sec. 6-1.

2-5. Jumps, Conditional Jumps, and Subroutines

A computer would be close to useless if it couldn't jump from one place in a program to another on the basis of various conditions. In particular a number of Z80 instructions set or reset another flag, the zero (Z) flag, which then allows a conditional jump. For example,

```
            LD      B,9        ;Routine to add integers 1 to 9
            LD      A,0
LOOP:       ADD     B          ;A <- A+B
            DEC     B
            JP      NZ,LOOP
```

decrements B 9 times and then falls through leaving the accumulator with the sum of the integers from 1 to 9 (45). Try it on your TRS-80 or Z80 starter kit. This is an example of an iteration loop (like a DO loop in Fortran or a FOR-NEXT loop in BASIC). To understand how this loop works, recall from Sec. 2-1 that the Program Counter (PC) always contains the address of the next instruction to be executed. When the JP NZ,LOOP instruction is executed, the PC is set equal to LOOP if the zero flag is reset to 0, i.e., if B is NonZero (NZ). If the Z flag =1, the PC is left pointing at the location following the JP NZ,LOOP instruction.

A shorter version of the above is given using the DJNZ (Decrement B and Jump on NonZero) instruction as follows:

```
            LD      B,9
            LD      A,0
LOOP:       ADD     B
            DJNZ    LOOP
```

One difference from the previous loop is that the DJNZ instruction doesn't touch the zero flag (or any other for that matter). Another difference is that the DJNZ jumps by a one-byte two's-complement displacement relative to the program counter. At the time of executing the DJNZ, the PC points at the instruction following the DJNZ. As a 2-byte instruction (JP nn is 3 bytes), DJNZ can only jump forward 7F bytes and backwards 80 (hex) bytes. The DJNZ LOOP instruction above assembles into 10 FD, the 10 for the op code, the FD for the negative displacement. In this regard, the JP nn is more powerful, since it can jump to any 16-bit address nn. But it takes three bytes to do so.

Another important flag is the carry (CY) flag. When you add 9+3 in decimal you have to carry a 1. That's part of what the CY is used for. The sequence

```
            LD      A,83
```

ADD   85

leaves the accumulator with the value 8 and CY with a 1, while if the LD had only loaded 73, A would equal 0F8 and CY would equal 0. The ADC r (add with carry) instruction sets A to A+r+CY. This allows one to add two n-byte numbers. The following calculates N1+N2, leaving the result in N1:

```
ADDN:    LD     HL,N2     ;Point at the number N2
         LD     DE,N1     ;DE points at N1
         LD     B,n       ;n is the desired # of bytes
         OR     A         ;Clear CY flag
LOOP:    LD     A,(DE)    ;Get next N1 byte
         ADC    (HL)      ;Add in next N2 byte plus CY
         LD     (DE),A    ;Store updated byte
         LD     B,n       ;n is the desired # of bytes
         OR     A         ;Clear CY flag
LOOP:    LD     A,(DE)    ;Get next N1 byte
         ADC    (HL)      ;Add in next N2 byte plus CY
         LD     (DE),A    ;Store updated byte
         INC    HL        ;Increment pointers
         INC    DE
         DJNZ   LOOP      ;Do all n bytes.
```

By replacing the ADC instruction by SBC (subtract with carry) here, you get N1-N2. For subtraction, the CY is set when a borrow is indicated and reset otherwise. SBC r sets A to A - r - CY.

The CY is affected by a number of other instructions. SCF sets it, CCF complements (inverts) it, OR's reset it (as used above), and CP (compare with accumulator) may modify it. This last instruction is very useful for character manipulation and deserves special attention. CP r and CP n compares the contents of the accumulator with the contents of register r or the constant n. If they're equal, the Z flag is set and can be used accordingly in conditional jumps. If the contents of the accumulator is smaller than that of the register or n, CY is set, and reset otherwise. These features are illustrated by the following string-manipulation program. By string we mean a group of letters stored sequentially in memory, egs., text or a message. The program searches a string of characters in memory for the first non-blank character and converts it to upper case if it happens to be lower case. The characters are stored as ASCII codes, which represent each one by a 7-bit code (see App. A). The program reads

```
         LD     HL,STRING ;Point at start of string
LOOP:    LD     A,(HL)    ;Get next character
         INC    HL        ;Point at following character
         CP     " "       ;Is it a blank?
         JP     Z,LOOP    ;Ignore blanks
         CP     "a"       ;Numerically lowest lower case letter
```

```
        JP     C,DONE    ;If smaller, cant be lower case
        CP     "z"+1     ;If smaller than "z"+1, is lower case
        JP     NC,DONE   ;So if No Carry, we're done
        RES    5,A       ;Convert to upper case (see ASCII
DONE:                    ; chart)
```

Two-byte relative jumps (see DJNZ description) exist for testing both the Z and CY flags. Their syntax is JR Z,away and JR C,away. Or, of course, JR NZ,away if you want to jump on NonZero to location away. In assembly language, you use the desired transfer address, here away. In machine language, you code in the relative displacement of that address. This is computed as discussed for the DJNZ instruction. You can do absolute (3-byte) jumps on the sign bit, bit 7. JP P,address jumps if the byte is positive (sign bit is 0) and JP M,address jumps if the byte is negative (sign bit is 1). You can also jump on Even or Odd parity. Check the reference manuals to see which instructions modify which flags.

The subroutine is such a valuable concept in computer programming that we introduce it here even though we have to wait until Sec. 2-7 to explain how it's implemented. Furthermore, we have to use it in the "hands-on" exercises right away. The subroutine is a group of instructions maybe with some data thrown in that may be "called" upon from anywhere in a program. The subroutine call might be described as a "boomerang" jump. It goes to the address specified, does its thing, and when done returns to the instruction following the call. Mathematical functions are usually implemented as subroutines. If you're interpreting data typed in on a keyboard, get-the-next-character is a subroutine (we name it CI for Console Input) that returns the next character in the accumulator. Sending a character to a computer terminal is done by calling a subroutine (CO) with the character in register C. For example, the following code simply echos whatever is typed on the keyboard, i.e., displays it on the terminal

```
LOOP:   CALL   CI        ;Get next keyboard character
        LD     C,A
        CALL   CO        ;Display it
        JP     R,LOOP    ;Loop forever
```

This particular loop is much handier than you might think, since it's helpful for debugging terminal interfaces. The neat thing here is that we don't have to be concerned with the details of the subroutines themselves. They can be changed as necessary to accomodate hardware changes, while the code above would remain the same. Furthermore, these subroutines can be called from many different places, obviating the need to repeat the code many times. Subroutines "modularize" your programming, helping you to "see the forest through the trees." In addition, they provide a powerful way to take advantage of your computer's operating system. You may be wondering how the subroutine knows where to return to, or how to write one. To find out, read Sec. 2-7.

2-6. Shifty registers

A very useful kind of manipulation is shifting a register's bits left or right. SLA r (Shift Left Arithmetic) shifts register r left one bit position, filling in bit 0 with a zero and setting CY=bit 7. In shorthand, one can describe this as $r[n+1] \leftarrow r[n]$, $CY \leftarrow$ bit 7, $r[0] \leftarrow 0$. This multiplies r by 2. SRL r (Shift Right Logical) shifts r right such that $r[n] \leftarrow r[n+1]$, $r[7] \leftarrow 0$, $CY \leftarrow r[0]$. SRA r (Shift Right Arithmetic) shifts the same way except that $r[7] \leftarrow r[7]$. This is a divide by 2 for both positive and negative numbers (represented in two's complement form). These instructions and several others work on all the 8-bit registers, but they take two bytes. For the accumulator alone several 1-byte quickies are available. RRCA (Rotate Right Circular Accumulator) is defined by $A[n] \leftarrow A[n+1]$, $A[7] \leftarrow A[0]$, $CY \leftarrow A[0]$. Doing this eight times leaves A the way it started, i.e., you go around in a circle. Similarly RLCA is defined by $A[n+1] \leftarrow A[n]$, $A[0] \leftarrow A[7]$, $CY \leftarrow A[7]$. The following program sets $CY \leftarrow A[n]$

```
        LD      B,n+1    ;Set B to the # of shifts needed
LOOP:   RRCA             ;Shift A right a bit
        DJNZ    LOOP
```

This program checks the bit specified by B. An alternative is to use the BIT instruction, which checks the bit specified in the operand field.

The Z80 has no hardware multiply instruction. Sigh! The Motorola 6809 has one. Maybe Zilog will come out with an updated version that does too. You can multiply using a program, of course, and some simple multiplies can be done by combinations of shifts. For fun, let's do some 16-bit cases, which can easily be applied to the accumulator also. ADD HL,HL multiplies HL by 2 by doing a 16-bit arithmetic left shift. So $H[0] \leftarrow L[7]$, among other things. To multiply HL by 10, just run

```
        ADD     HL,HL    ;HL0*2 (HL0 is HL starting value)
        LD      D,H      ;Save HL0*2
        LD      E,L
        ADD     HL,HL    ;Get HL0*8
        ADD     HL,HL
        ADD     HL,DE    ;HL0*8+HL0*2. Done in 6 bytes!
```

Try writing a program to multiply by 6. An extension of this technique allows one to multiply DE by A leaving the result in HL:

```
MULT:   LD      B,8      ;8 bits to think about
        LD      HL,0     ;Zero the result
LOOP:   RRCA             ;Check bit n
        JR      NC,NEXT  ;If 0, nothing to add
        ADD     HL,DE    ;Add in DE0*2**n
```

```
NEXT:     EX        DE,HL      ;Exchange DE with HL to double DE
          ADD       HL,HL      ; i.e., compute DE=DE0*2**n
          EX        DE,HL      ;Restore HL and get updated DE
          DJNZ      LOOP       ;14 bytes, could be worse!
```

2-7. Input/Output

All these manipulations are useless unless we can get data into and out of the computer. One possibility is to make your keyboard, video screen, disk drive, modem, analog/digital devices, etc. look like memory. The CPU wouldn't know; it just references some address you choose and your devices act like memory. That's the way the TRS-80 keyboard and video screen work, for example. An advantage of this approach is that you can use the extensive set of Z80 memory reference instructions. This method is used exclusively in the PDP11 series of minicomputers. It can be used on any computer, but it does have disadvantages. You tie up some of your memory address space (64K may seem like a lot, but for many projects it gets used up fast). Also when your program goes crazy, you may start writing all over your I/O devices (like your disk!). And you have to "decode" 16 address lines to recognize that a given device is being referenced. So most machines including the Z80 have special Input/Output (I/O) instructions as well.

The Z80 uses a one-byte I/O port address, giving 256 input ports and 256 output ports. You input to the accumulator from some port n with the instruction IN A,(n). You output from A to port n with OUT (n),A. For example, suppose you want to output a character to a terminal, which can accept characters at 9600 baud (about 1000 characters/second). The computer can output characters much faster than that, so you need to test an input status bit to see if the terminal is ready to take another character. With the usual system, a high status bit signals that another character can be shipped. The program is

```
CO:       IN        A,(CSTS)   ;Get status byte
          RRCA                 ;Check ready bit (0)
          JR        NC,CO
          LD        A,C        ;It's ready.  Get char from C
          OUT       (CDTA),A   ;Output character
          RET                  ;(We make this a subroutine)
```

This program shows you how to "poll" a device by constantly watching its status bits. It's one of four basic methods for synchronizing data flow between the CPU and I/O devices (see Chap. 3). There are other I/O instructions including block I/O instructions, but the IN and OUT are sufficient for our purposes. A companion input routine CI reads

```
CI:       IN        A,(CSTS)   ;Get status byte
```

```
BIT        1,A         ;Check ready bit (1)
JR         Z,CI
IN         A,(CDTA)    ;Input character
RET
```

2-8. The Stack

Now to another very important concept: the stack. This "data structure" is a consecutive bunch of locations in memory whose number and values change in a "Last In First Out" (LIFO) way. It's like the stack of plates in a restaurant: the last plate on the stack is the first one taken by some hungry soul. This is to be distinguished from the fiendish data structure known as the LINO (Last In Never Out!) To make this concept quite concrete, let's demonstrate one that interchanges the contents of the register pairs BC and DE:

```
LD         HL,STACK ;Point at the top of the stack
DEC        HL          ;Start one byte down
LD         (HL),B      ;Save BC on stack
DEC        HL          ; high byte above low byte
LD         (HL),C
LD         B,D
LD         C,E
LD         E,(HL)      ;Load saved BC values into DE
INC        HL
LD         D,(HL)
INC        HL          ;HL now points at STACK again.
```

Whew! If you had to do that it wouldn't be worth it (also you could interchange them easily using A for intermediate storage). But on the Z80 and on any other decent CPU a stack is also implemented with special instructions. First there's a Stack Pointer 16-bit register called SP, which we can load with LD SP,nn. Second, we can "push" the contents of the register pair rp onto the stack by PUSH rp and "pop" two bytes off the stack into rp by POP rp. Hence the program above can be written more simply by

```
LD         SP,STACK   ;Interchange BC and DE
PUSH       BC          ; using stack instructions
LD         B,D
LD         C,E
POP        DE
```

for a total of seven bytes. In fact, since the SP should always be set to something, the exchange itself only requires four bytes, although the six-byte sequence using the accumulator (did you figure it out?) executes faster.

In Sec. 2-4, we introduced the subroutine because it's such a useful concept we needed it right away for the hands-on exercises. Now that we have explained the stack, we can show how the subroutine knows where to return to. The CALL instruction PUSH's the address of the instruction following the CALL onto the stack and then jumps to the subroutine. The subroutine ends with a RET instruction which POP's the byte pair off the stack into the Program Counter. If this sounds complicated, maybe it is, but it has to be thoroughly understood or you're completely saved from computerholism! Computers don't work without subroutine calls any better than they work without conditional branching. Well only slightly better. An example should fix you just fine!

This example combines much of what we have learned. It returns the next nonblank character typed on a keyboard to the calling program with lower case converted to upper case.

```
        .
        .
        .
        CALL      CHAR        ;Calling statement in some program
                              ; somewhere.  CHAR returns here.
        .
        .
        .

CHAR:   CALL      CI          ;Get a character from Console Input
        CP        " "         ; (See end of Sec. 2-7 for CI)
        JR        Z,CHAR      ;Ignore blanks
        CP        "a"
        RET       C           ;Return if CY set (not lower case)
        CP        "z"+1
        RET       NC
        RES       5,A
        RET
```

That's it. If you understand all that, you're on your way! If not, read it over and discuss it with your friends. Treat it like a puzzle. Another powerful feature is that CALL's and RET's can be conditional just like the JP's. This can lead to very tight code. There are lot's of other neat things to do with the Z80 instruction set, but they're best learned in some useful context.

2-9. A Tiny Operating System

Now that we've gone through a viable subset of the Z80's instruction set, you may be asking yourself, how does the Z80 actually do it's thing? How does it access memory, I/O ports, how does it interact with the user, etc. The hardware aspects of these questions are the subject of the next and remaining chapters. But a large software problem remains. In fact, with hardware becoming so cheap these days, the real make or break occurs with the software. Inadequate programs can keep a potentially powerful computer system operating like a moron.

The most basic part of the whole software picture is the operating system. This is a set of programs written by human beings who make choices just like everyone else. There's nothing sacred about an operating system; it's just that it affects everything that depends on it, namely all the user-written programs. The operating system provides the interface between user's programs, compilers, assemblers, etc., and the input/output devices. Typically it consists of a bunch of subroutines to get the next character from the keyboards, to write or read a sector on a floppy disk, to print a file etc. It might also return the time of day or control the priorities for a set of users running seemingly simultaneously on the same machine.

To illustrate about the most simple operating system imaginable, consider the following. We have two I/O devices, a keyboard with hex input and 6 seven-segment display IC's (or an ASCII keyboard and a CRT screen on a TRS-80). You could set the system up so that when you turn the computer on or hit the reset button, the hardware jumps to the start of the system, which resides in Read Only Memory (ROM). The purpose of the little operating system is to accept hexadecimal numbers from the keyboard that either specify memory addresses to examine, or bytes to store in the memory. In addition to this memory examine/modify capability, the system can jump to an address you specify. That's it! Next to nothing, but with it you can type in a program in machine language and run it. Bigger operating systems are all just elaborations on this principle. The only advantage of this little one is that you can readily understand it. Once you do, you'll start to be able to understand substantially more complicated operating systems, such as the Z80 Starter System's operating system and ultimately disk operating systems like CP/M (if you can get your hands on the source code).

The tiny operating system is listed in App. E and consists of four parts: a command dispatcher, an examine/modify routine, a change memory address routine and a display routine. The command dispatcher jumps to routines according to the commands typed. But it first pushes a return address to itself onto the stack. This allows routines to RETurn to the dispatcher when they encounter a command from the keypad. The HL register is used throughout the system to contain the address of the memory location to be examined, modified or jumped to. HL is changed by the CHGADR routine jumped to when MON (on the Z80 Starter System) or M (on the TRS-80) is typed. Digits typed are shifted into HL from the right until a command is typed. Digits shifted out the left of HL are forgotten. So if you make a mistake, just keep typing until the address is what you want. HL is incremented when NEXT (space for TRS-80) is typed. After NEXT or MEMXAM (X for TRS-80) are typed, the examine/modify loop is entered. Digits typed are shifted into the chosen memory location (HL) from the right, and the digits shifted out the left are forgotten. When the system starts up, the dispatcher encounters a NEXT code and jumps to the examine/modify routine to examine the start of memory location (on the Z80 Starter Kit, this is 2000H). When the EXEC key is pressed (G on the TRS-80), the dispatcher jumps to (HL). Better have a program there or crash! Whenever HL or (HL) are modified, the display is updated by a call to DISPLY. This is a general routine except for the STORE subroutine, which assumes a memory mapped display and binary format. The keypad input routine KPDIN returns the next key value typed with CY set for a command and reset for a digit. This routine is given in App. F.

Problems

2-1. Write a subroutine to convert upper case letters to lower case.

2-2. Write a subroutine that returns with Z flag set if A contains an ASCII digit ("0" to "9").

2-3. Write a subroutine to test the bit in A specified by the binary number (0 to 7) in B.

2-4. Write code to multiply A by 9.

2-5. Write code to left shift HL by 1 place; to logical right shift HL by one place.

2-6. Write two-byte routine to interchange HL and BC.

2-7. Write a subroutine to compare HL to DE setting Z and CY flags as the CP instruction does for the accumulator.

2-8. Write two-byte code to set/reset the Z flag according to the non-zero/zero contents of HL.

2-9. Write a subroutine to compare two character strings terminated by ASCII nulls (binary 0). Set Z flag if and only if identical.

2-10. Write a subroutine to logically and the two 16-bit words whose addresses occur in line following the call statement. Any registers used must be restored before returning. Note: a normal return will bomb, since it tries to execute the first address pointer.

2-11. Write a routine to add (B) 16-bit numbers stored starting at HL. Hint: use EX (SP),HL and DE registers, but no other registers or memory.

2-12. The Z80's D_0-D_7 lines come to pins 7 thru 15 (skipping 11), but are numbered D_4, D_3, D_5, D_6, D_2, D_7, D_0 and D_1 respectively. To get a simple I/O connection without crossing any lines, write a program to unscramble these data lines, i.e., internal bit 0 should go to D_4, bit 1 to D_3, etc.

2-13. Rewrite the console input routine in Sec. 2-7 using memory mapped

I/O. Note that you can use bit instructions. An interesting variation is to point at the I/O port area of memory with one of the Z80's special index registers IX and IY. This takes some of the pressure off HL.

2-14. Write a routine to convert hexadecimal digits to 7-segment displays. Note that AbcdEF can all be represented nicely. Write a routine to convert hexadecimal digits to ASCII.

2-15. Write an EBCDIC (IBM's character code) to ASCII conversion routine. Hint: use a table lookup.

2-16. Write a divide routine to divide by 2^n.

2-17. Write a routine to divide by any 16-bit number. Hint: use 16-bit subtract instruction.

References

W. Barden, Jr., 1979, TRS-80 Assembly Language Programming, Radio Shack. A bargain for the price ($3.95).

K. Spracklen, 1979, Z80 and 8080 Assembly Language Programming, Hayden Book Co., Rochelle Park, NJ. This book uses TDL extended 8080 mnemonics for the Z80. Learn two instructions sets at the same time!

L. A. Leventhal, 1979, Z80 Assembly Language Programming, Osborne/McGraw-Hill, New York. Detailed and nicely laid out.

R. Zaks, 1980, How to program the Z80, Sibex Inc., Sold by Radio Shack stores. Contains a detailed discussion of every instruction and many examples.

Zilog Z80 Technical Manual, published by Zilog, Inc., 10460 Bubb Road, Cupertino, CA 95014. Also available from Mostek Co., 1215 W. Crosby Road, Carrollton, TX 75006. This is the primary hardware reference manual for the Z80.

Z80 Assembly Language Programming Manual, Zilog (address above). This defines and illustrates every Z80 instruction.

Chapter Three

Processor-Input/Output Interfacing

*Any sufficiently advanced technology is
indistinguishable from magic.*

-A. C. Clarke

OK, you say, out with it. (In with it?) How does a 40-pin dip do all
that? Sure it's got a bunch of 8-bit and 16-bit registers, but it has no additional memory of its own and no I/O ports. So how does it convince other
IC's to provide it with the necessary memory and I/O ports? Sounds like a
real con job! Well, as usual, it's just plain logic. This chapter defines the 40
pins of the Z80 and shows you how to connect them to memory and I/O
ports. It explains how "handshaking" conventions and interrupts are implemented to synchronize slow I/O devices to the CPU. It discusses wait
states and Direct Memory Access (DMA) methods for high speed data access
to the computer memory. A major fringe benefit is that understanding the
Z80 provides you with concepts common to all computer systems. The basic
principles are quite portable from machine to machine, although some details
vary.

3-1. The Forty Pins

As you see in Fig. 3-1, 16 of the Z80's 40 pins are the address lines A0-
A15 and are collectively referred to as the address bus. A high is a one and
a low is a zero, so you can read off an address with your voltmeter (if you
pull the $\overline{\text{WAIT}}$ line low: otherwise the Z80 keeps a given address out there
for less than a microsecond). Eight more lines are the data lines D0-D7,

Murray Sargent III and Richard L. Shoemaker, Interfacing Microcomputers to the Real World, ISBN 0-201-06879-6

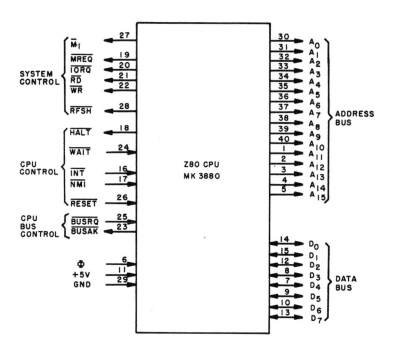

Fig. 3-1. Z80 Pin Configuration.

known as the data bus. This bus is bidirectional: the Z80 can output 8 values or it can input 8 values. The system control lines tell whether to input or output. As with the address bus, the data lines are high for 1's and low for 0's. Then there are the three life lines, +5 volts, ground, and the clock. The clock is a TTL-level (with a 330 Ω pull-up to 5 volts) square wave supplied by an external oscillator, such as that in Fig. 1-18. The Z80 does something every time the clock ticks (each period of the square wave), and if you stop the clock, you halt the Z80 in its tracks. The clock can run from 0 to 2.5 MHz for all Z80's, provided the low value is a maximum of 2 microseconds. So if you stop the Z80 by stopping its clock, stop the clock on the high level. The Z80A runs up to 4 MHz and the Z80B up to 6 MHz. A CMOS Z80 is available from Intersil, which runs 4 MHz or better with a five-volt supply and up to 10 MHz with a 12-volt supply. The pinouts of the CMOS version correspond to the Intel 8085, which has multiplexed low-address and data busses, along with a few other changes.

Now we get to the "control bus". This bus gives the Z80 arms to reach memory and I/O ports. All lines in the bus are active low. Thus $\overline{MREQ}$ (Memory REQuest) low means a stable memory address is on the address bus. $\overline{RD}$ (ReaD) low at the same time means that the Z80 wants to read a byte from memory at the address it has on the address bus, i.e., it wants the memory to put a byte onto the data bus. Now if there's no memory out there at that address, the Z80 just sees 0FFH, all ones, provided the data lines have pull-up resistors on them. If it's using this data as an instruction

(0FFH = RST 7), it CALL's location 38H. If a 0FFH or nothing is at 38H, the Z80 goes into a loop calling 38H, pushing return addresses on the stack forever writing all over any existing RAM in your system. Actually this generates easily recognizable address patterns for checking out Z80 controllers and CPU boards. More later about what the Z80 thinks is data and what it thinks are instructions (see the $\overline{M1}$ signal description below). If $\overline{WR}$ (WRite) goes low when $\overline{MREQ}$ is low, that means the Z80 wants to write the byte it's placing on the data bus into the memory address it's specifying on the address bus.

That takes care of referencing memory. Only two changes exist for reading and writing I/O ports. First, the Z80 puts $\overline{IORQ}$ (IO ReQuest) along with $\overline{RD}$ or $\overline{WR}$ low to indicate an I/O read or write is being made, and second, only the low eight address lines contain the port address (remember that there are only 256 input ports and 256 output ports?) Actually, the IN A,(n) and OUT (n),A instructions also stick the contents of A out on the high address byte, which you might find useful someday. So now you see how an I/O device could act like memory or like an I/O device; it simply chooses to respond either to $\overline{MREQ}$ or to $\overline{IORQ}$. The Z80 doesn't know who's out there, and doesn't even care. With so much intelligence, it's amazing that it doesn't care! But today anyhow computers are just automatons doing exactly what they're told to do without feelings. Similarly memory can pretend it's a set of I/O ports, and as such it's far less likely to be written over in the event of a stack crash (which fortunately isn't as serious as a stock crash). If memory or I/O devices cannot respond as fast as the CPU is running, they have the privilege to pull the $\overline{WAIT}$ line low, telling the CPU to wait until they release the $\overline{WAIT}$ line. Believe it or not, with these 5 control lines plus the address and data busses, you can do almost all of the interfacing you'll ever want to do.

Before the CPU can make any I/O requests, it has to read instructions from memory. This is done using $\overline{MREQ}$ and $\overline{RD}$, and to indicate that it's referencing an op code, it pulls $\overline{M1}$ low as well. For a Z80 to indicate that it is expecting an op code is more than an idle gesture, for it cues peripherals as to what's up. The sophisticated interrupt capabilities of the Z80 and its peripheral family (more about them all later) involve some instruction decoding by the peripherals themselves, so they need to know when op codes are being read. $\overline{M1}$ is also handy for human beings to synchronize their oscilloscopes to to get an idea of what's going on on the Z80's submicrosecond time scale. Suppose you execute the instruction

HERE: JP   HERE   ;Loop here forever

Put $\overline{M1}$ on the oscilloscope's channel A and sync to it, and then look at $\overline{MREQ}$, $\overline{RD}$ and the clock ϕ. The timing diagram in Fig. 3-2 summarizes the first part of what you should see, namely the op code "fetch" from memory (or whatever is out there pretending it's memory). The top line shows the clock (ϕ) ticking away, T_1, T_2, T_3, T_4. Remember that a clock is needed to let all lines settle to their correct levels. On a 2MHz (slow) system, the

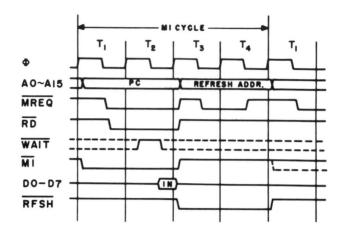

Fig. 3-2. Timing diagram for the Z80 op code fetch cycle. (From the Zilog Z80 manual, Fig. 4.0-1)

tick period is 500 nanoseconds, which you can check with your scope. Just after the positive edge of the T_1 period, the Z80 pulls $\overline{M1}$ low and puts the value of the Program Counter (PC) on the address bus. Just after the negative edge of T_1, the Z80 pulls $\overline{MREQ}$ and $\overline{RD}$ low, indicating that it wants to read the byte specified by the program counter. At the end of T_2 (unless some wait states are inserted by the memory), the Z80 reads whatever is on the data bus, and proceeds to interpret it as an op code. If the PC was pointing at data, crash! In the case of the JP instruction above, the Z80 reads memory two more times for the 2-byte address, so an oscilloscope trace shows three low values of $\overline{RD}$ for each low value of $\overline{M1}$. $\overline{MREQ}$ gets four low values, one coinciding with $\overline{RFSH}$, which we discuss shortly.

To see how the I/O control signals work try executing the program

```
LOOP:     OUT        (0),A        ;Write something to port 0
          JR         LOOP         ;The record ain't broke, the record ...
```

Look at $\overline{IORQ}$ (handy pin 20) on channel A and trigger on it (it goes low only once in the loop). Then examine $\overline{RD}$, $\overline{M1}$, $\overline{RD}$, $\overline{MREQ}$, etc. The output cycle itself is summarized by the timing diagram in Fig. 3-3. The top line shows the clock ticking away, T_1, T_2, $T_w{}^*$, T_3, T_4. Shortly after the rising edge of T_1, the Z80 asserts the port address on line A0-A7. Just after the rising edge of the T_2 period, the Z80 pulls $\overline{IORQ}$ low to tell any devices that care that an I/O request is being made. For reads, the Z80 pulls $\overline{RD}$ low at the same time as $\overline{IORQ}$ goes low. For writes, it pulls $\overline{WR}$ low instead of $\overline{RD}$, at a time after the data bus has had time to settle. The $T_w{}^*$ tick is a wait state that the Z80 automatically inserts on all I/O operations. An I/O device can insert more of its own by pulling the $\overline{WAIT}$ line low as soon as

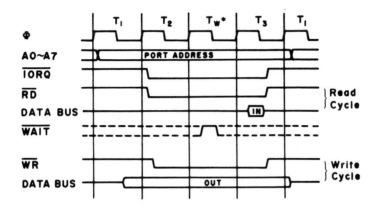

Fig. 3-3. Timing diagram for the Z80 input/output cycle. (From the Zilog Z80 manual, Fig. 4.0-3)

the device is addressed. Note that on input the Z80 samples the data bus substantially later than the beginning of the IORQ active time. This gives the input port the maximum time to respond and to let the data lines settle. On a 2 MHz system, more than one microsecond intervenes between the initiation and actual reading of data. This is adequate for any TTL port and most "smart" ports such as the Z80 PIO and CTC. The Zilog Z80 Technical Reference Manual has a number of other useful timing diagrams illustrating the use of wait states and interrupts. Read these over for a more complete understanding.

On to the remaining seven pins. One of these, the interrupt line INT, is so useful we devote Secs. 3-4 and 3-5 to it. An I/O device can pull this line low, causing the Z80 to literally CALL any location in memory. Specifically the Z80 pulls both M1 and IORQ low to acknowledge the interrupt and thereby asks the interrupting device to put a byte on the data bus explaining where the Z80 should call (more in Sec. 3-4). This combination of signals is usually called INTA for INTerrupt Acknowledge. If the Z80 has its interrupts enabled, this call can occur at the termination of any instruction, that is, right in the middle of some routine. The so-called interrupt handler, a program, must save whatever registers it needs to use, do its thing, restore the registers and RET. Section 3-5 illustrates this concept with a real time clock implementation, and Sec. 3-4 shows you how terminals can interrupt. What address the Z80 calls on an interrupt depends on the interrupt mode you choose as discussed in Sec. 3-4. Another interrupt line is available (NonMaskable Interrupt - NMI) that calls location 66H willy nilly! This interrupt line is particularly useful for handling disastrous situations such as power failure. Trouble is, you have to have a routine (or a JP to a routine) at location 66H. Consequently, it's best used in small systems having Read

Only Memory (ROM - see Sec. 6-1) or EPROM (Erasable Programmable ROM) in low memory. This is fine for controllers (see Sec. 6-2) and the TRS-80, but not so useful for the larger systems described in Chaps. 6 and 7, which require RAM in low memory. The $\overline{\text{NMI}}$ line is negative edge triggered, in contrast to $\overline{\text{INT}}$, which is active low. The edge trigger is necessary, since $\overline{\text{NMI}}$ is nonmaskable.

An interesting feature of the Z80 is the $\overline{\text{RFSH}}$ line. When this is low and $\overline{\text{MREQ}}$ is low, A0-A6 have a "refresh" address on them for refreshing dynamic RAM's. These RAM's store their bits on tiny capacitors that must be refreshed every 2 milliseconds or the charge will leak off and the computer will lose its memory! So the Z80 provides an address byte that scans through the "rows" of the dynamic RAMs keeping them refreshed. More on that in Sec. 6-1. The TRS-80 uses this feature to eliminate about four IC's. One thing to note: $\overline{\text{MREQ}}$ low does not by itself mean the Z80 wants to read or write memory. It may be putting a refresh address out on A0-A6, 0 on A7 and the interrupt-mode-2 address byte (see Sec. 3-4) on A8-A15. On the other hand, since the Z80 ignores the data bus during refresh, it doesn't matter if memory responds then. This fact is used in the mimimum Z80 system of Fig. 3-4. In the study of the JP to HERE instruction above, try comparing the $\overline{\text{MREQ}}$, $\overline{\text{RD}}$ and $\overline{\text{RFSH}}$ traces. You'll see that the $\overline{\text{MREQ}}$ pulse that doesn't have a $\overline{\text{RD}}$ low has a $\overline{\text{RFSH}}$ low instead.

$\overline{\text{HALT}}$ low means the Z80 has executed a HALT instruction. You can snap it out of its thumb twiddling (executing NOP's) by pulling $\overline{\text{INT}}$ low, $\overline{\text{NMI}}$ low or by pulling:

$\overline{\text{RESET}}$ low forces the program counter to 0 and initializes the interrupt registers as discussed in Sec. 3-4. It's sort of like an interrupt, except for this initialization and the fact that no return address is pushed onto the stack. $\overline{\text{RESET}}$ is used to restart your system typically when it has crashed or you've just turned the power on. Most computers have a switch connected to this line to restart the system.

We've now seen briefly three ways to synchronize data transfer between the computer and the I/O devices: polling, interrupts and wait states. Each has its advantages and disadvantages. For high speed operation (e.g., faster that 50 kbytes/sec), polling and interrupts are no longer feasible. A dedicated Z80A (operating with 4 MHz clock) with appropriate wait states can increase the data rate to 190 kbytes/sec using the block I/O instructions. But to get 1.2 MHz without CPU dedication, you have to resort to Direct Memory Access (DMA), the fourth of the synchronization methods. One DMA implementation utilizes the two remaining Z80 pins, $\overline{\text{BUSRQ}}$ and $\overline{\text{BUSAK}}$. The address, data and control lines, i.e., all output lines except $\overline{\text{BUSAK}}$ are tristate lines. Another CPU, a DMA controller or other I/O device can pull $\overline{\text{BUSRQ}}$ low, requesting that the Z80 "look the other way". The Z80 then simply vanishes, electrically speaking, from the show and some other device mans the address, data and control busses (everything except $\overline{\text{BUSAK}}$). The Z80 says OK to the bus request by pulling $\overline{\text{BUSAK}}$ (bus acknowlege) low. More about this in Sec. 3-7 on DMA, along with a more detailed comparison of the four synchronization methods.

That's all 40. You see that on chip the Z80 has only its registers for memory and no I/O ports, but with its various busses it can directly access 64K RAM, 256 input ports and 256 output ports. With a bit of imagination (perverse perhaps?), you see that the Z80 can rule the world!

3-2. Input/Output Ports

The Z80 is useless without devices to converse with. This section discusses some general principles about the devices and gives a simple example of a complete Z80 computer system. Two basic concepts are common to all I/O processes: latching the data and recognizing that the CPU is addressing you. As shown in the timing diagrams in Figs. 3-2 and 3-3, the CPU doesn't output or look at data very long. If you want to light up some LED's with a particular pattern, you can't just hang them on the data bus. For one thing, the Z80 outputs couldn't sink (or source) the required current. Use of 74LS04 buffers can get around this problem. But more important, the data bus is constantly changing, since instructions as well as I/O data are continually strobed back and forth across it. So you have to catch the data destined for the LED's and hold it in some flip-flops. This process is called latching the data, and an output port can be a simple latch (a collection of flip flops) such as the 74LS273 (Fig. 1-18). On input, latching may not be required as such, because the input data may be stable for a long time compared to CPU cycle times. If the data comes from a keyboard, for example, the key remains pressed for at least several milliseconds, so if the CPU examines the keyboard often enough, the keyboard data doesn't have to be latched. For such data a simple tristate buffer such as the 74LS244 (Fig. 1-12) is sufficient, along with some software to debounce the switches. This approach is used in the Z80 Starter Kit (see Sec. 3-7).

Secondly, the port has to know when it is being addressed. This is called address decoding and involves making a logical comparison between the address lines and the port number that you, the designer, choose for the port. Furthermore it requires the device to listen (for CPU output) or respond (for CPU input) just when the Z80 pulls $\overline{WR}$ or $\overline{RD}$ respectively and $\overline{IORQ}$ low. For a 74LS273 output latch, the combination of correct address, $\overline{IORQ}$ and $\overline{WR}$ low should pull the 74LS273 "enable" pin 11 low, causing the 74LS273 to latch the byte on the data bus. LED's or whatever can be attached to its output pins. Similarly on input the combination of correct address with $\overline{IORQ}$ and $\overline{RD}$ low should pull the 74LS244 tristate enable pins 1 and 19 low, which cause the 244 to stick its byte onto the data bus. If you decide to use different numbers for input and output, you can omit the $\overline{RD}$ and $\overline{WR}$ strobes in your decoding for these unidirectional ports. But don't then try to read an output port with this simplified decoding, since you'll write all ones into it (assuming the data lines are pulled up). Section 3-3 shows you how to hook up such input and output ports to your Z80 system. The Z80 Starter Kit shows a fairly tricky example of two 74LS273's in combination with a 74LS244 to run both the six 7-segment displays and the keypad. Such ports are called "parallel" since all eight bits are individually available as outputs, i.e., in parallel. Chapter 5 deals with serial ports which stream the bits in or out consecutively on single lines (useful for running terminals).

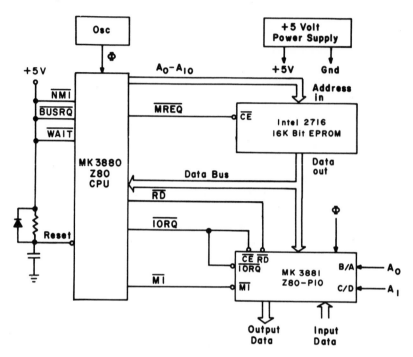

Fig. 3-4. Z80 minimum configuration. MK numbers refer to Mostek, one of the Z80's second sources. The configuration uses internal registers for RAM, EPROM for the programs and one smart parallel I/O port (PIO) for I/O.

Let's get an overview of the whole idea by considering the minimum Z80 computer system in Fig. 3-4. As with any Z80 system it includes five entities: the Z80, a 5 volt power supply, memory, a clock and I/O ports. It uses EPROM (see Sec. 6-1 for discussion) for memory with the idea that the 14 8-bit registers together with the IX and IY 16-bit registers might provide adequate RAM for a small application. The system has four I/O ports collected into a programmable I/O circuit called the Z80 PIO (Parallel I/O). Address decoding is simplified by letting the PIO worry about its four ports (chosen by A0 and A1) and addressing them for any combination of A2-A7. This multiplicity of addresses is called "redundant" decoding. The PIO has on-chip logic to respond or listen according to the values of $\overline{RD}$ and $\overline{IORQ}$. Note that $\overline{IORQ}$ low and $\overline{RD}$ high implies $\overline{WR}$ low, so that the PIO doesn't have to monitor $\overline{WR}$.

Just as the PIO in this system responds to all I/O requests, the EPROM responds to all memory requests, although it has only 2K bytes of its own (use the 2732 for 4K). So any combination of A11-A15 address the EPROM. Since no $\overline{RD}$ strobe is used (the 2716 has only one $\overline{CE}$ line), your EPROMed program shouldn't try to write to memory. The EPROM also puts data on the data bus during refresh, but the Z80 ignores it. Notice how the data bus is directly connected to both the EPROM and the PIO. This is possible because of their tristate outputs: only one responds at a time (the Z80 never pulls $\overline{MREQ}$ and $\overline{IORQ}$ low simultaneously).

More generally, we can add more memory and more I/O ports provided we beef up the logic driving the $\overline{CE}$ (Chip Enable) lines for the memory and I/O devices. Curiously enough, although the minimum system is simple to understand, it's not simple to use. You have to have a development system (bigger computer with disk, EPROM burner, etc.) to get it running. If you're dealing with a simple single unit application, you're better off with a single board computer like the Z80 Starter Kit, since you can enter data with a keypad. And if you're going to mass produce your simple system, you might be better off using a single-chip computer like the Zilog Z8 or Intel 8051. Nevertheless, we use slightly enlarged versions of the minimum systems for controllers (Sec. 6-2), since the Z80 code is so familiar and the systems can expand to meet future demands.

We close this section with a brief introduction to the "smart", i.e., programmable, parallel I/O circuit, the Z80 PIO. It's one of a number of smart parallel ports on the market, and as you'll see it has distinct advantages and disadvantages compared to other parallel ports, both smart and "dumb" (like

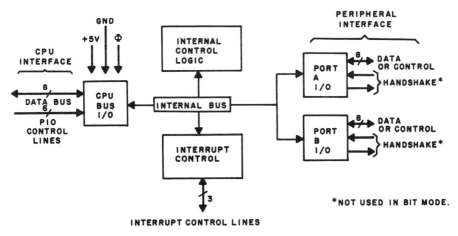

Fig. 3-5. Z80 PIO smart parallel port block diagram.

the 74LS273 and 74LS244 mentioned above). Figure 3-5 shows the Z80 PIO block diagram. On the left are the CPU interface lines: the Z80 data bus and six control lines $\overline{IORQ}$, $\overline{RD}$, $\overline{M1}$, $\overline{CE}$ and two others A/B and C/D. The A/B and C/D lines choose one of four I/O ports. Two of these are called data ports and can be attached to the real world out there. The other two are called control ports and provide the mechanisms to program the PIO and read its status. Specifically C/D high addresses a control port; C/D low addresses a data port. A/B high addresses port B's data or control port and A/B low addresses port A's data or control port. In the minimum system of Fig. 3-4, A/B is connected to the Z80 A0 line and C/D to the A1 line, giving a sequence to four ports for your software to worry about. Setting A2-A7=0, port A data is port 0, port B data is port 1, port A control is port 2 and port B control is port 3. Moving over to the right of Fig. 3-5, we see the two data ports together with "handshake" lines which allow the ports to be synchronized with peripheral devices. In the lower middle of Fig. 3-5, we see the interrupt control block, which provides the Z80 PIO with special power compared to other parallel ports. In fact, when any of a number of conditions is met, the Z80 PIO can literally CALL any location in memory! (discussed in Sec. 3-4).

The primary advantages of smart parallel ports vs the dumb ones is that 1) they can be dynamically programmed to be either input ports or output ports, 2) output ports can be read back in like memory, 3) status information is provided, 4) fewer dip pins are needed, and 4) interrupt control is implemented. Of course, you can do all that with TTL circuits, but many circuits are required. In particular, the Z80 PIO has four modes of operation: 0 for Output, 1 for Input, 2 for bidirectional (only available on port A) and 3 for bitwise control. You choose which mode along with interrupt features by writing to the appropriate control port. On some smart PIO's, e.g., the Synertek 6522, you can also read status information by reading the appropriate control port. Specific examples of this programming technique are given in later chapters, in the hands-on exercises and in the reference manuals.

With all these advantages, you ask why would anyone ever use a dumb port? Well that depends on your requirements. Dumb ports made out of 74LS244's and 74LS374's are bus drivers. They can take far more beating, source and sink much more current and are far less critical of their inputs (due to their Schmidt trigger character) than the smart ports. The smart ones are static sensitive, so bad handling can blow their minds! The dumb ones couldn't care less about static. So you may have to buffer the output of a smart port with a 74LS244 anyhow! Space and cost wise, the smart and dumb ports are more or less comparable bit for bit, unless you need the special features of the smart ports. For straight input, you can buy about four 74LS244's for the price of a Z80 PIO, so that's definitely cheaper. When several devices are best serviced under interrupt control and you use the Z80, you may save effort by using the Z80 smart ports (PIO, CTC, Combo, DMA, SIO - more about them all later). If drive power is unimportant, the most bits (24) for the money are given by the smart Intel 8255 PIO. But often in simpler applications in which you know just what you want for input and output, dumb parallel ports prove to the best choice.

3-3. Input/Output Address Decoding

This section introduces the IC's and concepts particularly valuable for wiring up custom I/O interfaces, or for understanding commercially available

I/O boards. Specifically it shows how an I/O device recognizes that the CPU is talking to it. The hands-on exercises implement these ideas on a wire-wrap board that decodes four input and four output ports. One input is based on the 74LS244 tristate octal buffer and one is from a 16 channel 8-bit Analog/Digital (A/D) converter. One output is based on the 74LS273 octal latch and two are for the A/D converter. The extra I/O port strobes are available for whatever you might need to wire up.

The wirewrap board can be configured to fit into any computer system, but we have chosen boards compatible with the S-100 bus standard. This bus (which is a collection of simpler busses, like address, data and control busses) is described in some detail in Sec. 6-3. We note here that the Z80 Starter Kit has two S-100 bus slots, allowing one to plug the wirewrap board right in. Furthermore, HuH Electronics manufactures an inexpensive TRS-80/S-100 adapter kit, so that the wirewrap board can be used equally easily with the TRS-80. And if you ultimately put together a larger computer system based on the S-100 standard, your board will plug in.

Four ports use up two address lines (A0 and A1), so we have six more lines to specify. Note that memory mapped I/O (using $\overline{MREQ}$ instead of $\overline{IORQ}$) requires specifying 14 more lines unless we permit redundant addressing. A handy IC to compare the six address lines to the desired address is

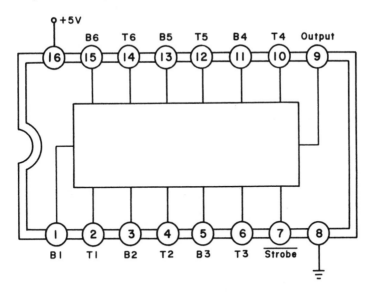

Fig. 3-6. Pinouts of the 8131 address comparator. CPU bus inputs B1-B6 are very low power Schmidt trigger inputs; comparison values T1-T6 are TTL type inputs. The output pin 9 (called $\overline{8131}$ in text) goes low if the Bn match the An in value.

the 8131, diagrammed in Fig. 3-6. Curiously enough, no 7400 number is currently assigned to this useful IC. Inputs from the bus are very low power Schmidt triggers, while the reference inputs are standard TTL. Typically the latter are pulled high by external pullup resistors, allowing dip switches

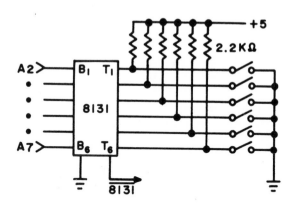

Fig. 3-7. Use of the 8131 to match an address chosen by a combination of high and low values. Values are high unless a dip switch grounds them.

to force a low value (Fig. 3-7). Alternatively, the desired address combination can be chosen by wiring the corresponding TTL inputs to +5v or ground. A low output on pin 9, which we call $\overline{8131}$, specifies that the bus and reference lines match. For address decoding, always wire the strobe line to ground, since a negative-going edge latches the inputs rather than enabling operation.

Now we have to know that the CPU is requesting I/O, and not referencing memory. We suppose two signals SINP and SOUT are available meaning that the CPU wants input and output respectively. These are trivially derived from $\overline{IORQ}$, $\overline{RD}$ and $\overline{WR}$ as shown in Fig. 3-8. If $\overline{8131}$ is low and SINP is high, then the CPU has selected one of the four input ports on the board. Which one is specified by the address lines A0 and A1. Given $\overline{8131}$, SOUT, SINP, A0 and A1, we can decide which of the eight ports is selected using a 74LS155, as shown in Fig. 3-9. The 74LS155 is a dual 1-out-of 4 data decoder. We use one half for input and the other half for output. The chosen port gets a low value on its 74LS155 connection (either a 1Yn if output, or a 2Yn if input).

We could hang our 74LS273 output latches and our 74LS244 input buffers right on the Z80 data bus, but the Z80 data lines can only drive a little more than one standard TTL load. Since we're designing an I/O card that plugs into a slot on a "backplane" (extension of the bus), we should follow the general rule of only one LS load per card. Specifically, we can buffer the data lines with the octal transceiver 74LS245 (Fig. 1-14). With a Z80

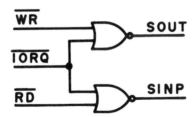

Fig. 3-8. Pair of NOR gates that can be used to generate the SINP and SOUT signals from the Z80's $\overline{IORQ}$, $\overline{RD}$ and $\overline{WR}$. SINP and SOUT are active high meaning that the CPU requests input or output respectively. These are S-100 signals (see Sec. 6-3), and with a Z80, they are the only I/O strobe signals required (the S-100 signals PDBIN and $\overline{PWR}$ are superfluous). However the Z80 smart peripherals work better with $\overline{IORQ}$ and $\overline{RD}$ in their interrupt modes.

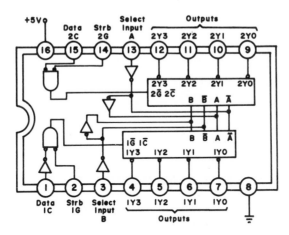

Fig. 3-9. Diagram showing how the 74LS155 is used to decode the CPU's selection of one of 8 possible ports (four for input, four for output). Only one of the eight values 1Yn, 2Yn, n=0-3 is selected at a time.

system, you always enable the 74LS245 outputs. Furthermore, you keep the direction going from the Z80 data bus to the board data bus, unless the board is selected for input. With these conventions, the $\overline{On}$ signals from the 74LS155 can be used as clocks for the 74LS273 output latches, since the data buffered by the 74LS245 is stable before SOUT goes high. It also allows the smart Z80 peripheral IC's like the Z80 PIO to decode the RETI (RET from Interrupt) instruction required for their interrupt operation (see Secs. 3-4, 3-5).

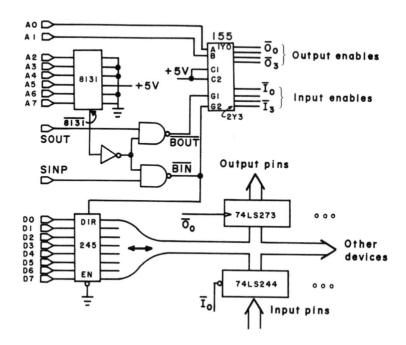

Fig. 3-10. Putting it altogether: complete I/O address decoding schematic diagram allowing four input and four output ports to be selected by individual active low lines.

Putting it all together, we have the schematic diagram in Fig. 3-10, which can interface four input and four output ports. Section 4-6 attaches a 16-channel, 8-bit A/D converter to the board's data bus. This device uses up an output port to specify which channel is desired, a second output for an initiate-data-conversion signal, an input port for the converted value, and a status bit indicating conversion complete. We attach the 74LS273 to various devices including buffers to drive relays and triacs for power control and to a DAC (Digital to Analog Converter). Room is left for some other I/O device.

The bidirectional buffering scheme of Fig. 3-10 works fine with the non-standard S-100 sockets on the Z80 Starter Kit. However, the S-100 standard officially has two 8-bit data busses, one for data out and one for data in. The S-100 expansion interface for the TRS-80 supports these two busses and does not work with the bidirectional buffering method. To satisfy the S-100 convention, we have to use two back-to-back 74LS244's (Fig. 1-13) to handle the two busses (see Fig. 8-6a). The reason the Z80 Starter Kit's S-100 slots work with the 74LS245 is that the two data busses are connected together, DO1 to DI1, etc. Since the I/O devices are run tristate, no 8-bit S-100 board can tell the difference, which also shows that only one data bus was needed in the first place.

As for the 74LS245 case, unless the board is selected for input, the output 74LS244 (from Z80 onto the board) should be enabled. In fact, Fig. 8-6a uses the inverse of the input 74LS244 enable for the output 72LS244. With these conventions, the $\overline{On}$ signals from the 74LS155 can be used as clocks for the 74LS273 output latches, since the data buffered by the output 74LS244 is stable before SOUT goes high. Note that the two-bus scheme is not easy to use with smart Z80 peripheral IC's like the Z80 PIO, since they need to read the input bus to decode the RETI instruction. These IC's were designed for a bidirectional data bus, and are seldom used on S-100 systems (except right on the CPU card) for that reason. If you don't mind being a bit nonstandard, connect the data busses together as on the Z80 Starter Kit and interface with a 74LS245. Then you can use the Z80 peripheral IC family. But you give up the S-100 16-bit data bus capability (see Sec. 6-3).

The 74LS273 and 74LS244 are much faster than the Z80, and wouldn't themselves require wait states. But what they're connected to might, or

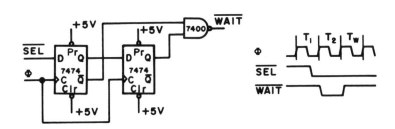

Fig. 3-11. Adding a wait state to the I/O port selected by the $\overline{SEL}$ line. To understand how this works, try starting with $\overline{SEL}$ and Q high and follow a couple of ticks after $\overline{SEL}$ goes low.

that extra device you tack on might, so Fig. 3-12 shows how to add one wait state, i.e., exactly one tick of the clock. Can you figure out how it works?

3-4. Interrupts

A computer's purpose in life is to read, write and manipulate data. While it's in the middle of processing data or waiting for some slow device to accept data, data from some other device may become available. If more than one piece of data comes in from that device, the older data will be overwritten and the computer will miss it altogether. A very valuable software/hardware method of avoiding this problem is the interrupt. When the data becomes available, the responsible device "taps the CPU on the shoulder" asking it to drop everything long enough to process the data and then go back to where it was. A prime example of this is the neglected keyboard. Your program is off in a loop somewhere; you'd like to stop it to see what's going on. Without interrupts, you'd have to restart the system losing all information about where the machine hung up. With keyboard interrupt capability (e.g., as provided in the Z80 Starter Kit), you can stop the program anywhere, look at the registers, stack, etc., and then continue as if you'd never looked in the first place. Just as when people are interrupted and have to remember where they were before the interrupt, the computer must save the program counter. The interrupt is an "asynchronous CALL", asynchronous because it can happen at any time, and CALL because the return address (current value of the PC) is pushed onto the stack and a jump to some location occurs. The routine that is CALLed, the interrupt handler, then simply returns (RET's) when it has processed the data. It must also leave every register exactly as it was before the interrupt, since the registers may well have values critical to the interrupted routine.

This section shows how interrupts are implemented in hardware and software and gives examples of their use. Two data rate ranges are discussed: medium speed (between 50 and 50000 bytes/sec) and slow speed (slower than 50 bytes/sec). High speed rates (> 50000 bytes/sec) are too fast for interrupts. Medium speed transfers typically require their own interrupt mechanisms, but slow speed transfers are easily overseen with periodic polling driven by interrupts from a Real Time Clock (RTC). As shown in Sec. 3-5, a single 60Hz RTC interrupt can greatly increase the power of a small computer system in the lab or home. We first consider the single interrupt system, and then the Z80's elegant multidevice daisy-chain interrupt facility.

Figure 3-12 shows a keyboard interface which works with many keyboards on the market. It can be used either without interrupts in a polled mode (see code for CI in Sec. 2-8) where the computer loops until the keyboard status bit goes high, or in an interrupt-driven mode. The open-collector buffer on $\overline{Q}$ allows other devices to interrupt also. Which one is determined by checking the status bits collected in port $\overline{10}$. Operation in the polled version uses little code (9 bytes), but either requires a dedicated CPU or takes a chance of missing characters.

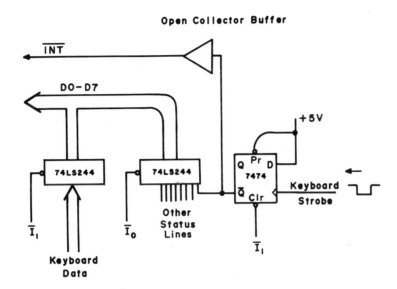

Fig. 3-12. Keyboard interface circuitry that allows for both interrupt and polled modes of operation. Other devices can be added to
this diagram by supplying additional 74LS244's for data input, con-
necting their status lines to the $\overline{I1}$ port and driving the $\overline{INT}$ line
with open collectors.   The $\overline{I0}$ and $\overline{I1}$ signals are generated as
shown for Fig. 3-10.

In interrupt-driven mode, the keyboard works as follows. When a key is
pressed, a keyboard strobe pulse is generated that clocks the 7474 flip-flop,
which, in turn, pulls INT low. When the Z80 see $\overline{INT}$ go low, it finishes the
instruction currently being executed, and then responds to the interrupt in
one of three ways. The type of response depends on which interrupt mode,
IM 0, IM 1, or IM 2, that the Z80 has been programmed for.

Interrupt mode 1 gives the simplest response: the Z80 CALLs location
38H, when $\overline{INT}$ goes low. Hence the interrupt handling routine, or a jump to
it must be located at 38H. To program this mode, execute

        IM   1   ;Put Z80 into Interrupt Mode 1
        EI   ;Enable interrupts.

The second instruction is needed because interrupts are disabled after a
reset, i.e., the Z80 ignores the $\overline{INT}$ line until an EI instruction is executed.
Interrupts are also disabled after an interrupt occurs. This is to prevent
further interrupts from interfering with an active one until any critical code
is executed.

Interrupt Mode 0 is slightly more flexible and is the default mode following reset. Only the EI instruction needs to be executed after reset to have
interrupts handled in this mode. In mode 0, which is identical to the 8080's

only interrupt mode, the Z80 expects the interrupting device to place a jump or a call on the data bus following the $\overline{\text{INT}}$ low. It requests the instruction by outputting an interrupt acknowledge signal ($\overline{\text{M1}}$ and $\overline{\text{IORQ}}$ both low). The simplest call is the RST n, where n is one of the eight memory locations 0, 8, 10H, 18H, 20H, 28H, 30H, or 38H. In particular, RST 38H (0FFH) calls 38H, like the IM 1 case. The advantage of the RST n instruction over the CALL nn is that it's only one byte long. If no special hardware is used and the data lines are pulled up, the default instruction is 0FFH, i.e., RST 38H. Alternatively, you can use a priority encoder IC like the Intel 8214. This IC outputs the binary encoding of the one of eight input lines having the highest priority. The three bits generated can be used to change the default 0FFH into any of the RST n instructions.

Interrupt Mode 2 is the most powerful, allowing a device to call any location in memory. Before describing this elegant approach, let's consider the software needed to handle the keyboard interrupt. An essential action of the interrupt handler is to input the keyboard data from port I1. In addition to getting the data for processing, the input strobe $\overline{\text{I1}}$ clears the interrupt flip flop, thereby releasing the $\overline{\text{INT}}$ line. After inputting the data (and only after, since the interrupt routine would otherwise be immediately reinterrupted for the same data), the interrupt routine can reenable interrupts by executing an EI instruction.

A minimal keyboard interrupt routine simply inputs and stores the interrupting character. Such a routine together with the Console Input (CI) routine to access the stored character is

```
CINT:    PUSH    AF          ;Be sure to save all registers
         IN      A,(DATA)    ; used in interrupt routines
         LD      (nn),A      ;Input and store character
         POP     AF
         EI                  ;Reenable interrupts & return to
         RET                 ; interrupted routine

CI:      PUSH    HL
         LD      HL,nn       ;Point at input location
CIWAIT:  LD      A,(HL)      ;Get potentially new character
         OR      A           ;Wait for nonnull character
         JR      Z,CIWAIT
         LD      (HL),0      ;Indicate no new characters
         POP     HL          ;Return with character
         RET
```

This CINT routine isn't particularly useful, unless the keyboard doesn't have a character latch. In contrast, a small addition makes CINT very useful. Specifically, CINT should check to see if the interrupting character is a special monitor character, e.g., ©X. If ©X is found, the routine jumps to a handy monitor (such as the DEMON - App. D) stored in EPROM which allows you to examine memory, etc., and then either to return where the ©X interrupted or to do something else. Trouble is, if more than one character is input before CI is called, only the last character is retrieved. And some programmers enjoy typing ahead of the system.

At the cost of some memory, we can remedy this lamentable situation by implementing a 128-byte FIFO (First In First Out) buffer. If this is too much space, it can be made smaller. The programs CONINT and CI listed below keep track of what's in the buffer with two one-byte pointers called C1 and C2, each of which indicates a position relative to BUFFER, the starting location of the buffer. The console interrupt handler CONINT uses C2 to know where to put incoming data, while the console input routine CI uses C1 to know where to retrieve data from the buffer. If C1=C2, no new characters have been input. Hence C1 effectively "chases" C2 around the buffer. Since the high bit of both C1 and C2 is always set to 0, the buffer is a 128-byte "circular" buffer, that is, byte 0 follows byte 127. This circular-buffer technique is a powerful method for interfacing two devices having different data rates. The code we use requires that the buffer start on a page boundary. We chose 0DD00H here, but any page boundary is OK. Two routines are needed: CONINT which stores a byte on interrupt and CI which gets the next character from the buffer. CI must be called regularly by whatever program is running in the computer. If either interrupt mode 1 or mode 0 with no special hardware is used, CONINT or a jump to CONINT must be located at 38H.

```
.RADIX   16                    ;Hexadecimal spoken here

BUFFER   EQU     0DD00      ;Up high on our system page
C1       EQU     BUFFER+80 ;Trailing offset pointer
C2       EQU     C1+1       ;Leading offset pointer

CONINT:  PUSH    AF         ;Save the registers used
         PUSH    HL
         LD      HL,C2      ;Increment leading buffer
         INC     (HL)       ; pointer
         LD      L,(HL)     ;Point HL at new byte position
         RES     7,L        ;Modulo 128 buffer
         IN      A,(DATA)   ;Get byte
         LD      (HL),A     ;Store it in buffer
         POP     HL         ;Restore registers
         POP     AF
         EI                 ;Reenable interrupts
         RET                ;Return to interrupted routine

CI:      PUSH    HL         ;Console Input routine; save HL
CI0:     LD      HL,C2      ;Point at leading (C2) buffer
         LD      A,(HL)     ; pointer and get it
         DEC     HL         ;Point at trailing (C1) pointer
         CMP     (HL)       ;If C1=C2, nothing new
```

```
JR      Z,CIO      ;Loop till a byte bites

INC     (HL)       ;Caught one! Increment C1
LD      L,(HL)     ;Point at next byte in buffer
RES     7,L        ;Wrap around at byte 127
LD      A,(HL)     ;Get next byte
POP     HL
RET
```

This routine prevents losing input characters unless 128 characters are typed before CI is called. Not likely, unless it's another computer that's typing (which it most definitely might be). This buffering feature is very useful. But it's just the start. Now that characters are read asynchronously, special functions can occur. With a bit more code in CONINT, you could stop program execution with a ©S (Press CTRL key and S simultaneously) by hanging in a loop inside the interrupt routine (after executing EI) and starting up again on receipt of a ©Q. Handy when the computer outputs a document onto a CRT screen too fast. You can also arrange to have special character sequences restart your system or interrogate registers. You can asynchronously "poke" (store bytes) into memory or output to ports. You can operate in a "line" mode for which CI only gets characters when a carriage return is received. This allows you to delete characters from the buffer so long as they're on the same input line. If you've used a time shared computer, you probably recognize some of these features. Such computers are all interrupt-driven and no person ever types fast enough to get ahead of them. But a microcomputer that pretends it's a terminal sure can (more on this in Sec. 5-4).

As mentioned earlier, the Z80 has three ways of being told where CONINT is: interrupt modes 0, 1, and 2. Ordinarily one wants to have interrupt handlers in ROM or EPROM, so they won't get bombed out by a program crash (it's very annoying to have your keyboard suddenly disappear!). Thus unless you have ROM on page 0 of memory, there's only one good choice: interrupt mode 2. For this mode, you choose a convenient page of memory on which to store a table of interrupt handler addresses. If there's only one handler, the table is just two bytes long. The Z80 saves the page number by executing the code

```
IM      2          ;Choose Interrupt Mode 2
LD      A,0F8
LD      I,A        ;Set table address high byte to 0F8
EI                 ;Enable Interrupts
```

Here we have chosen page 0F8 for nostalgic reasons. When the Z80 acknowledges INT low (pulls IORQ and M1 low simultaneously), it expects the interrupting device to supply the low byte that completes a 16-bit table address. The Z80 then CALL's the location specified by the byte pair at this table address (this is known as an indirect call). With our simple circuit in Fig. 3-12 nothing responds to the Z80 interrupt acknowledge, so the Z80 reads 0FFH. With the code above, this means that the Z80 will call whatever location is specified by the bytes at 0F8FFH and 0F900H. So you need to include the code

```
ORG     0F8FFH    ;Interrupt handler address location
DW      CONINT    ;Put CONINT's address here.
```

This assembly language code places the address CONINT into locations 0F8FFH and 0F900H. An illustration of interrupt mode 2 operation is given in Fig. 3-13. In the present example, our simple I/O device supplies 0FFH for the interrupt vector.

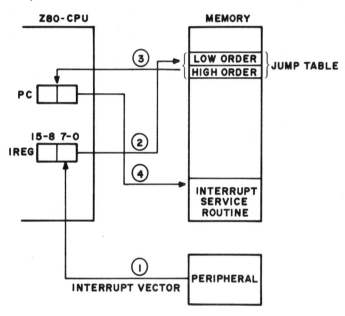

Fig. 3-13. Sequence by which an interrupting I/O device calls any location in memory under the Z80's interrupt mode 2. (From the Zilog application note on "The Z80 Family Program Interrupt Structure").

As mentioned above, several devices can pull $\overline{\text{INT}}$ low, causing an interrupt if interrupts are enabled. As soon as an interrupt occurs, interrupts are automatically disabled until another EI is executed. By reading a status port such as $\overline{\text{I0}}$ in Fig. 3-12, the computer can tell which port(s) has interrupted and then jump to the appropriate interrupt handler. This approach is simple and works on all sorts of computers. It also treats all devices on an equal priority basis, which may not be adequate for more sophisticated applications. Medium data rate devices (50 to 50000 bytes/sec) may require immediate attention to prevent loss of data.

The Z80 microcomputer family (CPU, PIO, CTC, SIO, Combo and DMA) incorporate an elegant interrupt facility complete with priority control.

First of all, the peripheral IC's can be programmed to respond to an interrupt acknowledge with user chosen low bytes. Consider the Z80 PIO, which has two data channels, A and B. Execute the code (CTLA is channel A's control port):

```
LD    A,97H    ;Enable the PIO for interrupts
OUT   (CTLA),A ; and specify low address byte.
LD    A,60H    ; Z80 peripherals want even table
OUT   (CTLA),A ; addresses (unlike the 0FFH above)
```

If channel A interrupts and the Z80's interrupt register contains 0F8H, the Z80 calls the location stored at 0F860H; if channel B interrupts, it calls the location at 0F862H. Since the table at 0F860H can have any values you want, the PIO can call any location in memory! Furthermore, if your usual address table is in EPROM and you want to debug a new interrupt handler in RAM, fine. Just tell the Z80 and the PIO where to find some new table in RAM and store the appropriate addresses. The method is completely dynamic, and is one of the distinguishing features of the Z80 microcomputer family. Interrupt handlers for the Z80 peripheral IC's must return by executing a RETI (RETurn from Interrupt) instruction or call a routine that RETI's. This reinitializes the IC's for further interrupts.

Secondly, the family supports an elegant prioritizing scheme called "daisy chaining", typically only found on larger machines. Each IC contains an interrupt enable input (IEI) and an interrupt enable output (IEO). Within the IC, each data channel (two on the PIO) has its own IEI's and IEO's. So long as a channel's IEI is high, it is allowed to interrupt, at which point it pulls its IEO low. If a channel's IEI is low, it may not interrupt and must pull its IEO low. Figure 3-14 shows a sequence of events with four channels, such as for two PIO's daisy chained together or one CTC (Counter/Timer Circuit, which has four channels). Channel 2 interrupts first and pulls its IEO low. This forces channel 3 to pull its IEO low too and prevents channel 3 from interrupting. While channel 2's interrupt handler is doing its thing, channel 1 decides to interrupt, which is allowed because its IEI is high. The Z80 calls the appropriate handler. When a RETI is executed, channel 1's IEO goes high. Typically this occurs at the end of the channel 1 interrupt handler, and channel 2's handler resumes its thing. When it in turn RETI's, channel 3 (and the others, of course) can interrupt. You may well not want to prevent interrupts for the entire duration of an interrupt service. If so, you can execute a CALL RETI, which calls the routine

```
ORG    0FFFCH    ;Put it at end of address space

RETI:  EI        ;Enable Interrupts
       RETI      ;Return from Interrupt resetting I/O device
       RET       ;CALLs to empty memory simply return
```

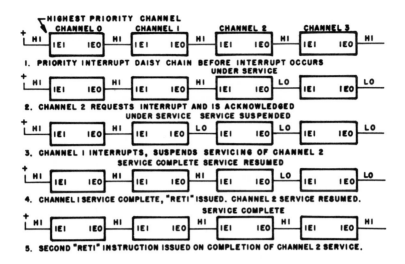

Fig. 3-14. Example of daisy chain interrupt servicing (from the Zilog Z80 CTC Technical Manual).

We store the routine at 0FFFCH in EPROM, so that any routine can take advantage of it. The ordinary RET at 0FFFFH is very useful when working with 2716 style EPROMS (see Sec. 6-1).

For many applications, the Z80 family interrupt scheme is a case of overkill. It also has problems in that signals "ripple" down the daisy chain thereby acquiring intolerable delays if more than four peripheral devices are used. Look ahead and wait state circuitry can get around this. In any event, the scheme is very flexible and may well save you effort. The ability to call any location in memory is particularly valuable, since it allows you to put your interrupt handlers in EPROM anywhere you choose, and overrule them for debugging purposes. The next section shows how a fairly powerful computer system can be organized using only a real-time-clock interrupt. For this approach, the software sets the interrupt priorities.

3-5. Real Time Clock Interrupt Scheme

In this section we show how a computer can keep accurate time with a minimum of hardware and give interrupt capability to an arbitrary number of slow speed (< 60 bytes/sec) devices. This might include a terminal, a modem talking at 30 bytes/sec to a remote computer and various keypads. The basic method is to convert the 60 Hz line voltage into a square wave (see Fig. 1-18) whose positive edges interrupt the computer 60 times a second. This single interrupt allows generation of the time of day and provides a frequent enough polling interval to check on the status of slow speed devices. In the absence of device action, the interrupt overhead is less than 3 msec/sec on a 4MHz Z80, which is unnoticeable to the user. We also show how the Z80 CTC can be used to generate a real time clock.

The hardware circuit is diagrammed in Fig. 1-19, which now takes on its complete meaning. In Sec. 1-6, it isn't possible to be precise about the $\overline{INT}$ line and the Z80's interrupt acknowledge signal ($\overline{M1}$ and $\overline{IORQ}$ both low), but an understanding of Sec. 3-4 clarifies this. On small systems that do not decode the interrupt-acknowledge signal, you can use a left over port or memory enable strobe (e.g., $\overline{I3}$ in Fig. 3-10).

The software is an extension of the console interrupt routines in 3-4. Specifically we use the Z80 interrupt mode 2 and put the interrupt address table (2 bytes worth) at 0F8FFH. We've used 0F8 for nostagic reasons (it can be anything you want) and 0FFH because we don't want to wire up circuitry to output a special byte on interrupt acknowledge. The initialization routine (executed on power-on or reset conditions) should include the code

```
IM     2            ;Choose Z80 Interrupt Mode 2
LD     A,0F8H       ;Interrupt address table on page 0F8
LD     I,A
EI                  ;Start the show
ORG    0F8FFH       ;Origin of address table
DW     CLOCK        ;Point at clock routine
```

Suppose now that only the keyboard is connected to the status byte (port 10 in Fig. 3-12). Seven other devices can be added with no increase in polling overhead. Then we use the following code to divide down to .1 sec intervals and poll the keyboard for action:

```
CLOCK:   PUSH  AF            ;Save what we're about to clobber
         EI
         IN    A,(STATUS)    ;Check status byte
         INC   A             ;Anyone low?
         CALL  Z,CONINT      ;If so, process the data
         LD    A,(PCOUNT)    ;Load the partial count
         INC   A
         CP    6             ;Down to .1 sec?
         JR    Z,RTC         ;If so, go to clock routine
         LD    (PCOUNT),A    ;Update byte
         POP   AF
         RET
```

Here we have simply called the CONINT routine of Sec 3-4 if any bit in the status byte is low. If more devices are to be polled, the STATUS byte must be examined and the handlers for corresponding 0 bits called. Note that CONINT doesn't have to PUSH AF in this context, since CLOCK already did so and doesn't have to have the old AF values on return.

The RTC routine that follows CLOCK divides from .1 second intervals down to seconds, minutes and hours. It's easy to extend this to the date with provision for leap year, etc. Furthermore, the RTC routine provides well defined time intervals for processing very slow data, such as every minute checks of various temperatures, the humidity, wind velocity, etc. It also lets you time out the motor on your disk drives after some number of seconds. We close this section with a minimal RTC routine that can be easily extended to fairly complicated applications like running a large mansion!

```
.RADIX   16                      ;As usual, all constants are hex
TENTH    DB      C1+10           ;Put time intervals near buffer ptrs
SEC      DB      TENTH+1         ;Seconds location
MIN      DB      TENTH+2         ;Minutes location
HOUR     DB      TENTH+3         ;Hour's location

RTC:     PUSH    HL              ;Save additional registers
         PUSH    DE
         PUSH    BC
         LD      B,4             ;Increment up to 4 time intervals
         LD      HL,TENTH        ;Point to time interval array
         LD      DE,CYCLE        ;Point to cycle array
RTCLP:   LD      A,(HL)          ;Get next time interval
         INR     A               ;Increment it
         OR      A               ;Clear CY for decimal arithmetic
         DAA                     ;Use packed decimal format for
         LD      (HL),A          ; easy display
         LD      A,(DE)          ;Complete cycle for this interval?
         CP      (HL)
         JR      NC,RTCS         ;If not, leave loop
         LD      (HL),0          ;Yes. 0 value and go onto next
         INC     HL
         INC     DE
         DJNZ    RTCLP           ;Do up to hours if necessary
```

;Real Time clock routines. HL -> interval being
;incremented. DE-> cycle top value (e.g., 9 for .1 sec)

```
RTCS:    LD      A,B             ;This code executed every .1 seconds
         CP      4               ;Only .1 sec incremented?
         JR      Z,RTCEND
         CP      3               ;This code executed every second
         NOP
         JR      Z,RTCEND
         NOP
         CP      2               ;This code executed every hour
         JR      Z,RTCEND
         NOP                     ;This code executed every day
RTCEND:  POP     BC              ;Restore registers
         POP     DE
         POP     HL
```

```
        POP    AF
        RET

CYCLE:  DB     9,59,59,23
```

The idea in the RTCS routine is to insert calls in place of the NOP's to whatever routines should be done every second, minute or hour at the indicated places.

Two potential problems to this simple, powerful method: 1) devices may have data rates in excess of 59 bytes/sec, and 2) excessive wait states such as used in some disk controllers can cause loss of counts. The first problem can be solved by assigning individual interrupts to the higher speed devices. The second problem can only be solved by using DMA instead of wait states or incrementing the counters an estimated amount.

If you have a Z80 CTC (Counter/Timer Circuit) available, as on the Z80 Starter Kit, for example, you can use it to make a RTC in two ways. First you can use it to divide the system clock down from the MHz range to something like 40Hz and then count down to 1 Hz intervals from there. This uses the CTC's timer mode. Alternatively, you can use it as a counter, either having it interrupt after each count (this allows periodic polling) or interrupt after 60 counts, which generates seconds directly.

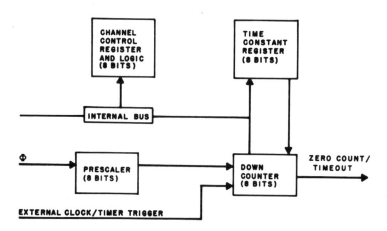

Fig. 3-15. The Z80 CTC (Counter/Timer Circuit) consists of four channels like the one diagrammed here.

The CTC has four of these counter/timer channels (see Fig. 3-15, which occupy four consecutive ports, CTC0, CTC1, CTC2 and CTC3. The low byte of the interrupt mode 2 address table is specified by outputing a byte with bit 0=0 to CTC0. Control bytes can be output to any channel, and have bit 0=1. For the most part you can ignore bits 1, 3 and 4 (see the Zilog or Mostek literature for more details). Bit 7=1 enables the channel to interrupt after a countdown completes. Bit 6=0 specifies timer mode; bit 6=1 specifies counter mode. In counter mode, the CTC channel counts down one for each period of a square wave on its external input pin. The initial count is given by a one-byte time constant. This byte is assumed to follow the control byte if bit 2=1. If bit 2=0, the previously loaded constant is used. Timer mode also decrements the count using an internally generated square wave derived from the system clock. Specifically if bit 5=0, the square wave has a period 16 times the system clock period, while if bit 5=1, the square wave period is 256 times the system clock's period. In other words, the system's clock frequency is divided (prescaled) by 16 and 256 respectively.

We illustrate these choices with three examples. First suppose the system clock has a frequency of 1,996,800 Hz (as in the Z80 Starter Kit). Executing the following code causes INTerrupt HANdler, INTHAN, to be called 40 times a second:

```
;This code initializes the CTC

START:   LD      A,20        ;Set Interrupt Mode 2 high byte
         LD      I,A         ;Store it in I register
         IM2                 ;Specify Interrupt Mode 2
         LD      A,60        ;Setup low byte for CTC0
         OUT     (CTC0),A    ; CTC1 outputs 62 on INTA, etc.
         LD      A,0A5       ;Enable CTC0 interrupts in timer
         OUT     (CTC0),A    ; mode with 256 prescale
         LD      A,0C3       ;Set time constant=195 (=0C3 hex)
         OUT     (CTC0),A    ; getting 1996800/(256*195)=40
         EI

;Continue with other code...

;Here is the interrupt jump table

         ORG     2060        ;CTC jump table
         DW      2040        ;CTC0 interrupt handler
         DW      CTC1IH      ;CTC1 Interrupt Handler, etc

;CTC0 Interrupt Handler

         ORG     2040
INTHAN:  PUSH    AF          ;Always save what you destroy
         LD      A,(PSEC)    ;Load Partial SECond count
         INC     A           ;Increment count
         CP      28          ;=40?
         JR      C,STORE     ;If < 40 counts, keep count
         XOR     A           ;If =40, 0 count
;
;Insert code here for seconds as above
```

```
STORE:    LD        (PSEC),A
          POP       AF
          EI
          RETI
```

To get a 60 Hz interrupt by connecting the Schmidt trigger output in Fig. 1-18 to CTC0 external trigger input, do as above, but output the control bytes

```
          LD        A,0C5      ;Enable interrupts in counter mode
          OUT       (CTC0),A
          LD        A,1        ;Interrupt every period, i.e, 60 Hz
          OUT       (CTC0),A
```

To get one second interrupts from the 60 Hz input, output a 3CH (=60) instead of the 1. We see more of the CTC in Sec. 4-5 on pulse generation. It can also be used for baud rate generation in serial communications.

3-6. Direct Memory Access (DMA)

At this point we have discussed three methods of synchronizing data transfers between the CPU and I/O devices: polling, interrupts and wait states. Section 3-5 showed a hybrid method which might be called periodic polling, namely polling based on a real time clock interrupt, as distinguished from what you might call dedicated polling. We've seen that periodic polling is a good technique for slow data rates (< 60 bytes/sec) and that interrupts are good for medium data rates (> 30 but < 50000 bytes/second). Dedicated polling such as that used in Sec. 2-8 for CI can be used for up to 60000 bytes/sec on a 4MHz Z80 and wait states together with the Z80's block I/O instructions (see INIR instruction) can be used up to 180000 bytes/sec.

Faster speeds require a different approach known as DMA. Two basic methods of DMA exist: use of dual-ported memories and transfers under the supervision of a DMA controller. Dual-ported memory is ordinary programmable memory that is connected to address and data-bus multiplexers. A multiplexer selects one of the two sets of lines and connnects them to the memory. Typically one set of address and data lines belongs to the Z80, while the other set is connected to some I/O device. The DMA controller, on the other hand, is a special purpose, high-speed CPU which shares the Z80's bus, and can take over on command to perform high speed data transfers. The dual-ported memory is less general, but is faster, limited only by the memory access speed. High speed memories can allow transfers in excess of 10 megabytes/sec. The dual-port approach is substantially more common than the DMA controller method because it's used extensively for terminal implementations. The TRS80, PET and Apple II all use this method. Storing into certain memory locations causes special hardware (see Sec. 4-7) to display the characters on corresponding locations on a TV screen. The data rate on a 16x64 display is 16x64 x (10 lines/char) x (60 frames/sec) = 614400 memory reads/sec, clearly too fast for the Z80 even if one didn't mind dedicating its operation. A 24x80 display has almost twice that data rate. Similarly video input into a computer is best handled with dual port memory. Because video input typically has grey levels, the amount of information (and hence the data rate) exceeds that for terminal operation. More on these topics in Sec. 4-7.

The DMA controller works differently from the dual-ported memory and

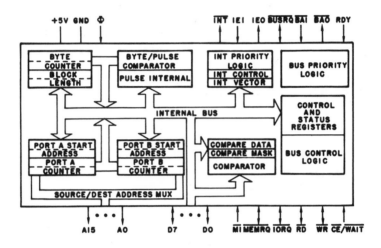

Fig. 3-16. Zilog DMA Internal Block Diagram (from Zilog Z80-DMA product specification)

has both advantages and disadvantages. Figure 3-16 shows a block diagram of the Z80 DMA controller. Its pin definitions resemble those of the Z80 itself. Essentially it is a high-speed, relatively limited version of the Z80. It has a small instruction repertoire allowing one to tell it to take over the Z80's busses (address, data and all control lines except $\overline{BUSAK}$). Among other things, it is set up to transfer bytes from any source, memory or I/O port, to any destination, memory or I/O port, until a specified number of bytes is reached or until a search byte is matched. As such it can be used to search memory for a given byte, transfer from an input device to an output device, transfer data between memory and I/O ports, etc. When I/O ports are involved, the transfers can be controlled by the RDY line and, of course, the $\overline{WAIT}$ line.

Compared to the dual-port method, the DMA controller offers complete flexibility as to source and destination, that is, any memory or any I/O port can be used, instead of specific memory connected to a specific I/O device.

It is limited, however, to about 1.2 MHz, and must be programmed to do what you want it to do. The programming is performed by a number of I/O instructions to the DMA controller, and unless at least 14 bytes are transferred, the CPU doesn't save any time over dedicated operation (of course, the data rate may not be slow enough for dedicated operation). If 256 bytes are transferred as for a double density floppy disk sector at 13 μsec/byte, the CPU does gain substantial freedom. In particular, it's then available to handle interrupts from slower devices, such as the real time clock. Such floppy disk transfers can also be handled using wait states, but then ticks of a 60Hz clock are lost. The various methods of synchronization are summarized in Table 3-1.

Method	Max Data Rate	CPU overhead
Interrupts	50,000 bytes/sec	part time (CINT - §3-4)
Polling		
periodic	RTC rate (60Hz)	little (RTC - §3-5)
dedicated	60,000 bytes/sec	full time (CI - §2-7)
Wait states	180,000 bytes/sec	full time (block I/O)
DMA		
controller	1.25 Mbytes/sec	little
2 port memory	memory access rate	none, unless wait states used on conflict

Table 3-1. Overview of synchronization methods for data transfers between CPU and I/O devices. All methods can be used for arbitrarily slow devices, but periodic polling or interrupts are preferred. Maximum interrupt and polling data rates are based on a 4MHz Z80 running the routines indicated in parentheses. The DMA methods are discussed in this section; the periodic polling method in Sec. 3-5; interrupts in Sec. 3-4; dedicated polling in Secs. 2-7 and 5-4; wait states in Secs. 3-1 and 3-3.

3-7. I/O Example: Multiplexed Keypad/Display

In controlling and monitoring devices with a computer, one has to decide how much work should be performed by hardware and how much by software. This section discusses a typical example, the multiplexed keypad/display, in which software is used to save on hardware. We do not particularly recommend this technique in practice, but it is illustrative of how software can replace hardware at the cost of either tying up the CPU or neglecting information. It also gives the CPU complete control over both keypad and display. The approach is used in the Z80 Starter Kit, in the KIM I and SYM I 6502 single-board computers, and for the TRS80 keyboard.

The Starter Kit's six 7-segment displays are run by outputting appropriate streams of bytes to two 74LS273 ports (see Fig. 3-17). The keypad data is encoded into unique binary codes for each key using one of these latches in combination with a 74LS244 input port. Consider the displays first. Each one consists of seven LED segments that light if they have both a current source and a current sink. One 74LS273 (IC U12) called SEGLH (SEGment LatcH) turns on transistors that source the seven segments. Referring to Fig. 3-17, we see that when pin 5 of U12 goes low (bit 1), transistor Q2 turns on, sourcing the b segments for all six display IC's. No b segment will light, of course, unless its IC has a current sink as well. The other 74LS273 called DIGLH (DIGit LatcH) determines which display IC's have current sinks. For example, when pin 2 of DIGLH goes high, a 75452 driver IC sinks current from the rightmost 7-segment display. The code

```
LD      A,0FD      ;Set bit 1 alone low
OUT     (SEGLH),A  ;Source all b segments
LD      A,1        ;Set bit 0 alone high
OUT     (DIGLH),A  ;Turn on rightmost display
```

turns on the b segment of the rightmost display. Don't do this very long because too much current flows through the rightmost b segment. Allowing for the voltage drop across the transistors (the 75452 has an open-collector output) and the LED, we find about 50 ma flows through the LED, which is too much for continuous use. The principle used is to drive each display about one sixth of the time, giving an average current of about 8 ma. A program loop is used to sink current from each display IC digit individually, while appropriate segments are sourced for that digit IC. Since the loop is executed many times a second, the eye can't see the flicker. This method is called time multiplexing. Each display IC gets turned on for a short period many times a second. Only seven sourcing and six sinking transistors are required to drive all six display IC's. Without multiplexing, 42 sourcing transistors would be required along with six 74LS273 latches (the sink latch wouldn't be required in this case). A subroutine (DISUP) that refreshes the displays in Fig. 3-17 is given in App. F.

The keypad can be encoded (i.e., each key gets its own binary code) by a similar multiplexing technique. When a given display has a current sink, so does one row of keys. The program that choses which display is sunk also knows which row is sunk. By reading the KBSEL port (the 74LS244 input port), the program can determine which (if any) keys are pressed in that row. If the low 5 bits are all high, no keys are pressed since the input lines are pulled high by 10K resistors. If a key is pressed, the corresponding bit goes low. For example, if the rightmost display is being sunk and the KBSEL port has bit 1 equal to 0, then the D key is being pressed. Hence the program that refreshes the 7-segment displays can also scan the keypad for closures. Appendix B includes a program called KPDIN (KeyPaD INput) that

Fig. 3-17. (adjacent page) Multiplexed keypad/display circuit used by the Z80 Starter Kit. The top 74LS273 (U12) latch is the output port that determines what segments have current sources. The lower 74LS273 latch is the output port that determines what display IC's and keypad rows have current sinks. The 74LS244 is the input port for the keypad columns.

calls the display-refresh routine DISUP and KPDSTS repeatedly until KPDSTS returns NZ, indicating a key closure. Register B then shows which row was being sunk and A indicates which key is pressed. KPDIN translates this information into a binary code, waits 20 msec to debounce the key and then waits until the key is released. KPDSTS is not used to determine when the release occurs (can you figure out why?). If two keys are pressed, the routine encodes the first one to make contact and ignores the second key.

One feature remains on Fig. 3-17, namely the role of the U15 IC in the lower right corner. This is a "one-shot" circuit (see Sec. 1-8). Given a low on its B input, it outputs a low on its $\overline{Q}$ for a time determined by the resistor and capacitor. The B input is connected to the keypad column containing NEXT, MON, SS and EXEC. If any of these is pressed, the one-shot shoots low for a time long enough for debouncing. Its output is connected to the Z80 CTC (Counter/Timer Circuit) which interrupts the Z80 if it has been programmed to do so (see Sec. 3-5). That's how the MON key gets you back to the monitor, even when the Z80 is in the middle of some other program.

Neat, you say, software can replace hardware and save money. Clearly the multiplexing could have been done by hardware that reads out a memory IC, or each port could have its own latch, etc. And the whole thing does provide an interesting I/O example. But what if someone presses a key when the CPU isn't looking? And what happens to the display when the CPU is executing a program? Nothing. The display isn't refreshed and the key closure goes unnoticed. For small time applications, e.g., controllers, such software/hardware tradeoffs are fine. But bigger applications can't afford to tie up the CPU that way. Three possibilities exist. One is to interrupt the Z80 every millisecond to drive the keypad/display software for half a millisecond. This returns half a Z80 to work on other projects. Another method is to beef up the hardware. For the keypad/display problem, the INTEL 8279 for less than $10 does everything but drive the LED's. All multiplexing, digit storage, 7-segment conversion, keypad encoding and debouncing, etc. is taken care of, although it's not as totally flexible as the straight Z80 method. The 8279 can be programmed to interrupt when a character is ready. If you're interested, read up on this interesting special purpose microprocessor. Alternatively, one can add another microprocessor to the system to handle the keypad, display and other things. It becomes a set of I/O ports to the CPU, or the two processors can communicate through some common memory locations. In fact for extensive control applications, you may have 20 or 30 microprocessors all working together, each thinking of

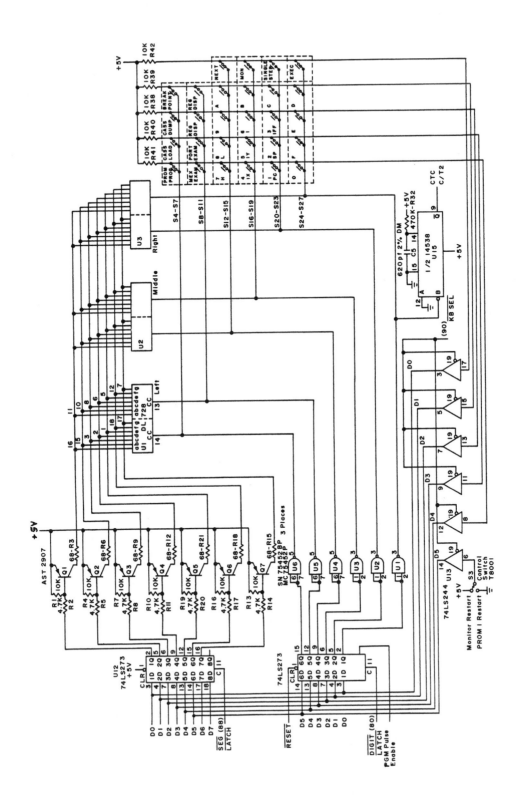

the others as programmable I/O devices. Because microprocessors are sold in large quantities, they're bargains for the price and are often cheaper even for a set of menial applications than the support IC's you might be tempted to buy.

Problems

3-1. What single character change needs to be made in the CINT and CI routines to make the circular buffer 64 characters long? 32 characters long? On what 64 or 32 byte blocks can these smaller buffers be placed?

3-2. Use the Z80's alternate register set (see EX AF,AF' and EXX instructions) to speed up the real time clock interrupt routine. You can use the alternate register B to store PCOUNT during the countdown to .1 seconds and then use it as a loop counter within the .1 second's routine. Note that to access the alternate register set from outside the interrupt routine, you must first disable interrupts (Why?). It's not a good idea to use the alternate set for interrupts on larger Z80 systems, since high level software may well use them and you'd have to save/restore their contents.

3-3. Use a 74LS138 to interface an arbitrary combination of eight I/O devices, i.e., ignore $\overline{RD}$ and $\overline{WR}$; only use $\overline{IORQ}$. What happens if you now read an output port?

3-4. Using two 74LS138's, design address decoding for eight input ports and eight output ports.

3-5. Using an octal latch output port, design a Z80 system with 8x64K = 512K bytes of memory. Hint: use different A_{15} lines for each bank, setting the appropriate value with the output port. This is a memory banked system in the small, and requires software to complete its implementation.

3-6. Write code for an interrupt driven time shared computer running an editor and operating system residing in the lower 32K of memory and various user data areas residing in individual 32K upper memory banks, one to each user. A particular 32K upper bank is enabled by a bit of the output port discussed in Prob. 3-5. Use a real time clock interrupt to periodically poll the user keyboards and switch from one user to another. Use spare time to poll output buffers.

3-7. Design eight bytes of output ports using the 74LS259 bit latches instead of 74LS273's to save 20% board space.

3-8. What problem occurs in an interrupt-driven system if the stack pointer is used to manipulate a data array? Moral: don't use the stack pointer in this way.

References

A. Osborne, 1979, An introduction to microcomputers, Vol. 3: Some real support devices, Osborne/McGraw-Hill, Berkeley, CA. The most complete compilation of peripheral IC's.

B. A. Artwick, 1980, Microcomputer interfacing, Prentice-Hall, Englewood Cliffs, NJ.

P. Horowitz and W. Hill, 1980, The art of electronics, Cambridge University Press, New York.

S. Libes, 1980, Interfacing to S-100 (IEEE-696) microcomputers, Osborne/McGraw-Hill, Berkeley, CA.

J. A. Titus, 1979, TRS-80 Interfacing, Howard Sams, Indianapolis, Indiana.

The TTL Data Book for Design Engineers, 1976, Texas Instruments, Dallas TX. The 7400 series Bible.

Chapter Four

Controlling/Monitoring Various Real World Devices

Intuition is necessary, but not sufficient.

In Chaps. 2 and 3, we have seen how to program and wire a microcomputer to read and write parallel I/O ports, including implementation of address decoding and data synchronization methods. The question now arises as to how the TTL level highs and lows interface to the real world quantities of switch closures, threshold detectors, analog signals, display devices and motor control. This chapter deals with the buffering and translation techniques required to interface the TTL world to the real one we live in, providing the computer with the necessary isolation to operate reliably. Section 4-1 treats mechanical and solid state switch closures. On output, switches are used to turn on devices of all power levels; on input, monitoring switch closures reveals the status of real world situations. The switch circuits are often isolated from the computer either optically or by relays, and power control is implemented with relays, SCR's and triacs. Section 4-2 treats digital-to-analog (D/A) conversion techniques. These allow one to display data on oscilloscopes and to control devices dependent on voltage levels. Section 4-3 discusses analog-to-digital (A/D) conversion methods, allowing one to measure voltages. Section 4-4 illustrates the D/A and A/D methods with a discussion of signal averaging and lock-in detection, which enable one to pick a signal out of noise. Section 4-5 develops waveform generation methods, including some discussion of computer-generated music. Waveform generation is used in Sec. 4-6 to control stepper

Murray Sargent III and Richard L. Shoemaker, Interfacing Microcomputers to the Real World, ISBN 0-201-06879-6

motors. Section 4-7 explains how raster displays work. These displays are useful for implementing smart multichannel analysers, processing pictures digitally and presenting information graphically. The techniques discussed in this chapter can be used to interface to most devices in your home or in a scientific or engineering laboratory. A major omission is communication with other computers or with computer terminals. This subject is developed in Chap. 5.

4-1. Switch Closures, Input and Output

In this section, we are concerned with the setting and monitoring of individual bits, namely switch closures, either for input or for output. We consider input first. If a switch is located in or near the computer and turns on a positive voltage 2.5 to five volts, the computer can read it directly using 74LS244 buffers as discussed in Sec. 3-3. But if the circuit involves other voltages, or travels over some distance, the input should probably be

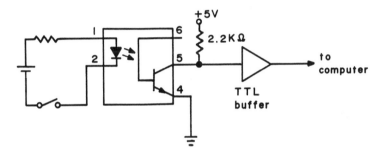

Fig. 4-1. Optoisolator dip is used to isolate computer's circuit from that of a switch. The switch can involve AC or DC voltages totally outside the 5 volt world of TTL.

optically isolated from the computer. The 6-pin optoisolator used in Fig. 4-1 is a convenient package that allows the computer to literally look at a bit of information (namely whether a switch is on or off), with typically 1500 volts or more of electrical isolation. The package combines an LED and a phototransistor and is available from many manufacturers. Currents of 10 to 20 ma through the LED cause it to emit light and turn the phototransistor on. This, in turn, pulls pin 5 of the optoisolator low. Hence the computer can see if the switch in Fig. 4-1 is closed. The switch's circuit is electrically isolated from the computer's. It can involve AC or relatively high voltages and can handle discharges from static electricity, which may be as much as 1500 volts, without affecting the computer's circuit. Figure 4-2 shows how an optoisolator can be used to generate a 60 Hz signal from the line voltage.

Many kinds of real world information can be presented as switch closures. Doors and windows can be monitored, room lights can be detected (see Fig. 4-3), water levels can be reported, temperature and humidity

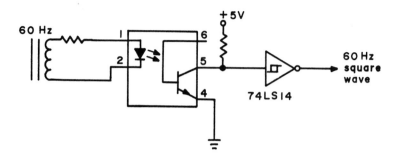

Fig. 4-2. Circuit to get 60 Hz square wave from the power line illustrates isolation from a non-TTL environment. Fig. 1-20 provides an alternative circuit.

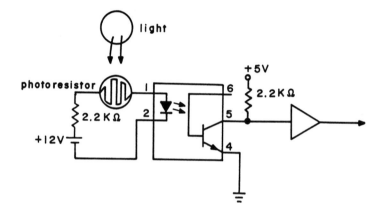

Fig. 4-3. The on/off status of a light can be monitored by using a photoresistor as the LED's current limiting resistor. If the photoresistor circuit uses more than five volts, an extra current limiting resistor may be needed (LED current shouldn't exceed 30 ma).

thresholds can be monitored. Burglar devices like LED beams and sonar alarms also typically use switch closures to indicate intrusion.

In addition, you may want to turn on devices, like lights, motors, sirens, etc., or open door latches. These things can be done by having the computer close switches, either relays or solid-state analogs like transistors, Silicon Controlled Rectifiers (SCR), and TRIAC's (TRIode AC). Status LED's can be driven directly from output latches like the 74LS273 (Fig. 1-18). Small speakers for audio output need more power, which can be supplied by a transistor as shown in Fig. 4-4. The 75452 NAND gate can also be used in this capacity, and can sink up to 300 ma and withstand off-state collector voltages up to 30 volts. The 7406 open collector hex inverter can also withstand 30 volts, but sinks a maximum of 40 ma per gate.

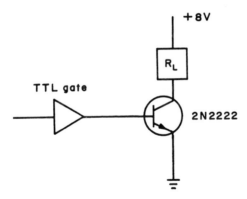

Fig. 4-4. A 2N2222 logic transistor is used to drive a small speaker. This transistor can sink up to 150 ma. TTL circuits can source the 3 ma required to turn the 2N2222 on. Typically one uses a current-limiting resistor in the transistor's base circuit. For ordinary TTL, this isn't necessary, but with the 74LS244 it is.

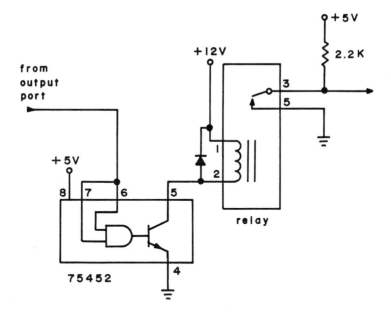

Fig. 4-5. Small relay circuit allows computer to turn on currents up to 1 ampere at voltages outside those of the TTL world.

Higher currents can be driven with bigger transistors and with relays. A simple relay circuit is shown in Fig. 4-5. Some relays work with 5 volts, and small relays requiring higher voltages can be operated with the 7406 (or with the 7407 noninverting open collector buffer). To protect the open collector from seeing excessive voltages when the relay is turned off (inductors generate high voltages when a current suddenly stops flowing through them), a reverse diode is included. This diode shorts out the voltage spike. The little relays are typically rated at 1 ampere, and can be used for driving bigger relays and devices. They have no on-state voltage drop (as transistors do) and isolate the output circuit from the computer's. On the negative side, they have slow response times (on the order of 1 msec), can arc and wear out under high repetition rates.

In somewhat different applications, optoisolators coupled to SCR's (Silicon Controlled Rectifiers) and TRIAC's (AC TRIodes) play important roles. The SCR switches current on in one direction only, while the triac switches AC currents. Since the triac acts something like a parallel pair of reversed

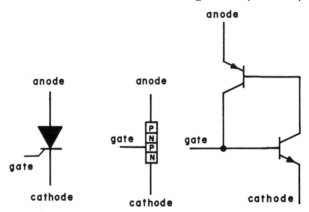

Fig. 4-6. Silicon Controlled Rectifier (SCR) symbol, junction configuration and equivalent circuit. Once turned on, the SCR stays on until the anode-cathode current falls below the holding value.

SCR's, we describe the SCR first. Figure 4-6 shows the SCR symbol, junction configuration and equivalent circuit, and Fig. 4-7 shows the current-voltage characteristic. The SCR acts like a diode that can be switched on by raising the voltage of the gate relative to the cathode. Once the SCR is on, it stays on as long as a minimum current flows from the anode to the cathode. This happens because the two effective transistors "egg each other on." When the lower (NPN) transistor is turned on by the gate, the upper (PNP) transistor is forward biased, and therefore turned on also. But once the upper transistor is on, the lower is forward biased and remains on. Thus once you turn the SCR on, it stays on until the current flow quits or tries to reverse direction. This is fine for DC currents if you want a latching switch, but there's no simple way to turn it off (except manually!) The SCR is easier to use with AC voltages, which reverse polarity on a regular basis. If the gate is held positive, the SCR provides a half-wave rectified signal as shown in Fig. 4-8a. By delaying the gate voltage relative to the AC voltage, the SCR turns on later in the cycle (Fig. 4-8b). This is how room light dimmers work, and a computer could easily provide the desired gate delays. SCR's come in all sizes, from 300 ma varieties which include optoisolation of the gate (optoSCR) to 500 ampere varieties used in mining

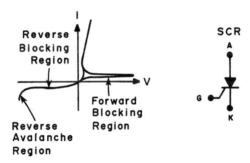

Fig. 4-7. SCR current/voltage characteristic. SCR has two possible forward biased outputs unlike an ordinary diode. If it has a minimum anode-cathode current, it offers very little resistance. For smaller currents, it has high resistance blocking current flow unless a large voltage is applied.

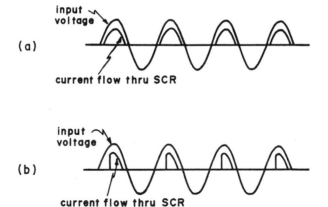

Fig. 4-8. SCR response to AC input signal with a DC positive gate, and with a gate that lags the input signal (useful for dimmers).

equipment. They respond substantially faster than relays, don't arc, and provide dimming capability. On the negative side, they're hard to turn off for DC applications, and introduce a voltage drop unlike relays.

If a controllable AC switch is desired, the triac (Fig. 4-9) may suffice. While the SCR rectifies an AC signal, the TRIAC passes both directions when its gate (G) has the same polarity as its MT2 (Main Terminal 2). The device acts very much like two SCR's of opposing polarity connected in parallel and fired by a common gate. A triac can be driven by the MOC3011 optotriac as shown in Fig. 4-10. One problem can occur in switching inductive loads, for which the current lags the voltage in time. The triac is supposed to turn

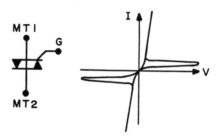

Fig. 4-9. TRIAC (AC TRIode) symbol and current/voltage characteristic. Acts as an AC switch.

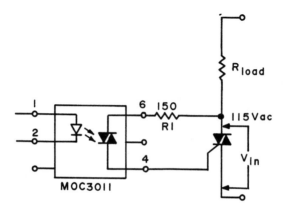

Fig. 4-10. Optocoupled triac circuit allows computer to switch AC voltages (from Motorola MOC3011 Ap. Note).

off for currents less than a minimum holding current. At this point, the voltage is increasing to its maximum value, so that suddenly the triac is supposed to block a large voltage. Triacs cannot block instantaneously, and consequently the rate of change in voltage across the triac must be kept below the manufacturer's specification. Otherwise the triac may stay on once triggered, regardless of the gate voltage. The rate of change of the voltage can be reduced by "snubbing" the triac with an RC network as shown in Fig. 4-11. Alternatively, you can buy a circuit similar to Fig. 4-11's all potted neatly in a case about .5"x1.5"x1.2". Known as a solid-state relay, this module plugs into a pc board that's UL approved for up to 220 volts AC. The convenience may well be worth the extra cost. Furthermore they can be driven by low-power CMOS circuits (good for battery operation).

Many AC devices are controlled by 24 VAC rather than 110 VAC. This "low voltage" doesn't develop fire danger and hence is hardly mentioned in the National Electricians Code (but don't run 24 VAC lines in the same con-

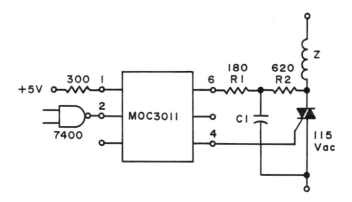

NOTE: Circuit supplies 25 mA drive to gate of triac at V_{in}= 25 V and T_A≤70°C.

LOAD POWER FACTOR	C
1.0	0
0.75	0.22µF
0.5	0.33µF

Fig. 4-11. "Snubber" RC network is used to limit time rate of change of voltage across triac as the triac tries to turn off while driving an inductive load. The power factor is the cosine of the angle between the voltage and the current (for a resistor, this angle is zero (cosine=1), but it can be 60° (cosine=.5) for significantly inductive loads (from Motorola MOC3011 Ap. Note).

duit as 110 VAC). In particular, thermostats, sprinkler system values, and low voltage relays can all run on 24 VAC. So your computer can run a home with the circuit in Fig. 4-11. Another useful device is the low voltage latching relay shown in Fig. 4-12. This device turns on up to 20 amperes at 277 VAC. It acts just like an ordinary wall switch, except that to turn it on, you momentarily (.1 sec) apply 24 VAC between the white and red leads, while to turn it off, you momentarily apply the voltage between the white and blue leads. In practice, the white lead is always connected to one side of the 24 VAC line, and a pair of optotriac circuits (Fig. 4-10) or small relays are used to turn the big relay on and off. In addition, any number of local momentary contact switches can be used to turn the relay on and off, i.e., it provides "N-way" switching. The relay fits readily into a standard junction box and passes the National Electrician Code. As such it's ideal for the control of 110 VAC lights, motors and other fairly heavy duty equipment.

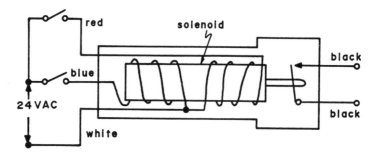

Fig. 4-12. Sierra latching relay is turned on by a momentary 24 VAC across the red and white lines and turned off by the voltage across the blue and white lines. Inside the solenoid cylinder is a smaller metal cylinder. The latter is pulled inside a turned-on coil. The relay fits in junction boxes and passes the National Electrician's Code.

4-2. Digital to Analog Conversion

Reading and setting switch closures provides a computer with substantial I/O capability. However some applications require more than a single bit of depth, and for these we need to interface to the variable voltage or analog world. This section deals with outputting analog voltage levels (D/A conversion), while the following section handles analog input. One reason for this order of presentation is that many analog to digital (input) devices use Digital to Analog Converters (DAC's) in their conversion. Uses of DAC's include setting mirror deflections and rotor positions, choosing temperature and pressure levels, controlling motors, voltage controlled oscillators and amplifiers, generating waveforms, and most important, displaying graphical data.

A DAC consists of four main parts: a voltage reference, a resistor network, a digitally controlled set of analog switches and in most cases an output buffer that converts current to a voltage. The buffer is an operational amplifier (op amp) and is so useful here and elsewhere that we review it first. Figure 4-13 shows an op amp used in a typical application: amplifying an input voltage V_i to give an output voltage $V_o = -R_o V_i / R_i$. This relationship can be understood quickly if you're willing to swallow the characteristics of the ideal op amp. These are: infinite input impedance, infinite gain and zero output impedance. If you're not familiar with the term impedance, don't worry. It's just resistance, generalized to include the resistance of inductors and capacitors to the flow of AC currents. It's measured in ohms, like ordinary DC resistance. The op amp's infinite input impedance means that no appreciable current can flow into the inputs because they look like a very large resistance to external signals, typically 10^6 - 10^{12}

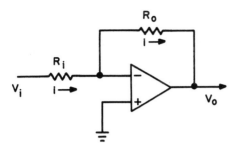

Fig. 4-13. Typical op amp circuit. − input is held at ground potential and accepts no current. Input current is pulled through the
output resistor R_O by the op amp's output voltage V_O. $V_O =$-
$R_O V_i / R_i$.

ohms in real devices. Infinite gain means that any voltage difference
between the + and − inputs is amplified by a very large factor, so that even
the smallest voltage difference at the inputs produces a relatively huge
output voltage. In real devices, this gain is typically 10^5 - 10^6. Zero
output impedance means that the output can supply whatever amount of
current is needed to maintain its output voltage. Real devices typically
have output impedances of 10 - 100 ohms.

The infinite gain property implies that the voltage difference between
the + and − inputs is zero, since we divide a finite output voltage by infinity
to get the input voltage. In Fig. 4-13, this means that the − input is at
ground potential, since the + input is connected to ground. Furthermore,
since no current can flow into an infinite impedance, the input current must
all flow through R_O. The voltage V_O that keeps the input current flowing in
the same direction past the ground potential, has to have opposite sign from
V_i. By Ohm's law, we have the input current $i = V_i/R_i = -V_O/R_O$, i.e., $V_O =$
$-R_O V_i / R_i$. Since R_O can be bigger than R_i, the op amp can yield gain in a
precise way. There's much more to op amps than this (especially their
finite response times), but it's all you need to know for the moment.

Figure 4-14 shows the simplest kind of DAC, namely one based on a
binary weighted resistance ladder. An output latch is connected to the DAC
inputs and its contents determine which switches are closed. Thus the computer controls the DAC output by writing different numbers into the latch.
By calculating the total resistance of the resistors switched to V_{ref}, we find
the effective input resistance R_i to the op amp. Using this in the op amp
voltage relation, we find

$$V_O = -V_i(b_3/2 + b_2/4 + b_1/8 + b_0/16),$$

where b_0 is the least significant bit, and b_3 the most significant bit. By
adding more switches attached to increasingly higher resistances, one can

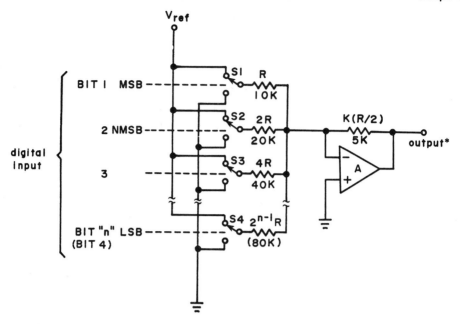

Fig. 4-14. DAC using binary weighted resistor network.

make DAC's with higher resolution. Eight bit DAC's are cheap and twelve bit DAC's are within reason. But few DAC's use the binary weighted resistance ladder, since it's hard to match the resistances accurately.

Instead the R-2R network illustrated in Fig. 4-15 is used. For this all resistors can be made up of a single resistance R, which is relatively easy to achieve. The R-2R network can be analyzed using Norton's theorem. To get a rough idea as to how the network works, treat the voltage source V_{ref} as having zero resistance to ground. Then the resistance to ground from the bottom node is 2R through either path, regardless of the corresponding switch position. Similarly the resistance to ground for the next-to-bottom node is 2R through either path, etc., on up the ladder. A current flowing into the top node thus sees two paths with equal resistance to ground and splits into two, etc., on down the ladder. A switch n nodes from the op-amp's minus input gets $1/2^n$ of the current flowing through the output resistor. Hence it contributes $1/2^n$ of its voltage (V_{ref} or ground) to the output voltage. For the network shown, the voltage output is the same as that for the binary weighted ladder case of Fig. 4-14. Both kinds of DAC's are called multiplying DAC's, since they multiply the reference voltage by a digital value.

The heart of the DAC is the resistance ladder coupled to the digitally controlled analog switches. As such the DAC is in the first instance a current device, which is converted to voltage by use of one or more op amps. If the desired application requires an analog current proportional a digital value, then the output op amp can be eliminated. Inexpensive op amps are limited in response time, and hence high speed voltage DAC's have to use

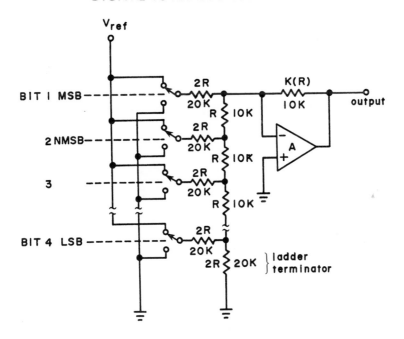

Fig. 4-15. DAC using R-2R resistor network.

premium op amps. Another advantage of the current mode is that currents are less susceptible to noise when traveling over long lengths of wire.

A critical part of a DAC is the analog reference, either current or voltage. The precision voltage reference is usually based on a zener diode, which you connect up backwards (see Sec. 1-4)! All diodes conduct in the wrong direction if the voltage applied exceeds their breakdown value, the Zener voltage. The zener diode is constructed to break down at a precise voltage value, which then can be used as a voltage reference.

Figure 4-16 shows both an inexpensive 8-bit DAC (MC 1408, currently $4) and a relatively high performance 12-bit DAC (Burr Brown DAC80, currently $30). The MC1408 requires external reference voltages, runs in current mode, and settles to 8-bit accuracy within 300 nsec. The DAC80 generates its own voltage reference from the +15 VDC supply voltage, by using an internal zener diode. It can be purchased with or without the output op amp (the current model comes without), features user selectable output voltage ranges of -2.5 to 2.5, -5 to 5, -10 to 10, 0 to 5 or 0 to 10, settles to 12-bit accuracy within 5 microseconds, and offers four different digital encoding schemes.

The most straightforward encoding schemes are the straight binary and complement binary. These are used for unipolar outputs, e.g., 0 to 10 volts. For the straight binary code, all 0's gives 0 volts; all 1's gives the reference voltage minus one bit's worth. The complement binary gives the same outputs with a bitwise complemented input. Bipolar voltage ranges, e.g., -10 to 10, require a less obvious encoding. 2's complement coding effectively

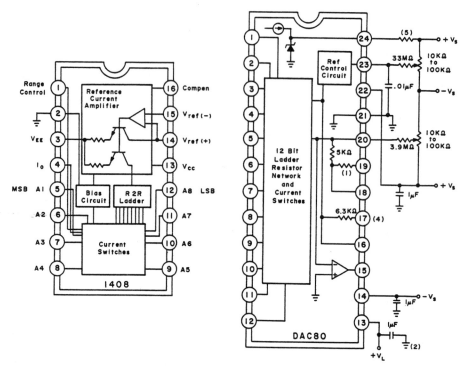

Fig. 4-16. Motorola MC1408 8-bit DAC and Burr Brown DAC80 12-bit DAC.

multiplies the reference voltage by the 2's complement number (see Sec. 2-2), which makes it trivial to use with 2's complement machines like the Z80. Offset binary is also used, for which all 0's gives the most negative voltage, and all 1's the most positive. This is easy to use too, since you just add an appropriate offset value to the computer's 2's complement number.

To output several voltages, several DAC's (and the output port latches to drive them) can be used. Alternatively, you can multiplex the DAC's output by using an analog switch IC and several sample and hold's as shown in Fig. 4-17. The sample and holds (Fig. 4-17b) use op amps to read voltages stored on input capacitors by the DAC circuit (Fig. 4-17a). Since the voltages leak away, a refresh circuit is employed to have the DAC rewrite the voltages many times a second. The system shown is part of the Diablo HyTYPE II 1345A printer used to typeset this book. The scheme is fine if the voltages are supposed to change slowly as in the Diablo, but it would be unworkable for video applications.

Another useful application of a DAC is to display waveforms on vector CRT's, e.g., on an oscilloscope with an x-y input. For this, the DAC traces out curves in rapid succession. Several traces can be displayed together, limited only by the combined DAC and computer response times. The approach is very simple, requiring only a modest amount of software and a DAC. To free up the computer from continually refreshing the CRT screen,

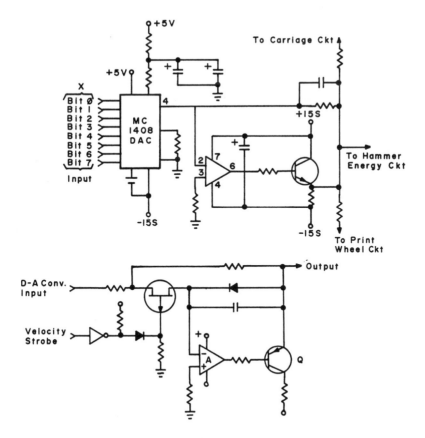

Fig. 4-17. Use of MC1408 DAC in a refresh mode as used in the Diablo 1345A HyTYPE II Printer (used to typeset this book). Hammer energy refers to the hammer that hits the daisy wheel to type a letter. A built-in microprocessor continually feeds the 1408 numbers while pulsing the appropriate "velocity strobes."
ate "velocity strobes."

you might prefer the self-refreshing, bit-mapped raster displays discussed in Sec. 4-7. These are substantially more expensive (unless you don't have an oscilloscope), but are very flexible.

4-3. Analog to Digital Conversion

This section describes five basic ways to convert analog signals to binary numbers, in the order of increasing speed. The first is called the integrating analog-to-digital converter (ADC) and is used primarily in digital voltmeters. The next three employ DAC's and comparators in feedback circuits that ultimately match the voltage to be measured, and the fifth method called "flash" conversion matches the input voltage directly in a flash! The first four methods are all capable of 12-bit resolution, but flash conversion is seldom seen with more than 6 to 8 bits. The section concludes with a discussion of a convenient 8-bit analog data acquisition package boasting 100 μsec conversion times and 16 analog input channels.

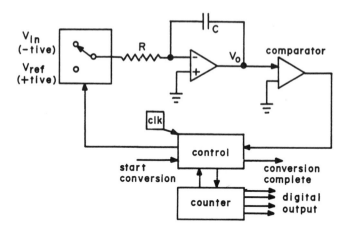

Fig. 4-18. Integrating A/D converter integrates a positive input voltage V_{in} for a time t_1 reaching some maximum op amp output voltage. It then integrates the negative reference voltage V_{ref} driving V_0 back to zero. The time t_2 it takes to get back to zero is a measure of V_{in}.

The dual-slope integrating A/D converter is illustrated in Fig. 4-18. At the start of the conversion, the control unit zeroes the op amp output, V_0, switches the op amp input to the voltage to be measured, V_{in}, and starts the counter counting from zero. While the counter ticks away, the output voltage V_0 gives the time integral of the input voltage. If V_{in} is a constant, $V_0 = -V_{in} t/RC$, where t is the time from the start. The control unit lets the counter tick away to a specific time t_1, when it zeroes the counter and switches the input to the reference voltage V_{ref}. V_{ref} is chosen to have opposite sign from V_{in}, so that the integrating op amp then integrates V_0 back to zero. The comparator fires at time t_2 when V_0 crosses zero. The controller stops the counter and signals that the counter's output has the desired numerical output. To see this, note that the maximum V_0 is given by both $-V_{in} t_1/RC$ and by $V_{ref} t_2/RC$. Equating these two expressions, we have $V_{in} = -(V_{ref}/t_1)t_2$. Since V_{ref} and t_1 are fixed, t_2, the time it takes the known reference voltage to integrate back to zero, is proportional to V_{in}. In particular, the proportionality constant can be chosen to give V_{in} in the desired units. The method is simple, can give 12-bit accuracy and averages out noise fluctuations by virtue of the integrations. It's also slow, however, typically 100 msec per conversion, so it's usually found in digital voltmeters, rather than in computer ADC's. Although the value of RC cancels out, these components should be stable, and the counter should be crystal controlled.

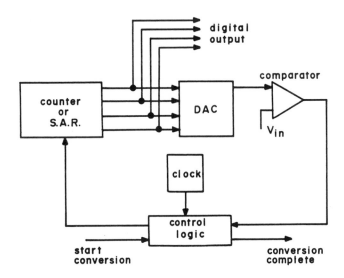

Fig. 4-19. Counter A/D method counts up from zero driving the DAC output up from zero until the comparator flips its output. The counter's output is then proportional to V_{in}. Substitution of a Successive Approximation Register (SAR) for the counter implements a binary search algorithm and is called the SAR A/D conversion method.

Another counter technique, is used in the "counter" ADC, illustrated in Fig. 4-19. At the start of conversion, the control unit starts the counter counting from zero. The DAC converts the count into a well-defined reference voltage which is compared to the input voltage V_{in}. When V_{in} is passed, the comparator flips its output, causing the control logic to freeze the count with the desired numerical output. The accuracy of this method is limited only by the DAC, and for V_{in}'s that vary little in the count time, 12 bits is quite possible. Problem is, of course, that it can take a long time to match a voltage at the upper end of the conversion range, maybe 10 msec. The method is certainly faster than the integrating method, but you immediately start to conjure up better search algorithms.

In particular, imagine a slightly more complicated system that has an up/down counter. Then as V_{in} changes, the control logic can have the counter follow or "track" V_{in}. The initial lock-on time is as long as with the unidirectional counter, but if V_{in} varies slowly compared to the counter-DAC rate, the counter can continually give an up-to-date reading.

Neat you say, but surely a binary search algorithm is a better way to get tracking in the first place. It's like that number game you play against the computer. The computer says, "I've got a number between 0 and 100. Can you (simple-minded human) guess it?" Naturally you could start at 1 like the counter ADC, but why not start in the middle at 50? And when computer says "Sorry, it's bigger", you respond with 75, i.e., you always guess half way between the limits established in the dialogue. Let's assume the computer doesn't change its conniving mind in the middle of the conversion, and pretty soon out comes "Whoops, you did it you clever so and so; how about playing again?" We know, it's a silly game, but that's exactly how the very popular successive approximation A/D conversion technique works. Just replace the counter in Fig. 4-19 by a SAR, i.e., a Successive Approximation Register. At the start of conversion, the SAR sets the Most Significant Bit and resets the rest of the bits. If the comparator indicates the DAC output is too big, the SAR resets the MSB; else it leaves it on. Then it sets the NMSB (Next MSB), etc. If the V_{in} changes in the middle of all this, of course, we're in trouble! So for signals that may vary appreciably (more than a LSB) during the conversion time, it's best to sample and hold V_{in} at the start of conversion. The SAR method can be both fast (50 μsec) and accurate (12-bits). It's a common conversion technique in computer applications.

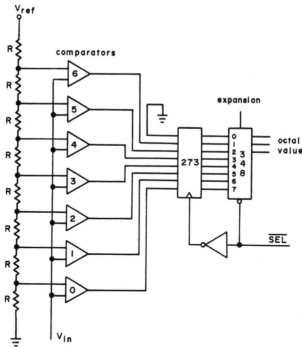

Fig. 4-20. Flash A/D conversion method simultaneously compares input voltage to a set of equally spaced reference voltages. The priority encoder yields the digital value of the comparator with closest reference voltage greater than V_{in}.

Before looking at a real live system, let's glance at flash conversion. Figure. 4-20 shows a 3-bit version. A precision resistor chain divides the reference voltage V_{ref} up into a set of equally spaced smaller reference voltages. The input voltage V_{in} is simultaneously compared to these reference voltages yielding comparator outputs equal to 1 (H) for V_{in} Higher than the corresponding references and 0's (L) for those Lower. A data read ($\overline{SEL}$) causes a 74273 to latch the comparator outputs and a 74348 priority encoder to translate to the appropriate octal number. All this within 50 nsec! But you need 2^{n-1} comparators and 2^n resistors. So for 7 bit accuracy, that's already 127 comparators, and 12-bit is 4095 comparators. Needless-to-say, 12-bit versions aren't commonplace!

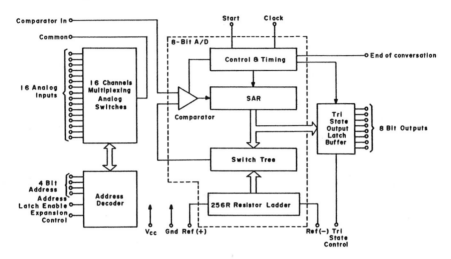

Fig. 4-21. Block diagram of National Semiconductor ADC0816 single chip data acquisition system. Provides 8-bit accuracy on any of 16 analog input channels with latched tristate control making microprocessor interfacing a snap. Uses SAR A/D method for conversion times under 100 μsec.

Figure 4-21 shows the block diagram of the ADC0816 single chip data acquisition system. This 40-pin dip (under $30 in single quantity) uses the SAR ADC method to convert any one of 16 inputs to 8-bit accuracy within 100 μsec. The digital interface provides latched tristate outputs and latched address (telling which of the 16 lines to convert) inputs, making microprocessor interfacing easy. We simply add it onto the bus in Fig. 3-10 as discussed in Exercise. 11. Now let's turn to some applications of our DAC's and ADC's.

By combining an ADC with a DAC, one can record and display waveforms. This effectively gives one a multichannel storage oscilloscope capability. With a disk system, you can store traces for later computation or retrieval. If you continually record an input signal, you also have the flexibility of "triggering" on any feature, that is, you choose the feature of interest and display data before and after. The 30 megasamples/second 8-bit TRW flash ADC's are very handy in this regard and reasonably priced considering their bandwidth. As discussed in Sec. 4-2, you may prefer the use of bit-mapped raster displays to the vector type, since they free the computer from refreshing the CRT.

4-4. Signal Averaging and Lock-in Detection

We have seen how DAC's and ADC's can greatly broaden the scope of computer monitor and control, even to the point of providing a multitrace storage oscilloscope of sorts. In this section, we see how the computer can literally pull some kinds of signals out of the noise in situations where you wouldn't be able to deduce a thing with an ordinary analog oscilloscope. Two methods are considered: signal averaging and lock-in detection. Both involve the repetitive addition of noisy signals in a fashion that is synchronized to the signal. Because the noise is not so synchronized, it ultimately contributes only a uniform background level (in signal averaging), or it subtracts as often as it adds, preventing it from contributing appreciably to the sum (lock-in detection). Meanwhile, the signal contributions are always in phase with one another, causing the signal summations to grow faster than the noise

Signal averaging is nicely introduced with an example from the medical profession. Suppose a person is unconscious and it's important to know if he can hear. Or suppose a leg is badly damaged and it's important to know if the nerves in his feet are still functional. Signal averaging can answer these and similar questions rapidly and effectively. The brain emits brain waves that can be monitored by electrodes attached to the skin. The analog signals that are picked up are the superposition of many responses. The brain is something like a CPU running many tasks at the same time. Consequently the ears, eyes, nerves, nose as well as thought are constantly influencing the brain waves. Now suppose that at a specific time, we clap our hands near the patient and digitize the ensuing brain-wave response at .1 sec intervals for 10 seconds in our computer. This gives 100 "time slots", with each of which we associate one 16-bit word (two bytes) of memory. The curve so taken looks essentially random because of the large amount of noise present. Then we clap and record again, adding each data value to the memory word for its time slot. After some number of claps and data taking, a characteristic curve emerges revealing the brain wave due to the clap response alone, independent of everything else going on in the brain. That's signal averaging.

The technique is very useful in other areas as well. In Fig. 4-22, you see a diagram of the apparatus in hands-on exercise 11 (Sec. 8-7). The idea is to measure the shape of a square wave covered up with noisy fluctuations. The curves in Fig. 4-23 shows an example of signal averaging as obtained in exercise 11. Curve (c) is the sum of 16 response curves (divided by an overall scale factor to make it fit nicely on the page), and curve (d) is the sum of 256 response curves. You see a well defined curve emerge with very little noise.

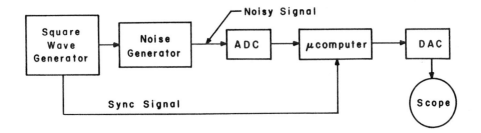

Fig. 4-22. Example of signal averaging: experimental apparatus for measuring a very noisy square wave. The noise generator used in exercise 11 is shown in Fig. 8-9.

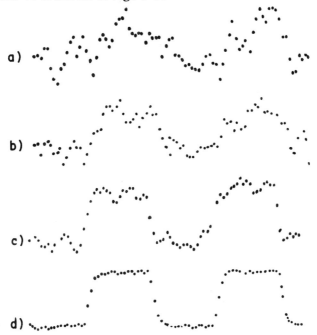

Fig. 4-23. Addition of 16 time responses like curves (a) and (b) yields curve (c). Addition of 256 responses yields curve (d). Although individual response curves are noisy, the averaged curves show less and less noise.

A program to do signal averaging is easy to write and provides another way to understand the technique. The following program zeroes a 512 byte area reserved for the time-slot data sums. Two bytes are reserved for each time slot. The ADC is read at regular time intervals following the trigger signal and the value added to the appropriate sum. We have

```
SIGAV:   XOR    A            ;Zero curve summation memory
```

```
            MOV     B,A       ;Do 2*256 bytes of memory
            LD      HL,CRVMEM ;Point at curve memory
ZRLOOP:     LD      (HL),A    ;Zero a byte
            INC     HL
            LD      (HL),A    ;Zero next one too (whole 16-bits)
            INC     HL
            DJNZ    ZLOOP     ;Zero 'em all

            LD      C,NADD    ;C counts # additions to do
AVLOOP:     LD      B,NPOINTS ;Calculate NPOINTS sums
            LD      HL,CRVMEM ;Start with first sum
            LD      A,1       ;Send out perturbation
            OUT     (SYNC),A  ;This synchronizes CPU to response

RSLOOP:     CALL    ADC       ;Read response voltage (answer
            ADD     A,(HL)    ; in A; add it
            LD      (HL),A
            INC     HL        ;Point to high byte
            JR      NC,NCY    ;If no CY, leave high byte alone
            INC     (HL)      ;Add in CY
NCY:        INC     HL        ;Get ready for next sum
            DJNZ    RSLOOP    ;Do all the points

            DEC     C         ;Do NADD summations
            JR      NZ,AVLOOP
            RET

ADC:        LD      A,20      ;Select ADC0816 channel 0
            OUT     (ADC),A   ; (See Fig. 8-6b)
            LD      A,10      ;Start conversion
            OUT     (ADC),A
DELAY:      DEC     A         ;Wait 100 microseconds
            JR      NZ,DELAY
            OUT     (ADC),A   ;Turn off start conversion strobe
            IN      A,(ADC)   ;Get value
            RET
```

The code assumes that the event you're measuring is produced by a trigger signal from the computer [the OUT (SYNC),A instruction]. If an external trigger is available that is synchronous with the signal, one would replace the code with a loop that monitors the input signal until it sees the appropriate rising or falling edge.

At the end of the code, you'd probably branch to a display routine to show the results. If the time interval is long enough, you could have the computer display the results while waiting, or execute a display loop continuously, running the RSLOOP routine under interrupt control. That way you watch the signal emerge from the noise. Beautiful, eh? Later we consider raster display devices that display continuously independently of the CPU (as a terminal displays independently). Then you can have your cake and eat it too.

A number of facts about signal averaging are worth mentioning. The signal to noise ratio (S/N) is proportional to the square root of the number of repetitions of the experiment. Thus going from 1 to 256 repetitions increase the Signal/Noise by a factor of 16. But to get another factor of 16, you have to go to 64K repetitions. Even such numbers can be possible to deal with, however, since you can go away and let the computer run overnight collecting data. Computers work much faster than human beings, but they can also work much longer, since they don't have to eat, sleep, etc. In this regard, digital signal averaging is better (and cheaper) than analog signal averaging. The analog version depends on sample and hold circuits that don't work for very long periods of integration time (charge leaks off the capacitors). Finally, note that if you keep adding numbers to a 16-bit integer sum, it "wraps around" at 64K. To prevent this, the number of bytes for the sum locations should be increased to handle the largest sum. The signal-averaging technique produces a background value equal to the sum of the noise. Part of this background may be sensitive to the running of the experiment itself. This contribution may be measurable by running the experiment without the signal. The final answers can then be obtained by subtracting this background average from the average obtained with the signal on.

An incredible example of signal averaging involves the 1 bit flash ADC, i.e., a single comparator or a TTL gate. This works very well provided you have enough noise! Consider the case in which the Signal/Noise (S/N) $\ll$ 1. You adjust the input so that the average noise amplitude occurs at the gate high-low threshold. Adding up many response curves yields the signal superimposed on top of a large constant background. To increase the data rate into the microcomputer, periodically output the comparator into a shift register (e.g., 74LS164) to convert to byte format. If you have dual ported 250 nsec memory, this gives a 30 MHz rate into your micro!

For small S/N, you don't gain anything with more than one bit accuracy, and the high conversion speed may be a major advantage. As the S/N increases, higher accuracy is useful. Furthermore for S/N=1, faithful signal reproduction depends on random noise with probability amplitude distributed uniformly from 0 to 1 bit's worth. The central limit theorem of probability theory tells us that such square distributions are the exception rather than the rule. The rule is Gaussian distributions. For nonsquare distributions, you have to divide out by the distribution shape. For example, Gaussian distributions centered at zero amplitude would weight large signals more than the smaller ones, and distort the averaged curve accordingly. The moral of this story is to use the 1-bit ADC for cases with S/N$\ll$1, but use the convenient ADC's for larger S/N's.

Two other names are given to signal averagers: MultiChannel Analysers (MCA) and transient digitizers. The MCA was the first device to become popular, specifically in nuclear physics.   There people want to plot the number of gamma rays impinging on a detector vs the energy of the rays, i.e., a gamma ray spectrum.   The x axis for these measurements is gamma ray energy and not time, but it's still signal averaging.   MCA's can, of course, have any variable for the x axis, and contemporary MCA's are just fancy microprocessor based systems.   Transient digitizers are simply high-speed signal averagers with time for the x axis.   Your own microcomputer can have substantially more flexibility than commercial MCA's and transient digitizers, but you'll have to go to some effort to compete with their elaborate (and convenient) ADC's and other front-end equipment.   For slow speed work (100 kHz or less), you'll save a bundle by using a microcomputer and in addition have the convenience of general purpose computing at your fingertips.

While signal averaging is particularly useful for distilling a time response curve out of the noise, lock-in detection is useful for pulling a constant or slowly-varying signal out of the noise.   The basic idea is to switch the signal on and off for equal periods of time.   When the signal is on, you add the input a number of times.   When it is off, you subtract the input the same number of times.   Any frequency that differs from the on/off (chopping) frequency is added and subtracted equally, averaging its contribution to zero.   The signal, on the other hand, adds and adds and adds. This procedure

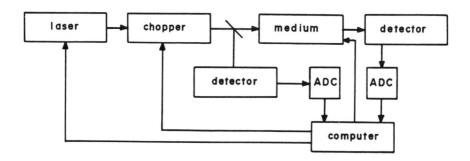

Fig. 4-24. Example of lock-in detection: measurement of absorption coefficient of a medium.   Here the computer controls the chopper.   It's also possible to have the computer synchronized to a free-running chopper

is diagrammed in Fig. 4-24.   Two points: 1) the signal must vary slowly compared to the chopping frequency, and its value recorded before it changes appreciably, and 2) no phase shift should exist between the signal switch and the adder/subtracter.   In particular, if a 90° phase shift exists, the signal itself is averaged to zero along with the noise.   Analog lock-in amplifiers include a phase shift control to compensate for shifts between signal and reference.   In a computer, one can simply introduce a delay loop. A program that performs a digital lock-in goes as follows:

```
LOCKIN:  LD      C,NAV       ;Do NAV periods
         LD      D,0         ;Zero high byte of 16-bit register
         LD      HL,0        ;Zero sum (answer goes here)
AVLOOP:  LD      A,1         ;Turn signal on
         OUT     (SIG),A     ;Computer must be set up to do so
         LD      B,10        ;Add 10 times (or whatever's good)
ONLOOP:  CALL    ADC         ;Get a value (leaves answer in A)
         LD      E,A
         ADD     HL,DE       ;Add since signal is on
         DJNZ    ONLOOP      ;Add a bunch of times
         LD      A,0         ;Turn signal off
         OUT     (SIG),A
         LD      B,10        ;Subtract same number of times
OFLOOP:  CALL    ADC
         LD      E,A
         OR      A           ;Clear CY
         SBC     HL,DE       ;Subtract since signal is off
         DJNZ    OFLOOP
         DEC     C           ;Iterate NAV times (signal should
         JR      NZ,AVLOOP ; remain constant during iteration)
         RET
```

In practice, the computer is usually programmed to vary some parameter in the experiment and then to repeat the lock-in call. By running off 100 parameter steps, you can generate a curve, ready for publication!

4-5. Waveform Generation and Recognition

One of the kinds of data that can be manipulated by computers is an input or output voltage that is a function of time, generally called a waveform. Data which can be regarded as waveforms include speech, music, digital recording of data on tape and disk, responses of various media to perturbations, motor and relay control signals, head load delays on disk drives, etc. This section considers some of these waveforms, starting with binary varieties and concluding with analog signals encountered in music and noise. The methods can be characterized by the degree to which programming is involved. Software-intensive methods are based on timing loops, while hardware methods use sophisticated peripheral IC's that contain appropriate internal programming to produce complex waveforms. In general the software methods require dedicated operation of the CPU and are sensitive to variations in CPU clock speed, wait states, interrupts and code changes, while the hardware methods are more expensive, relatively insensitive to CPU timing and less easily modified.

Timing loops can create one shots and square waves like the hardware versions considered in Sec. 1-8. The simplest timing loop for the Z80 is

```
          LD       B,n           ;Load count value
HERE:     DJNZ     HERE          ;Loop to here n times
```

This loop lasts 13n+7 t states. On a 4MHz Z80 system, this gives a range of 5 to 836 microseconds in 3.25 µsec steps. To produce a one shot on some parallel port bit, you have to turn the bit on and off as well. This leads to code like

```
          LD       B,n
          LD       A,1           ;Turn bit on
          OUT      (PORT),A
HERE:     DJNZ     HERE
          XOR      A             ;Turn bit off
          OUT      (PORT),A
```

Hence the one shot code includes an extra 14 t states (one OUT instruction and the XOR A). For longer delays, 38n t states can be added to this loop by including two EX (SP),HL instructions, which as a pair do nothing. This provides up to 3.27 msecs delay on a 4MHz machine. Even longer delays are conveniently generated using a 16-bit register pair:

```
          LD       BC,nn
LOOP:     DEC      BC
          LD       A,B
          OR       C
          JR       NZ,LOOP
```

This gives 26nn+10 t states, with a range from 9 to 425995 microseconds. Adding the 38nn t states from two EX (SP),HL instructions gives a maximum of 1.05 seconds. Longer loops can be written that call delay subroutines containing such timing loops.

Symmetric or nonsymmetric square waves can be generated with slight elaborations on this scheme. An example consists of a way to encode ones and zeroes on cassette tape. Each bit is represented by a low interval and a specific high interval. The high for ones last COUNT1 program loops, while the high for zeroes last COUNT0 loops. Specifically the code reads

```
ONE:      PUSH     BC           ;Entry to output a one's waveform
          LD       C,COUNT1 ;Get one's high count
          JP       EITHER
ZERO:     PUSH     BC           ;Entry to output a zero's waveform
          LD       C,COUNT0
EITHER:   LD       B,18         ;Wait a low interval of 18 loops for
LOW:      DJNZ     LOW          ; both ones and zeroes (noncritical)
          LD       A,1          ;Output appropriate high interval
          LD       B,C
```

```
         OUT    (CASIO),A
HIGH:    DJNZ   HIGH
         XOR    A          ;Go back to low value.  Rest of routine
         OUT    (CASIO),A ;is executed in noncritical low
         POP    BC         ; interval
         RET
```

This approach can be used to provide recording rates of approximately 3000 bits/second on ordinary cassette recorders provided one defeats the automatic volume controls so that saturated recording can be obtained. One of us has used this technique with great success using inexpensive GE 3-5121 recorders.

Very similar loops can be written to recognize a one shot's duration or to tell the difference between a one and a zero in this cassette format. For example, to measure the duration of a high value, use

```
         LD     B,0         ;Zero loop counter
LOWLP:   IN     A,(PORT) ;Wait for bit to go low
         RLCA               ;Suppose we want Bit 7
         JR     NC,LOWLP
HIGHLP:  INC    B
         IN     A,(PORT)
         RLCA
         JP     C,HIGHLP ;Relative jumps take longer
```

2/0253

The measured high time is then 28*B t states or 7*B microseconds. Another popular way of storing ones and zeroes on tape consists of representing a one by 8 periods of a 2400 Hz square wave and a zero by four periods of a 1200Hz wave (the Kansas-City format). This format has one tenth the data rate of the high-period modulated scheme, but runs on anything! This method is an example of Frequency-Shift Keying (FSK). Other examples include representing a one simply by a high for a "baudrate" period and a zero by a low for the baudrate period. This is the format used in connecting terminals to computers as discussed in Chap. 5. The TRS-80 cassette tape format records clock pulses at 2 msec intervals and represents ones or zeroes by the presence or absence of a pulse in between. Single-density floppy disk formats are similar, but have greater than 40 times the data rate and require hardware bit-stream generation.

Two major problems with this kind of waveform generation and recognition are 1) a dedicated CPU is required, and 2) the timing is distorted by wait states, interrupts and CPU clock changes. For long delay times, a viable alternative exists if you've implemented an interrupt-driven real time clock. Suppose you want to wait n tenth seconds and that the real-time-clock routine stores the current value in the location TENTHS. Then the following code works

```
         LD     B,n
```

```
WAIT:   LD      A,(TENTHS)
        CP      C           ;Has TENTHS changed since last time
        JR      Z,WAIT      ; thru loop?
        LD      C,A         ;Yep. Update current value
        DJNZ    WAIT        ;Wait n tenths.
```

The first time through the loop, the chances are that C has something other than what's in TENTHS. Consequently there's up to .1 seconds error in this approach, but there would be if you preloaded the C register too. For more accuracy, a smaller time interval must be used. Since the program timing is no longer important, code to do other things, such as polling, can be included in the WAIT loop. Such an approach was used by one of the authors in a controller that deposits adhesives on printed circuit boards for programmable lengths of time.

In addition to pulsing TTL one shots, a number of programmable counter/timer circuits are available for the microprocessor system. The Z80 CTC discussed in Sec. 3-5 is a good choice, especially if the elegant Z80 interrupt structure leads to appreciable software simplification. As a timer, a CTC channel generates a 1 microsecond pulse every time it counts down an 8-bit programmable value. The count periods are programmed to equal either 16 or 256 CPU clock periods. The very nonsymmetrical output can be turned into a square wave by dividing the output by two with a 7474, and other variations can be obtained by pulsing one shot IC's like the 74221. Programmable-length one shots can be generated by having the circuit interrupt the CPU at count completion, and disabling the timer. In counter mode, a channel can interrupt after counting an 8-bit programmable number of external events.

Unless the interrupt vectoring is particularly convenient, the Intel 8253 provides more powerful counter/timers. The 8253 houses three 16-bit counter/timers in a 24-pin dip. Each channel can interrupt on count completions, can generate symmetric square waves, and can produce one shots with or without interrupting the CPU at count completion. The substantially increased counting resolution (from 8 to 16 bits) allows one to generate audio square waves well within human ability to distinguish pitch, and baud rates can be easily generated from any CPU clock speed.

Another interesting smart peripheral is the Synertec 6522 PIO, which contains two counter/timers and a serial shift register in addition to two parallel I/O channels, all in a 40-pin dip. Serial I/O (Chap. 5) involves generating and recognizing TTL waveforms and can be done by dedicating the Z80 to monitoring and setting one-bit ports. To relieve the CPU from translating to and from standard serial bit streams, special purpose IC's such as the UART and USART IC's were developed (see Sec. 5-1). Similarly the Western Digital 1771 floppy disk controller family handles much of the conversion for floppy disk formats. Disk data rates are too high for Z80 generation and recognition in any case.

Analog waveform generation and recognition use DAC's and ADC's respectively. Sections 4-3 and 4-4 discuss the measurement of analog waveforms. Recognizing waveforms goes a large step further in that a fit to some function is made. This falls into the realm of numerical analysis and is outside the scope of this book. A large variety of analog waveforms can be generated easily on microcomputers and used to probe the response of media in the laboratory, and to produce music. We discuss a few of these and then describe the General Instruments AY-3-8910 sound generator IC.

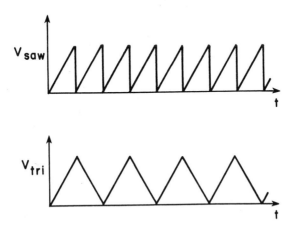

Fig. 4-25. Sawtooth and triangular waveforms simply generated by program loops.

Some simple analog waveforms such as sawtooth and triangular waves (Fig. 4-25) can be computed directly. For example, the following code generates a sawtooth

```
          XOR     A          ;Zero counter and value
LOOP:     OUT     (DAC),A
          ADD     A,n
          JP      LOOP       ;A wraps around at 255
```

A 4MHz Z80 executes this loop $579n$ times a second. Delays can be incorporated to reduce the frequency. Similarly a triangular wave can be produced by the code

```
          XOR     A
LOOP:     OUT     (DAC),A
          ADD     A,n
          JP      P,MULTWO
          NEG                ;Take absolute value
MULTWO:   RLCA               ;Multiply by two to fill range
          JP      LOOP
```

More generally an arbitrary periodic waveform can be generated by reading a table to the DAC. A 256 byte table is particularly convenient for micros as illustrated by the following code

```
        LD      HL,TABLE
LOOP:   LD      A,(HL)
        OUT     (DAC),A
        INC     L               ;Increment pointer, wrapping around
        JP      LOOP            ; at page boundary
```

In a fascinating article on music generated by micros, Chamberlin has described how to generalize this concept to yield frequency (pitch) and envelope variations. The pitch variations come from skipping entries in the table, much as one adds an increment greater than 1 in the sawtooth code. However the increment must have a fractional part to sound reasonable, a feature which could be included in the sawtooth code too.   Hence the pointer is three bytes long: page #, byte # and fractional part. Calling the latter two POINTR and the corresponding 16-bit increment INC, we have the following code

```
LOOP:   LD      HL,(POINTR) ;Get pointer L byte and fraction
        LD      DE,(INC)    ;Get increment
        ADD     HL,DE
        LD      (POINTR),HL ;Save updated value
        LD      L,H         ;Make table pointer
        LD      H,PAGE
        LD      A,(HL)      ;Get table value
        OUT     (DAC),A
        JP      LOOP
```

This code can be repeated to add more voices to the DAC's output. For a single voice, the code can be shortened appreciably by using registers alone, and a second voice can be added in this fashion by using the Z80 alternate register set. Musical instruments are characterized by both the waveform and a slowly-varying envelope. For example, a plucked instrument has a sharp attack and slow decay, while an organ has a mostly uniform amplitude. An envelope can be added by feeding the DAC output into a programmable amplifier, and using a different DAC-amplifier combination for each voice. Alternatively a more faithful reproduction can be obtained with a single DAC by using a set of waveforms for different points in time. This requires more memory (not much by 64K standards), but allows the waveforms to change shape as well as amplitude as time proceeds. As Chamberlin explains, the various harmonics present in an instrument's sound have different envelopes, and consequently a set of waveforms can sound more realistic than a single waveform multiplied by an envelope. It adds a new dimension to waveform synthesis, and Chamberlin uses it to invent new instruments, such as the "blither"! Another feature of computer-generated sound is that a musician has potential access to infinitely many different instruments with a single kind of keyboard. This is a huge extension on the concept of the pipe organ.

We conclude this section with a brief description of the General Instrument AY-3-9810 Programmable Sound Generator (PSG) IC. This IC generates various sounds purely digitally, using techniques like those described in

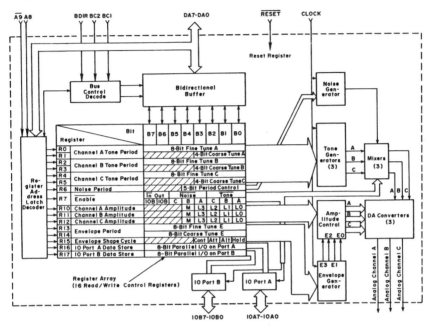

Fig. 4-26. The GI AY-3-9810 Programmable Sound Generator IC

this section and contains its own DAC's. Figure 4-26 is a block diagram of the PSG, revealing 16 8-bit registers that control a noise generator, three tone generators, three tone-noise mixers, three amplitude controls, an envelope generator, three DAC's and two general purpose parallel ports. Fourteen registers are used to program the sound generator characteristics and two are used for the parallel ports. The noise generator outputs a frequency-modulated, pseudo-random-pulse-width square wave. That's not gibberish, that's noise! The noise generator modulation period = $16t_C$*(5-bit programmable value), where t_C is the CPU clock period. Each tone generator yields a square wave with period = $256t_C$*(12-bit programmable value). This affords a good pitch resolution, although the steps are perceptible, particularly at higher values. Each channel's mixer can be programmed to provide 1) the noise generator output, 2) the tone generator output, 3) both, or 4) neither. Each mixer's output is then converted to an analog output with amplitude given by a programmable 4-bit value and multiplied by an envelope if desired. The envelope is the same for all three channels and has a period = $256t_C$*(16-bit programmable value). A number of sawtooth, triangular and one-shot shapes can be chosen. The DAC outputs are logarithmic, corresponding to the logarithmic response of the human ear.

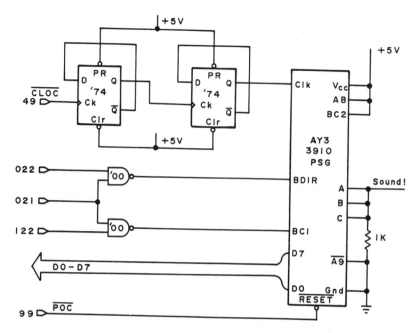

Fig. 4-27. Schematic incorporating the GI PSG into our interface
board.

The register address and data lines are multiplexed, unlike the Z80's.
Figure 4-27 shows a simple way to interface the PSG as two I/O ports: an
output port used to specify the desired register's address and a bidirectional
data port. Once a register's address is specified, all I/O takes place to and
from that register until another's address is output. Detailed instructions on
command values are given in the manufacturer's specification sheet and in
the article by Ciarcia. Here are some software examples here that illustrate just a few of the possible sounds that can be generated by the PSG as
wired up in Fig. 4-27. Nothing like ending a section with a bang (generator)!

```
LASER:    LD      HL,TABLB    ;This routine makes the sound of
          CALL    SETPSG      ; a Star Wars laser gun
          LD      HL,1B40     ;Sweep channel A frequency
          LD      B,3
          CALL    SWEEP
          LD      HL,TABLS
          JR      SETPSG      ;Set PSG and return

BOMB:     LD      HL,TABLB    ;This makes the sound of a
          CALL    SETPSG      ; whistling bomb
          LD      HL,1B6B     ;Sweep channel A frequency
          LD      B,19
          CALL    SWEEP
```

```
          LD        HL,TABLE    ;This makes the sound of an explosion
```

;This subroutine transfers data into all the sound generator
;registers from a table in memory. On entry HL points at the
;desired table.

```
SETPSG:   PUSH      HL
          XOR       A           ;A = register #
          LD        C,VAL
SETLP:    OUT       (REG),A     ;Set PSG to proper register
          OUTI                  ;Put data into register & inc pointer
          INC       A           ;Increment register #
          CP        0E          ;Fill registers 0 thru 0D
          JR        NZ,SETLP
          POP       HL
          RET
```

;This subroutine sweeps the frequency of channel A upward.
;On entry the sweep rate must be in B, the starting frequency
;in H and the end frequency in L.

```
SWEEP:    XOR       A
          OUT       (REG),A
MSEC:     PUSH      BC          ;Delay 1 msec on 4MHz Z80
MSEC1:    LD        A,0D2       ;(Adjust this constant for different
MSEC2:    DEC       A           ; CPU clock speeds)
          JR        NZ,MSEC2
          DJNZ      MSEC1
          POP       BC
          INC       H
          LD        A,H
          OUT       (VAL),A
          CP        L
          JR        NZ,MSEC
          RET

TABLE:    DB        00,00,00,00,00,00,1F,07
          DB        10,10,10,00,1F,00
TABLB:    DB        1B,00,00,00,00,00,00,3E
          DB        0F,00,00,00,00,00
TABLS:    DB        00,00,00,00,00,00,00,00
          DB        00,00,00,00,00,00

          END
```

4-6. Motor Control

We have seen how computers can read and set switches and analog volt-ages. These capabilities already cover burglar alarm equipment, much environmental control, soil-humidity-driven sprinkler systems, phone answering and dialing, much laboratory control and monitoring, etc. In addition, however, one would like to give the computer "hands." For this, we need motor control. A basic tenet of motion control is that changes in position are monitored and used to control further change. An obvious example is a person driving a car. The person instructs the car to move along the road according to what he sees. If the car moves a bit too far to the right, the person counteracts with a bit of a turn to the left. This con-cept is called "feedback": the system, e.g., car and driver, is driven by inputs consisting of the difference between the actual position and the

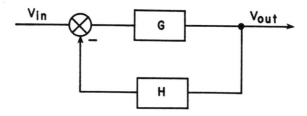

Fig. 4-28. Block diagram of a closed-loop control system. Part of the output is fed back into the input to generate an error signal. To minimize this signal, the output follows the input.

desired position as depicted in Fig. 4-28. In this section, we consider two approaches to this problem. The first uses the stepper motor, a device whose output position is known reliably from knowing what pulses are sent to it. Once calibrated and initialized, no feedback of the rotor's position is necessary, unless the speed demanded is too high or the torque required is too great. Running a motor this way without feedback is called "open-loop". The second method uses feedback, is a "closed-loop" approach and is called a servo system. The servo system can respond more quickly and accurately than the open-loop stepper motor system and is relatively insen-sitive to hardware variations. But it requires position sensors or transducers to tell where the motor has turned as well as relatively complicated drive electronics to ensure stability. Servo concepts are not limited to motor control; consider the smart thermostat developed in Prob. 4-6.

The permanent-magnet stepper motor is pictured in Fig. 4-29, and as all motors, consists of a rotor (thing that rotates) and a stator (thing that's stationary). But you'll notice the rotor features two gear-like cylinders that are turned one half a tooth spacing with respect to one another. One gear is a permanent magnetic North pole, the other is the South pole. The stator is also gear-like and has a different number of teeth than the rotor poles. In the stator, however, each tooth is an electromagnet and can be

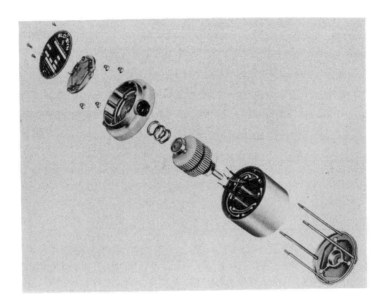

Fig. 4-29. Exploded view of permanent magnet stepper motor. The rotor consists of two groups of gearlike teeth, one group being north poles and the other south. The stator also consists of two groups of matching teeth that can individually be made north or south poles (photo courtesy of Superior Electric).

made into a N or S pole by driving a current through its winding. A simplified three-tooth rotor interacting with a four-tooth stator is illustrated in Fig. 4-30, adapted from Giacomo's excellent introductory article in Byte Magazine (see references). In Fig. 4-30a, currents flow in the A and C stator windings creating N and S poles respectively. The rotor's upper S tooth is attracted to the stator N pole, while the rotor's lower N tooth is attracted to the stator S pole. By now deenergizing the A and C stator teeth and turning on currents to make B and D into N and S poles respectively, we cause the rotor to turn clockwise one position. Alternatively, one could make B and D into S and N poles, respectively, and the rotor would turn counterclockwise one position. Similar combinations of stator coil currents turn the rotor further around as shown in Figs. 4-30c and d.

Two methods of coil windings are popular. The first assigns a single coil to each stator tooth. To reverse the polarity, you must reverse the current flowing through the coil, which typically requires a bipolar power supply. The other approach is the bifilar motor which has two windings for each tooth, such that current flow through one winding creates an N pole, while flow through the other creates an S pole. The bifilar motor thus can be

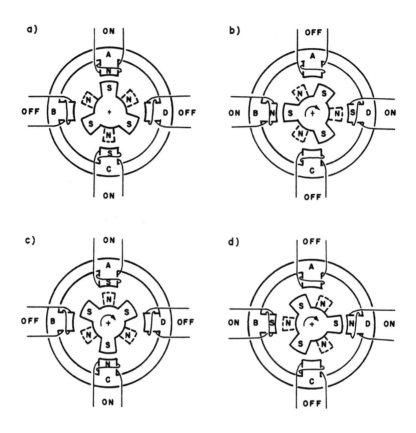

Fig. 4-30. Four-tooth permanent magnet stepper motor illustrates way that motor can be turned to discrete positions. Adapted from Giacomo (1979).

driven with a single-ended power supply. To fit both coils in the same place as a single one occupies, one uses thinner wire, which has higher resistance. The two coils each belong to distinct circuits called phases that contain many other coils on other teeth in series. In addition, the two coils for adjacent stator teeth belong to two new circuits. The total number used is four, and consequently the bifilar motor is called a four-phase motor. Because of their permanent magnet rotors, both two-phase and bifilar motors have a residual torque holding the rotor in a given position when no current flows. This torque is substantially less than that produced with current flow. You can feel the difference by advancing the paper on a daisy-wheel printer like the Diablo daisy-wheel printers with the power on and off. The paper feed mechanism on these printers use two-phase stepper motors with a bipolar power supply. Three phase "variable reluctance" motors are also popular, and have an unmagnetized rotor. These motors can also run from a single-ended power supply, since the unmagnetized rotor responds equally well to either magnetic polarity. Since they have no permanent magnet, the variable reluctance motors have no residual torque in the absence of current flow.

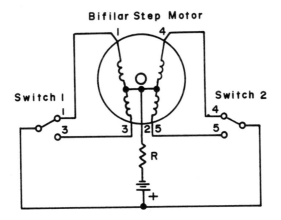

Fig. 4-31. Schematic diagram of a four-phase bifilar permanent-magnet stepper motor. Appropriate drive circuitry is shown in Fig. 8-10. By running current through the different windings, sets of stator teeth can be made into North or South poles, causing the rotor to move to particular positions.

Figure 4-31 shows a schematic diagram of a bifilar four-phase permanent-magnet stepper motor. Appropriate drive circuitry is shown in Fig. 8-10. There the power transistor used to drive the winding is protected by a diode, because as discussed in Sec. 4-1, a coil tries to keep the same current flowing even after the transistor turns off. This can produce transient high voltages across the transistor and burn it out. Power resistors are inserted between the coils and the positive supply terminal to improve the inductance to resistance (L/R) ratio. Just as inductors don't want to turn off, neither do they want to turn on. A decrease in the L/R ratio allows the current to start up faster, with a corresponding increase in performance as

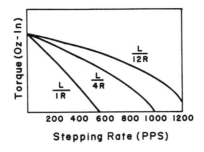

Fig. 4-32. Torque vs L/R ratio for stepper motor.

illustrated in Fig. 4-32. Adding the resistance helps the torque, but wastes energy and requires larger power supplies. The bifilar winding has higher built-in resistance, which helps the torque in this way. More elegant methods use variable voltage supplies that provide a large voltage to start the current flowing through the inductor and then automatically reduce the voltage as the current flows more easily. One can implement these methods using microcomputers among other ways, but usually one sticks to the simple series resistance method.

To drive a four-phase stepper motor, we need to energize the four phases for appropriate lengths of time. The simplest way to do this is to drive four bits of a parallel port connected to the drivers in Fig. 8-10. Due to somewhat more complicated construction than that of the motor in Fig. 4-30, real bifilar motors have three distinct stepping methods: single-phase, dual-phase and half-step. The method discussed in connection with Fig. 4-30 is single-phase. Dual phase can also be used there, by making two adjacent coils the same polarity. This leads to a position half way in between the single phase positions. The half-step method capitalizes on this feature to rotate in half steps. First a single phase is energized, then two phases, then a single, etc. The dual-phase method offers the most torque, but requires more power. All three methods can produce about equal motor speeds, provided their torque ranges are not exceeded.

The three methods can all be implemented with the same program using appropriate tables. On successive calls, the C register is incremented or decremented to turn the rotor clockwise or counterclockwise respectively. On entry, the B register is assumed to contain the desired stepping method: 1 for single-phase, 2 for dual and 3 for half-step. The routine outputs four bits to the port MOTOR, and assumes that a 0 value turns a phase on. We have (routine clobbers A, DE and HL, so you may want to save them)

```
STEPPR:  LD     A,B          ;Make sure 0<B<4
         AND    3
         RET    Z
         LD     DE,8         ;Calculate desired table origin
         LD     HL,TABLE-8   ;Each table is 8 bytes long
LOOP:    ADD    HL,DE
         DEC    A
         JR     NZ,LOOP
         LD     A,C          ;Add in counter offset
         AND    7            ;Keep count offset between 0 & 7
         LD     E,A
         ADD    HL,DE
         LD     A,(HL)       ;Get next set of phase bits: 0 value
         OUT    (MOTOR),A    ; turns on phase.
         CALL   DELAY        ;Delay a bit or go do something else
         RET

TABLE:   DB     07,0E,0D,0B,07,0E,0D,0B  ;Single-phase values
         DB     06,0C,09,03,06,0C,09,03  ;Dual-phase values
         DB     06,0E,0C,0D,09,0B,03,07  ;Half-step values
```

Clearly the stepping sequences can also be implemented in hardware so as to respond to simple output strobes, one for forward motion and one for backward. In fact, special LSI stepper-motor controllers exist. Hardware implementations have the advantage of relieving the CPU from dedicated timing loops, and they are failsafe, should the CPU crash. But they're more expensive, especially if they implement all three stepping methods. Furthermore, the CPU still has to know when it can send the next pulse. This can be done on a polled or interrupt-driven basis.

When the rotor position yields a well-defined output, the open-loop stepper-motor approach suffices. For example, stepper motors can be used to turn knobs on pre-digital, but otherwise excellent laboratory equipment that everyone throws away these days. The stepper motor position is then calibrated to the desired equipment response through the use of appropriate conversion tables contained in a program. In many other situations, especially where high speed is required, the response achieved in this fashion is not adequate, and one must resort to a closed-loop method. The carriage and print-wheel circuits on the Diablo printers are examples. Very high performance is required and the printers use a combination of hardware and software to implement servo loops.

We illustrate the servo concept with a simpler example, an automobile automatic cruise control. The cruise control matches a desired speed specified by a knob to the actual speed measured by a speedometer by driving the gasoline throttle with a function of the difference between the two. In principle, the car speed stays essentially constant in spite of changes in the road grade. But the problem is not completely trivial. Changing the amount of gasoline changes the engine torque and hence the car's acceleration. The velocity is the integral of this quantity, and hence the induced change in velocity may overshoot the desired value. The throttle is then reversed, but overshoots in the opposite sense may occur. The system may become unstable, with increasingly large oscillations about the desired speed, leading to a very jerky ride. This illustrates a major problem with servos: instability. To counteract this problem, the feedback circuits have to be appropriately designed to damp out for all incipient oscillations. When the output speed can be specified as a function of the desired input value, that function (called the transfer function) must always relax to the input value, regardless of road conditions. In mathematical terms, the Laplace transform of the transfer function can have no poles in the right-half complex plane, for such poles represent exponentially increasing deviations as time goes on. This observation forms the basis for an analytical approach to servo design called "root locus". Such an approach is beyond the scope of this book, but we note that it requires an analytic formula for the transfer function. Good approximations exist for the cruise control problem, but often the formulas prove to be elusive or impossible to write down. In these cases, one simulates the servo using analog or digital computers, and varies parameters until the thing works. Experience with the analytically solvable problems is particularly helpful here in providing intuition about what changes to make in the simulations. The digital simulations are particularly interesting in today's world because part of the simulation may well become a final part of the servo loop, namely in the form of a microcomputer. The microcomputer not only can close a loop by controlling motors and monitoring position or velocity transducers, but also can provide information to other computers and to human beings as to what is going on. Furthermore if instabilities in the final system do develop due to inadequate simulation, there's a good chance that the system can be fixed simply by modifying the microcomputer's program, rather than by making relatively difficult hardware changes. Microcomputers win again! But in all honesty, sometimes it's incredibly hard to get those programs debugged. For an excellent discussion of servo systems involving microcomputers, see the book by Bibbero given in the references.

4-7. Raster Displays

One of the most important devices a computer must interface to is a raster display, such as a video terminal (often called a CRT for Cathode Ray Tube). This is most easily done by connecting the terminal to the computer with a serial link as described in Chap. 5. However substantially higher performance (more speed and flexibility) can be obtained with displays based in the microcomputer itself. This is particularly noticable with word-processing and high-resolution graphics applications, where the serial link proves to be slow (even at transmission rates of 1920 characters per second, i.e., 19,200 baud). In this section, we describe how raster displays work, show how they can be integrated into microcomputer systems, and give an example of graphics software. We concentrate on the "memory-mapped" display, i.e., a display whose memory is directly accessible by the microprocessor in a dual port (Sec. 3-6) mode. Some of the computer's memory space is used up in this fashion, although it is also straightforward to "bank" the video memory by having it replace other memory whenever video changes are desired.

The displays we want to talk about are called "raster" displays, because the picture or text is produced on the display screen by repeatedly scanning an electron beam across the screen to form a uniform pattern of closely spaced horizontal lines (the raster), which covers the entire screen. The screen's surface is covered with a phosphor that glows when the electron beam hits it, so that pictures can be formed on the screen by turning the beam on or off as the beam scans across the screen face.

The ordinary TV is the most familiar raster display device. The video monitors used for computer displays are basically high quality TV sets whose electronics are designed to handle the relatively wide signal bandwidths (10-20 MHz vs. the TV's 4.5 MHz) required to display small details clearly. The raster is formed by scanning the electron beam from left to right starting in the upper lefthand corner. At the end of each horizontal scan line, the beam is blanked (turned off) and returned to the lefthand side of the screen ready to begin the next scan line below the one just written. Standard TV systems have a horizontal sweep frequency of 15,750 Hz, with each scan line requiring about 53.5 μsec plus 10 μsec for the horizontal retrace. There are 262.5 lines requiring 16.7 msec per complete field, so that 60 fields are displayed per second. Only about 242 of these lines are visible on the screen, however, since 1.25 msec is required for the vertical retrace, which brings the beam back to the top of the screen after a field has been completed.

In most computer displays each field contains the entire picture or text being displayed. In normal broadcast television and in some high resolution displays, two successive fields are required to make one complete picture or frame. The second field is shifted down by one-half a line, so that its scan lines fall between the lines of the first field. This is called an "interlaced" picture and gives 525 lines of vertical resolution. One potential problem with an interlaced display is flicker. The full picture is only refreshed 30 times per second, and with the standard P4 picture tube phosphor, one finds that small details in the picture tend to flicker on and off. This problem can be solved by using a picture tube having a yellow-green (P39) long persistence phosphor or by using a linear polarizer of the type used in sunglasses to reduce glare and enhance picture contrast. When placed in front of the CRT face, these polarizers are quite effective in eliminating flicker (available in large sheets from Edmund Scientific).

In an actual computer text display, the number of lines used depends on the display format. Consider a standard 24 character-line by 80 character-

Line Number		Line Counter Mode 0	Line Counter Mode 1
0	□ □ □ □ □ □ □	0000	1001
1	□ □ □ ■ □ □ □	0001	0000
2	□ □ ■ □ ■ □ □	0010	0001
3	□ ■ □ □ □ ■ □	0011	0010
4	□ ■ □ □ □ ■ □	0100	0011
5	□ ■ ■ ■ ■ ■ □	0101	0100
6	□ ■ □ □ □ ■ □	0110	0101
7	□ ■ □ □ □ ■ □	0111	0110
8	□ □ □ □ □ □ □	1000	0111
9	□ □ □ □ □ □ □	1001	1000

Fig. 4-33. Representation of the character "A" as a 5x7 dot matrix. This approach is used for raster displays and dot-matrix printers. 7x9 displays are also popular and offer better looking characters at the cost of 80% more dots per character.

width screen, with character defined by the dots on a 5x7 matrix (see Fig. 4-33). Each character is separated by two dots for visibility. Hence a raster line is 80x7=560 dots long. The characters are drawn raster line by raster line as depicted in Fig. 4-34. Character rows are separated by three raster lines, which allows descenders on lower-case letters like g. Hence 24x10=240 raster lines are required, which is nearly all of the available 242

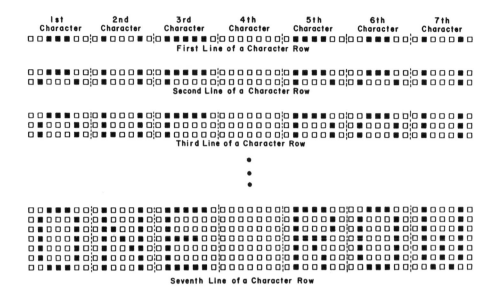

Fig. 4-34. Illustration of drawing a set of characters on a raster. Each character line consists of many raster lines. For the 5x7 dot matrix used, typically 10 raster lines are used to allow for lower-case descenders and interline spacing. Figure taken from Intel specification on the Intel 8275 Programmable CRT Controller IC.

lines. The total number of dots on the screen is 240x560x60 = 8,064,000. The minimum bandwidth for such a display is thus about 10 MHz.

To synchronize the horizontal and vertical beam movements to the video data, coarse and fine adjustments are used. The coarse adjustments are made using the horizontal and vertical hold knobs on the monitor, which change the approximate oscillation frequencies of the beam sweep circuits. The fine adjustment is made through the use of horizontal and vertical sync signals, which are used to synchronize the horizontal and vertical oscillators to the data stream. Usually these sync signals are combined with the dot stream itself to form a "composite video" signal. A bright spot is caused by a high signal (about 1.8 volts), a dark spot by an intermediate voltage about .4 volts, and a sync signal by pulses of zero volts (see Fig 4-35). The horizontal sync signal is distinguished from the vertical sync signal by being a much shorter pulse (5 vs 50 μsec). The brightness control changes the on-off threshold of the dot data, while the contrast control changes the video signal gain.

Two popular methods exist to refresh a screen of text. One is to store a value for every possible dot position on the screen as a bit in a memory, and read the memory out to the video monitor 60 times a second. This "bit-mapped" method requires about 80x7x24x10 = 134,000 bits, which is a little more than 16K bytes of memory. It allows one to display any character, subject to the limitations of a dot matrix. But it requires substantial

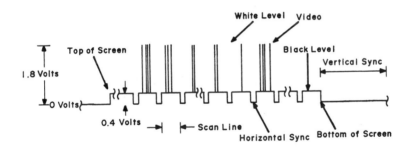

Fig. 4-35. Illustration of composite video output taken from the TRS-80 Microcomputer technical reference handbook.

memory and CPU time to create the characters. An alternative is to store only the ASCII values, i.e., one byte/character, instead of 7x10/8=9 bytes/character, and then to expand the ASCII value into the dot matrix format using a character generator. This second method is block diagrammed in Fig. 4-36, along with subsystems for timing signal generation and memory access control. According to this diagram, the CPU can read or write the video memeory any time it wishes. This simplified approach produces glitches on the screen as CPU accesses occur. Glitch-free displays typically use wait states to allow CPU access only during horizontal and vertical retrace times. On the Motorola 6800 series microprocessors, the CRT driver accesses can be made during the second phase of a two-phase CPU clock. During this second phase, the CPU never accesses memory. In this respect, the Z80's single phase clock is a disadvantage compared to the 6800 dual-phase clock. Clever use of a 4 MHz Z80's refresh cycle allows you to do much the same thing, but you need a FIFO (First-In First-Out memory buffer) since the refresh cycles aren't evenly spaced.

The timing signals such as horizontal and vertical blanking ($\overline{HZBL}$ and $\overline{VTBL}$) and next-character-load (LOAD) are generated by dividing a high frequency clock down appropriately. For our 5x7 matrix format, each character in memory is read 10 times and presented as seven or eight low order address bits to the character-generator ROM (which can be an EPROM). The higher-order address bits define which of the 10 raster rows is to be output by the ROM. When the LOAD signal is active, the ROM output is loaded into the shift register, which then proceeds to shift the bits out in a serial data stream. This data is combined with blanking and synchronization signals to form the composite video signal. The TRS-80 provides a good example of ths approach on a 16 character-line by 64 character-width display. The TRS-80 Microcomputer Technical Reference Manual walks you through the entire display circuitry and is very much worth reading.

There are many ways of improving this simple concept. Various LSI smart video IC's generate all the timing signals, resolve video memory conflicts, and add neat attributes such as reverse video (black on white), cursor generation, underlining, blinking, intensification, special line buffering, etc.

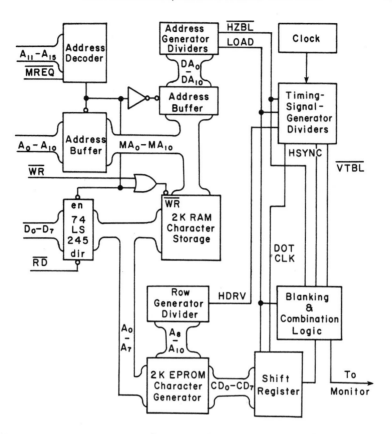

Fig. 4-36. Diagram of a simple memory-mapped text display driver. The CPU bus has access to 2K RAM character storage through tristate buffers. The 2K RAM is translated into dot-matrix raster format by the character generator and shifted out serially in accord with appropriate timing signals.

A number of boards of various levels of sophistication are available that generate memory-mapped displays. We note here an interesting combination board for S-100 microcomputers called the CAT-100. This board has a 7x9 matrix character generator, a 32K-byte RAM, both character-generator and bit-mapped display modes, a 4-bit flash converter for digitizing a TV camera picture, along with color and light pen options. The 32K RAM is enough for a 512x512 display or a 256x256 display with 16 grey levels. This kind of system is very useful in the laboratory, since it provides both text and graphics modes of operation. In particular, the multitrace storage scope idea mentioned in Sec. 4-3 can be readily implemented by using this board in combination with an ADC.

To use bit-mapped systems to display lines, we have to translate from the natural vector format of the data into the raster format. Because this is a critically important routine for use in the laboratory and a very useful one in general, we give it here in BASIC so that it can be used on any computer.

```
10 '    -- DRAW LINE FROM IX,IY TO X,Y --
20 DX=X-IX: DY=Y-IY: SX=1: SY=1              'calc delta-x, delta-y
30 IF DX<0 THEN SX=-1                        'store sign of DX, DY
40 IF DY<0 THEN SY=-1
50 DX=ABS(DX): DY=ABS(DY)                    'compute |DX|, |DY|
60 IF DY>=DX GOTO 160
70 ER=2*DY-DX: SWAP X,IX: SWAP Y,IY          'init ER; swap start-end pts
80 FOR QQ=1 TO DX
90 GOSUB 300                                 'output a point
100 IF ER>0 GOTO 120                         'check sign of error term
110 ER=ER+2*DY: GOTO 130                     'adjust error term value
120 Y=Y+SY: ER=ER+2*DY-2*DX                  'calc X and Y for next point
130 X=X+SX: NEXT QQ                          ' accordingly
140 SWAP X,IX: SWAP Y,IY: GOSUB 300          'swap back, do last point
150 RETURN
160 ER=2*DX-DY: SWAP X,IX: SWAP Y,IY         'DY>=DX case done here
170 FOR Q=1 TO DY
180 GOSUB 300
190 IF ER>0 GOTO 210
200 ER=ER+2*DX: GOTO 220
210 X=X+SX: ER=ER+2*DX-2*DY
220 Y=Y+SY: NEXT Q
230 GOTO 140

300 'Insert subroutine here to output a point on the screen at X, Y.
```

This routine uses a clever technique called Bresenham's algorithm which allows lines to be drawn without doing any floating-point multiplications or divisions. To see how it works, plot a few points by hand using it. For further discussion, see the book by Newman and Sproull.

Problems

4-1. Write a program and design the corresponding hardware to distinguish between a telephone busy signal and ring signal.

4-2. Write an assembly-language routine to write vectors in raster format.

4-3. Write a "printer plot" routine, i.e., make some device act like a chart recorder.

4-4. Write code to dial the phone with a relay. Assume the number is stored as an ASCII character string terminated by a null and pointed to by HL.

4-5. Determine the temperature measured by a thermistor by including the thermistor as part of an RC circuit driving a 555 astable multivibrator.

4-6. Design a smart thermostat controller to allow the heat in a home to go down after signaled that everyone's gone to bed, and to turn the heat back up before ringing a wakeup alarm in the morning. Include both hardware and software in the design. Use the ADC0816 A/D converter with a temperature-dependent current source.

4-7. Design a smart sprinkler system that turns on according to the time of day and the soil humidity.

4-8. Design a solar energy controller that pumps water according to ambient temperature and presence of sunlight.

4-9. Design a wind-driven pool skimmer controller. Include enough hysteresis in the program loops to prevent turning the pool motor on and off every 15 minutes.

4-10. Design a water alarm using a clothes pin with electrodes on each face separated by an aspirin tablet.

References

S. A. Hoenig and F. L. Payne, 1973, How to Build and Use Electronic Devices Without Frustration, Panic, Mountains of Money or an Engineering Degree, Little Brown, Boston.

W. M. Newman and R. F. Sproull, 1979, Principles of Interactive Computer Graphics, McGraw-Hill, New York.

H. S. Howe, Jr, 1975, Electronic Music Synthesis, W. W. Norton.

W. Bateman, 1975, Introduction to Computer Music, John Wiley, New York.

R. J. Bibbero, 1977, Microcomputers Instrumentation and Control, Wiley, New York.

Motorola Power Device Data book, 1978, Motorola, Inc., Phoenix AZ.

S. Ciarcia, 1979, "Sound Off!" Byte **4**, No. 6, p. 34. Steve's many Byte articles are of special interest in connection with this chapter. A number of them are collected in the Byte Book Ciarcia's Circuit Cellar, McGraw-Hill, New York (1979).

P. Giacomo, 1979, "A Stepping motor primer," Byte **4**, No. 2, p. 90, and **4**, No. 3, p. 142.

H. Chamberlin, 1980, "Advanced real-time music synthesis techniques," Byte **4**, No. 4, p. 70. See also his earlier article, "Techniques for computer performance of music," 1977, Byte Magazine **2**, No. 9, p. 62.

G. F. Franklen and J. D. Powell, 1980, Digital Control of Dynamic Systems, Addison-Wesley, Reading, MA.

Chapter Five

Serial Input/Output

I/O, I/O, it's off to work we go...

--The Seven Dwarfs

So far our interfaces have all input or output 8 bits at a time in parallel at TTL voltage levels. This is convenient and in many cases straightforward. On the other hand it is very susceptible to noise if more than a few feet are involved. Eight data lines are required (16 for simultaneous input and output), and finally, simple as it is in concept, parallel operation is nonstandard. Each implementation seems to have its own special set of handshake signals. Even the very flexible smart PIO's can't be programmed to handle some of these, e.g., most of the inexpensive dot-matrix printers (which themselves are controlled by microprocessors!) Sigh. A standard way around the noise, multiplicity of lines, and lack of conventions is to use serial I/O. In fact serially coded ASCII (American Standard Code for Information Interchange) is the most generally applicable way of exchanging information between computers. Virtually any other way requires special programming. Serial I/O involves shipping bytes a bit at a time, LSB first, with a few extra bits to keep it all synchronized. It's slower, sure; but it's general.

This chapter describes the software and hardware of serial I/O, defines serial ASCII encoding, defines the voltage and current conventions commonly used (RS232-C and current loop), describes modems (MOdulator / DEModulators) used for sending serial data over phone lines, shows how to

Murray Sargent III and Richard L. Shoemaker, Interfacing Microcomputers to the Real World, ISBN 0-201-06879-6

connect any computer to any other over the phone line, and finally describes the increasingly popular serial transmission media of rf (radio), fiber optics and power lines. Although serial I/O is not as commonly used for experimental control as parallel I/O, it is invaluable in connecting small lab computers up to bigger machines to take advantage of big machine data bases, crunch power and expensive peripherals (like microfilm recorders). It's also used to interface terminals to computers or to modems. And it's relatively easy....

5-1. Parallel/Serial Conversion: the USART

An essential feature of a serial bit stream is time dependence: the bits are represented by codes with specific time durations.. The standard asynchronous serial formats used in data communications all allocate a time interval known as a "baud period" to each bit. The word baud is used in honor of a Frenchman named Baudot, who studied various serial encoding schemes back in the 1800's. In the simplest form, we imagine a one is represented by a TTL high voltage, i.e., 2.5-5 volts, for a baud period and a zero by a TTL low voltage for a baud period. To send information encoded this way, we have to synchronize the transmitter and receiver clocks, which define the baud period. As for raster displays (see Sec. 4-7), the two clock oscillators have slightly different frequencies and unrelated phases. With the asynchronous formats or protocols that we consider here, the absence of data is indicated by a high value, often called a "mark". The transmitter signals the receiver that a character is about to start by sending a low bit

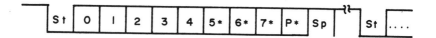

Fig. 5-1. Serial bit stream format. Character is preceded by a low-level start bit, which synchronizes the receiver and transmitter baud-rate periods. Character (5, 6, 7 or 8 bits) follows, LSB first. * flags optional bits. An optional parity bit and one or more stop (high level) bits terminate the character.

known as the "start bit", as shown in Fig. 5-1. The data bits follow, LSB first, each lasting one baud-rate period. A one is transmitted as a high period and a zero as a low period. Serial receivers and transmitters can be instructed to convert as few as 5 or as many as 8 bits between serial and parallel formats (but they must agree on how many!). In the figure, we flag these optional bits by asterisks.

After the desired number of bits is sent out, an optional parity bit P may follow. The parity bit P is useful if the data line is suspected to be too noisy for accurate transmission. For even parity, you set P=1 if the number of one's in the character is odd and set P=0 if the number of one's is even. That is, you choose P so that the number of one's including P is even. For odd parity, you choose P so that the number of one's including P is odd. In our example, we mean by "you" the remote transmitter, of course. The local receiver checks to make sure that the parity is still the same in spite of the noise incurred over the phone line. If the parity has changed, some bit has flipped its lid, and the receiver sets the parity-error flag in its status register (which the CPU can read if it wants to).

At the end of these bits, the transmitter inserts one or more high "stop" bits into the stream. Basically the line must come high long enough to allow the receiver to synchronize its conversion with the next start bit. The transmitting and receiving baud rates are bound to differ a bit (up to 4% will still work well), and therein lies the source of the synchronization problem. Typically one high baud-rate period suffices for a stop bit, although transmitters can be instructed to insert 1, 1.5 or 2 stop bits under program control. Because the high interval following a character's transmission can be any amount of time longer than the desired number of stop bits, the method is called asynchronous. We see that at least two (start and stop) extra bits are required to transmit asynchronous data. So if you want whole bytes without parity, that's 10 bits. Just as in any business, you have to pay for overhead.

The popular baud rates are 50 (HAM radio with 5-bit characters; some people can decode this speed by ear! Blame the HAM's predicament on the FCC), 110 (yetch, it's an old teletype, better known as a klunk klunk!), 134.5 (ugh, it's an IBM 2741!) 150 (too slow), 300 (also very slow, but goes great over phone lines), 1200 (better, also goes over phone lines and becoming popular), 2400, 4800, 9600 and 19200 (now you're talking!). CRT (tube) terminals usually can work at any of these rates. Hardcopy devices usually are restricted to the lower rates. For an 8-bit character, no parity and one stop bit, we have a total of 10 bits, for which 300 baud yields 30 characters/second.

We've seen in Sec. 4-5 that a computer can generate many kinds of waveforms. In particular it can convert a byte into an asynchronous serial bit stream, which it methodically outputs to some pin of a parallel port. The output bits are then buffered by one of the standard conventions (see Sec. 5-2) and out they go to a terminal or modem. Early personal computer systems used this software method. The trouble is that it really ties up the CPU and prevents the use of higher speed transmissions. Early in the days of LSI circuits, a special IC called the UART was developed to simultaneously transmit and receive serial data, performing the appropriate parallel/serial conversions and inserting or checking the extra bits used to keep the serial data synchronized. UART is an acronym for Universal Asynchronous Receiver Transmitter. A UART is typically configured as four ports: an input status port, an output control port, an output data port that converts bytes into a standard-format bit stream for transmission (hence

Transmitter), and an input data port that converts an incoming bit stream into bytes for reception (hence Receiver). Since a byte can start at any time, the serial format is called Asynchronous. The name Universal applies because the device can work with all popular asynchronous serial formats.

Simultaneous conversion of an incoming and an outgoing serial data stream is called full duplex, and requires two data carriers. These carriers could be three wires: one for the outgoing stream, one for the incoming stream and the third for a common ground line. Half duplex is sometimes used, which allows two-way communications, hence the name duplex, but only one direction is active at a time. It's similar to using walkie talkies, for which you have to say, "over," when you're finished talking and want to let the other guy talk back. A UART requires some extra circuitry to run in a half duplex mode, since the data stream direction has to be "turned around" electronically. The UART does provide for standard full duplex handshaking conventions.

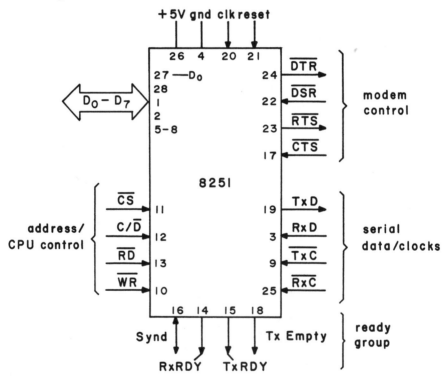

Fig. 5-2. Pinouts of the Intel 8251 USART grouping the pins into the bidirectional data bus and five groups of four pins (total of 28 pins).

Figure 5-2 shows a more general IC, the Intel 8251 USART, which can be used for some Synchronous as well as all popular asynchronous serial formats. It comes in a 28-pin dip instead of the UART's 40-pin dip, and is more flexible in a number of ways. We use this USART here and in Exercise

13 of Chap. 8 to illustrate serial I/O conventions. First we define the USART's pins, and then we explain how to program it. The 28 pins consist of eight tristate bidirectional data lines, and five groups of four lines. The supply and address groups are similar to those we've seen in other smart peripheral IC's. The supply group contains the 5 volt line, ground, CPU clock (or a clock between .75 and 2.5 MHz) and a reset line. The address group contains $\overline{CS}$ (chip select), C/$\overline{D}$ which specifies a control port if high and a data port if low, $\overline{RD}$ which causes the chosen input port to assert its data on D0-D7, and $\overline{WR}$ which loads the appropriate output port with the data on D0-D7.

The serial data group contains the receive data line RxD, the transmit data line TxD, and the read ($\overline{RxC}$) and transmit ($\overline{TxC}$) clock lines, which are used to time the length of the bits in the serial bit streams. These four lines comprise the soul of a UART or USART. The baud rate is derived from the TxC or RxC clocks. Typically these clocks have 16 times the desired baud-rate frequency. UARTs require the 16 factor to be able to sample the bit values in the middle of the baud-rate periods. The edges of the periods may not be precisely defined, due to limited bandwidth of the carrier medium and to relative shifts between receiver and transmitter clocks. The USART has a high frequency clock as mentioned above, and consequently can figure out where the middle of a bit period is even when TxC or RxC have the same frequency as the baud rate. The USART can be programmed to use such a "1x" baud rate clock, to use the standard 16x clock, or to use a 64x clock. Ordinarily, you connect TxC and RxC to the same clock line, so that both incoming and outgoing data streams have the same baud rate. The Signetics 2651 USART is very similar to the 8251 and can be programmed to generate and use any of the standard baud rates, while the older Intel 8251 requires external baud-rate generation. Another advantage of the 2651 is that its interrupt lines (coming up) are open collectors, and hence can be connected directly to the Z80's $\overline{INT}$ line. Unfortunately, the 2651 is not as widely available as the 8251.

The fourth of the five groups in Fig. 5-2 is the status group containing three output status lines RxRDY, TxRDY, TxEMPTY, and one bidirectional status line, Synd. The USART sets RxRDY high when it has assembled an input character from the RxD line. The CPU can read this character, at which point RxRDY is reset to low. The RxRDY state (and those of TxRDY, TxEMPTY and Synd) is also available as a bit in the USART input status register, where it can be polled. Its existence as a pin on the USART IC allows one to generate input interrupts. Similarly TxRDY goes high when the transmitter is ready to accept another character. This occurs if 1) the transmitter input register is empty, 2) $\overline{CTS}$ is low, and 3) the transmitter is enabled (see bit 0 of the command byte in Fig. 5-4). The TxRDY pin can be used for interrupts with $\overline{CTS}$ providing a "handshake" capability (explained next). The TxEMPTY indicates that two characters can be shipped to the USART for transmission: the transmitter effectively has a two-byte FIFO. If you write an output interrupt service routine, you halve the number of interrupts by interrupting on TxEMPTY and outputting two characters from the CPU output buffer. TxEMPTY was originally intended for use with half-duplex communications. We refer the reader to the Intel 8251 specification for a discussion of the Synd status line, which has to do with synchronous transmission.

The last of the five groups is the modem control group, consisting of two outputs, $\overline{DTR}$ and $\overline{RTS}$, and two inputs, $\overline{DSR}$ and $\overline{CTS}$. The traditional hand-shaking convention goes as follows: the Terminal pulls $\overline{DTR}$ (Data Terminal Ready) and $\overline{RTS}$ (Request To Send) low, indicating to the Data Set, e.g., a modem or computer, that the terminal is alive, kicking and requests permission to send. The terminal's $\overline{DTR}$ and $\overline{RTS}$ are connected to the data set's $\overline{DSR}$ (Data Set Ready) and $\overline{CTS}$, (Clear To Send) respectively. Correspondingly, the data set pulls its $\overline{DTR}$ and $\overline{RTS}$ lines low, which are connected to the terminal's $\overline{DSR}$ and $\overline{CTS}$ lines. Just who is the terminal and who is the data set depends on your point of view. A given USART thinks of itself as the terminal, but it may well be communicating with another USART. In any event, one USART's $\overline{DTR}$ line should be connected to the other's $\overline{DSR}$ line and vice versa. Similarly, one USART's $\overline{RTS}$ should be connected to the other's $\overline{CTS}$ and vice versa. As discussed in Sec. 5-2, modems tend to use all four of these lines. For computer-computer communications (see Sec. 5-4), the $\overline{DTR}$ lines can be very useful to synchronize data transmission. But typical time-shared terminal to computer applications can ignore them all (just tie $\overline{CTS}$ low!), since the user at the terminal knows if the computer responds or not.

That's all 28 pins. Now let's see how to program the USART to convert according to the various asynchronous serial formats. Two command bytes

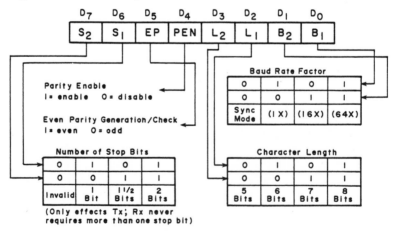

Fig. 5-3. 8251 USART mode command format. Command byte is output to USART control port.

are required. The first is called the mode byte and is defined in Fig. 5-3. This byte specifies how many bits/character and stop bits are desired, whether even, odd or no parity is desired, and what multiple of the baud rate is to be input on the TxC and RxC clock lines. The second command

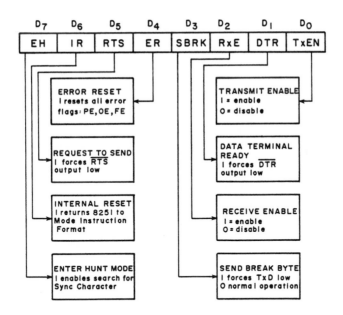

Fig. 5-4. 8251 USART control command format. Command byte is output to USART control port.

byte is called the control command byte and is defined in Fig. 5-4. The TxEN, DTR, RxE and RTS bits are hopefully self-explanatory in view of the discussion above. The SBRK bit is used to signal the remote device that transmission is complete, or that the line should be turned around if half duplex operation is involved, i.e., like the walkie talkie "over." The ER bit resets error flags in the status register, which is defined in Fig. 5-5. The IR bit allows one to reset the USART under program control as well as by the reset pin. The EH line is used for synchronous communications, which we ignore, but which can be very useful (see Intel 8251 specifications).

Both command bytes are output to the USART control port. The USART interprets the first command byte it gets after a reset (internal or external) as the mode byte and all successive bytes as command bytes, unless a reset occurs. Problem is, how can you make sure the device is reset? For example, after the power is turned on, the USART is reset by most systems (there's a Power On Clear signal $\overline{POC}$ that goes to the reset pin). An initialization program ships out the mode and control commands in that order. Now if you execute that initialization program again without the power on clear, both commands will be treated as control commands, unless you ship a reset command first. An easy way around this problem is to send a command that doesn't reset if it's interpreted as a control command and is reasonable as a mode command, e.g., 0BE. The next command has to be interpreted as a control command, so you ship 40, which resets the USART. Then the desired mode and control commands can be sent in peace.

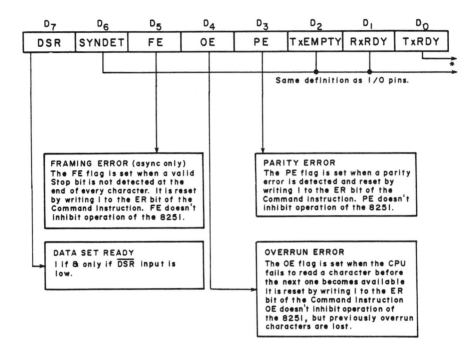

Fig. 5-5. 8251 USART status register format. Status byte is input from USART control port. *This bit is high if the transmitter input register is empty, regardless of the level of the $\overline{CTS}$ pin and of the value of the TxEN command bit. This differs from the TxRDY pin, which goes high only when the transmitter input register is empty and both $\overline{CTS}$ and TxEN are active. As such, the USART's $\overline{CTS}$ input is useful as a handshake input only in interrupt-driven operation run by the TxRDY pin; for polled operation, ground $\overline{CTS}$ and use the $\overline{DSR}$ input for handshaking instead.

Suppose we want to initialize the USART to run full duplex communications with eight bits/character, no parity, 1 stop bit, and a 16x clock. The general code is:

```
INIT:     LD      A,0BE      ;Be sure USART interprets reset
          OUT     (CTRL),A   ;command as a control command
          LD      A,40       ;Output reset command
          OUT     (CTRL),A
          LD      A,4E       ;16x clock, 8 bits/character, no
          OUT     (CTRL),A   ;parity, one stop bit
          LD      A,37       ;Enable receiver and transmitter,
          OUT     (CTRL),A   ;reset errors, set DTR, RTS low
```

That's it. Now use either the interrupt or polling methods to synchronize the devilishly fast computer with the serial communication link. For polling, you input the CTRL port and check the desired bit (TxRDY,

TxEMPTY or RxRDY) for your application. Handshaking can be accomplished by checking the DSR bit as described in Sec. 5-4.

5-2. RS232 and Current-Loop Conventions

Now that we've seen how a USART converts parallel data to and from TTL-compatible serial bit streams, we need to know how to send these streams over a distance. The two most popular ways are RS232, a voltage level convention, and the current loop method, which dates from early telegraph days. For low data rates, current loop can go across the country, which is why it was used for telegraph. Current loop is also easily implemented in an optically isolated way, which makes it ideal for connecting student lab computers up to bigger computers. In contrast, RS232 is not as ideal, for if improperly connected it could throw the big machine into its own kind of loop. The RS232 convention is rated for up to 50 feet, but in practice can go at 9600 baud at least 100 feet (more at slower rates or with proper shielding). RS232 is often used for terminal-modem and terminal-nearby computer combinations. Since current loop is simpler, we define it first.

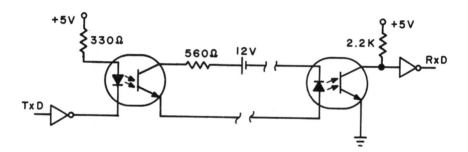

Fig. 5-6. Single-path optically-isolated 20-ma current loop circuit. A pair of these makes a full duplex link, although modem controls are missing. 1's are represented by 20 ma current flow; 0's by absence of current flow.

Figure 5-6 shows a circuit connecting the TxD serial output line of one USART (or UART) to the RxD of a different USART some distance away. Both USARTs are optoisolated from the current loop connecting path, which has its own power supply. The current loop supply voltage and resistor are chosen to maintain about 20 ma flowing in the loop when TxD is high. A low value yields no current flow. So a 1 is represented by a baud period of 20 ma and a 0 by a period of 0 ma. Two loops of the kind in Fig. 5-6 are needed for full duplex operation, i.e., 4 wires. To check out your circuit, connect the TxD current loop output to the same USART's RxD current loop input. Your USART should then act like a slow, expensive one-byte memory. If not, try connecting the USART TxD directly to its RxD. If the

USART still doesn't act like a memory byte, check your USART wiring and initialization code.

Ordinarily, current loop doesn't support the modem control signals $\overline{DTR}$, $\overline{DSR}$, $\overline{RTS}$ and $\overline{CTS}$, so you just tie $\overline{CTS}$ low and do the handshaking by seeing if your typing generates a response. A handshake signal can be derived from the RxD line by determining if RxD stays low for more than one character time, i.e., if no current flows for more than a character time. Specifically, NOR the RxD with the Q output of a 74123 retriggerable one shot clocked by RxD. The one-shot is chosen to time out at the end of a character time. So long as the remote device sends characters, the one-shot Q stays high and keeps the NOR output low. Alternatively if the device is idling (RxD high), the NOR gate output stays low. If no current flows for more than one character frame, RxD is low and the one shot times out giving a low, causing the NOR output to go high.

The other communications method is a voltage level convention using RS232. This not only supports $\overline{DTR}$, $\overline{DSR}$, $\overline{RTS}$ and $\overline{CTS}$, but a host of other signals as well. Somehow the writers of the RS232 convention defined every pin on the ubiquitous 25-pin D-type connector. Fortunately a maximum of 9 pins are typically used, and if you're willing to cut a few corners, you may get by with only 2! To increase the noise immunity over that of TTL, RS232 represents 1's by -3 to -20 volts, and 0's by 3 to 20 volts. This gives a larger voltage swing as well as a zero crossing, which is more noise immune. Two IC's handle the TTL-RS232 conversion: the 1488 (Fig. 5-7a) has three NAND gates and one inverter that convert from TTL to RS232 and the 1489 (Fig. 5-7b) has four inverters that go from RS232 to TTL. One wishes they'd make a single IC that has two transmitters and two receivers, since many applications only need one or two conversions per direction. Table 5-1 defines the nine most commonly used pins of the 25-pin connectors both from the point of view of a terminal and from that of a modem or computer. Note that the meanings of six lines are interchanged between the two points of view, since, for example, the terminal's TxD has to go to the computer's RxD. The convention assigns a male connector to the terminal and a female connector to the modem or computer. If you use RS232, you can "dummy out" various control lines. Specifically, by connecting pin 4 to 5, you dummy out the RTS/CTS protocol, and by connecting pin 6 to pin 20, you dummy out the DTR/DSR protocol. You may have to dummy out the carrier detect line 8 by connecting it to pin 6. But whatever you do, be sure to use a male connector (DB25-P) for the terminal, a female connector (DB25-S) for the modem or computer, and to observe the corresponding definitions of pins 2 and 3. A minimal installation just connects up 2 and 3 appropriately and depends on the built-in chassis grounds to complete the circuits. In fact, we've run 9600 baud communications around a house that way, although the dedicated ground lines on pins 1 and 7 are highly recommended if noise is a problem (or if the building's wiring lacks the chassis ground wire required by the National Electrician Code).

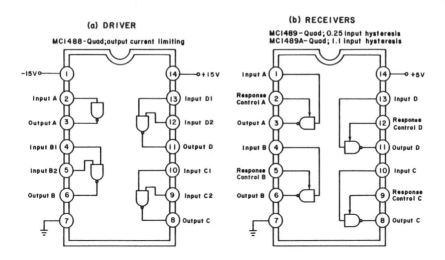

Fig. 5-7. (a) The 1488 TTL-to-RS232 converter and (b) the 1489 RS232-to-TTL converter. Each package converts four lines. The 1489 receiver IC includes a hysteresis input to reduce its high frequency response (increase low data rate noise rejection). The positive and negative supply voltages for the 1488 do not have to be symmetric. The positive voltage can range from 7 to 15 volts, and the negative from -2.5 to -15.

RS232 definition	I/O	Terminal	Modem
Signal ground		1	1
Transmit Data (TxD)	O	2	3
Receive Data (RxD)	I	3	2
Request To Send (RTS)	O	4	5
Clear To Send (CTS)	I	5	4
Data Set Ready (DSR)	I	6	20
Chassis ground		7	7
Carrier Detect (CD)		8 (input)	8 (output)
Data Terminal Ready (DTR)	O	20	6

Table 5-1. Pin numbers for the most commonly used RS232 lines, both from terminal and modem (or computer) points of view. By connecting wires straight through, e.g., 2 to 2, 3 to 3, etc., a terminal's transmitted data is the modem's received data, etc. To connect two devices of the same nature together such as two terminals, one device's 2 must be connected to the other's 3, etc. The associated cabling is called a "null modem."

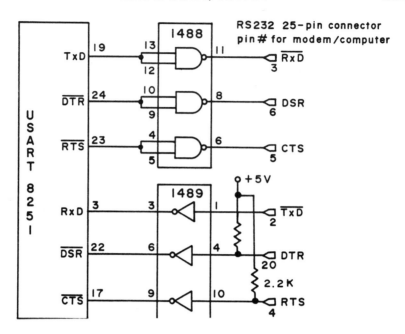

Fig. 5-8. Computer (or modem) RS232 interface supporting the DTR, DSR, RTS and CTS modem control lines. The 25-pin connector pins are labeled from the terminal's point of view, while the inverted computer labels appear on the USART.

Figure 5-8 shows an RS232 interface circuit that supports TxD, RxD, DTR, DSR, RTS and CTS. Note that this interface works with or without the control protocol, since the input handshake lines are pulled up. Most interfaces work this way, so you only need to define pins 2 and 3. But connect up the ground pins (1 and 7), if only for good luck.

5-3. Modems

When two devices are sufficiently close to one another, you can wire them together using the RS232 or current loop conventions. This approach allows the highest baud rates to be used. But for devices separated by substantial distances, the phone line may be the only practical method. In this section, we describe how the phone can be used for low-speed data communications, typically at 300 baud. Although this data rate is not very desirable for interactive programming, it's fine for shipping files between computers while you do something else.

The phone was designed to carry voice communications by various wizards who discovered that a frequency bandwidth of 3000 Hz provided adequate fidelity. They also invented an ingenious device called the duplexer, which allows two wires to carry voices in both directions at the same time. This "duplexing" is a special case of multiplexing for which many signals are carried over the same line. For distances less than 100 miles or so, you can argue with a friend over the phone, both talking at once. This is "full" duplex, as discussed earlier. For longer distances, the finite speed of the electrical signals would lead to a returned echo somewhat after you say something, making it very hard to talk. Consequently long distance communications use "echo suppressors", requiring the talkers to take turns talking. This is "half" duplex operation. If you've ever fiddled with your phone wires, you've probably discovered that only two of the three or more wires are necessary not only for talking, but also for ringing the bell and dialing. In the four-conductor modular telephone cable, the middle pair, one red, one green, do the job. Taking the phone off the hook actually closes the phone circuit, drawing current and connecting you up with the local switching station. By touch tone, ordinary dialing, or by rapidly pushing the hook buttons, you can dial a number.

More recent inventors from the same company (Ma Bell) figured out how to use this convenient facility to transmit low speed data in both directions simultaneously, i.e., full duplex. Specifically they allocated a frequency band from about 2025 to 2225 Hz to be used by the device that answers a phone call, and a band from about 1070 to 1270 Hz for the device that origi-

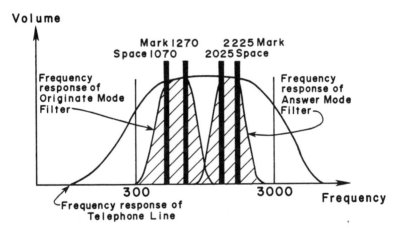

Fig. 5-9. Originate and answer mode frequency bandpasses used for full-duplex, 300-baud data communication on phone lines.

nated the phone call (see Fig. 5-9). The one's level or "mark" is represented by 2225 and 1270 for the answerer and originator, respectively. The 2025 and 1070 are used for the corresponding zero's level or "space." The device that translates the USART's bit stream into these frequencies is called a modem, short for MOdulator DEModulator. The modulation technique is called frequency shift keying (FSK). The modem answering the phone puts a 2225 Hz tone on the phone line, causing the modem on the originating end to reply with a 1270 Hz tone. When this handshake has occurred, both modems pull their respective CTS lines active, allowing communications to proceed.

The most familiar modem is, perhaps, the acoustic modem, which features a cradle to lie the phone handle in. The cradle has a microphone and a speaker, and you can even listen in on the data conversation if you're quiet (else all sorts of jibberish gets interjected). To start the communication process, you dial the remote computer and wait for the 2225 Hz signal. Then you press the phone handle into the modem cradle. The beauty of this method is that you don't have to connect any hard wires to the phone line; the connection is electrically isolated by a sound link.

Alternatively, the modem output can be coupled to the phone lines via an isolation transformer, with an increase in the signal to noise ratio. Both to protect the phone network from the modem and the modem from the phone network, this kind of connection is required and regulated by the Federal Communications Commission. The connector is called a Data Access Arrangement (DAA) and typically includes ring detection and off hook capability. These features provide a modem interface with the lines to answer the phone and to dial out. To take advantage of both facilities, such an interface must be able to transmit and receive either as an originator or an answerer. In general transmit filters should be characterized by six or more poles and receive filters by eight or more. This leads to quite reliable data communication over ordinary phone lines. The filters essentially prevent a modem from hearing an echo of the modem's own transmission, and consequently the echo suppressors used for long distance voice communications are not needed. The echo suppressors turn off automatically when modem frequencies are detected, allowing full duplex data communications to take place. Excellent originate/answer/auto-dial modems for S-100 and Apple systems are sold by Hayes Microcomputer Products.

Recently 1200-baud full-duplex asynchronous modems have become available. Two encoding conventions are used, one due to Racal Vadic Corporation and the other to Ma Bell. The Vadic convention tends to be better for acoustic modems. For a number of years, it has been possible to communicate at 2400 and 4800 baud rates using synchronous half-duplex methods over "conditioned" lines. You can also rent multiple lines allowing the bandwidth and hence the data rate to be increased.

5-4. Computer-Computer Communication Methods

There are many software protocols for computer-computer communications, ranging from "hands on" to automatic. If the computers in question both use hardware and software compatible secondary storage (e.g., CP/M single-density, IBM-compatible full-size floppy diskettes), the transfer just involves moving a diskette from one machine to the other. If this is inconvenient or impossible, other methods must be used. The simplest and most general of these is to make the originate computer act like a computer terminal. Timesharing computers systems support terminal interactions by their very natures. The disadvantage of this method is that a human being has to oversee the transfer. The concept is illustrated in Fig. 5-10 and is

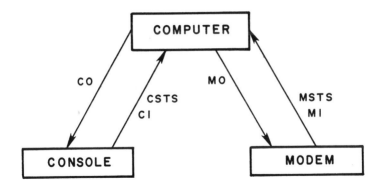

Fig. 5-10. Diagram showing how characters typed on local terminal are relayed by the local computer to the modem and vice versa. One special local character is reserved, e.g., ©R, to return to the local computer's operating system.

implemented by the "modem" loop:

```
MODEM:  CALL    MSTS        ;Modem character received?
        JR      Z,CTEST
        CALL    MI          ;Yes. Get it (call Modem Input)
        LD      C,A
        CALL    CO          ;Output it to local console
CTEST:  CALL    CSTS        ;Local character typed?
        JR      Z,MODEM
        CALL    CI          ;Yes. Get it (call Console Input)
        LD      (CRFLG),A   ;Turn on modem rdr flag (see Prob. 5-10)
        CP      "R"-40H     ;©R?
        RET     Z           ;If so, return to local system
        CALL    MO          ;No. Send character to modem
        JR      MODEM

MSTS:   IN      A,(MSTAT)   ;Modem input status routine
        BIT     1,A         ;USART convention
        RET

MI:     CALL    MSTS        ;Modem input routine
        JR      Z,MI
        IN      A,(MDATA)
        RET
MO:     IN      A,(MSTAT)   ;Modem output routine
        BIT     0,A         ;USART convention
        JR      Z,MO
        LD      A,C         ;Output character passed in C
        OUT     (MDATA),A
        RET
```

This modem loop ships whatever you type on the local keyboard to the remote computer, and displays whatever the remote computer sends on the local CRT. Exercise 14 in Chap. 8 gives you a chance to actually try this for yourself. To transfer a file to the remote computer, you first execute MODEM to log onto the remote computer. You then tell the remote computer to copy from the terminal to a disk file. On a Digital Equipment DEC10, for example, you type

.PIP file=TTY: (cr)

(the "." is typed by the DEC10, which we indicate by underlining). (cr) means carriage return. On a Data General Eclipse, you type

) COPY file @CONSOLE (cr)

Each timeshared computer has its own COPY-from-terminal command. After typing the copy command, you type ©R to return to your local system. You then type an appropriate local command to transfer the file from memory, disk or wherever to the modem output (MO). When done, you execute the MODEM loop again and type an end-of-file character. This is ©Z for a DEC10 and ©D for an Eclipse.

Transferring a file from the remote computer to the local is slightly harder. You log on as before and type

.TYPE file

The trouble is that as soon as the carriage return for this command is typed, the remote may start typing the file before you've had a chance to instruct the local computer to read the modem input into local storage. There are a couple of ways to get around this problem. One possibility is to have the modem reader routine MDMRDR (see Prob. 5-10) type the CR. The MODEM routine sets a flag (CRFLG in the code above) requesting the MDMRDR to send the CR and turn the flag off. In Exercise 14, we present a somewhat more elegant approach, in which you return to your local monitor after logging on the remote computer and type an L (for Load) command. This command is followed by a string of characters constituting the appropriate command to the remote computer, e.g., TYPE filename. This string is terminated by a break character, and followed, in turn, by a destination address in the local computer. When you type CR locally, the L command program sends the TYPE command to the remote computer and the transfer occurs. For either a DEC10 or an Eclipse, you can type

>Ltype file©R100 (CR)

where the > is the local monitor prompt character (like the DEC10's ".") and where the string "type file" is sent to the remote computer. The address we want the file to be transferred to in the local computer memory follows the ©R, (in the example, hex location 100). The L program echos the received characters on the screen, so that you know what is being transferred. When no more characters are being sent, you can type ©R, which terminates the L command and returns to the local monitor program. You can then resume communications with the remote computer, using the MODEM program. During the transfer, characters other than ©R typed on the local keyboard are sent to the remote computer. This is particularly useful for sending control characters.

A couple of practices are helpful or even necessary. To speed up data transmission from remote to local, instruct the remote computer that your "terminal" has hardware tabs. Turn off the page mode on the remote (if it has one). For local to remote transfers, turn off the echo on the remote. Although timesharing systems usually can accept data all day at 300 baud, they tend to get behind in echoing at this rate, and you'll loose data. Higher baud rates require some kind of regular handshaking. For example, the DEC10 sends a ©S when it wants the terminal to stop sending data and sends a ©Q when it's ready to receive again.   Such a protocol is imple-mented by the output routine

```
MOS:     CALL    MSTS      ;Remote input available?
         JR      Z,MO
         CALL    MI        ;Yep. Get it
         CP      "S"-40H    ;©S?
         JR      NZ,MO
WAITQ:   CALL    MI        ;Yep. Hang for a ©Q
         CP      "Q"-40H
         JR      NZ,WAITQ
MO:                        ;Continue with MO routine above
```

Alternatively, for hardwired communications through USART's, you can use the DTR signal to control data transmission. This approach is sometimes called "reverse channel."   For this method, the MO routine requires both TxRDY (or TxEMPTY) and DSR to be active before shipping a character. By pulling its DTR bit low, the destination computer can then deactivate the source computer's DSR to stop data transfer. The corresponding MO routine becomes (bit meanings appropriate for USART)

```
MODTR:   IN      A,(MSTAT) ;Check USART status byte
         XOR     81        ;Both bit 7 and bit 0 must be high
         AND     81        ; for transmission to occur
         JR      NZ,MODTR
         LD      A,C
         OUT     (MDATA),A
         RET
```

If neither the ©S nor the DTR techniques can be used, have the destination computer echo the characters it receives and wait for an echoed character before sending another. For some reason or another, this approach never seems to work as reliably as the ©S and DTR techniques. Remote computers love to send out "helpful" additional characters.

A related technique can be used in the absence of a modem program. You hook up a "modem box" using a four-pole double-throw switch and a

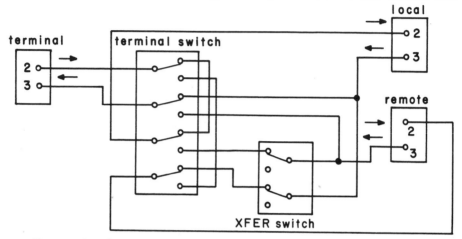

Fig. 5-1l. The "modem box", a passive "dumb" device with two switches that allows one to connect any computer to any other, provided they both use the same character codes, e.g., ASCII. The box is shown with the terminal connected to the local device and the remote receiving the local's output, e.g., set up for shipping a file to the remote.

double-pole single-throw switch as shown in Fig. 5-11. This box allows a terminal to be alternately connected to a local and to a remote computer. After instructing the destination computer (which can be either the local or remote computer) to copy from the terminal, you switch to the source computer and tell it to type the file. Before typing the carriage return, you flip the XFER switch which allows the destination computer "listen in" on the typing. At the end of the transfer, switch back to the destination computer to send an end of file if necessary. Here too, it's a good idea to use hardware tabs and to turn off the echo on the destination computer.

5-5. RF, Fiber-optic and Power-line Carriers

In Secs. 5-1 through 5-4, we have seen common serial communications techniques typically used to transmit ASCII codes between computers and terminals. The transmission media used are wires or phone lines. In this section, we consider other kinds of transmission media and other kinds of codes. The media are optical fibers, radio waves and 110 VAC power lines. Each has special advantages and limitations. Codes other than ASCII enter, due to variations in the natures of the media and the information transmitted. The optical fibers are primarily useful for high-speed data transfers and/or environments in which electric and magnetic fields would seriously impair wire links. The power-line and RF methods are useful for remote control applications.

Light waves traveling down optical fibers have become an important communications medium. The lowest-loss fibers consist of a solid cylindrical glass core surrounded by a cylindrical glass "cladding." The cladding has a lower index of refraction than the core, so that light waves propagating down the fiber are trapped inside by total internal reflection. The best fibers have losses less than 1 dB/km, that is, it takes about two miles to cut the light intensity in half! The fibers are used extensively in phone communications, ships, airplanes and wherever electrical noise is a problem. Since one end of the fiber system literally only looks at light, no electrical connection is made, and no electrical noise is picked up. The fibers can be run without problems in environments with large ambient electric and magnetic fields. This is particularly handy on airplanes and ships, since the powerful motors induce large voltage variations in wire systems. In addition, the data transmission capacity of fibers is substantially greater than that of coaxial cables, providing up to 100 times the data handling capability in the same volume. Around the home, you can run fibers on the wall: just paint over them, and no one will notice. Of course, you can also run 36 gage wire (about the thickness of a hair) on the wall, and no one's likely to notice it either. The wire has the advantage that kinks are OK. As a rule of thumb, optical fibers shouldn't be bent in a circle with less than a 2" diameter. Turns even of this size can be lossy if the fibers are painted over.

The major problem with the fibers is shining the light into them and detecting the light on the other end. Typically infrared LED's or injection lasers and matched photodiodes are used to generate and detect the light. In some commercial systems, a short length of fiber is bonded directly onto the LED emitter surface, and a similar fiber is bonded onto the photodiode detector surface. Optical fiber connectors are then used to connect the short fibers to the main fiber optic cable. Lenses can also be used to focus the light down into the fiber (about .1 mm thick) and to recover the transmitted light. Light coupling kits are available for less than $100 from Motorola and other companies. See in particular the TI 74LS462/463 encoder/decoder pair. These 20-pin IC's are all you need to interface TTL to the LED and photodiode. Bytes are input to the 74LS462 and are delivered by the 74LS463 at the other end of the cable. The data is transmitted serially up to 1 megabit/second over the fiber in a phase encoded format. The overall cost is still a lot more than the cost for a RS232 wire link if the noise and distance limitations of the wire link are unimportant. But the technology is improving rapidly and the cost is bound to decrease markedly. Commercially available single-fiber systems are simplex, that is, unidirectional. Two fibers are used for full-duplex operation. It is possible, however, to transmit bidirectionally on a single fiber, using duplexer devices analogous to those in two-wire phone communications.

A good way to encode data over optical fibers at 1 MHz or slower data rates is analogous to current loop with light playing the role of current. Light on means a mark; light off means a space. With this approach, you modulate the LED current with TTL and transmit ASCII. Higher data rates may require fancier encoding techniques.

A very different concept employs the 110 VAC (or 220VAC) wiring common in all buildings. In the United States, this wiring has 60 Hz current flowing through it. Since the middle of World War II, radio amateurs have known that the wiring can also be used for transmitting voice around a building and even elsewhere, provided the inductance in outside power transformers doesn't provide too much impedance (the impedance or ac resistance of an inductor is proportional to the frequency of the ac current). Radio Shack and others have marketed FM-intercom systems that modulate the power lines, and you can transmit Hi-Fi sound all over the house in this way.

More recently, a British company BSR has developed and marketed a set of 110-VAC triac modules that respond to serial codes impressed on a 120 kHz carrier wave. This high frequency wave is then transmitted on the AC lines. Three kinds of modules are available: 5-ampere appliance modules that plug into the wall and provide a socket for the appliance, 2-ampere lamp modules that plug in the same way and have a dimmer capability, and 2-ampere wall-switch dimmer modules that replace the usual wall switch. Up to 256 modules can operate in the same system, and each can be selectively turned on or off. They can be turned on or off in groups of 16 simultaneously, and dimmer modules can be dimmed or brightened. The 16-module groups are each assigned a "house code," so that each module has both a house code ("A"-"P") and a unit code (1 to 16). The idea is that the most any one home might need is 16 modules, and by choosing different house codes, one home's control signals won't affect a neighbor's in cases where no power transformer blocks the 120 kHz signals. The modules and controllers are marketed by Sears, Radio Shack and JSA. Special computer-based controllers for the modules are marketed by a number of firms; check the microcomputer magazines for advertising.

We now discuss the codes used by BSR and show a way of putting them on the power lines using a microcomputer and $20 worth of optoisolated hardware. We are indebted to Jim T. Fulton for the hardware schematic, a description of his system using the Apple 2 computer, and for several helpful discussions. Alternative methods include interfacing to the special remote-control sonor module marketed by Sears, etc., as described by Ciarcia (see references). Such interfaces can control only the 16 units corresponding to one house code. Since it's very easy to modulate the power lines directly and to access all 256 module combinations, we have chosen that method for presentation. Of course, you could write codes for your own receiving modules, e.g., other computers, but the wide availability of the BSR modules makes them particularly attractive. We discuss the hardware first, and then the codes together with a Z80 program for generating them.

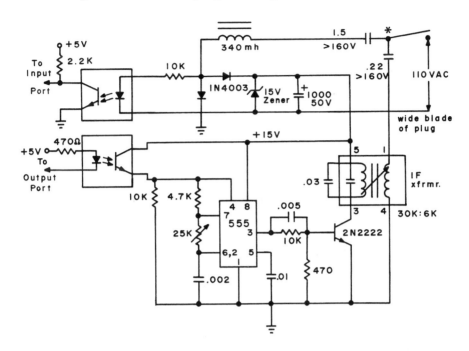

Fig. 5-12. Schematic of simple 60 Hz power-line modulation circuit. It provides the computer with an optoisolated TTL square
wave for zero crossing detection, and accepts a TTL serial output
stream for delivery to the power lines on a 120 kHz carrier voltage. *Touching this point is even more dangerous than reading this
book! We cannot assume any liability for doing either.

Fulton's circuit is shown in Fig. 5-12. Two capacitors are connected to
the 110 VAC line, one for the 15-volt power supply and one to transfer the
codes. Since one side of the power supply is connected to ground, you
should use a three-pronged plug, which forces the wide blade to be the
ground side of the AC power circuit. First consider the power supply, which
is essentially the same as that used in the BSR controller. The 340 mh
inductor is used to prevent the code frequencies from getting into the power
supply. The two diodes make a full-wave unipolar bridge that charges up
the 1000 μfd capacitor. The Zener diode limits the maximum voltage to 15
volts. The top optoisolator (see Sec. 4-1) converts the 60 Hz sine wave
into a TTL level square wave, which the microcomputer uses to spot zero
crossings (it can also be used for a real-time clock as discussed in Sec. 3-
5). The output circuit is driven by an optoisolator connected to one bit of
an output port. When this bit is low, the optoisolator turns on, pulling pin 4
of the 555 oscillator (see Sec. 1-6) high. This turns the 555 on, and it generates a 120 kHz square wave. The 555 output is amplified by a 2N2222
NPN transistor, which drives the IF transformer T1. The transformer output

is coupled to the power lines by the .22 fd capacitor.

The codes are binary numbers which are translated into pulse groups as

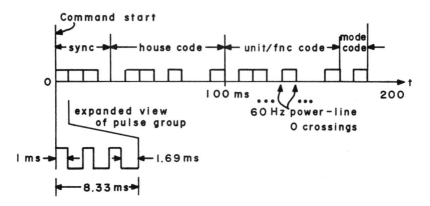

Fig. 5-13. BSR command sequence. The sequence consists of a
sync code, a house code, a unit/function code, and a mode code.
Each 1 bit is composed of three pulses with 1 millisecond highs and
about 1.69 msec lows, yielding a total of about 8.1 msec. The
software extends the last low enough to synchronize the bits to the
power-line zero crossings. These crossings are separated by 8.33
msecs. The zero bits (spaces) are similarly 8.33 msec long and
synchronized to the zero crossings.

illustrated in Fig. 5-13. A 1 bit is represented by three pulses superimposed
on a 120 kHz carrier wave. Each pulse high lasts 1 msec, while the lows
last about 1.69 msec. The last low is extended so that the sum of the three
pulse times fits into a half cycle of the 60 Hz power-line period. This time
is 1000/120 = 8.33 msec. The zero crossing input in Fig. 5-12 is used to
synchronize the computer program that generates the pulse group. Similarly
a 0 bit (space) is timed to fit one half cycle (8.33 msec).

The codes are chosen to give nearly equal numbers of 1's and 0's, to help
transmission through the power lines. A command sequence starts with a
sync code, which contains the only possible combination of three 1's (nine
pulses) in a row. After a space, one of 16 possible house codes follows,
represented by 8 bits. Actually these bits are all grouped into pairs of
either 01 or 10. Hence only 16 combinations occur. Calling the 01 pair a
"zero" and the 10 pair a "one", you might expect to find the 16 house codes
numbered sequentially, but they aren't. The house code is followed by 8
bits giving either the encoded unit of one of the 16 modules or the desired
function code. The 16 unit/function codes are encoded the same way as
the house codes, as shown in Table 5-2. There are six function codes: all of
one house code off/on, individual on/off, and dim/bright. These function
codes are represented by 4-bit codes 0 to 5, respectively. The sync, house
and unit/function codes are followed by the 2-bit mode code: 01 specifies
the unit/function code to be a function, and 10 to be a unit. Optionally, the

house	unit	function	hex	decimal	4-bit
A	1		69	105	0110
B	2		a9	169	1110
C	3	on	59	89	0010
D	4		99	153	1010
E	5	all on	56	86	0001
F	6		96	150	1001
G	7	bright	66	102	0101
H	8		a6	166	1101
I	9		6a	106	0111
J	10		aa	170	1111
K	11	off	5a	90	0011
L	12		9a	154	1011
M	13	all off	55	85	0000
N	14		95	149	1000
O	15	dim	65	101	0100
P	16		a5	165	1100

Table 5-2. 8-bit house, unit and function codes for BSR power-line modules. The four-bit code divides the eight bits into four bit pairs and substitutes a 1 for a 10 pair and a 0 for a 01 pair.

complete command sequence can be followed by a 4-bit sync sequence. We have suppressed the optional sync, to speed up the two-command (unit, then function) sequence.

It's easy to convince the Z80 to generate these codes. We include two subroutines: BSRUNT, which sends a unit command sequence, and BSRFNC, which sends a function sequence. The house code, ASCII "A" to "P" (1 to 16 works too), is passed in register D, and the unit/function code (1 to 16) in passed in register E. The function code numbers are defined in Table 5-2. For tighter code packing, you might want to number the house codes 0 to 15, i.e., one hex digit, and similarly the unit/function codes 0 to 15. If so, delete the "DEC A" and "AND 0F" instructions in the TRANS routine. Change the port numbers for LINE (zero crossing input bit) and F555 (555 oscillator output bit) to fit your configuration. The numbers nn for the delays in the pulses routine (see LD DE,nn instructions) are chosen for a 2 MHz CPU clock frequency and should be changed appropriately for other frequencies. Other times are synchronized to the 60 Hz line crossing. Note: as of press time, we have not verified that this routine works. If you check it out, please let us know what happens!

```
.RADIX    16                      ;All numbers are hexadecimal
LINE      EQU    0                ;Bit 0 of input port 0 gives line xing
F555      EQU    0                ;Bit 0 of output port 0 -> 555

BSRUNT:   LD     B,2              ;Routine to send unit code
          JR     BSR
BSRFND:   LD     B,1              ;Routine to send function
BSR:      PUSH   BC               ;Save mode code
          LD     A,D              ;Translate house code
          CALL   TRANS
          LD     D,L              ;Save it
          LD     A,E              ;Translate unit or function code
          CALL   TRANS
          LD     H,D              ;HL has 16-bit command code

          CALL   SYNC             ;Send out sync pulses and a space
          LD     B,10             ;Ship out 16 bits in HL
WORD:     ADD    HL,HL            ;Shift leftmost bit into CY
          CALL   PULSPA           ;Pulses if CY=1, space if CY=0
          DJNZ   WORD

          POP    AF               ;Send out 2-bit mode code
          LD     B,2
MODE:     RRA
          CALL   PULSPA
          DJNZ   MODE
          RET                     ;Delete RET for optional trailing sync

SYNC:     LD     B,3              ;Send 3 sync pulses
SYNC1:    CALL   PULSES
          DJNZ   SYNC1            ;Fall thru to a space

SPACE:    CALL   WAITZX           ;Wait for 0 xing and debounce it

MSEC:     LD     DE,51            ;Wait for about 1 msec
DELAY:    DEC    DE               ;Delay (DE*24+37) t states
          LD     A,D              ; (37 is for LD DE,nn, CALL & RET
          OR     E                ;  instructions)
          JP     NZ,DELAY
          RET

PULSPA:   JR     NC,SPACE         ;Pulses or space?
PULSES:   CALL   WAITZX
          LD     C,3              ;Send out 3 pulses
PULOOP:   XOR    A                ;Sink opto, turning on 120 kHz
          OUT    (F555),A
          CALL   MSEC             ;Delay 1 msec
          LD     A,0FF            ;Turn off opto and 120 kHz
```

```
         OUT     (F555),A
         LD      DE,137.      ;Delay about 1.67 msec
         CALL    DELAY
         DEC     C
         JR      NZ,PULOOP
         RET                  ;Total PULOOP time about 8.1 msec

WAITZX:  IN      A,(LINE)     ;Wait for zero xing
         LD      D,A
WAIT:    IN      A,(LINE)     ;Has value changed?
         XOR     D
         AND     1            ;Assume input bit is bit 0
         JR      Z,WAIT
         RET


TRANS:   DEC     A            ;Convert 1-16 to 0-15
         AND     0F           ;Mask out letter bits (for "A" - "P")
         LD      B,0
         LD      C,A
         LD      HL,CODES
         ADD     HL,BC        ;Compute code address
         LD      L,(HL)       ;Load code into L
         RET

CODES:   DB      69,0a9,59,99,56,96,66,0a6    ;0-7
         DB      6a,0aa,5a,9a,55,95,65,0a5    ;8-15

         END
```

The third of our exotic communications media uses radio waves with codes impressed on a 360 MHz RF carrier wave. This approach is copied from the Sears garage-door opener system, and works with up to 200 feet between the transmitter and receiver. The approach is not trivial to implement, since the test equipment has to have about 400 MHz bandwidth, and all sorts of little things (like leads that stick out too far) can change the operating characteristics of the circuit. If you want to build such devices, choosing the 72 or 75 MHz radio control bands or the 27 or 49 MHz unlicensed bands might be better choices. The FCC does have its rules, so even if you keep the power output under 100 mW, you need their permission. In this connection, it's amusing to note that the remote smoke detectors that use 360 MHz radio waves are only allowed to turn on the transmitters for about a second. It's OK to have your house burn down, but not to emit any extra RF!

Figure 5-14 shows the transmitter of a garage door opener. Consider the strange emblem on the right side. That's a rough idea of the circuit-board trace that plays the role of both a small inductor and the transmitter antenna. This inductor, the .36 μh coil, the small capacitors and the 42017

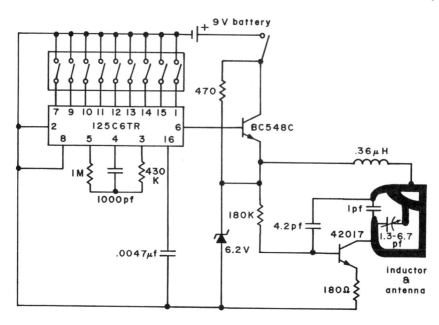

Fig. 5-14. Transmitter circuit of Sears garage door opener. Strange emblem on right is the circuit-board trace used as an inductor and antenna.

transistor make up the oscillator portion of the transmitter. They emit between about 290 and 430 MHz, depending on the setting of the 1.3-6.7 pf variable capacitor. This range fits comfortably between the TV channels 7-13, which range from 174 to 216 MHz, and the UHF channels 14-83, which range between 470 to 890 MHz. The BC548C transistor controls the power supply for the oscillator. By switching this transistor on and off, it is possible to amplitude-modulate the 360 MHz carrier with a serial data stream. The custom Motorola 125C6TR IC does this (the AMI S2743 is similar, but more elegant), and outputs a start bit followed by the binary number given by the nine dip switches connected to its inputs. Each bit is represented by a 4 msec rectangular wave. For a high input (dip switch off), the 4 msec starts with a 3 msec high, followed by a 1 msec low. For a low input (switch on), the 4 msec starts with a 1 msec high followed by a 3 msec low. The start bit has the same encoding as a high input. The pattern is repeated every 76 msec as long as the power switch is closed, with a low value occurring in the intervening 36 msecs. These waveforms are easy to see with an inexpensive oscilloscope. With a high speed spectrum analyzer, you can spot the 360 MHz transmitted through space, and then recover the codes from the RF signal.

    The receiver circuit shown in Fig. 5-15 is more complicated than the matching transmitter circuit of Fig. 5-14, because the weak RF signal has to be amplified and the 360 MHz carrier eliminated. Transistor Q1 amplifies the RF signal, provided it matches the circuit's resonant frequency.

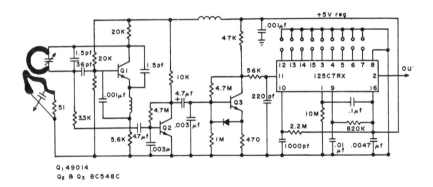

Q₁ 49014
Q₂ & Q₃ BC548C

Fig. 5-15. Receiver circuit for garage door opener. Transistor Q1 is a 49014 and amplifies the input 360 MHz signal. Transistors Q2 and Q3 are BC548C's and amplify the kHz envelope signals, while attenuating the 360 MHz carrier.

Transistors Q2 and Q3 are both low-pass amplifiers, that is, they amplify the serial kHz envelope of the 360 MHz carrier, while attenuating the carrier itself. The 0.003 µF capacitors connecting the transistor bases to ground have an impedance of about 33K for 10 kHz, while they have only 1 Ω for the 360 MHz, thereby effectively shorting the carrier out. If the receiver's tuning matches the transmitter's, the resulting waveform on pin 11 of the custom CMOS IC decoder 125C7RX is the inverse of that on pin 6 of the transmitter's 125C6TR IC. The 125C7RX compares this binary encoded signal to the binary number on its inputs. If the two agree, it sets its output pin 2 high. The circuit is analogous to BSR modules in that the tuned circuit at the input acts as a "house code", to keep a home owner from opening his neighbor's garage door, and the unit code is the binary number. Many more combinations are possible here, since the tuned circuit has at least 16 mutually exclusive positions, and the binary unit code has 2^9=512 values. The AMI S2743/S2742 encoder/decoder pair include a 3-bit preamble code, further increasing the number of combinations.

For a garage door opener, all you want to do is to open the door, i.e., one command. Suppose, however, that you want to control a TV set, or your whole house. One possibility is to have a set of 125C7RX receivers, each wired to respond to different transmitter dip-switch settings, one for each device. One of us (MS3) has six such circuits attached to his home computer and enjoys turning the sprinkler system on and off to adjust the flow rates without getting wet. Or walking outside at night and turning all the lights off to observe the beautiful Arizona sky. Or saying, "Let there be light!" and light there is, in quantity. Then saying "Open sesame!" and the front door opens. It's only barely short of incredible to see a tiny dip switch flick on a kilowatt of light plus the Hi-Fi!

A problem with this approach is that many receiver IC's are required. It is possible to dedicate the computer to decoding the input stream appearing at 125C7RX pin 11, which then yields 512 possibilities. This approach could even be carried out under interrupt control, reducing the computer overhead. But by appropriately driving the BC548C transistor, you can impress any serial code you want. In particular the AMI S2600 encoder IC can be used, which encodes and serializes up to a 31 key keyboard. The companion AMI S2601 receiver presents the result as a 5-bit binary number. It furthermore features remote-keypad controllable on/off, 2.44 Hz pulse-train, and analog outputs. This IC pair (and similar pairs made by Motorola) were designed for remote control of TV's. They work very well with computers as well, and allow you to control a house from your chair or back yard.

One problem with both the BSR and RF approaches is that they can be "jammed." A persona non grata can come to the house and distribute all kinds of RF radiation to ruin the RF communications, and plug in a strong 120 kHz square wave to upset the BSR communications. Hard wired (or fiber optic) communication systems cannot be so jammed, unless the wires are accessible. Consequently for security purposes, the hard-wired approach may be required. With the relative ease of the radio and BSR methods though, we don't recommend parallel wiring, except perhaps for new buildings or maximum security.

Problems

5-1. Write an interrupt-driven console output routine using a circular output buffer.

5-2. Include DSR in the console output routine protocol. Specifically, do not output a byte to the USART unless both TxEMT and DTR are high. This technique is particularly useful for sending data at high baud rates to a controller containing a FIFO. When the FIFO is nearly full, the controller pulls its DTR low. Provided the host computer recognizes DSR, no data is lost.

5-3. Write a subroutine to determine the baud rate of a serial terminal, given RxD on some input pin. Assume the terminal sends an odd ASCII character to begin with, e.g., ©A, ©C, carriage return, A, C, etc. What might you do if you don't know whether the characters are odd or even?

5-4. Write a software UART routine able to recognize a serial data stream with one start bit, 8 data bits and two stop bits. What is the practical upper baud rate limit for a 4 MHz Z80?

5-5. Write a software UART routine using a programmable clock interrupt based on a 16-bit programmable counter that divides the system clock down (e.g., Intel 8253).

5-6. Write a buffered input routine that sends ©S when the buffer is ten bytes from filling up, and sends a ©Q when the buffer gets down to eight bytes from being empty. This protocol is supported by Digital

Equipment Corporation and Data General Corporation computers and works fine over the phone lines.

5-7. Design a keypad serial interface circuit around the AMI 2600/2601 remote control chip set (often used for TV control).

5-8. Write a routine to decode the BSR signals. Assume a bandpass filter is used to eliminate input frequencies outside the .4 to 10 kHz range, i.e., that you see waveforms like those in Fig. 5-13.

5-9. Using a 7474 and two Schmidt-trigger inverters, design a 120 Hz interrupt circuit and write a program to shift out BSR codes under interrupt control. The advantage is that the computer is tied up only on the 1's, i.e., about half the time used in the program of Sec. 5-5, and the real time clock never loses a tick. What higher interrupt rate would allow you to output the 1 pulse highs under interrupt control as well?

5-10. Write a modem reader routine that checks the flag CRFLG referred to in the MODEM loop of Sec. 5-4. If CRFLG $\neq$ 0, the routine ships a carriage return to the remote computer, sets CRFLG = 0, and then waits for an input character. If CRFLG = 0, it just waits for an input character. The purpose of this feature is to send the carriage return of a TYPE-filename command when the reader is ready to read (and not before).

References

Jim T. Fulton, Letter to editor, 1980, Byte **5**, No. 6, p. 14.

S. Ciarcia, "Computerize a home," 1980, Byte **5**, No. 1, p. 28.

P. R. Rony, D. G. Larsen, J. A. Titus and C. A. Titus, 1979, Interfacing & scientific data communications experiments, Howard W. Sams, Indianapolis, Indiana. Includes parts of data sheets on Intel 8251 and Signetics 2651 USART's as well as sheets on various UART's.

See also references for Chap. 4, and data sheets on serial I/O IC's from Intel, Zilog, Signetics and others.

Chapter Six

Microcomputer Systems

Perfection is to be strived for, but not attained.

At this point we have covered many details of computer interface techniques: the way that machine instructions cause devices to respond to the CPU, ways to buffer alien voltage and current requirements, and ways to synchronize data rates between peripheral devices and the CPU. To implement these interfacing concepts in a real system, two general ingredients must be added: 1) ways to store programs and data conveniently, and 2) libraries of programs to instruct the computers to carry out the desired tasks. This second ingredient, software, is every bit as important as the hardware itself. Without programs, the hardware is totally useless. We devote Chap. 7 to this crucial topic, and consider here storage devices and the making of microcomputer systems. Section 6-1 discusses dynamic and static Random Access Memory (RAM), Erasable Programmable Read-Only Memory (EPROM), floppy disks and hard disks. Whatever system you choose, some or all of these ingredients are required. Section 6-2 considers a couple of small controller computers, so small that you just wirewrap them up and use them. One of these is based on the Intel 8048 single-chip microcomputer. Including some mention of this interesting family of tiny computers is irresistible, since it can have useful applications in the laboratory and requires fewer integrated circuits for the really small controller applications. To deal with larger systems, you can buy so-called "appliance computers" like the TRS-80 that come in a package, and still larger systems

Murray Sargent III and Richard L. Shoemaker, Interfacing Microcomputers to the Real World, ISBN 0-201-06879-6

can be configured around boxes supporting a motherboard. A motherboard is a printed circuit board with many parallel wires (the bus), and sockets connected to the bus into which you plug computer boards.

Section 6-3 discusses various Z80 microcomputer busses. First we describe the very popular S-100 bus. This bus is distinguished in a number of ways, notably in having substantially more different kinds of CPU's (>12) and boards running on it than any other bus, regardless of machine size. It's a hobbyist's heaven (sometimes nightmare) and when configured by the right people it can provide very solid computing at cost significantly below that demanded by well-known computer companies. Both authors of this book have had Z80 S-100 systems running in their homes and labs for over three years and find their systems very viable indeed. Then we describe the TRS-80 bus, which is the second most common computer bus. This bus can be buffered into an S-100 chassis, as implemented by the HuH Electronics Mini 8100 module, and it can be used to drive the smaller STD bus. As such, the TRS-80 makes a surprisingly powerful laboratory computer complete with built-in screen and keyboard for a low price. The STD bus is a commercially popular bus based on 56 pins and can be used with the Z80, 8080, 8085 and 6800 microprocessors. Many of the signals on the S-100 bus are absent on these smaller busses, which makes them easier to work with, but more limited in the variety of CPU's they can support. The STD bus provides well-defined systems with a flexibility appropriate for small machines in the laboratory at reasonable cost (although somewhat higher than S-100 equipment). Some discussion is given to two other bus concepts, the General Purpose Interface Bus (GPIB, IEEE 488) and the Intel Multibus. The GPIB is widely used in laboratory instrumentation, and the Multibus provides a popular alternative to the S-100 and STD busses. Section 6-4 gives some advice about buying microcomputer systems and describes some sample systems suitable for laboratory monitoring and control. Some discussion is also given to the needs of word processing, since both developing laboratory software and documenting the techniques and results requires word processing capabilities.

6-1. RAM, EPROM, Hard and Floppy Disks

Two kinds of high speed memory are required for microcomputers: RAM (Random–Access Memory) and ROM (Read-Only Memory). Either can be used for programs and data that do not change. The difference is, RAM is easily modified and looses its memory when the power is turned off, while ROM is hard to change but retains its memory when the power is turned off. Two general categories of RAM are popular: static and dynamic. The static variety consists of flip-flops like those in a 74LS273, typically arranged in a square or rectangular array. Unlike the 74LS273, the bits are not all on pins ready to connect to output devices. Instead an address is presented to the memory IC and the corresponding data comes out on one or more pins a short time later. Static memory retains its bits as long as the power is on.

The memory cells are either flipped or flopped! This kind of architecture is easy to work with, but requires about six transistors per bit inside the chip. In contrast, dynamic memories require only one transistor per bit and hence use substantially less power and space. Essentially each bit cell is a sample and hold circuit in which a capacitor is charged (for a 1) or discharged (for a 0). By reading all rows of the memory matrix at least once every two milliseconds, the dynamic memory IC's refresh the status of the bits, i.e., the capacitors having a "1" are recharged. If this refresh procedure is neglected, the bits will be lost, since charge leaks off the capacitors.

The Z80 has built-in refresh capability. When the $\overline{\text{RFSH}}$ line goes low, and the $\overline{\text{MREQ}}$ line goes low (during M1 cycles), a valid row refresh address between 0 and 127 is present on the low address byte. The TRS-80 uses this feature to refresh its dynamic RAM's and the TRS-80 microcomputer technical reference handbook describes the procedure in some detail (a schematic is included also). Potential problems occur when the Z80's $\overline{\text{WAIT}}$ line is pulled low to synchronize data flow to and from peripheral devices. During $\overline{\text{WAIT}}$ states, the Z80's address and data lines are frozen and no refresh occurs (see Exercise 1 in Chap. 8). If the wait states last too long, goodbye memory! Consequently, many dynamic RAM boards have on-board "invisible" refresh, and do not depend on the Z80's $\overline{\text{RFSH}}$ line. However, many of these "invisible refresh" schemes are critically dependent on timing of the CPU signals, and work only with certain CPU boards. Let the user beware!

Many computer systems use dynamic memories because of their substantially reduced cost. Currently the most popular dynamic RAM IC is the 4116 (see Fig. 6-1), a 16Kx1-bit 16-pin dip. In addition to the TRS-80, the Apple, Digital Equipment's LSI 11, Intertec's Superbrain, many minicomputers and many large computers use the 4116 or one of its equivalents. Now several companies are selling the 4164, a 64Kx1 dynamic RAM, and the 256Kx1 dynamic RAM's are coming. Because of the potential problems with dynamic RAM's, it can be very helpful to have some static RAM boards around to debug with if trouble occurs. Static RAM's like the 2114 1Kx4 (see Fig. 6-1) either fail hard or work right. Make sure in either case that you buy RAM's rated for the access times you need. Running at 4MHz, the Z80 has a minimum memory access time of 375 nsecs, which occurs when $\overline{\text{M1}}$ is active. Other memory references last 500 nsecs. So even 450 nsec memory should work fine if you include a wait state when $\overline{\text{M1}}$ is active. With static RAM's, we've never had any problems here, but dynamic RAM's rated at 375 nsec do not always work with a 4 MHz system even with wait states every time $\overline{\text{MREQ}}$ is low. The moral there is to slow down and live, or buy faster dynamic memory. It is interesting to note that while the 4116 RAM's have four times the bit capacity of the 2114's, they cost less and require about the same power.

Read-Only Memories, ROM's, are only sold in large quantities, since a special mask with the desired ones and zeros has to be made. PROM's (Programmable ROM's) can be programmed once using a PROM "burner," which

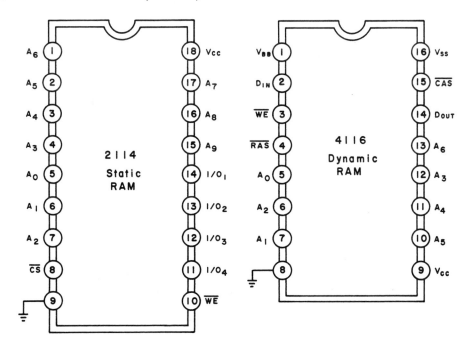

Fig. 6-1. Popular dynamic (4116) and static (2114) RAM IC's. The 4116 is a 16Kx1 RAM, so that 16K bytes requires eight IC's. The 2114 is a 1Kx4 RAM, so that 1K bytes is given by 2 IC's.

literally burns up fused links in a memory array. For most small quantity purposes, the Erasable Programmable Read-Only Memory (EPROM) is used. The most popular EPROM today is the 2716 2K byte (see Fig. 6-2), 5-volt-only circuit pioneered by Intel and second-sourced by many companies. Other 5-volt EPROM's include the 2732 (4K byte) and the 2764 (8K byte). Texas Instruments markets equivalents with a 25 prefix instead of the 27 to distinguish its TMS2716 3-voltage (+5, +12 and -5 volts) 2K-byte EPROMS. Don't plug an Intel 2716 into a TMS 2716 socket! Of course a few trace modifications allow switching from one to the other.

Some ROM is necessary in any computer system, since otherwise the computer has no program in it when it's turned on. Toggling programs in using front panel switches is a hassle no one wants to go through except for some initial learning experience. Almost all commercially available small computers have ROM, so that they do something when the power is turned on.

2716 EPROM's are easy to program on a Z80 system, because the $\overline{\text{WAIT}}$ line can be used to "latch" the address and data bytes directly (see Prob. 6-6). You just move the data from RAM into the EPROM with appropriate numbers of wait states. But look out if you wait too long with dynamic memories! The data movement must be accompanied by the correct 25 volt pulse. This is good and bad: accidentally writing over EPROM is very unlikely, since you need the 25 volts. On the other hand, you need an

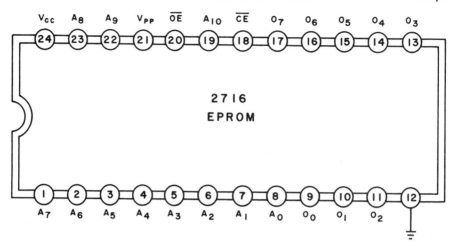

Fig. 6-2. Intel 2716 EPROM provides easy programmability at moderate IC cost. Thanks to large competition, notably from Japanese companies like Hitachi and Fujitsu, the price is less than $10 in 100 quantity.

EPROM "burner" (a pulsed 25 volt source under software control) to do the job. An EPROM is erased by exposing its quartz window to shortwave (230 nm) ultraviolet radiation for about 20 minutes. When done, all bits should register as 1's. Any one can then be turned into a zero by pumping some charge into the EPROM memory cell with the 25 v pulse. In fact with the 5-volt EPROM's individual bytes can be changed anytime you put them into the EPROM burner. But it's a oneway street: ones go to zeroes. To turn a zero back into a one, you must erase the whole EPROM. Some systems, like the Z80 Starter Kit, have a built-in EPROM burner. Just supply the 25 volts and you're ready to go.

Z80 systems address 64K=65536 locations directly. You can add more 64K chunks by "memory banking" as discussed in the problems. One thing is clear: there must be a way to load in and to save programs and data other than in ROM or EPROM. Various technologies are developing rapidly such as CCD's, and bubble memories, but for now the most convenient large scale, i.e., much greater than 64K, memories are provided by floppy disks and hard disks. These devices record data in serial bit streams on the magnetic surfaces of platters much like phonograph records. Each platter surface is divided into a set of concentric circles called tracks, and each track is divided into equal arcs called sectors. The data along with control bits is then stored on these tracks in a serial bit stream. The floppy-disk platters are called diskettes. They bend and their read/write heads contact the magnetic surface when reading or writing. The diskettes provide anywhere from 70K bytes for single-sided, single-density minifloppies (5.25 inch diameter) typically used on TRS-80 disk systems to over 1 megabyte for double-sided, double-density full size (8 inch diameter) floppies.

IBM invented the floppy-disk concept and introduced a special format (IBM 3740) for storing data in a reliable fashion on the diskettes. Each sector has a 128-byte data field, a 28-byte postamble, and a 51-byte prologue containing the track and sector number, some delay gaps and Cyclic Redundancy Checks (sum of all data bytes modulo 256). One little hole near the center of the diskette identifies sector 1. This format scheme is called IBM soft-sectored, and has been extended to deal with double-density diskettes, which have 256-byte records contained in the same disk area as a single-density sector. Soft-sectored methods are the most widely used today for microcomputers. Other manufacturers have used "hard-sectored" methods, in which each sector start is identified by its own hole near the center of the diskette. These methods tend to allow more information to be stored on the diskette, since special bit patterns identifying sector origins are not needed. Hard-sector methods have the disadvantage of being incompatible with the majority. Incompatibility is nevertheless widespread even among IBM-formated diskettes, what with all kinds of permutations of full vs mini, double-sided vs single-sided, double-density vs single-density, and would you believe quad-density vs the rest (but no quad-sided!). In any event, we cannot emphasize enough how valuable floppy disk drives can be for development of microcomputer software and data storage. Many systems include cassettes, e.g., the TRS-80. Unless you have at least one floppy-disk drive, however, you are just playing games or you're using a controller that is tied to a larger system with disk storage. Serious laboratory computing cannot be done efficiently without disk storage.

The most important considerations in choosing a disk drive and controller are reliability, disk capacity, and compatibility with other systems. We favor Shugart, Siemens or Persci drives with disk controllers that use the Western Digital WD1771 and WD1791 controller IC's, e.g., the SD Systems Versafloppy boards. Controllers using wait states for synchronization are easier to get running than DMA controllers, especially if dynamic memory is being used. On the other hand, DMA doesn't cause a real-time clock to lose ticks, and lengthy wait states can cause a RAM board dependent on the Z80's refresh capability to forget its data. 8" drives with their large capacity (250 Kbytes for single-sided, single-density up to 1 Mbyte for double-sided, double-density) are generally preferable, although new 96-track 5.25" drives with similar capacities are now becoming available and may be a better choice in the near future.

Floppy diskettes are great for most word-processing and laboratory data storage. For more demanding requirements such as large data bases, frequent compilations (see Chap. 7), several users, etc., hard disks are desirable or even necessary. The hard-disk platters don't bend and the read/write heads don't touch the magnetic surface. The most popular hard-disk drives for microcomputers are the Winchester drives, which are hermetically sealed to prevent dust particles from entering and causing a head crash or scratches on the disk. Like the floppy disk, this hard-disk technology was also invented at IBM. The name "Winchester" comes from the fact that one of the earliest such drives was called the 3030 drive. This part number reminded people of the Winchester 30-30 shotgun - hence the name. They can be bought with anywhere from 5 megabytes to 400 megabytes. The smaller numbers like 10 to 28 megabytes are becoming quite inexpensive, certainly less than a cheap car, and provide a large-size microcomputer with lots of room to work with. One general point about all disks is that all important data should be "backed up", that is, at least two copies should exist.

6-2. Small Controller Systems

In Sec. 3-2, we considered a minimum system consisting of the Z80, a 2716 EPROM, a PIO, and a clock circuit, and assumed that the internal memory of the Z80 provided sufficient RAM. As a practical matter, such a small amount of RAM is inadequate for any potential applications. In this section, we add a few IC's to make a practical Z80 minimum system, which is powerful and easy to program and modify, what with the great profusion of Z80/8080 software described in Chap. 7. We also consider a less powerful microcomputer that nevertheless does include enough RAM to perform very useful tasks, namely the Intel 8035 microprocessor with a 2716 EPROM. Should such a small controller suffice and many copies be desired, you can combine even these two IC's in the form of the 8048 single-chip microcomputer. The single-chip microcomputers are very popular in large volume applications and are becoming more powerful by the minute!

Our recommended miminum Z80 computer is diagrammed in Fig. 6-3. The memory consists of a 5-volt-only 2716 EPROM (2K bytes) and two 2114 static RAM's (1K bytes), which are easy to wirewrap up. The address decoding is redundant: many combinations of address lines access either the RAM or the EPROM, but no combination accesses them both. It's worth having a jumper option to run a 2732 in place of the 2716, in case more memory is called for (you always need more memory than originally planned, because controllers always end up doing things no one ever thought they'd do). One 74LS138 provides decoding for eight RAM/EPROM chip selects and the other for eight I/O chip selects. In particular the EPROM responds to the address 0000, which is where the Z80 starts execution after a reset. Each I/O device has the use of three low-order address lines, which is handy for smart peripherals like the 2651 USART. If four memory and four I/O strobes suffice, the two 74LS138's can be replaced by a single 74LS139. Alternatively, you can use one 74LS138 and memory map the I/O ports, which then respond to any of a large number of memory references. Note that reading a dumb output port like the 74LS374 above writes new data into that port! So you have to be a bit careful in writing the software for these simple decoding schemes. Furthermore since the $\overline{RD}$ signal is not used for accessing memory, a brief fight occurs if you try to write EPROM memory. Such compromises make sense in a small controller, but should be avoided in more general machines.

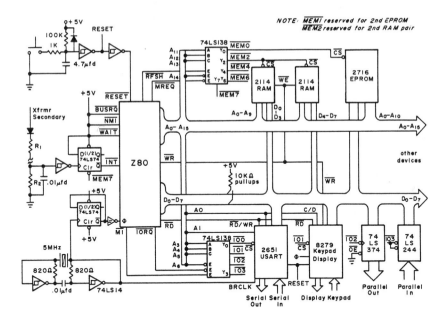

Fig. 6-3. Diagram of a small Z80 controller that includes 1K RAM, 2K EPROM, serial I/O with programmable baud rates, a keypad/display driver, one parallel output port and one parallel input port. If TTL drive power is not required, these parallel ports can be replaced by the Intel 8255 smart port, which provides up to 24 I/O lines for about $5. More devices can be hung on the address and data busses.

The system clock is chosen to be 5 MHz, which is a good rate for the 2651 USART. A 74LS74 divides this rate by two for a 2.5 MHz CPU clock, which works with all Z80 IC's (although 6-MHz Z80's can also be bought). The other half of the 74LS74 is used for the real-time-clock circuit discussed in Sec. 3-5, or it can be used for some other kind of interrupt. We have used one of the memory chip selects to act as an "interrupt acknowledge" to clear the flip-flop. The remaining I/O chip selects can be used for whatever needs exist in the application. Figure 6-3 includes the Intel 8279 keypad/display controller, a 74LS374 for a byte of output (with bus driving power!), and a 74LS244 for input (with Schmidt triggers).

The 10K pull-up resistors on the data lines may well be too small to ensure that the Z80 reads 0FFH when no device responds to the decoding, e.g., for interrupt acknowledge. Smaller resistors can be used, but a compromise must be reached between the number of IC's added to the Z80's bus and the reliability of the 0FFH value. This value is convenient both for Z80 mode-2 interrupts (see Sec. 3-4) and for determining if an optional IC is present (e.g., the USART). In the single-interrupt controller, mode-1 interrupts can be used to bypass the data-bus response. If many devices are to be used and the 0FFH value is important, then the data lines should be buffered with a 74LS245.

The USART plays a crucial role in an inexpensive debug process and may well be valuable in the application itself to tie the controller into a larger computer system. The first EPROM you use might contain the DEbug MONitor listed in App. D. This 1K program allows you to get into the controller to see what its environment looks like and to down load programs into RAM for trial runs. When everything works as you want, you PROM in the desired programs and the controller comes alive. The expensive method is to buy a fancy microcomputer development system ($10000 to $20000) complete with a simulation dip plug that plugs into the controller's Z80 socket. This works great and makes economic sense in industry, but requires a very generous budget. For a smaller pocketbook, the DEMON-USART approach is ideal and is almost as easy to work with. Of course, you do need a dual-trace, 15-MHz oscilloscope and a big brother computer to write the software on. How about a TRS-80 with dual disks?! Contrary to popular opinion, designing microprocessor controllers doesn't have to be an expensive operation. But it does require keen, clean programming.

So far in this book we have featured the Z80 because it packs a great deal into a very popular, small, inexpensive package. Quantities of excellent software (and quantities of mediocre too!) are available and many different hardware configurations are possible. For very small controllers, the Z80 is really too big, especially if many units are required. Figure 6-3 shows about the smallest reasonable IC count for a Z80 system, although the four-IC Fig. 3-4 might work in some cases. A neat alternative is to use one of the many single-chip microcomputer families. We consider here briefly the popular Intel 8048 8-bit family and note that several viable competitors exist (egs., the Mostek 3870, Zilog Z8, Motorola 6801). At first glance, this family is for the big consumer/military applications companies. The 8048 itself is housed in a 40-pin dip and has on chip 1K ROM, 64 bytes RAM, 27 I/O lines, an eight-bit programmable counter/timer, and clock generation circuitry. The ROM's the catch: you have to pay an expensive mask charge ($1000 to $3000 today) and order at least 1000 units. You can use the EPROM version, the 8748, but that's about $70 and is hard to program compared to a 2716. But there are other members of the family that don't have the internal ROM, namely the 8035 and 8039. These have 64 and 128 bytes of internal RAM, respectively, are cheaper than the 8048's and can be interfaced to the ubiquitous 2716 EPROM! So you can design a small controller with this family and bypass the real-time-clock circuitry, the address decoding, and extra IC's. If you're headed toward multi-thousand quantity, you can go over to the 8048 when your system is debugged. The 8048/8035 instruction set is different from and considerably more limited than the Z80's. But the spirit is similar enough to start programming quickly and assemblers are available for it (Digital Research's macroassembler works fine with its I8048 macros). A major design philosophy behind the instruction set was to provide bit, digit and byte manipulation capability without the paraphernalia of large address space access and 16-bit arithmetic codes. The result is a simple instruction set that typically requires fewer bytes to program many controller algorithms than the Z80. One problem with the approach is that, like the smart I/O ports, the 8035 is limited in drive power. Either you have to buffer the lines with 74LS244's, or you can use higher-power drivers such as power FET transistors. The latter allow you to drive a 100 volt 8 ampere load virtually right off the 8035! Some solid-state relays can also be driven with sufficiently low currents.

The 8048 family has been substantially improved with the addition of the more powerful 8051, and we can look forward to an increasing number of single-chip microcomputers (SCM's) in the future. The Intel 8085 offers a nice degree of compactness with its built-in clock circuit and companion 8155 RAM/timer/IO and 8355 ROM/IO "combo" IC's. It has several extra interrupt inputs, but as Sec. 3-5 shows, a single fast clock interrupt is preferable for most situations. More important, the 8085 only has the 8080 instruction set (plus two serial instructions) and once spoiled with the Z80's bit, shift, block-move, expanded 16-bit arithmetic, relative-jump and indexed instructions, it's painful to have to downgrade to the 8080 subset! National Semiconductor has come out with a CMOS Z80 called the NSC800 featuring 8085 pinouts and CMOS combo IC's like the 8155 and 8355. Sounds super if the price is right. A very Z80-like SCM is available from NEC called the μPD7801/7802, featuring 4/6 Kbytes ROM, 128 bytes RAM, up to 48 I/O lines, a 12-bit timer, a serial port, and 16 external address lines (comes in a 64-pin Quad-In-Line package). It would be nice to have a single-chip Z80 computer, with 16-bit multiply/divide, increased symmetry between the HL, IX and IY registers, 4K RAM, 32K ROM, 30 I/O lines, two 16-bit counter/timers, a 10-MHz clock rate, and a programmable baud-rate USART all in an $8 40-pin dip. Are we dreaming? By no means. Count on it within five years! Just think what we'll have in ten years....

In many cases it is desirable to share processor demand among two or more processors. One possibility is to configure a multiprocessor system using the BUSRQ and BUSAK lines. Another possibility is to add various small controllers to a host microcomputer. A problem arises in that a small computer cannot poll the main CPU's data lines fast enough to respond directly to commands. Two or more latched buffers are required between the processors. This can be accomplished with smart parallel IC's like the Intel 8255. For large volume applications (>1000 quantity), you might want to consider the Intel 8041, which is an 8048 with the appropriate high-speed buffers on the AD lines. This controller cannot be used with external EPROM as we've done with the 8035, since the external AD lines are devoted to the processor-processor communication interface. There is an EPROM version, the 8741, available to simplify debugging. Intel (and others) not only supports this IC for customers, but has programmed up a number of special controllers itself. The Intel Data book describes the 8278 Keypad/Display controller, the 8291 GPIB Talker/Listener, the 8292 GPIB Controller, the 8294 Data Encryption Unit and the 8295 Dot Matrix Printer Controller. All of these IC's have the standard 8048 pinouts, but give special names to the various data lines.

The human factor again needs to be cited: if you know a machine well, you will save time using it rather than learning a new system. If you're the type that cannot keep hands off a new toy, maybe you want to learn about the 8048 family and save board space. Buy the IMSAI 8048 control computer equiped with an 8035, 2716, some external RAM, relays, keypad and display and enjoy. Otherwise stick with the Z80 (or whatever) for tiny, small and some medium-size applications.

6-3. Z80 Computer Busses

When you need more power than a single-board computer can offer, you should consider bus systems used to interconnect several boards. A bus is usually incorporated into a "mother board" with various wires assigned for the address lines, for the data lines, the control lines and the power lines. Many microcomputer busses have sprung up in the past 6 years. This section describes several of the most useful busses to emerge for the Z80. One of the first, and certainly the most popular, is the Altair/Imsai bus, better known today as the S-100 (IEEE-696) bus. The name means Standard 100 pin bus. It was created back in 1975 by a company called MITS in Albuquerque, NM, specifically for the Intel 8080 microprocessor. An early microprocessor, the 8080 has somewhat awkward control signals by Z80 standards, and the S-100 bus provided for them all. In particular, the 8080 has the concept of status signals to tell board tristate buffers that an output or input operation will happen shortly, so that they can open or go tristated as need be. Then the write or read strobes follow. As we have seen in Chap. 3, the Z80 merely asserts $\overline{IORQ}$, and either $\overline{RD}$ or $\overline{WR}$. No status is proclaimed or needed. The way around the buffer tristate problem is simple: the onboard going data buffers stay enabled unless the Z80 asks for input data from the board. So, for example, the S-100's $\overline{SWO}$ (CPU will write data) is a useless signal from the Z80's point of view. In fact, as is revealed by the success of more recent smaller busses, more than half the S-100's control signals are unneeded for a Z80. That's no problem for custom interfaces; you just ignore all but SOUT, SINP, SMEMR and MWRITE. But just try designing a general purpose CPU card! Mike Simmons, one of the designers of the first Z80 S-100 card, the TDL ZPU, says he never wants to look at another S-100 card! It doesn't matter that several people have done an excellent job really standardizing the bus with the new IEEE specification (see App. B for Bus). Once burned, you tend to be more careful the next time. Meanwhile, Mike and Co. have built the incredible Hex-29 minicomputer around the AMD 2901 bit slice, but that's another story. We have had no major difficulties interfacing to our Z80 S-100 machines. A couple of evenings or less has almost always sufficed to get a new card up and running. One exception: the feature-packed SD Systems SBC-100, a single board computer with 1K RAM, Z80-CTC, 1 byte parallel out, 1 byte in, 4 EPROM sockets, 8251 USART and RS232 or current loop, and options to put memory just about anywhere. The trouble is, we wanted to run the SBC-100 with IMSAI front panels, and that's a chore!

Another anomaly with the bus is the use of two unidirectional data busses, eight lines for data out and eight for data in. Clearly this buys nothing over a bidirectional data bus, and complicates the use of Z80 peripheral IC's off the CPU board to the point of abandonment. In fact, most boards promptly recombine the two busses back into an onboard bidirectional bus. But there's a silver lining to this cloud: 16 lines are already allocated to data. So supporting 16-bit CPU's is a straightforward operation. The designers of the new S-100 standard have two extra control signals called sXTRQ* (16-bit request) and SIXTN* (16-bit acknowledge). If a CPU asks to use the combined data busses as a single bidirectional 16-bit bus, the responding board is supposed to pull the SIXTN* low. This allows one to mix true 16-bit boards with the older 8-bit boards. The new S-100 specification also assigns address lines up to A_{23}. This supports 16 megabytes, more than enough for one's home computer!

One effect of all the extra control lines is that the S-100 bus is able to support many CPU's, a true first in digital computing. There's no doubt that any given CPU suffers from superfluous control overhead, but the sheer variety of support boards may well simplify the remaining system configuration. Furthermore the great popularity of the bus (more S-100 systems exist than any other: IBM, DEC, TRS-80, APPLE, you name it!) has led to some of the least expensive computing on quality printed circuit boards. See Sec. 6-4 for some examples.

The second most prolific bus in existence is dedicated to the Z80 alone: the TRS-80 bus. This little 40-pin gem (see App. B) contains essentially all you need to extend the power of the TRS-80's Z80 to additional boards. Adapters are readily available to interface to the S-100 bus (HuH Electronics Mini 8100) and to the STD bus (Xitex Corp.). Unfortunately, with its new model III computer, Radio Shack has chosen to change this bus to a new bus with 50 pins. While changing, they should have switched to the STD bus! Fortunately, complete software compatibility is maintained with the model I.

The STD bus (App. B) uses 4.5" by 6.5" cards and features 56 pins. This allows for all data and address lines, the Z80 control signals, the daisy-chain interrupt lines, and various power supply lines. Because the STD bus is used primarily in industry and lacks the hobbyist volume, it tends to be more expensive and has fewer cards. Furthermore it supports only 8-bit microprocessors. But it is compact, reliable and easier to interface to than the S-100 bus.

Another popular industrial bus is the Intel Multibus. In contrast to the STD bus, the multibus has more lines than the S-100 bus, including, for example, special signals for battery-backup operation. Curiously enough, it is not as faithful to the original 8080 microprocessor, for which it was designed, as the S-100 bus is. The differences prove to be advantageous, since they implement a simpler set of control signals.

A bus that allows one to interconnect many laboratory instruments with a host computer is the 16-line IEEE-488 General Purpose Interface Bus. This consists of eight data lines and eight control lines. The host computer has the role of the controller, while the various devices, egs., voltmeters, pressure sensors, waveform generators, motor controllers, etc., are "talker/listeners." The bus can be routed over larger distances than the busses described above, although the data rates are reduced. The protocol to support communication on the bus is well defined, but complicated. We refer the interested reader to the IEEE-488 specification, and to the write-ups of the Intel 8291 GPIB Talker/Listener and 8292 GPIB Controller IC's. As noted above, these two IC's are just suitably programmed 8041 controllers.

6-4. Examples of Larger Microcomputers

The TRS-80 is a good example of what might be called an "appliance" computer. You buy it, plug it in and it runs. To add capabilities, you add the "expansion interface" or one of the motherboard adapters, which allow you to add more memory, disk, serial I/O, printers, etc. Alternatively, greater power can be obtained from larger systems based directly on the motherboard bus concept described in Sec. 6-3. These allow one to put many boards into a computer box, greatly expanding the power and flexibility of the microcomputer. For example, the IMSAI 8080 and Cromemco boxes provide the user with 21 S-100 bus slots along with generous power supplies. In this section, we consider a number of possible Z80 microcomputer systems.

Perhaps the best advice is to buy a complete system from a local firm that offers both reasonably-priced equipment and service. Service is usually limited to disk drives, but an occasional IC fails after the so-called "infant mortality" period. As discussed in Chap. 7, the computer should probably use the CP/M disk operating system (or certain upward compatible extensions) due to its very widespread use. By sticking with standard computers and disk systems, you'll save a large amount of personal effort. Some good S-100 names for complete systems include Cromemco, SSM, Ithaca Intersystems, Vector-Graphics, Industrial MicroSystems, North-Star, California Computer Systems, and Dynabyte. Myriads of companies exist that sell both complete systems and special boards. The old IMSAI-8080 mainframe is still a bargain for the hobbyist. Just replace the 8080 card with one of 20 or so Z80 cards. One very popular firm is SD Systems, which makes the SBC-100 mentioned in Sec. 6-3, disk controllers, dynamic RAM boards, video boards, etc. This company also makes the Z80 Starter System featured along with the TRS-80 in the hands-on exercises of Chap. 8.

If you'd like to configure your own system, buying a set of SD Systems boards is a high-quality, inexpensive way to start. You can buy industrial-grade boxes with power supplies for cards and disk drives from Integrand. A good laboratory computer typically includes 48 to 64K RAM, 4 to 8 K

EPROM (often on the CPU card), a disk controller with two 8" floppy-disk drives, one or two serial I/O ports and some parallel I/O ports. A very handy addition is a bit-mapped video display, which can double for the system CRT. Alternatively a number of video boards can be used with a video monitor and a keyboard to build in a terminal (see Sec. 4-7). The EPROM's can be both burned and stored on SSM's inexpensive EPROM-burner board. One general principle: don't compromise on enclosures, motherboards or cables. Most maintenance problems occur with connections, not IC's.

A great deal of computing can be carried out on a CRT screen conveniently. When you make a typing mistake, you can rub it right off the screen. At some point, however, you need hard copy, i.e., a printout. This is useful to get a more global feel than a screenful can give, to present information to someone else, and to provide an ultimate backup copy in case your diskettes get zapped. Many printer options exist with various speeds, quality, convenience and flexibility. For inexpensive dot-matrix printing (like that on a CRT screen), the Paper Tiger is a good buy (under $1000 including a "bit-mapped" graphics option). Such printers are convenient, but are not up to letter quality. The IBM Selectric typewriters are letter-quality and can be driven by computers. They have largely been replaced by the superior (and more expensive - $2400 to $3900) Diablo and Qume daisy-wheel printers, which print from two to three times faster than the Selectric (up to 55 cps), have numerous type fonts, and have horizontal resolution of 1/120" and vertical resolution of 1/48". The NEC Spinwriter is a very competitive alternative, using a "thimble" in place of the daisy wheel and having up to 128 characters on a single thimble. One disadvantage of the daisy-wheel/thimble approach is that only one font is on-line at a time. The double-daisy Qume has two daisies on-line for almost double the price. What should be very interesting are the inexpensive ink-jet printers, laser printers, and other devices that allow the type fonts to be software controlled.

This book was printed on a Scroll Systems printer, which consists of a Diablo HyType II daisy-wheel printer controlled by the Retroscroller™ firmware board. This board proportionally spaces and right justifies the text, handles over/underlining, sub/superscripts, centering, boldface, figure insertion, pagination, conditional output, hyphenation, etc. As such it makes daisy-wheel (and Spinwriter) printers virtually into typesetters as you can see, and runs with virtually any computer and any text editor. These printers also cost about $3500, but you get what you pay for! To get a more detailed idea of what's being offered, check the microcomputer magazines like Byte, Kilobaud Microcomputing, Interface Age, and others listed in the references.

Problems

6-1.   Modify the controller in Fig. 6-3 to use a 74LS139 for the memory address decoder.

6-2.   Is the $\overline{\text{RFSH}}$ line a necessary part of the memory address decoding? Does the EPROM decoding require use of the $\overline{\text{RD}}$ line? What is a practical limit to the number of 74LS374 or 74LS244 ports you can put directly on the Z80's bus?

6-3.   Configure an SBC controller to translate one serial stream into another that includes additional information. For example, the output stream might contain proportional spacing and right justification information for a dumb daisy-wheel printer (an elaborate version of this idea converted the "dumb" daisy wheel printer used to typeset this book).

6-4.   Configure and price a word-processing system containing 64K RAM, a bank-switched, memory-mapped video board, dual full-size floppy-disk drives, and a daisy-wheel printer.

6-5.   Configure a system to run a laboratory experiment interfacing: a) two detectors, b) two stepper motors, c) a link to a remote computer.

6-6.   Design a memory-mapped EPROM burner for the 5-volt 2716 EPROM family (2758, 2716, 2732, 2764) using a 50-msec one shot controlling the Z80's $\overline{\text{WAIT}}$ line. A clean 25-volt pulse should be applied to the V_{pp} pin during the wait period. This method is used in the SSM EPROM-burner board. The software to drive this burner consists simply of move and verify memory commands, e.g., the M and V commands of the DEMON monitor in App. D.

6-7.   A big but very illuminating project: wire wrap up the Z80 controller in Fig. 6-3. Include enough decoupling capacitors. Choose the I/O IC's to suit your purposes. The following is a bottom-up debug procedure: First check supply-pin voltages on all IC sockets. Then insert the 74LS14 and check the clock with an oscilloscope. Then insert the Z80 without RAM, EPROM or IO IC's. Using an oscilloscope, see that the A_{15} line blinks at about 2 Hz, the A_{14} line at about 4 Hz, etc., as you expect from execution of the 0FFH (RST 7) instruction. Then put in the EPROM with a JP 0 instruction at location 0. Check to see that the EPROM is being accessed and that the address and control lines are correct. Then EPROM a program that ships 41H ("A") to the USART whenever TxEMPTY is high (see Sec. 5-1), install the USART, and check that the USART TxD pin has the correct waveform on it. Then check that the RS232 1488 outputs are correct. Then EPROM a USART echo loop that doesn't use RAM (no CALL's) and hook up a terminal to check out the RS232 connection. Then put the DEMON (App. D) into EPROM, install the RAM and see if it runs. If not, perhaps the RAM has problems, so EPROM in a small RAM test program. The idea is to "divide and conquer" if you have bugs. When the DEMON is running, you've got it made. Congratulations, and welcome to the fascinating world of microprocessor control.

References

Each year, the EDN (Electronic Design News) November issue summarizes the popular microprocessors, single-chip microcomputers, support IC's and operating systems. In general EDN makes fascinating reading.

The most important sources of microcomputer information are the micro-computer magazines, including: Byte, Creative Computing, EDN, Dr. Dobb's Journal of Computer Calisthenics and Orthodontia, Interface Age, Kilobaud Microcomputing, Electronics, Digital Design, Mini-Micro Systems, On Com-puting, Popular Electronics, Computer Design, to name a few.

See also the mini/microcomputer newspapers Computerworld and Datama-tion. A good library has all these publications and more, but you'll probably want to subscribe to a couple.

The manufacturers' data books provide essential design information. See the data books by Intel, Zilog, Mostek, National Semiconductor, Texas Instruments, Motorola, etc. The IC Update Master is an expensive ($80) but useful reference.

E. C. Poe and J. C. Goodwin, 1979, S-100 and other micro busses, Howard W. Sams, Indianapolis, Indiana (doesn't have IEEE 696 standard).

S. Libes, 1980, Interfacing to S-100 (IEEE-696) microcomputers, Osborne/McGraw-Hill, Berkely, CA.

A. Osborne, 1979, An introduction to microcomputers, Vol. 3: Some real support devices, Osborne/McGraw-Hill, Berkeley, CA.

Chapter Seven

Software

*Inside every large program, there is a small
program struggling to get out.*

-C. A. R. Hoare

The main purpose of computerizing laboratory experiments, devices, control applications, your house or whatever is to replace hardware logic by software, which is relatively easy to design, modify and pay for. The software is nevertheless often not trivial. There must be a new Peter principle, namely that whenever a discipline becomes easy, it will be extended until it gets difficult again. So be it with software. Half to three quarters the cost of computerization lies in software purchase and development. In this book, the programs are quite simple, because we are showing how to interface devices, one at a time. But in most applications, not only are many devices involved, but also usually less than 10% of the code deals with I/O. To cope with the software task, it's essential to have development tools known as editors, assemblers, operating systems, interpreters and compilers. This chapter explains the nature of these tools and describes some of the larger repertoire of software available for Z80-based computers. Use of these tools requires a "development system." This can be a $20,000 machine having extensive disk storage, RAM, software, a big name and an act that's thoroughly together. On a lower level, you can buy a TRS-80 with a pair of disk drives for under $3000. Or you can buy something in between (see Sec. 6-4). As emphasized in Chap. 6, today, at least, disk drives are an essential, not an optional, accessory for serious software development.

Murray Sargent III and Richard L. Shoemaker, Interfacing Microcomputers to the Real World, ISBN 0-201-06879-6

This chapter gives an overview of the system software tools you need for computerizing things. More detailed discussion of the tools and the programming languages are given in the references. We assume, for example, that the reader has some familiarity with a high-level language like Fortran IV or BASIC. It's even better if you've had something "structured" like ALGOL or Pascal. The hope is that this chapter gives perspective in general, and guides the reader to some excellent software for the Z80 (most of which works on the 8080/8085 as well).

Section 7-1 describes the tool you'll probably spend 60-80% of your time with: the editor. This is a program that allows you to enter and change programs and other text, e.g., this book! into computer storage. To facilitate this important process, you should have a good <u>screen</u> editor. Microcomputers have a major advantage here over their big brothers, since their CPU's are inexpensive and can be dedicated to one thing at a time, e.g., you and your editing. A brief discussion is also given to word processing, since it's so useful and microcomputers are so good at it! Section 7-2 discusses assemblers, which are programs that translate assembly language into machine language (see Sec. 2-1 if you're not clear about the distinction between assembly and machine language). Auxiliary programs such as linkers, debuggers and disassemblers are also considered. Section 7-3 discusses high-level language interpreters and compilers, which are translators too, but deal with relatively machine-independent languages like Fortran IV, BASIC, Pascal, Forth, PL/I, etc. Interpreters minimize program debug time at the cost of slower execution, while the reverse is true for compilers. The last section (7-4) shows how to store and access these "system" programs and your own custom programs, namely with the aid of a disk operating system.

7-1. Editors

An editor is a program which allows you to create and modify text files. These files can be programs, letters, manuals, books, contract proposals, phone directories, etc. Many editors exist, since most computers need editors for program entry, let alone the preparation of letters, etc. Editors written in the 1960's and early 1970's are mostly "context" editors. You specify one-letter commands with optional numbers that move a "cursor" somewhere in a file. You can then use other commands to insert or delete characters at the cursor position as desired. Typically you can only see and work on one line at a time. It's also possible to write little text-processing programs, called macros, that can modify major portions of your file in a hurry. If you get into using macros much, make copies (backups) of your files at regular intervals, since you can totally destroy your RAM copy by mistake. The most famous of these editors is probably TECO on the Digital Equipment computers, and available in similar form on many other computers including microcomputers. With the advent of microcomputers and inexpensive CRT terminals, however, newer "screen" editors have become very popular. They allow you to look at a whole screen-full of text at a time and have simple one-stroke commands to move the cursor around by lines, words, characters, etc. When you're used to a screen editor, the pure context editors make you feel blind. The first of the microcomputer screen editors is Michael Shrayer's Electric Pencil, which has substantial print format capability. Others include Wordstar and Magic Wand. For the most part, the screen editors haven't included the handy macro facility of the context editors. An exception is Michael Aronson's Text Editor, MATE, which can be loosely described as a screen editor version of TECO (although the commands differ somewhat). This book was written using MATE, and it's really slick the way you can whiz around a file, moving paragraphs, deleting and inserting words, etc., all with a few keystrokes. MATE has another advantage, in that it works well with any CRT (having at least direct cursor positioning), rather than just the memory-mapped video boards described in Sec. 4-7. It also supports smart CRT-terminal features, e.g., insert/delete line or character to speed up screen updating. So we run MATE on all our microcomputer systems. One deficiency of these editors, MATE included, is that you still have to figure out what to write! Try as we have, we haven't been able to make the computer read your mind and correct the grammar. Come to think of it, we're not sure we want computers to read our minds; they might start to control us even more than they already do!

The CRT terminals provide both text entry and display, but you'll inevitably need hardcopy printed output. This is useful for looking over a program away from the computer, or when the computer is doing something else, for providing an ultimate "backup" for your files (what if everything crashes in a thunderstorm?), and for seeing more than a screenful of text at a time. Many "dot matrix" printers are available for well under $1000. This book was printed on a $3500 "daisy-wheel" printer, a Diablo Systems HyType II printer equipped with the Scroll Systems Retroscroller™ Text-Output controller. You just type in your text, include some control sequences, and presto! Out comes this book. (We did go through a couple of rough drafts, in addition to much rewriting right on screen). After all, if you're going to go to the trouble of writing a book, a manual, or even a computer program, you want to make it easy on yourself!

This discussion illustrates a generalization of editing called word processing, which can be defined as computer-aided preparation of documents. As you already knew, or have gathered by now, word processing is easy on a microcomputer. The Z80 is a character-oriented machine and word processing is ultimately character processing. More generally, 8-bit microprocessors are good at manipulating characters, while bigger machines tend to be a bit awkward at it. This shows up in the code, which is typically more compact on a Z80 than on mini and maxicomputers. In summary, use a good screen editor to enter and modify your program files.

7-2. Assemblers, Linkers, and Debuggers

The preceding chapters have included program segments and subroutines in Z80 assembly language, that is, mnemonics are used for op codes and register names, and programmer-chosen symbols are used for branch labels and storage. Needless-to-say, the use of these suggestive names is considerably more meaningful than the strings of hexadecimal digits comprising the corresponding machine language. Since an assembler program automatically computes the addresses of the labels, etc., insertion or deletion of code doesn't cause the programmer any trouble. You just reassemble the program. In addition to the op codes, the assembler has various "pseudo" op codes that provide for saving storage, conditional assembly and other handy features. This section introduces the assembler and the associated programs known as linkers, debuggers and disassemblers. Then it mentions four complete assembler development packages.

The assembler translates an assembly-language program into a machine language module stored in one of a number of formats. One of these is the popular Intel hex format, consisting solely of the ASCII characters 0-9, A-F, :, carriage return and linefeed. This format includes a checksum for spotting errors, and it can be printed and sent over phone lines. One drawback is that it's not very compact, since more than two characters are required to represent each byte of machine language. It is an absolutely locatable format, that is, each record goes to a specific place in RAM. The machine language module is loaded into memory by a program, which may be either a simple loader, a linker or a debugger (coming up shortly). Other assembler output formats include a binary version of the Intel hex format, i.e., two hex digits are packed into a byte, and various relocatable formats. The latter are particularly useful for all but the smallest programs, and have the essential property that the loader or linker can relocate the module anywhere in memory (except on top of the loading program!). In addition, linker programs provide the capability to link a number of separately assembled relocatable modules together to make one big one. This is very handy, since you only have to reassemble the programs with changes in them, rather than some big monster program. The most popular relocatable format is the Microsoft format, which is very compact, but unreadable (except by the linker) since it's a bit stream: the instructions are not aligned on byte boundaries.

Linkers also typically allow you to assign data storage to one area, program storage to another, etc., at link time, rather than at assembly time. This also saves the amount of assembly required. For example, you may want to debug code for a controller in your convenient development system at one set of locations and then relink at alternate locations for EPROM to go into the controller. Another handy feature is that linkers can search "libraries" of useful subroutines, like math or plot functions, and include any that your routines call for. To identify the needed functions to the linker, you use assembler pseudo-op codes like ".extern name" to ask that a routine called "name" be included, and ".entry name" to tell the linker that "name" is in the current module.

Because of their powerful and detailed nature, assembly language programs can be very difficult to debug merely by running them. To alleviate this problem, you can use a debug monitor or "debugger." Appendix D has a small monitor of this nature called DEMON which was derived from a subset of the old TDL Zapple monitor. The full Zapple monitor, which is quite powerful, is sold by Computer Design Laboratories. The DEMON provides a number of standard debugger features such as the ability to examine and modify memory and registers, and to set breakpoints. You set a breakpoint at any program location where you'd like to stop execution. The debugger automatically saves all register values and lets you perform any monitor function. In particular, you can change memory and register values, set new breakpoints and continue from where program execution was interupted or from anywhere else. The idea is that if your program fails in some way, you can set breakpoints along the execution path to monitor progress. The technique is exceedingly powerful and works on any interactive computer, big or small. The TRS-80 has a debugger available called TBUG. Although much less convenient to use than DEMON, it is inexpensive ($15) and provides cassette tape load and save facilities. A more powerful TRS-80 debugger is available from Microsoft Consumer Products as part of an editor-assembler package called EDTASM-PLUS.

Debuggers fancier than the little DEMON in App. D include several ways of displaying memory; hex, decimal, ASCII and instruction mnemonics. The last is particularly useful, since you don't have to look up or memorize machine-language op codes. It also provides you with a low-level disassembler, that is, you can recover the assembly language from any machine language program, admittedly without comments and descriptive labels. EDTASM-PLUS provides this facility for the TRS-80. Furthermore you have to identify tables, character strings, and other non-op-code bytes yourself. Full-fledged disassemblers are quite sophisticated, and allow interactive definition of labels, can spot tables, character strings, etc. RESOURCE, a program available from the CP/M Users Group is a good example of such a disassembler.

We mention four companies that market excellent Z80 assembler/linker/debugger software packages: Phoenix Software Associates (PSA), Microsoft, Cromemco and Digital Research. Of course, Zilog and Mostek, among others, have their own packages too. PSA sells improved versions of the original Technical Design Laboratories (TDL) package and assembles both the TDL "extended 8080" mnemonics and the official Zilog mnemonics. The advantages of the extended 8080 mnemonics are 1) that the prolific 8080 code runs without changes with this system, 2) you end up knowing two microcomputers for the effort of learning one, and 3) you have less to type. However there are more op codes to learn. So aside from specific plusses of one system over another, it boils down to a matter of taste and what you're used to. We authors are split on the issue, one using TDL mnemonics primarily and one using Microsoft's.

The PSA linker can accept mixed Microsoft and TDL relocatable modules, which means you don't have to convert completely over to one system or the other. The Microsoft M80 assembler and L80 linker is an excellent package that runs on 8080/8085's as well as Z80's (PSA takes advantage of all those neat extra Z80 codes), and features Zilog mnemonics. Their relocatable format has become the de facto industry standard and is compatible with their excellent line of high-level language software. Similarly both Digital Research (responsible for the ubiquitous CP/M disk operating system - see Sec. 7-4) and Cromemco have excellent packages. The latter's is cheaper and can be run on CP/M systems with the aid of a wildcat program called ADAPT (marketed by The Software Works). This may be attractive if you want to use Cromemco's high-level languages. In any event, you'll certainly save money by using Cromemco's package if you have a Cromemco system.

7-3. Interpreters and Compilers

Assembly language has three serious disadvantages: it's patently machine dependent, it's hard to "see the forest through the trees," and it's probably harder to learn. So while it can be very run-time and storage efficient, it's typically not programmer efficient. One technique that can help with the tree-forest problem is flow charting. Figures 7-1 and 8-5 provide examples of how to flow chart a computer program. We don't recommend flow charting everything in sight, but flow charting complicated logical algorithms may well be the only way you'll get them to work. In addition to this aid, software designers back in the 1950's decided they needed to have programs that translate relatively English-like languages, called "high-level" languages, into machine language. Two basic approaches are used: interpreters and compilers (plus a few mixtures). Both have advantages over each other, and the ideal is to have both for any given high-level language. This section discusses these programs, and then considers four (among many) high-level languages that are popular on microcomputers (BASIC, Fortran IV, Pascal and Forth). As elsewhere in this chapter, this section is only an overview. The references for the chapter guide the reader to specific understanding of the languages. We hope that the reader has had experience with at least one of the four high-level languages we consider. At the end of the section, we present a lock-in detector program in six versions: flowchart, assembly language, BASIC, Fortran IV, Pascal and Forth. With experience in one or more of these idioms, you can get an idea of what it's like to program in the others.

An interpreter runs programs by examining each byte of a program either exactly as it was typed or in a slightly compacted form. Consequently you can change a program and then run it again immediately. No initial translation into machine language (as with an assembler) needs to be performed, since interpreters continually translate as they execute. This "instantaneous" modification capability speeds up the debugging process. It also introduces substantial runtime overhead, slowing the execution way down compared to an assembly-language coded routine (often by a factor of 100 or more). But if you're just debugging an algorithm, or if your program doesn't do much calculation, the interpreter may well get the job done the fastest. Furthermore, interpreters are interactive by nature. You can always interrupt the execution, perform a few calculations, examine and change variable values and then resume execution where you interrupted it or somewhere else. Does that sound like the debuggers of Sec. 7-2? Sure does, but with the difference that here a high-level language is used.

Compilers translate programs all the way into machine code. The speed of execution and size of the machine code relative to optimally coded assembly language depends on the compiler. Some compilers are quick and dirty, i.e., good for debugging, but slow for execution and wasteful of memory. Others turn out optimized code at the cost of extra compile time and disk banging. For many computational purposes, compilers work as well or better than most programmers code assembly language. A disadvantage relative to interpreters is that compilers (like assemblers) require both compilation and link steps, which take substantial amounts of time on microcomputers. Furthermore whatever interaction you want to have with the program must be programmed explicitly, rather than being there automatically as with interpreters. Hence it's nice to have both interpreters and compilers for a given language. Unfortunately, the only high level language extensively supported by both is BASIC.

A major advantage of high-level languages is their portability. Code them up on one machine and transport them over to another. An experienced assembly language programmer can do the same with assembly language, but at far greater effort per statement. One general rule is to beware those neat but nonstandard features in various high-level languages. Code in a subset that runs on most machines. As time goes on, of course, the portable subset grows. Nobody uses the LET in BASIC anymore, and most people are using BASIC's IF-THEN-ELSE construction, which was absent in the original Dartmouth implementation. Similarly quotation marks can be used in place of the Hollerith count in all contemporary Fortrans. Code that is definitely not portable should be confined to subroutines well labeled as trouble makers. Some operations aren't suited to various high-level languages, because of speed, memory, I/O or other reasons, and these can be coded in assembly language. A good high-level language compiler/linker system allows you to link in the assembled machine code. This mixture of languages can provide tremendous speed and power when used properly.

The most widespread high-level language on microcomputers is a modern, interpreted version of BASIC written by Microsoft for the TRS-80, Apple II and many other machines. Chances are there are more of these BASIC interpreters around than all other compilers and interpreters combined! Curiously enough, a number of the popular constructs in this BASIC are not supported by most big machine BASICs. Microsoft also markets a compiler version of their BASIC, which can be linked together with modules generated by other Microsoft compilers. Another popular implementation is CBASIC-2, a compiler BASIC that unfortunately differs substantially from Microsoft's BASIC in a number of ways, although it is possible to write in a portable subset. BASIC is easy to learn and use. The most common criticism is that it's hard to follow the program logic, because of gobs of statement labels (each line gets a statement number in the interpreter versions) and "unstructured" GOTO's. The major BASIC's do have limited structures, including IF-THEN-ELSE with the capability of including several statements after both the THEN and the ELSE. This helps to reveal the program flow. BASIC is available from Microsoft and many others (try Lifeboat Associates, a large software distributor).

The next most popular language around (excluding COBOL which wins in the business world) is Fortran IV. This language is in the process of being upgraded in very essential, useful ways, so it's hard to pigeon-hole it the way we could before the recent Fortran 77 specifications were written. One irresistable historical point is that the character-string data type, the IF-THEN-ELSE construct and a number of other features of Fortran 77 should have been in the original IBM 1964 Fortran IV, but were omitted for reasons known only to the designers. The features were well known from COBOL and ALGOL at the time, and shortly thereafter IBM released PL/I, which includes every construct but the kitchen sink! On big machines, carefully written Fortran IV is probably the most portable language around. Every machine has optimizing compilers for it. It has the capability for treating huge problems, partly because subroutines can be separately compiled and can communicate together via "labeled common." It also has complex variables, which are very useful in scientific applications. The only competitive language for these cases is PL/I, which is extensively used only on IBM equipment. The new Fortran 77 promises to be supported on all machines as well, and erases many of the very annoying features of Fortran IV. Although Fortran isn't beautiful, the fact that it is so widespread gives it power and advantages that no other language has. If you like structured code, try RATFOR (RATional FORtran), a preprocessor that compiles into ordinary Fortran IV. It runs on most computers, including the 8080/8085/Z80 family. Fortran IV is available from Microsoft and Cromemco. These compilers are essentially the same thing, except for their relationship to the operating system. RATFOR is available from the CP/M user's group and The Software Works.

Our third language is Pascal, which might be called an Algol derivative with powerful data-type capability. It has all the neat structures you need to write with few or no GOTO's, so your programs tend to have the clarity of flow charts. It also provides extensive runtime error detection capability. On microcomputers, you typically need 48-56K of RAM to compile, substantially more than with Fortran IV. Pascal is widely available; try Lifeboat Associates for a delicious menu! Pascal is discussed in some detail in August 1978 issue of Byte magazine, which also gives good lists of books on Pascal.

Our fourth language is Forth (only five letter words were permitted on the IBM 1130, the first Forth machine). This language is an extensible reverse Polish (like the HP calculators) language, that lends itself admirably to control applications. Unlike the previous three, a disk version of Forth can run with as little as 16K of memory, and has the advantages of an interpreter with some of the speed of a compiler. The language is heavily structured and lacks a GOTO altogether. It runs on virtually every computer known to mankind, and is used by Atari in many of their game programs. If you're interested in small (or not so small) control applications and prefer a high-level language, consider Forth. After reading this book, you should have a healthy appreciation for the stack, which is the central data structure in Forth. In this connection, Forth's data handling capabilities have to be organized by the programmer. Pascal's formidable data type declarations are totally missing. The August 1980 issue of Byte is dedicated to Forth and is highly recommended for further information.

We conclude this section with six ways of writing a simple lock-in detection algorithm (lock-in techniques are discussed in Sec. 4-4). The first is the flow chart. The algorithm isn't really complicated enough to merit a flow chart, but hopefully it's a clear way to say what we're doing. INP(n) is a function that returns the value at input port n. DELAY is a user-coded phase delay routine, which plays the role of the "phase" knob on analog lock-in amplifiers. The assembly-language version should be self-explanatory by now, that is, with the comments given. It produces only 34 bytes of code, substantially less than any of the other methods. The BASIC program uses the WAIT function, which waits until the exclusive or of the first and third arguments ANDed with the second is nonzero. The GOTO 200 is for the DELAY call. Since BASIC runs slowly, this may not be needed. The Pascal program looks just like Algol in this simple application. No fancy data structures are involved. To reveal the program logic, we have indented all versions of the program, although the second **begin** in the Pascal program didn't get an additional level of indentation. We don't feel increased clarity results in this case, and more complicated programs get shoved past the right margin with such a habit! The Forth program is the smallest of the five. As in many controller applications, the limited data handling involved can be easily relegated to the program stack, making the algorithm very compact in Forth.

In the programs below, input ports 1 and 2 are connected to the signal to-be-averaged and reference, respectively.

Assembly Language

```
;On entry BC has the desired count; on exit HL has the lockin value

LOCKIN:   LD     H,0          ;HL accumulates the lockin sum
          LD     D,H
NEXT:     IN     A,(2)        ;Get current reference flag: 1 for on
          LD     E,A          ; 0 for off
```

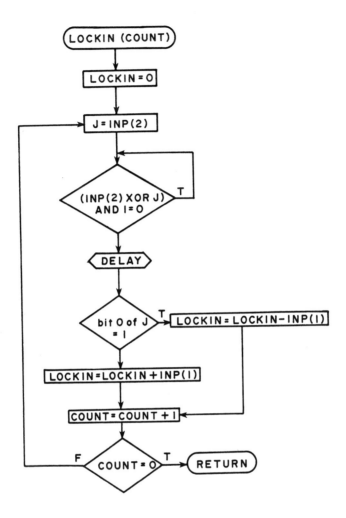

Fig. 7-1. Flow chart of a lock-in detection algorithm. The delay function can be anything desired and can implement the phase delay required in some applications (see Sec. 4-4). This algorithm is implemented in five forms in this section: assembly language, BASIC, Fortran IV, Pascal and Forth

```
CHNGLP:   IN      A,(2)         ;Wait for it to change
          XOR     E
          AND     1             ;Only check bit 0
          JR      Z,CHNGLP
          CALL    DELAY
          BIT     0,E           ;Was signal on?
          IN      A,(1)
          LD      E,A
          JR      Z,ADD
          SBC     HL,DE         ;No: subtract input
```

```
            JR      INC
ADD:        ADD     HL,DE        ;Yes: add input
INC:        DEC     BC           ;BC has desired count on entry
            LD      A,C          ;Is it 0?
            OR      A,B
            JR      NZ,NEXT
            RET
```

BASIC

```
100 LOCKIN = 0
110 FOR I = 1 TO COUNT
120 J = INP(2)
130 WAIT INP(2),1,J
140 GOSUB 200
150 IF (J AND 1)>0 THEN LOCKIN = LOCKIN - INP(1)
    ELSE LOCKIN = LOCKIN + INP(1)
160 NEXT I
170 RETURN
200 'Delay subroutine goes here (if needed)
```

Fortran IV

```
        FUNCTION LOCKIN(COUNT)
        LOCKIN = 0

        DO 30 I = 1,COUNT
            J = INP(2)
10          IF(((J.XOR.INP(2)).AND.1).EQ.0) GO TO 10
            CALL DELAY
            IF((J.AND.1).EQ.0) GO TO 20
                LOCKIN = LOCKIN - INP(1)
                GO TO 30
20          LOCKIN = LOCKIN + INP(1)
30          CONTINUE

        RETURN
        END
```

Pascal

```
function lockin(count: integer): integer;
    var i,j: integer;
    begin
        lockin := 0;
        for i := 1 to count do begin
            j := inp(2);
```

```
while (xor(j,inp(2)) and 1) = 0 do;
delay;
if j and 1 then lockin := lockin - inp(1)
else lockin := lockin + inp(1);
end;
end;
```

Forth

(On entry, COUNT is on top of the stack; on exit lockin value is there)

```
: LOCKIN 0 SWAP 0            ( Stack has: 0 lockin value, COUNT, 0)
  DO
    2 INP                     ( Stack has: lockin value, INP(2))
    BEGIN  DUP 2 INP XOR  1 AND  UNTIL
    DELAY
    1 INP  SWAP               ( Stack has: lockin value, INP(1), old
                                INP(2))
    1 AND IF + ELSE - THEN
  LOOP;
```

Ordinarily, we comment more heavily than here; the flow chart provides most of the commenting needed (we hope!)

7-4. Disk Operating Systems

To develop software or write papers, you need a disk operating system. This is a program that handles I/O to the console, printer and disk controller. Typically you just type commands in and things happen. For example, the editor loads into memory from a floppy disk, opens a file and you're ready to make changes. Or you command the assembler to assemble a program, or the Fortran compiler to compile a subroutine. You can have the system type a file (e.g., program) on the CRT console, or print it on the printer. You can display the names of files on the current disk. This section describes the most popular disk operating system for microcomputers, Digital Research's CP/M, which stands for Control Program for Microcomputers. Widely used on S-100 computer systems, CP/M is also available for the TRS-80, the Apple II, STD-bus systems, and in general any 8080/8085/Z80 computer. In fact, it's now available for the new 16-bit microprocessors like the Intel 8086 and Zilog Z8000. Unlike some of the high-level language compilers and interpreters on the micros, CP/M is not elegant by mini/maxi computer standards. It's a skeleton. But for most program development and word processing, it's all you need. The skeleton is sturdy and can be beautifully fleshed out with quantities of software, readily available from various software houses. The important point is that CP/M has become a standard, much the way the S-100 bus and Fortran IV are standards. While all three are far from the ultimate, the fact that so many people follow their conventions has made them often more useful than their betters. CP/M is a single-user system; Digital Research also markets a multiuser system called MP/M. The beautiful UNIX operating system is also available for 8080/8085/Z80 micros. There are two versions of CP/M in wide use, CP/M 1.4 and CP/M 2.2. This chapter gives an overview of CP/M features common to both, with the thought that you'll read the manuals for actual usage. The references provide further discussion. At the end of the section, we discuss TRSDOS, the disk operating system sold by Radio Shack for the TRS-80.

CP/M is a program that is typically loaded automatically on reset, at the termination of large programs, and whenever you type control C (press CTRL key and C together). It signs on by typing

A>

on the console. We use boldface here to indicate that the system typed the A>, not the user. The A> notifies you that disk drive A is initialized and that you can type anything you want. Five built-in commands are available: TYPE, DIR, ERA, REN and SAVE. The code for handling these commands doesn't touch the user memory area. The command

A>type filename

types the file "filename" on the console. You can abort the typing by entering a control C. Control S stops the typing and control Q starts it up again. The filename consists of one to eight alphanumeric characters (plus a few special characters like $) optionally followed by a period and one to three additional characters known as the extension. The extension is handy to identify files of a given type, such as FOR for Fortran files, MAC as macroassembler files, and COM as machine-language "command" modules. The filename can also be preceeded by a disk-drive specification in the form x:, where x=A,B,C,D (or more on CP/M 2.2). If this specification is omitted, the current disk drive is assumed. To change this drive, type x: to go to drive x. For example, typing B: as in

A>B:

causes the system to respond with

B>

indicating that drive B is now initialized.

The REN command renames a file according to the format

A>ren newflnam=oldflnam

A useful case is

A>ren chapter.7=chapter.bak

which you would do if you clobber the file "chapter.7" and want to recover the previous version from a backup file "chapter.bak". The SAVE command allows you to copy a memory image into a disk file. Although inelegant, this command can be both extremely useful and is a lifesaver in the event of weird crashes. The syntax is

A>save n filename

where n is the decimal number of 256-byte records called pages you want to save starting at location 100_{16}.

DIR types the name(s) of one or more files on the console and ERA erases one or more files from the disk. Several "wild-card" characters can be used to indicate more than one file, but the most useful is *. This stands for an arbitrary number of legal characters, providing they fit the eight-three filename format. For example,

A>dir filename.*

types all files with the name "filename", regardless of their extensions. If you have an assembly-language program called FOO.ASM, a relocatable binary file called FOO.REL and an executable memory image called FOO.COM, the following sequence can take place

```
A>dir foo.*
A:FOO    ASM
A:FOO    REL
A:FOO    COM
```

Similarly ERA FOO.* erases them all, while ERA FOO.REL erases only FOO.REL. Note that you can mix upper and lower case; CP/M automatically converts your commands to upper case for its use.

If it encouters any command other than the five mentioned above, CP/M searches the current disk for a file with that command name and the extension COM. If you say

A>pip

it looks for a program PIP.COM on the current disk, and tells you FILE NOT FOUND if it's missing. You can buy all kinds of COM files: editors, assemblers, compilers, games, etc., and you can make them yourself using linkers, loaders and the built-in SAVE command. So it's easy to add new commands to CP/M's built-in five. One difference: CP/M loads the COM file called for at location 100_{16} and transfers execution to this location. If you have something there, it's written over. For the most part, this is fine, but there are cases when you may want to be careful. Although various CP/M extensions, such as CDOS (Cromemco Disk Operating System) can begin execution anywhere, CP/M always branches to 100_{16} (unless you fake it out - coming up!).

CP/M comes on a diskette with a number of COM files, including an 8080 assembler and debugger, a file transfer program called PIP.COM (like the Digital Equipment computers), an extended DIR program called STAT.COM, a program to reconfigure CP/M for a different memory size called MOVCPM.COM and something that claims to be an editor called ED.COM. PIP is a very useful program allowing you to transfer files either singly or with wild characters from any place to any place, including the printer (LPT:) and console (CON:). The MOVCPM program is useful when you add more memory. The others are very much outclassed by programs available either from the CP/M user's group or on the general market. ED is close to absurd when you're used to using one of the premium screen editors that run under CP/M like MATE, Electric Pencil or Wordstar. Digital Research itself has a considerably better macroassembler/debugger combination. The point is, you can throw ED or whatever away: there're quantities of COM files out there for you to use, so be choosy! Unlike on bigger machines, you don't have to stick with inferior vendor-supplied software that costs an arm and a leg. $150 buys a great deal in the microcomputer world.

The one CP/M omission that we find particularly unfortunate is the failure to mark files with the last time and date modifed. You may have the same file on several diskettes and not know which is the latest. With text files, you should get into the habit of entering the date religiously into the file. A large library of files can be cataloged with a special set of catalog programs (CAT, UCAT, FMAP) available from the CP/M Users Group.

Now some tricks. We've hardly showed you how to use CP/M and we go into some details Digital Research doesn't even tell you about! The thought here is that the CP/M manuals and other references are quite good at teaching the basics, and we recommend them highly. After using the system a bit, you'll become familiar with it, but it's those hard to discover tricks that you then need to know. If you aren't familiar with CP/M or some operating system, go try it out. Otherwise what follows is pure gibberish!

First of all, it's very useful to have a little EPROM monitor underneath CP/M, that you can branch to with a control X. If something goes wrong, which does happen occasionally (a power surge maybe), you'd like to be able to save all that text you've just typed in. Or you want to delete a few files back in CP/M and then continue executing where you left off. On a big machine like a DEC10, this is easy. You just type control C, do some housekeeping and then type CON. CP/M doesn't have this feature, so a handy control X to jump to your little monitor (the DEMON in App. D is fine) can give you substantial power. The question is, how do you implement the control X? Two ways. The more elegant is to use an interrupt-driven keyboard as described in Sec. 3-4. CP/M doesn't know where its console input comes from; it just calls a particular location. You can have a nice interrupt-driven circular buffer collecting characters and handing them to CP/M when requested. Or a one character buffer is adequate. Control X can then be spotted. Alternatively you can simulate an interrupt by including some extra code in the CP/M BIOS console status routine CONST. CP/M, BASIC and many other programs constantly call CONST to see if anything has been typed. So in finding out, the CONST routine can get a typed character and see if it's a control X. If so, branch to your monitor's breakpoint entry, which saves registers, etc., for possible resumption of execution from where you left off. The CONST routine can also be used to poll a printer device to see if it can take another character. This allows you to "spool" a file out to the printer, while using the computer for something else. Digital Research does market a package to do this (DESPOOL). What you're doing is adding a bit of a multitasking system to CP/M, which is basically a single-task operating system. A real-time clock interrupt provides another way to run many tasks "simultaneously" as described in Sec. 3-5.

Sometimes you want CP/M to load a file into memory and then you want to work with the file using your EPROM monitor. But CP/M executes any COM file it loads in, right? Not necessarily. If you put a space followed by an illegal character after the filename, CP/M loads the file, types a ? and gives you back its prompt (A>). Then with your control X, you're home free. The file has to have the extension COM, but anything can be in it.

Your own COM files have to get back to CP/M eventually. There are two ways: jump to 0 to reboot CP/M from disk (assuming you haven't clobbered the jump to the reboot routine stored at 0 at the last booting), or simply return by executing a RET. CP/M calls location 100_{16} after loading in the COM file. The return approach is nicer if you don't need all the memory you can get. Be sure to save the stack pointer and restore it if more than a couple pushes or calls are performed by your program. CP/M consists of two parts: a Console Command Processor (CCP) and a Basic Disk Operating System (BDOS). Many programs clobber the CCP (lies under BDOS), thinking they need the space, and then reboot to restore it. So unless you need the extra 2K, the CCP can stay there, and your program can return.

BDOS provides many useful runtime I/O facilities. The basic idea is to put a code in register C, data or an address (if needed) in DE and CALL location 5. When CP/M is booted, location 5 is filled with a jump instruction to BDOS. The codes specify what kind of I/O operation is desired. 27 codes in CP/M 1.4 are documented in detail in the CP/M manuals. A number of undocumented codes also exist to help foil the competition. Many other groups have adopted CP/M codes so that their software is "CP/M compatible," except for those rarely used special codes. Naturally people have disassembled CP/M and discovered all the secrets, and dealers can buy the source code. The references to this chapter guide you to their discoveries (it's more fun than playing Star Wars).

CP/M is I/O-device independent. It relies on a program called BIOS (Basic I/O System) to connect its requests to actual I/O instructions. A standard set of jump vectors sits at the end of CP/M, which jump to the various low-level I/O routines. For example, CP/M calls the fourth vector to get a console character and the fourteenth vector to read a sector from the disk. The complete set of vectors appears in the CP/M manuals. A handy trick here is to intercept the usual jump to some EPROMed routine. Jump to your own patch routine, and then decide whether to continue to the original. This is useful both for debugging new low-level I/O drivers and for temporary patches. For example, the PSA debugger is quite happy to type disassembled code on the console. But suppose you want to print it or put it in a disk file. Ordinarily typing a control P to CP/M toggles the "print" flag, which causes whatever goes to the console also to go the printer. But the PSA debugger bypasses the CP/M console routines (as do many BASIC's and editors) so that the control P and control C aren't trapped. Specifically this program calls the BIOS jump vectors directly (it knows where they are by looking at the warm-start jump vector at location 0, which jumps to the second BIOS jump vector). So to print your disassembly, replace the BIOS jump vector to the console out routine with one to a patch area that calls the printer and then jumps to the console out routine. Or you can write a handy disk routine (using various calls to location 5) to save the output on disk. The CP/M BIOS jump vector table concept is very flexible and is part of the reason for CP/M's enormous success.

A note here: Cromemco's DOS is for the most part compatible with the CP/M BDOS entry calls, so most CP/M-compatible software can run under CDOS. But they changed a couple of calls and scattered the BIOS jump table entries to keep people from buying their bargain-priced software (Fortran IV is only $99) and running it on other manufacturer's equipment. Since they've made their fortune, we tell you two ways to circumvent this trick: either unscatter the BIOS calls, or use a program called ADAPT, available from The Software Works. At some point, Cromemco may go back to the standard. Since their scatter techniques have been circumvented, they might as well. Of course you can also pay more and get Microsoft's CP/M-compatible software which is as good, better, or nearly identical to Cromemco's, depending on the package in question.

One final trick. To keep up with the disk transfer rate, CP/M skips a number of physical sectors on a diskette between what it considers logically consecutive sectors. On single-density diskettes, for example, it skips five and occasionally six sectors. Although this gives CP/M time to think, it means that program loading takes about four times as long as it would if the logical sectors corresponded to consecutive physical sectors. You can fix this problem up by having a special track buffer in your BIOS code. Whenever CP/M asks for a sector from a new track, your BIOS could read in the whole track on a consecutive-sector basis. So long as CP/M doesn't change tracks or modify the current one, the BIOS can then transfer data immediately at RAM rates, rather than waiting for the disk to go around. You'll find the disk response better than with big machines!

TRSDOS

Radio Shack sells a disk operating system similar in power to CP/M, but unfortunately incompatible. The major advantage of TRSDOS over CP/M on the TRS-80 is that many TRS-80 programs are only available in the TRSDOS format (10 sectors/track, 256 bytes/sector). TRSDOS also has a number of annoying flaws that have been corrected in NEWDOS, a disk operating system sold by Apparat, Inc. One example of TRSDOS limitations is that the FORMAT program formats an entire diskette and then verifies the tracks. If more than 3 tracks fail, the diskette is declared unfit for use. A much better approach is to format tracks one at a time, verifying each as the formatting proceeds. If a track fails to verify, it is formatted again, up to ten times. If it fails to verify all ten times, then it really is a failure! Even then, probably only one sector is bad, and this could be marked bad in the directory (CP/M doesn't have this feature, although it's easy to implement using a dummy file name). We refer the reader to the book The TRS-80 Disk and Other Mysteries for further information about TRSDOS versus NEWDOS. We think Radio Shack should simply replace TRSDOS with NEWDOS, or better yet, switch to CP/M! In this latter connection, the only way to fully implement CP/M is to switch the memory around under software control, since ROM resides in most of the first 16K of memory. A board to do just this has been made by Omikron.

7-5. Computer Hierarchies

At this point we've seen how to interface microcomputers to the real world, that is, to laboratory devices, to buildings, to various kinds of machinery, to printers, to other computers, etc. We've surveyed the large range of software available for microcomputers, and various systems putting the whole thing together. What remains is to glance at the position of the microcomputer in the overall world of computing. When do you use a microcomputer; when a Cray I supercomputer? This particular comparison is extreme. Today at least, each has its place, and you'd probably never use one where you'd use the other.

We've seen that microcomputers based on the Z80 and microprocessors of similar power (8080, 6502, 6809, etc.) are very good machines to interface devices with, and to run experiments. They are hard to beat for sophisticated word processing. They are great for numerous games and for simple calculations. There are several areas, however, where the microcomputer doesn't live up to its bigger brothers, at least at the present time. It computes more slowly. A 64-bit floating point multiply takes about 1 msec on a Z80, or .1 msec if you use the 9512 hardware-multiply IC. A new multiply of this accuracy can begin every 12.5 nsec on a Cray I: that's four to five orders of magnititude faster! So clearly if you're number-crunch bound, you'd use the Cray I. The Z80 would never finish a complicated weather calculation. Meanwhile, the Cray I cannot even be used directly to control an experiment, and it would be a waste of both the Cray I and the programmer's time to use it for text editing. Of course, we fully anticipate having micros with the power of a Cray I in our homes in ten years. But since the years go by so fast, we aren't rushing it. As the saying goes, every year things get better, so if you wait to buy your computer equipment until you die, it'll be fantastic!

There's a whole spectrum of compute power in between the Cray I and the Z80. In addition to their raw computational power, big machines have big data bases and elegant peripherals. These are major advantages, and are primarily responsible for why big computer centers are still, and will probably remain, useful. But using an elegant time-shared computer like a DEC-10 for teaching students BASIC is ludicrous. A TRS-80 does a much better job, faster and cheaper. On the other hand, a DEC-10 typically has the ability to handle large data bases, useful in business and scientific applications. It has immediate access to a wide variety of software and typically has its data bases backed up adequately on magnetic tape. Big machines often offer large memories for big problems. And big machines are expensive.

Wouldn't it be nice to have the advantages of both when you want them? You can! That's where computer hierarchies come in. On the low level, running experiments, editing text or doing simple calculations, you use one of your microcomputers. When you need the large machine facilities, you connect the microcomputer to the big machine via a serial link. If the two are in the same building, the data rate can be 9600 baud. At worst it would be 300 baud over an ordinary phone line. For example, you could collect data from an experiment and then ship it to the big one to number crunch. In turn the big one ships the results back for the micro to display on a screen or on paper. Or the big machine plots the results on its fancy microfilm recorder, ready for the publisher! You pay for the big machine only when you need its power, not for the trivia of entering text at a snail's pace. Meanwhile, you don't personally have to maintain all that fancy equipment that makes the big machine so powerful and expensive. By "big machine," we also include large minicomputer systems such as Digital Equipment PDP 11/70's, Data General Eclipse S/230's, and certainly their newer cousins the VAX 11/780 and MV/8000, etc. They are expensive and powerful by Z80 standards. A major revolution is brewing in which they'll be beaten by the new generation of microprocessors. For example, Intel is tooling up to produce its iAPX-432 chip set which is claimed to have the computing and number-crunch capability of a $300,000 IBM 370/168. Then the kind of problem that's too big for today's Z80's can be done in the laboratory with tomorrow's microcomputers and the lines in the hierarchy will have to be redrawn.

An important aspect of setting up the ideal computer hierarchy concerns what the people involved are used to. If you know an older machine well, you can save substantial time just sticking with it. Or if the people around you know some particular system, you're better off working with it than with a machine that otherwise might be better suited. This book features the Z80. But if you have competent helpful friends who use LSI 11's or Apple II's, you're better off switching to their machines. Knowledge is the key, for a great deal of knowledge is required in sophisticated computer applications. You can save days, even weeks, with the right 15 minutes' worth of knowledge.

One infamous problem in sticking with familiar territory in computer circles: every five years brings a new computer generation. Unwillingness to learn new systems does save time in the present, but obsoletes you in the nearby future. Of course, we never claimed that computing was a safe business. Computing is like a double-edged sword: you can cut with it, but it can also cut you. It leads to one perilous adventure after another, never a dull moment, and maybe after any number of humiliating experiences you finally reach that pot of gold at the end of the rainbow. Then you breathe a sigh of elated relief and you're all ready for the next adventure!

Problems

7-1. Summarize the advantages and disadvantages of using interpreters versus compilers. Of using high-level languages versus assembly language. Of using structured languages versus unstructured languages.

7-2. What are the necessary and desirable features of an editor?

7-3. What is a debugger? A breakpoint? A disassembler? A loader? A linker?

7-4. What is a file? A prompt? A disk specification? What five built-in commands exist in CP/M?

7-5. Where do non-built-in CP/M commands come from? Where do they execute in memory? Where and what is BIOS? What are the advantages of CP/M over other disk operating systems?

7-6. What are microcomputers particularly good at? What are they poor at? How can you combine the "best of both worlds" if a large computer is readily available?

References

R. Zaks, 1980, CP/M handbook with MP/M, Sybex, Berkeley.

H. C. Pennington, 1980, The TRS-80 Disk and Other Mysteries, International Jewelry Guild, Inc., IJG Computer Services, Upland, CA 91768.

CP/M manuals available from Digital Research or Lifeboat Associates.

The MATE editor is available from Phoenix Software Associates and Scroll Systems.

The programming languages Fortran, Pascal, Forth, and Basic are described in numerous books available in book stores and by mail. If you are familiar with one high-level language, you probably only need to read the language manual that comes with the software to use a new language. For Basic, the TRS-80 Basic manual is a good place to start (TRS-80 Basic was written by Microsoft).

Addresses of companies referenced in this book

Advanced Micro Devices, 901 Thompson Place, Sunnyvale, CA 94086 (408) 732-2400.

American Microsystems, Inc., 3800 Homestead Rd., Santa Clara, CA 95051 (408) 246-0330.

Apparat, 4401 South Tamarac Parkway, Denver, CO 90237 (303) 741-1778.

Apple Computer, 10260 Bandley Drive, Cupertino, CA 95014 (800) 662-9238 (in CA); (800) 538-9696 (elswhere in USA).

BSR, see Radio Shack or Sears for BSR modules.

Burr Brown Research Corporation, 6730 S. Tucson Blvd, Tucson, AZ 85706 (602) 746-1111.

California Computer Systems, 309 Laurelwood Rd., Santa Clara, CA 95050 (408) 988-1620.

CP/M Users Group, 1651 Third Avenue, N.Y., NY 10028.

Commodore Business Machines, Inc., 950 Written House Road, North Town, PA 19401 (215) 666-7950

Computer Design Laboratories, 342 Columbus Ave., Trenton, NJ 08629 (609) 599-2146.

Cromemco, 280 Bernardo Ave., Mountain View, CA 94040 (415) 964-7400.

Data General Corporation, 4400 Computer Drive, Westboro, MA 01580 (617) 366-8911.

Diablo Systems, 24500 Industrial Blvd, Hayward, CA 94545 (415) 786-5000.

Digital Equipment Corporation, One Iron Way, Marlboro, MA 01752 (617) 467-7000.

Digital Graphic Systems, 441 California Ave., Palo Alto, CA 94306 (415) 494-6088. (CAT-100 bit-mapped display)

Digital Research, P. O. Box 579, 801 Lighthouse Avenue, Pacific Grove, CA 93950 (408) 649-3896.

Dynabyte, 115 Independence Drive, Menlo Park, CA 94025 (415) 329-8021.

E-Z Hook Corp, 114 E. St. Joseph St., Arcadia, CA 91006 (213) 446-6175.

General Instruments Corp., 600 W. John St., Hicksville, NY 11802 (516) 733-3107.

Global Specialties Corp., 70 Fulton Terrace, New Haven, CT 06509 (203) 624-3103.

Hayes Microcomputer Products, 5835 Peachtree Corners East, Norcross, GA 30092 (404) 449-8791.

HuH Electronics, see California Computer Systems.

Industrial Micro Systems, 628 N. Eckhoff, Orange, CA 92668 (714) 978-6966.

Integral Data Systems, 14 Tech Circle, Natick, MA 01760 (617) 237-7610. (Paper Tiger printer).

Integrand, 8474 Ave. 296, Visalia, CA 93277 (209) 733-9288.

Intel Corp., 3065 Bowers Avenue, Santa Clara, CA 95051 (408) 987-8080.

Ithaca Intersystems Inc., 1650 Hanshaw Road, P.O. Box 91, Ithaca, NY 14850 (607) 257-0190.

Lifeboat Associates, 2248 Broadway, N.Y., NY 10024 (212) 580-0082.

Michael Shrayer Software, Inc., 1198 Los Robles Drive, Palm Springs, CA 92262 (714) 323-1400 (Electric Pencil).

MicroPro International Corporation, 1299 4th Street, San Rafael, CA 94901 (415) 457-8990 (Wordstar).

Microsoft, 10800 NE 8th, Suite 819, Bellevue, WA 98004 (206) 455-8080.

Motorola Integrated Circuits Division, 3501 Ed Bluestein Blvd, Austin TX 78721 (512) 928-6800.

Mostek Corporation, 1215 W. Crosby Road, Carrollton, TX 75006 (214) 242-0444.

Mullen Computer Systems, 2306 American Av., Hayward, CA 94545 (415) 783-2866.

National Semiconductor Corporation, 2900 Semiconductor Drive, Santa Clara, CA 95051 (408) 737-5000.

NEC Information Systems, 5 Militia Dr., Lexington, MA 02173 (617) 862-3120.

North Star Computers, Inc., 1440 Fourth Street, Berkeley, CA 94710 (415) 527-6950.

OK Machine & Tool Corp, 3455 Conner Street, Bronx, NY 10475 (212) 994-6600.

Omikron, 1127 Hearst St., Berkeley, CA 94702 (415) 845-8013.

Page Digital Electronics, 1858 Evergreen Street, Duarte, CA (213) 357-5005.

Phoenix Software Associates, Ltd., 1395 Main Street, Waltham, MA 02154 (617) 899-7383.

Pro-Log Corp., 2411 Garden Road, Monterey, CA 93940 (408) 372-4593.

Qume Corp., 2350 Qume Dr., San Jose, CA 95131 (408) 942-4000.

Radio Shack, see your local phone book.

Rapidsyn, 11901 Burke St., Sante Fe Springs, CA 90670 (213) 698-2595.

Scroll Systems, 6930 E. Acoma Place, Tucson AZ 85715 (602) 885-1633.

SD Systems, P. O. Box 28810, Dallas, TX 75228 (214) 271-4667.

Shugart Associates, 475 Oakmead Parkway, Sunnyvale, CA 94086 (408) 733-0100.

Signetics, 811 E Arques Avenue, Sunnyvale, CA 94086 (408) 739-7700.

The Software Works, 8369 Vickers, San Diego, CA 92111 (714) 569-1721 (ADAPT program).

SSM Microcomputer Products, 2190 Paragon Drive, San Jose, CA 95131 (408) 946-7400.

Superior Electric Co., 383 Middle St., Bristol, CN 06010 (203) 582-9561.

Synertek, 3001 Stender Way, Santa Clara, CA 95052 (408) 988-5600.

Racal Vadic Corp., 222 Caspian Dr., Sunnyvale, CA 94086 (408) 744-0810.

Texas Instruments, P.O. Box 1443, Houston, TX 77001 (713) 778-6690.

TRW LSI Products, P.O. Box 1125, Redondo Beach, CA 90278 (213) 535-1831.

Vector Electronic Co, 12460 Gladstone Av, Sylmar, CA 91342 (213) 365-9661.

Vector Graphics, Inc., 31364 Via Colinas, Westlake Village, CA 91362 (213) 991-2302.

Western Digital Corp., 3128 Red Hill Av., Newport Beach, CA 92663 (714) 557-3550.

Xitex Corp., 9861 Chartwell Dr., Dallas, TX 75243 (214) 349-2490.

Zilog, Inc., 10460 Bubb Road, Cupertino, CA 95014 (408) 446-4666.

Chapter Eight

Hands-on Experience

Experiments should be reproducible; they shall all fail in the same way.

Experience is directly proportional to the amount of equipment ruined.

-Murphy

Merely reading about microcomputers and microprocessor interfacing is not sufficient to really gain mastery of the subject. Some actual experience is needed to test your theoretical concepts against reality, and to see abstract ideas implemented in working hardware. This chapter presents a series of 14 experiments which illustrate many of the major ideas presented in the text. These experiments have arisen from a laboratory course on microprocessor interfacing we have taught. Together they contain somewhat more material than can be covered in a one semester course.

To do real experiments, one is forced to choose a specific computer system to work with. The experiments here are oriented toward two systems: SD System's Z80 Starter System (about $300 in kit form), and Radio Shack's TRS-80 (about $850 for a model I with level II Basic and 16K of memory) with an HUH Electronics mini 8100 TRS-80 to S-100 bus adapter (about $99 in kit form). The new TRS-80 model III is fully software compatible with the model I and thus can also be used for the experiments as soon as an S-100 bus adapter becomes available for it. Another alternative would be to use any S-100 bus computer.

The Z80 Starter system has several very attractive features. It is very inexpensive for a stand-alone Z80 computer system. Since it is a single-board computer, all the circuitry is out in the open where it can be examined. This feature helps to dispel the feeling a beginner has that the com-

Murray Sargent III and Richard L. Shoemaker, Interfacing Microcomputers to the Real World, ISBN 0-201-06879-6

puter is some mysterious black box. Its monitor program is simple and easily learned so that the student can master the machine in a very short time. It is also easily expandable.   There is an on-board wire-wrap area where custom modifications can be installed, and, most importantly, it has two S-100 bus slots on board. This means that the standard S-100 bus wire-wrap boards are available to build interfaces on, as well as a wide variety of ready-built boards and kits. Another nice feature is the presence of an on-board EPROM programmer so that one can extend, modify, or even replace the built-in ZBUG monitor if desired (with the DEMON monitor of App. D for example). All in all the Z80 Starter System is well suited for beginners doing microcomputer experiments. Its major drawback is that it can only be programmed manually in machine language, and this mode of operation becomes rather tedious and time consuming for all but the simplest programs. Also, there is no built-in serial port where one can hook up a CRT terminal (although such a port can easily be added).

The Radio Shack TRS-80 is an alternative computer to use for learning about microcomputers. It's a more expensive and sophisticated computer than the Z80 Starter System, and in fact can form the basis for a viable general-purpose computer system. In the beginning, however, the added capability and sophistication can be confusing to someone working with microcomputers for the first time. All the circuitry is sealed up inside so that the computer presents itself as a "black box". Furthermore, the machine comes up running Basic and one must follow a sequence of (initially) mysterious instructions to program it in machine language (by using a monitor program like TBUG which is loaded in from a cassette recorder). For more advanced interfacing projects, on the other hand, the TRS-80 is very powerful. The built-in CRT display allows the use of editor and assembler programs which speed up the process of producing machine language programs (once one learns how to use them). Large amounts of data can be easily displayed and there is even low-resolution graphics. The system is also easily expanded to include floppy disks for fast mass storage.

A TRS-80 together with a Z80 Starter System provides a nearly ideal combination as a teaching tool. One can begin using only the Starter System and then add on the TRS-80 via a serial link, using it as a smart terminal for the Starter System (and the cost of a TRS-80 is comparable to the cost of an ordinary dumb terminal!). Alternatively, one can switch entirely to the TRS-80 for later experiments. With the HUH TRS-80 to S-100 adapter, the same interface boards can be used in either computer. The TRS-80 and Z80 Starter System pair can also be used to illustrate computer-to-computer communications.

The only major piece of equipment needed for these experiments besides an SD Starter System or a TRS-80 with bus adapter, is an oscilloscope. Many of the experiments can be done without it, but it is a most useful, and often essential, tool. Other basic equipment includes a breadboard (such as the Global Specialties PB-6 Proto-board), power supplies (+5V at 3A, +15V and -15V at 0.1A), and a voltmeter. We have found that the cheap $9.95

Radio Shack voltmeters work very well if the ends of the test leads are cut off and replaced by XM micro-hooks made by E-Z-Hook Corp. These micro-hooks are indispensible for making connections to closely spaced wire-wrap pins. You should also have several jumper wires with these hooks on the end available. For a few measurements it is also handy to have a more accurate digital multimeter available. A stepper motor is needed for one of the experiments. Any kind of stepper will do; just make sure you have the right power supply available to drive it. We used a fairly expensive 1.8 degree precision stepper (Rapidsyn 23D-6102, about $95). This stepper runs on +5V which is very convenient. Finally, a non-essential but useful piece of equipment is a logic probe. These cost about $40 and are available either hand-held or as an S-100 extender board (the Mullen extender board).

The computer interfaces are all constructed on a Vector 8800V wire wrap board (about $22). Wire wrap is faster and more reliable than other construction techniques and is highly recommended for all digital electronics work. Kits of precut 30-gauge wire-wrap wire are sold by Page Corp. (900 pieces for $10). You should buy the modified hand wire-wrapping tool (OK Machine and Tool, about $7) which puts one turn of insulated wire around the wire wrap post before the stripped end is connected. This adds strength and helps avoid problems with shorts to adjacent circuitry. You will also need a variety of three-level wire-wrap sockets, some wire-wrap posts (such as Vector T46-4-9), assorted resistors and capacitors, and of course, a variety of integrated circuits. These are mostly inexpensive ($.30 to $2 each) except for the ADC and DAC which are about $30 each.

The 14 exercises which follow are arranged in roughly the same order as the material presented in the preceeding chapters. Section 8-1 introduces TTL integrated circuits and illustrates some of the logic circuits discussed in Chap. 1, and Sec. 8-2 contains simple programming exercises which provide experience with the programming concepts introduced in Chap. 2. Section 8-3 shows how to build an interface board which provides the computer with advanced I/O capabilities and is used in most of the later exercises. Sections 8-4 and 8-5 complement the material on Z80 timing signals and inter-rupts presented in Chap. 3. Sections 8-6, 8-7, and 8-8 provide experience with interfacing the computer to a wide variety of devices such as switches for ac and dc current, analog to digital and digital to analog converters, and stepper motors. These exercises illustrate the material covered in Chap. 4. Finally, Sec. 8-9 deals with serial and computer-computer communications, complementing the discussions in Chap. 5.

Happy interfacing!

8-1. TTL Logic

The two exercises in this section are intended to teach you some of the basics of working with the TTL digital logic circuits discussed in Chap. 1. Before you start doing any experiments make sure you understand the following basic techniques for working with digital circuitry:

- Always wire up your circuits with the power OFF. When you are finished wiring, double check that the circuit is wired correctly BEFORE you turn the power on. The alternative is to check the circuit after the power is on and to observe which components have smoke rising from them.

- To minimize the possibility of shorting the +5V supply to ground, connect only +5V to the upper pair of horizontal bus lines on the breadboard and only ground to the lower pair. Always put a capacitor (.01 to .1 µF) between +5 and ground to reduce noise spikes. This is known as a bypass capacitor.

- Use both hands to insert IC's into the breadboard, being careful to use even pressure so both ends go in together. If the pins are spread too wide to go into the holes, place the IC on its side on a table and apply pressure on top with both hands to reduce the spacing. To remove IC's never use your fingers. One end always sticks, resulting in bent pins. After this happens a couple of times the pins break off, giving you a collection of interesting but unusable 13 and 15 pin IC's. Instead, pry on alternate ends with a tweezers or a screwdriver so that both ends of the IC come out at the same time.

-If you don't know how to find pin 1 on an IC, refer to the diagrams in Fig. 8-1.

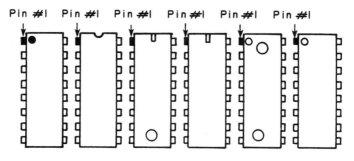

Fig. 8-1. Finding pin 1 on an integrated circuit DIP.

- Resistors are marked by a standard color code. If you don't already know this code, learn it.

Now try your hand at the following experiments:

EXERCISE 1

a) Besides measuring voltage and resistance, the ohms scale on the little Radio Shack voltmeters can be used to determine LED, diode or transistor polarity and failure. The technique is based on the fact that the voltmeter measures ohms by outputting a voltage (about 1.5 volts) and measuring the current drawn. Put your voltmeter on the ohms scale and borrow another voltmeter to find out which lead is + (its usually the black common lead, just the opposite of what you'd expect). Now measure the resistance of a diode or LED, first with the + lead on one side of the diode, then with it on the other. One measurement should be infinity, the other a few kilohms. If you think about it a little, it should be obvious that when you got the low resistance reading you had the + lead on the anode. If either reading gave zero resistance or both readings gave infinity, then the diode or LED was defective and should be thrown out. The same technique can be used to check both diodes (collector-base and emitter-base) of a transistor. Try it! If you use a voltmeter other than the little Radio Shack meter, check it out carefully first. Some voltmeters provide either too much or too little voltage when they measure resistance, resulting in possible damage or improper readings.

b) Wire a NAND gate (7400) on the breadboard and build an LED indicator

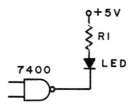

Fig. 8-2. LED logic indicator circuit

on the output as shown in Fig. 8-2. By wiring one input high or low, change the output state so the LED turns on or off. Notice that the LED lights up when the output is low. Change the value of resistor R1 and observe its effect on the LED brightness. Select a value that gives a convenient level of brightness. Also measure the value of the output voltage (for both high and low outputs) with a voltmeter. Does the presence of the LED indicator change the value of the output voltages?

c) Replace the 7400 with a 7405 open-collector inverter. Repeat part (a) above for this IC. Make sure you understand why this gate acts the way it does. Also connect 2 outputs of the 7405 together to the LED cathode and vary the 7405 inputs. This illustrates the "wired-or" capability of the open collector.

d) By connecting the inputs of a NOR gate (7402) to +5V or ground, verify its truth table. Next take several NOR gates and construct a 2-input NAND gate out of them. Verify that your circuit gives the correct truth table for all input combinations.

e) Connect a 100 ohm pot between +V and ground as shown in Fig. 8-3. Connect the wiper of the pot thru a current meter (you will need a more sensitive scale than the one on the little Radio Shack voltmeters) to the

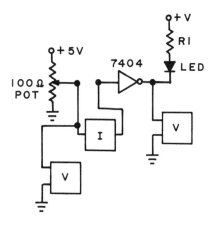

Fig. 8-3. Circuit to measure input/output characteristics of a TTL gate.

input of a 7404 inverter. Vary the voltage of the pot wiper between 0 and +5 volts and record how the input current and output voltage change. This should give you a good idea of the input-output characteristics of a typical TTL gate.

f) Have someone give you a TTL gate with the markings removed or covered up. Determine what kind of gate or gates this circuit contains. HINT: guess that the +5 volt and ground pins are in their standard positions and connect them up. Then use a 1kΩ resistor connected to +5 or ground to try and pull the other pins up or down. If they are willing to be pulled, they must be inputs.

EXERCISE 2

This exercise introduces some of the more complex but very common TTL circuits discussed in Secs. 1-5 through 1-8.

a) Let's begin by looking at switches. Because of the way they are constructed, the contacts of electromechanical switches bounce when they are closed, and thus are unsuitable for direct use with most TTL circuits. You can see this for yourself by doing the following: Connect an SPDT (single pole double throw) switch to the input of a 7404 inverter, and look at the output on an oscilloscope. Have one side of the switch connected to +5V and the other side connected to ground as shown in Fig. 8-4. When the switch is flipped, the inverter output will change and you want to look on the scope to see if it changes cleanly. The scope should be set up for internally-triggered normal operation (not automatic) and 0.2 msec/cm sweep speed. When the trigger level is properly adjusted, you should see a single trace flash across the screen when the switch is flipped. Dim the room lights and turn up the trace intensity so you can see it easily. You should

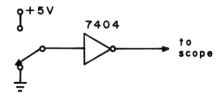

Fig. 8-4. Measuring contact bounce on a switch

find that the switch bounces on going from +5V to ground, but doesn't appear to bounce going from ground to +5V. You should be able to explain this if you recall that open TTL inputs usually pull themselves up. Also note the time scale over which bouncing occurs.

b) Now construct a bounceless switch using the circuit shown in Fig. 1-16. Note that no bouncing can occur with this circuit. Make sure you understand how the circuit works because it is the most elementary example of a flip-flop.

c) Wire up a 7474 D-type flip-flop using your bounceless switch as the clock input. By wiring the data, set, and reset inputs to +5V or ground, determine the truth table for this type of flip-flop. Note especially that the flip-flop acts as a latch by recording the state of the D input when enabled by a clock transition.

d) For further experiments we need an oscillator. One of the most useful is the 555 timer discussed in Sec. 1-6. Read about how this circuit works and then wire up one (see Fig. 1-22) to produce a square-wave output somewhere in the 50-70 Hz frequency range. A 0.18 μF capacitor is a convenient size for C.

e) Hook up a 7474 as a divide-by-four counter and connect your f=50-70 Hz oscillator to the input so that an f/4 Hz output is obtained. Next connect the LED probe circuit of Exercise #1 to the f/4, f/2, and f Hz signals present in the circuit to determine at what frequency you can no longer see the LED flicker on and off. This should give you an idea of how often a visual display must be refreshed in order to appear flicker-free.

f) To produce pulses of variable length or duty cycle, a one-shot is typically used (Sec. 1-8). Replace the 0.18 μF capacitor on your 555 oscillator by a 0.001 μF so that an output frequency of about 10 kHz is produced. Now wire up a 74121 to produce a 10 microsecond pulse on every rising edge of the 555's square wave output (see Fig. 1-25). Observe the waveforms on an oscilloscope to verify that everything is working correctly.

8-2. Assembly Language Programming

In these two exercises we begin working with the computer, and the first order of business is to learn how to operate a machine-language monitor. If you have a Z80 Starter System the monitor is built in on a ROM chip. The details of how to use this monitor (called ZBUG) to enter and run programs can be found in the Z80 Starter System manual. The sections in the manual you should read are Secs. 3-1 thru 3-10, 3-14, and 3-18 thru 3-20. If you have a TRS-80 you need to load in some kind of machine language monitor program such as Radio Shack's TBUG or the ZBUG monitor in Microsoft's Editor/Assembler-plus. Read the introduction and the description of monitor commands in the manual supplied with your software. Throughout the rest of this chapter we will assume that TBUG is being used when monitor and program start addresses for the TRS-80 are given. With Microsoft ZBUG on the TRS-80, 4380H is the monitor start address (instead of 43A0H) and 5B80H is the lowest free RAM address (instead of 4980H).

EXERCISE 3

a)   After you've gotten some vague notion of how to use the monitor from the manual, carefully work your way thru the following programming example:

address	op code	mnemonics		comments
2000	3E 50	LD	A,50H	;load 1st number in A
2002	06 70	LD	B,70H	;load 2nd in B
2004	80	ADD	A,B	;add them
2005	C3 F4 00	JP	00F4H	;return to monitor

This version of the program is for the Z80 Starter System. For a TRS-80 enter the program starting at address 4980H instead of 2000H, and change the last instruction to:

4985	C3 A0 43	JP	43A0H	;return to monitor

Enter the op codes into the computer and then run the program using the single-step command or setting breakpoints to see the effect of each instruction (TBUG has no single-step command). If you have a Starter System you may want to read the manual's Sec. 5-1, which goes thru an example program very similar to the one above.

The program above shows the proper layout for an assembly-language program. The address of the instruction is written first (in hex), followed by the op code. Then the assembly language source code appears, followed (optionally) by a semicolon and a comment explaining what's going on. Always use this standard format and never write a program without com-

ments!   Note that machine-language addresses are entered "backwards",
i.e. low byte first, high byte second.   This places the "low byte lower in
memory".   In the rest of this chapter we follow the convention used by
most computer assembler programs: all addresses appearing as part of a
computer instruction are written as a single four digit number.   It is
assumed that the reader knows enough to interchange the low and high
bytes when he enters the code into the machine.   Thus the previous instruction would be given as:

```
4985    C3  43A0       JP      43A0H          ;return to monitor
```

b) Hopefully you're now ready to do your own hand assembly of a computer
program.   If not, try it anyway!   Think of it as a jigsaw puzzle.   Below is
an assembly-language source program which gets the number stored in location 2100H (for a Starter System), adds the number in location 2101H to it,
and stores the result back in location 2100H.   Convert this program into
machine language, enter it into the computer, and run it.   You should play
with this program until you understand it, using the single step, register
examine, and breakpoint commands to aid in verifying that the program
actually operates the way you think it does.

```
2000              LD     HL,2100H    ;point to first number
                  LD     A,(HL)      ;get it
                  INC    HL
                  ADD    A,(HL)      ;add second number
                  DEC    HL
                  LD     (HL),A      ;store in loc of first number
                  JP     00F4H       ;restart monitor
```

If you have a TRS-80 you should modify this program as in the previous
example: Change 2000 to 4980, 2100 to 4A80, and 00F4 to 43A0.

c) Now write a program of your own that does the same thing as the above
program except that you should subtract the second number from the first,
and you should not use HL as a pointer.   Instead use the LD A,(nn) instruction to get the two numbers and LD (nn),A to put the result back.   Assemble
your program, run it and verify that it does what you expect it to.   Note
that this technique requires more bytes of code than the pointer approach.

d) Finally, try writing a program that gets the 16-bit number 5678H from
locations 2100-2101H, adds the constant 96H to it and stores the result back
in 2100-2101H.   For a TRS-80 use locations 4A80-4A81H.

EXERCISE 4

a) Below is a program which displays the contents of the HL and A registers
on the Starter System LED display or on the TRS-80 CRT screen.   Study this

program so that you understand how it works, and then enter it into the computer. Remember to exchange low and high bytes of all addresses which appear as part of a computer instruction. An explanation of how the Starter System display hardware works is given in Sec. 3-7 and a description of the TRS-80 display hardware can be found in the TRS-80 Microcomputer Technical Reference Handbook (see also Sec. 4-7). Next write a little program that fills the HL and A registers with known values and then calls the OUTPUT routine for a Starter System or the OUTPT routine for a TRS-80. Note that with a Starter System you will have to have a loop which calls OUTPUT repeatedly. Otherwise the display will only light up for a millisecond or so. The TRS-80 refreshes its own display in hardware so OUTPT need only be executed once and then you can jump back to TBUG's entry point at 43A0. BEFORE you attempt to execute the program, save a copy of the machine code on a cassette tape. Read about the procedure required to do this in either the Starter System or the TBUG manual. It is good practice to always save a copy of a new program on tape so that you don't have to enter it again by hand when the program bombs and wipes out the entire memory. After you've saved the program on tape, erase the last few steps of the program from memory and then load the program back in from the cassette recorder. In this way you can verify that the program was properly recorded. Finally, execute the program and see that it works as advertised. Note that the Starter System output routine requires that you also enter the subroutine DISUP at location 2357 (see App. F for a listing). Also note that the Starter System displays hex digits directly, while the TRS-80 requires each hex digit to be translated into ASCII code before it can be displayed. See App. A for a chart of how this code works.

OUTPUT routine for SD Starter System

```
                .RADIX    16        ;all numbers here are hexadecimal

                ; External addresses

2380            DISMEM    EQU   2380        ;RAM storage for LED's

2357            DISUP:    --------            ;App.  F  display  routine
                                             ;starts at this location

                ORG       2080    ;start program at loc. 2080

                ;This routine displays HL and A on the seven segment
                ;LED's of a Z80 Starter System.

2080  11 2380   OUTPUT: LD      DE,DISMEM ;point to display area
2083  F5                PUSH    AF        ;save copy of A
2084  7C                LD      A,H       ;store H
2085  CD 2095           CALL    OUTA
2088  7D                LD      A,L       ;store L
```

```
2089  CD 2095                CALL  OUTA
208C  F1                     POP   AF       ;restore A and store it
208D  CD 2095                CALL  OUTA
2090  CD 2357     REPEAT:    CALL  DISUP    ;display storage area
2093  C9                     RET
```

;This subroutine converts a binary byte in A into two
;hex digits and stores them in the locations pointed
;to by DE and DE+1

```
2094  F5          OUTA:      PUSH  AF       ;save copy of A
2095  0F                     RRCA           ;put high nibble in low
2096  0F                     RRCA
2097  0F                     RRCA
2098  0F                     RRCA
2099  E6  0F                 AND   0F       ;mask off top 4 bits
209B  12                     LD    (DE),A   ;store in display area
209C  13                     INC   DE
209D  F1                     POP   AF       ;get A back
209E  E6  0F                 AND   0F       ;mask off high nibble
20A0  12                     LD    (DE),A   ;store in display area
20A1  13                     INC   DE
20A2  C9                     RET
```

OUTPT routine for TRS-80

```
            .RADIX   16       ;all numbers here are hexadecimal

            ; External addresses

4020        CURSOR  EQU  4020
0033        DISPLY  EQU  0033
002B        KEYBRD  EQU  002B

            ORG  4A00          ;start program at loc. 4A00
```

;This routine displays HL and A on the CRT
;screen of a TRS-80

```
4A00  F5          OUTPT:     PUSH  AF       ;save A and HL
4A01  3E  1C                 LD    A,1C     ;clear the CRT screen
4A03  CD 0033                CALL  DISPLY
4A06  3E  1F                 LD    A,1F
4A08  CD 0033                CALL  DISPLY
4A0B  11  3120               LD    DE,3120  ;set cursor position to
4A0E  ED 53 4020             LD    (CURSOR),DE ;middle of screen
4A12  3E  20                 LD    A,20     ;output initial blank
4A14  CD 0033                CALL  DISPLY
```

4A17	7C		LD	A,H	;display H
4A18	CD 4A24		CALL	OUTAC	
4A1B	7D		LD	A,L	;display L
4A1C	CD 4A24		CALL	OUTAC	
4A1F	3E 20		LD	A,20	;output another blank
4A21	CD 0033		CALL	DISPLY	
4A24	F1		POP	AF	;display A
4A25	CD 4A24		CALL	OUTAC	
4A28	C9		RET		

;This subroutine converts a binary byte in A into two
;ASCII digits and displays them on the CRT screen.

4A29	F5	OUTAC:	PUSH	AF	;save copy of A
4A2A	0F		RRCA		;shift high nibble into low
4A2B	0F		RRCA		
4A2C	0F		RRCA		
4A2D	0F		RRCA		
4A2E	CD 4A2D		CALL	HEXASC	;translate and display
4A31	F1		POP	AF	;now do low nibble
4A32	E6 0F	HEXASC:	AND	0F	;mask off high nibble
4A34	C6 30		ADD	A,30	;add 30H if 0-9
4A36	FE 3A		CP	3A	
4A38	38 02		JR	C,SKIP	
4A3A	C6 07		ADD	A,07	;add 37H if A-F
4A3C	CD 0033	SKIP:	CALL	DISPLY	;display on CRT screen
4A3F	C9		RET		

b) Now you should be ready to write a more substantial assembly language program which uses the above display routines. Write a program that finds the largest number in a table of sixteen eight-bit numbers and displays this number along with its address. A flow chart of how this program should proceed is given in Fig. 8-5. Use OUTPUT or OUTPT to translate your results to hexadecimal digits and display them. Assemble and run your program, and verify that it works properly no matter what numbers the table contains.

8-3. Building an Interface Board

This exercise describes how to build an interface board that allows you to couple the Z80 Starter System or a TRS-80 to a wide variety of real world devices. The interface can be built on a Vector 8800V wire-wrap board. This is an S-100 bus compatible board and it can be inserted directly into a Starter System, an HUH Electronics TRS-80 to S-100 adapter, or any S-100 bus computer.

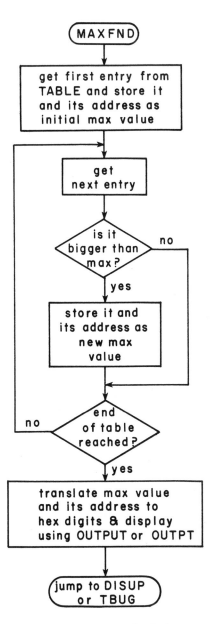

Fig. 8-5. Flowchart of program to find the maximum number in a table of 16 bit numbers.

The first thing we need to install on the Vector board is the decoding circuitry that allows each I/O port to recognize when it is being addressed by the CPU. This circuitry is discussed in Sec. 3-3. A circuit which handles 4 input ports, 4 output ports and an 8251 USART is shown in Fig. 8-6. You will also need data sheets for the various IC's being used. The S-100 computer bus signals and their meanings are given in Appendix B. Make sure

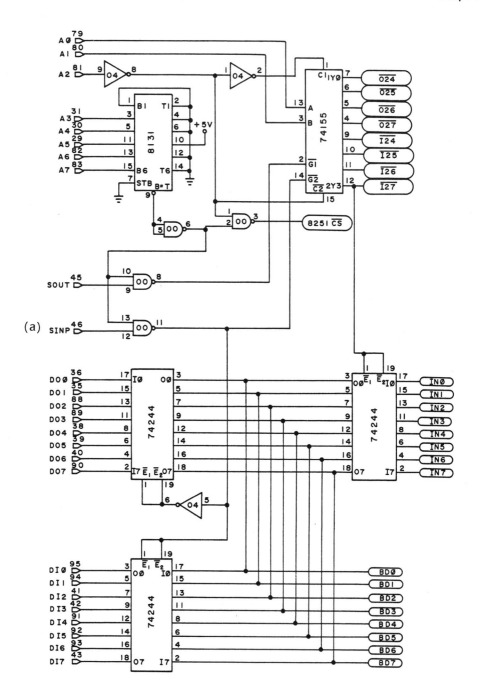

Fig. 8-6. Schematic diagram of S-100 interface board used for hands-on exercises. Board may be used with TRS-80, SD Z80 Starter System, or with any S-100 system. (a) S-100 interface, decoding circuitry, and parallel input port. (b) ADC, DAC, and parallel output port. (c) serial I/O port.

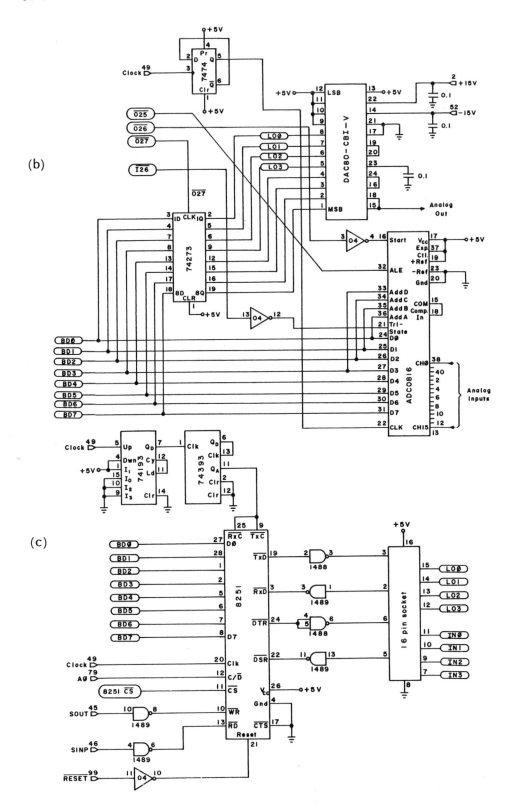

(b)

(c)

Fig. 8-7. Interface board photograph

you understand how this decoding circuitry works and why each component is present, as it is the foundation for all of the later devices we will add.

The circuit is constructed using wire-wrap techniques. The long end of the OK Machine and Tool wire-wrap tool has a center hole and a small side hole. To wrap a wire first determine the length of wire required and insert one of the stripped ends as far as it will go into the small side hole. Pre-stripped wire of various lengths make the wrapping faster. It is best to choose a wire long enough so that there is a bit of slack in the connection. That way one can wriggle the wires around with a tweezers later when you want to see which wire is which. Using random colors for the wire or using a color coding scheme can also help you disinguish one wire from another. With the wire inserted, slip the center hole of the tool over the post and turn clockwise until all the wire in the tool is wrapped around the post (about 12 turns). When doing this don't push down or pull up on the tool. The weight of the tool is about the right pressure to apply. The first wrap on a post should start at board level, not up higher, and the coils should be tight with no gaps between them. Subsequent wires wrapped on the same post (up to two more) should follow with no intervening spaces. If you make a mistake, you can simply unwrap the wire. To unwrap use the short end of the wire-wrap tool. Simply slip it over the socket post and turn counter-clockwise until you see the wire begin to move. Then pull the tool off. If you've done it properly, the wire will come off with the tool. You may find it easiest to cut the wire near the post before unwrapping it. Just make sure you cut the right wire!

EXERCISE 5

a) To actually build the decoding circuit on the Vector board, proceed as follows:

1. Insert Vector wire-wrap pins for all the S-100 bus connections needed. This is best done by cutting a short length of small copper or brass tubing and holding it vertically in a clamp or vise. Insert a pin into the board by hand and then place the board on top of the tubing so that the pin extends thru the board and into the tubing. You can now pound the pin all the way in with a hammer. The tubing supports the board around the pin area and prevents it from breaking. Insert all pins so that they stick out on the WIRING side of the board. When the pins have been inserted, solder each pin in place.

2. Next solder decoupling capacitors between the power and ground planes at the positions indicated on the board photo shown in Fig. 8-7.

3. If you plan to run the board from a regulated 5-volt power supply, install a jumper wire across the regulator pads as shown on the photo. The other option is to power the board from an 8-volt supply and use a

7805 voltage regulator on the board. The literature supplied with the 8800V board shows where to install the regulator and its heat sink. You should also put electrolytic or tantalum decoupling capacitors of about 20-40 μF on the regulator input and output (see Fig. 1-15).

4. Now use a small dab of 5-minute epoxy to glue ONE row of sockets in place on the component side of the board without slopping any glue on the wire-wrap pins themselves. If you have trouble with your wire-wrap connections later, you may have accidentally gotten glue on the pins. Put the sockets in the positions shown in the board photo (Fig. 8-7), making sure you use the proper size socket for each IC. Pin 1 of each socket is indicated by a chopped off corner or a notch in the pin 1 end of the socket. Make sure all the pin 1's point to the upper left corner of the board and are inserted into holes marked as pin 1 on the Vector board (except for the three 74LS244 sockets).

5. Next put in the power and ground connections to each chip by wire wrapping one end of a short wire onto the socket and soldering the other end to the power or ground plane. The power plane is the component side of the board. +5 volts is present everywhere here. All of the wiring side of the board is connected to ground. If you've never wire wrapped before, practice a bit on a spare socket before you try the real thing.

6. Now repeat steps 4 and 5 for any additional rows of sockets you wish to install, one row at a time. If you do all the sockets at once you will find it very difficult to get your soldering iron in between them to connect power and ground.

7. At this point it is a good idea to put a label between the pins of each socket (on the wiring side of the board) identifying the IC that goes there. This simple step can save a lot of agony later on.

8. Now you're ready to wire up the decoding circuitry itself. The key word here is ACCURACY. You can either double check the accuracy of every connection as you make it, or you can spend hours later on trying to figure out which one of 300 wires you put in wrong. A good technique is to write down on the circuit diagram the IC pin numbers for every wire as you attach it and/or to use a colored marker pen on a copy of the circuit diagram to show which wires you have attached. Alternatively, you can make a wire list showing the connections for every wire on the board. This is the method most often used by professionals.

When you've finished wiring the board, check it over carefully to see that nothing has been omitted. Then insert it into the Z80 Starter System or the S-100 bus adapter and verify that all the I/O strobes (the 8 outputs of the 74155) work properly. If they don't, then go back and test the SINP and SOUT signals as well as the 8131 output to see if they are working properly. Testing signals of this sort is a little bit tricky because a strobe signal is just a 1.25 microsecond long active-low pulse. The best tool is a logic probe. You can attach it to the circuit and put it in the "pulse catcher" mode. If even one pulse longer than a few nanoseconds occurs, the probe will turn on a signal indicating a pulse and leave that signal on . You can create the pulse by using the PORT EXAM function on the Starter System or by using the Basic commands OUT ADDR,DATA and INP(ADDR) with a TRS-80. Here ADDR is the port address (in decimal!) and DATA can be any number 0-255. If you don't have a logic probe, an oscilloscope can be used. Low repetition rate signals are hard to see, so it's best to use a little loop:

```
LOOP:       OUT  (PORT),A    ;change to IN A,(PORT) for an input strobe
            JR   LOOP
```

where PORT is the address of the port whose strobe you want to look at. Running this program will give you a strobe pulse on the 74155 about every 12 microseconds. If the strobe is not working properly, check SOUT, SINP, and $\overline{8131}$. Note that $\overline{8131}$ goes low often simply because of the Z80's refresh cycle.

b) Once the decoding circuitry is working, add a parallel input port and a parallel output port as shown in Fig. 8-6. The output port is just a 74LS273 (a set of eight flip-flops) with an output strobe connected as the "clock" that enters data into them. The input port is a tristate buffer (74LS244) which enables input data onto the bus when its enable line, which is connected to an input strobe, is pulled low.

8-4. Looking at CPU Signals

It is difficult if not impossible to do any serious interfacing projects without a good working knowledge of the signals sent back and forth between the CPU and its peripheral devices. This topic is discussed at length in Sec. 3-1. In the exercise below we look at two different ways of observing how the CPU signals tell other devices what to do, and we also get a brief introduction to the use of parallel output ports (see Sec. 3-2).

EXERCISE 6

a) One way of examining the CPU signals is by stopping the computer in the middle of a machine cycle and looking at the signal levels present on the various bus lines. This approach doesn't need an oscilloscope. To stop the computer we attach a lead to the $\overline{\text{WAIT}}$ line and ground it. When the $\overline{\text{WAIT}}$ line is grounded, the CPU is forced to stop and wait until the requesting device (in this case, you!) is finished and allows the line to go high again. On the Starter System the $\overline{\text{WAIT}}$ line can be controlled by lifting pin 10 of U37 (otherwise you'll short it out) and attaching a clip lead to the CPU side of R36. For a TRS-80 you should get a 40 pin card edge connector that fits

the expansion port on the back of the keyboard, label the pins on the connector so that you can see where the address, data, and control signals are,
and attach a clip lead to the $\overline{WAIT}$ line. Whenever the clip lead is grounded,
the computer will be forced to stop and wait until you remove it from
ground.

If you are using a Starter System, enter the following program into
memory and execute it:

```
2000   01 2100              LD    BC,2100    ;initialize registers
2003   21 2102              LD    HL,2102
2006   7E           LOOP:   LD    A,(HL)     ;read from memory
2007   02                   LD    (BC),A     ;write into memory
2008   DB 63                IN    A,(63)     ;input data
200A   D3 64                OUT   (64),A     ;output data
200C   18 F8                JR    LOOP       ;loop forever
```

There are no I/O ports at 63 or 64, but that doesn't matter because we
just want to look at the signals the Z80 is sending. Now ground the clip
lead and use a voltmeter, or a logic probe if you have one, to check the
state of the 16 address lines (A0-A15), the 8 data lines (D0-D7), and the
control lines ($\overline{MREQ}$, $\overline{IORQ}$, $\overline{RD}$, $\overline{WR}$, M1). From this data you should be able
to determine where the CPU has stopped. There are twelve possible
machine cycles in the loop where the CPU could stop. Five of these are
instruction fetches, four are memory read cycles, and the remaining three
are a memory write cycle, an input cycle, and an output cycle. Refer to
the timing diagrams in Chapter 3 or your Z80 technical manual to see what
the state of the various lines are for these operations. The CPU will stop at
the point in the timing diagram where the $\overline{WAIT}$ line is sampled. Next
release the $\overline{WAIT}$ line, ground it again to stop at another point in the loop,
and again determine where the CPU has stopped. Repeat this process until
you've managed to stop at most of the various possibilities.

If you are using a TRS-80, the procedure above won't work very well
because the programmable memory is all dynamic RAM. When you pull the
$\overline{WAIT}$ line low, the RAM is no longer refreshed, and the TRS-80 forgets the
program you've entered as well as TBUG. Since it's very time consuming to
reload TBUG every time you stop the machine, let's not use it. Instead we
can enter a somewhat shorter program directly from Basic, and resign our-
selves to re-entering it after each time we pull the $\overline{WAIT}$ line low. Here's
the program we'll use:

```
20100   219   99      LOOP:  IN    A,(63)
20102   211   100            OUT   (64),A
20104   24    250            JR    LOOP
```

Notice that the machine language here is given in decimal, not hex. We can
enter this directly from Basic using the POKE command. Just turn on the
machine, enter POKE 20100,219 and then enter POKE 20101,99 et cetera.

You can check whether you entered the data properly by using PEEK(20100), PEEK(20101), etc. Once the program is in the computer you can execute it by typing SYSTEM. The TRS-80 responds with *? to which you reply /20100. The program will start executing as soon as you hit the enter key. Stop the machine by grounding the $\overline{\text{WAIT}}$ line on the TRS-80's 40-pin bus output connector (see App. B for pinouts). Now see if you can determine the state of the machine by examining the data, address and control lines. The control signals are simple combinations of Z80 signals. RD* is $\overline{\text{MREQ}}$ anded with the Z80 $\overline{\text{RD}}$, WR* is $\overline{\text{MREQ}}$ anded with the Z80 $\overline{\text{WR}}$, IN* is $\overline{\text{IORQ}}$ anded with the Z80 $\overline{\text{RD}}$, and OUT* is $\overline{\text{IORQ}}$ anded with the Z80 $\overline{\text{WR}}$. $\overline{\text{M1}}$ is unfortunately not present on the connector. There are eight possible machine cycles where the CPU can stop: Three instruction fetches plus three memory read cycles and the input and output cycles. After you've determined the machine state you've stopped in (see the Starter System paragraph above for details), you can lift the $\overline{\text{WAIT}}$ line from ground. The computer will promptly go crazy since it's lost all its memory contents, so you'll have to use the reset button or turn the machine off and back on again to get started properly. Then re-enter the program and repeat the process until you've seen most of the posssible machine states.

b) To see what Z80 signals look like when the CPU is running at full speed, enter and run the simple program:

```
D3  83        HERE:    OUT   (83),A
18  FC                 JR    HERE
```

Look at the CPU signals with a oscilloscope while this program is running. Trigger the scope on SOUT (OUT* for a TRS-80) and observe the various control signals which are active during this loop: $\overline{\text{RFSH}}$, $\overline{\text{RD}}$, $\overline{\text{WR}}$, $\overline{\text{MREQ}}$, $\overline{\text{IORQ}}$, CLOCK, and $\overline{\text{M1}}$ (only RD* and OUT* can be seen on a TRS-80). If possible use a dual-trace scope for these observations so that you can look at two signals at once and observe their relative timings.

SKIP PART (c) IF YOU ARE USING A TRS-80

c) Next let's look at an example of an output port. The Starter System has two I/O ports on board in the form of a Z80 PIO (Parallel I/O) chip. Although the chip has some very sophisicated modes of operation, it can also be easily used as a simple input port or output port. The chip has two identical ports, A and B. Consider only port B for the moment. Port B looks like two I/O ports to the computer. Port 81 is used for the actual input or output of data, and port 83 is a write-only register which controls the mode of port 81. For example, if we write the number 0F to port 83, port 81 becomes a simple output port. If we write a 4F to port 83, port 81 becomes an input port.

The PORT EXAM function of the Starter System can be used to set the mode and input or output data without writing a program. See the Starter

System manual for details on how to use this function. Connect a voltmeter to bit 0 of port B and use PORT EXAM to set the bit high and low. Next convert the port to an input port, and then (NOT BEFORE!) connect a jumper wire from bit 0 to +5 volts or ground and see that it inputs data properly.

d) A very general method of looking at CPU signals for any instruction or set of instructions is to use one bit of an output port as the scope trigger. On the Starter System the built-in PIO provides us with the port we need, and we can control it as follows:

```
          LD    A,0F        ;make PIO port B into an output port
          OUT   (83),A
LOOP:     LD    A,01        ;set bit 0 of PIO port B high
          OUT   (81),A
          XXX                ;put any instruction(s) you like here
          XOR   A           ;set bit 0 of PIO port B low
          OUT   (81),A
          JP    LOOP        ;loop forever
```

You can insert any instruction(s) you want into the spot marked XXX and observe the CPU signals on a scope if the scope is set up to trigger on a rising edge at bit 0 of the output port. Try inserting various instructions into the loop and observe how the CPU control signals behave on the oscilloscope.

With a TRS-80 there is no built-in output port so you will have to somehow provide one. If you have built the interface card described in Section 8-3, you are all set. Alternatively, you can add an I/O port onto the keyboard edge connector (see for example Ciarcia's article in the May 1980 issue of Byte), or if you have an expansion interface you can use the parallel port for the printer. Once you have an output port hooked up you can use the program above with the first two instructions deleted and the 81 in the OUT (81),A replaced by the number of the port you are using.

8-5. Interrupts and Real-time Clocks

As discussed in Sec. 3-4, interrupts can be a very powerful tool in microcomputer systems, particularly for real-time applications. One of the most useful ways to implement interrupts is to build a clock into the computer so that it knows what time it is and thus can perform tasks at prescheduled times (see Sec. 3-5). In the exercise below we'll do this using the 60 Hz line frequency as our timing reference, and an interrupt-driven service routine as a means of keeping track of the time of day and performing prescheduled tasks. We use interrupt mode 1 since it requires no interrupt acknowledge hardware and is very easy to use.

EXERCISE 7

a) To get 60 Hz pulses from the ac line, we must first change a high voltage 60 Hz sine wave into a TTL-compatible square wave. To do this, build the circuit shown in Fig. 1-20 on a breadboard. The 5-10 volt ac input can be tapped off the secondary of your computer power-supply transformer, or you can use a separate transformer. Check your circuit with an oscilloscope to make certain it's giving a TTL square wave before you hook it up to anything else. To produce interrupts from this clock, use the simple flip-flop circuit shown in Fig. 1-20. $\overline{Q}$ will be connected to the $\overline{INT}$ line on the computer, and one of the output strobes on your interface board should be connected to the flip-flop CLR line. Don't connect the wire to the $\overline{INT}$ line until after you've started executing the program described in part b.

b) To finish the clock, all we need is software. The Starter System and the TRS-80 have ROM in low memory so we cannot simply put an interrupt service routine at location 0038 (all addresses here are hexadecimal). However, the ROMs have a JP into RAM memory at 0038, so we can still use mode 1 interrupts. With a Starter System the first thing we need to do is to put another jump instruction at 23D3 (the instruction at 0038 is JP 23D3) because it's in the middle of the Starter System's scratch-pad area. The interrupt service routine can then be located at some convenient place like 2100. With a TRS-80, the jump at 0038 is JP 4012. We need to put another jump here because 4012 is just below the keyboard and video-display control block areas. Insert a JP 4A80 instruction at 4012 so your interrupt service routine can be located at 4A80.

To test the hardware and general organization of your programs, let's first have the interrupt service routine be one which just increments a memory location. When you write the routine, remember to save and restore any registers you use and to re-enable interrupts before returning. Failure to save registers is a common cause of senility in interrupt-driven computer programs. To run the program on the Starter System set up the memory as follows:

```
2000  3E 47           LD    A,47       ;turn off interrupts from CTC
2002  D3 86           OUT   (CTC2),A
2004  ED 56           IM1              ;set interrupt mode 1
2006  FB              EI
2007  C3 2007  LOOP:  JP    LOOP       ;loop forever

2100           INT:   ---------        ;put interrupt service routine
                                        here

23D3  C3 2100         JP    INT
```

On the TRS-80, set the memory up this way:

```
4012  C3 4A80            JP      INT

4980  ED 56              IM1                 ;set interrupt mode 1
4982  FB                 EI
4983  C3 4983   LOOP:    JP      LOOP        ;loop forever

4A80            INT:     ---------           ;put interrupt service routine
                                              here
```

Enter your programs into memory and start executing the program (at 2000 for the Starter System, at 4980 for the TRS-80). Then (and only then) you can connect the flip-flop output to INT. To terminate execution of the program you will have to press RESET.

c) Now that we have 60 Hz interrupts working, let's change the interrupt service routine into one that keeps the time of day. In particular, we want to keep a seconds count in some location SEC, and a minutes count in some location MIN. In order to see the time on the CRT screen or LED display, the instruction LOOP: JP LOOP must be replaced with a loop which continually outputs the contents of SEC and MIN onto the display (we won't worry about keeping track of hours). The easiest way to handle the display is to use the subroutines OUTPUT or OUTPT given in Exercise #4. Remember that with a Starter System you must have the subroutine DISUP (see App. F) present in order for OUTPUT to work. With these routines you should be able to write the clock display routine rather easily. If you want the time displayed in decimal, it can be done easily by executing a DAA instruction (e.g., if you want to increment the seconds count, clear the carry, put the count in A, increment it and execute DAA. This instruction treats the two nibbles in A as two BCD digits and propagates a carry correctly between them).

When you (finally!!) get the clock to work, congratulate yourself. You now have the world's most expensive non-portable stopwatch.

d) As a final embellishment to the program, you might like to connect a piezoelectric buzzer to one bit of an output port and modify your software so that the buzzer turns on for one second every minute.

8-6. Using I/O Ports as Device Controllers

In this set of exercises we get some experience using parallel I/O ports to control and/or monitor a variety of devices. The first exercise illustrates some of the versatility of the computer. We make it into a signal generator, a frequency counter, and a musical instrument, all just by playing with one bit of a parallel I/O port! The second exercise provides some experience in controlling a number of common electrical devices such as relays, switches, lights, etc., that do not use TTL logic levels (see Sec. 4-1). Since computers are relatively delicate, the key concept here is to isolate the external circuit or device from the computer, i.e., never allow electrical contact between them. With a Starter System either your interface board or the built-in PIO can be used as the I/O port. With a TRS-80, you will need to use either the interface board or one of the alternatives described at the end of Exercise 6.

EXERCISE 8

a) Output ports can be used as programmable signal sources. Try writing a program that outputs a one second long pulse on bit 0 of your output port each time the program is executed. Hint: Make use of a delay subroutine like the one shown below and your program can be written very easily.

```
DELAY:  LD    HL,0000    ;this routine delays for about 1 second
DELY1:  DEC   HL         ;decrement counter
        NOP              ;waste some time
        LD    A,H        ;check for HL=0
        OR    L
        JR    NZ,DELY1
```

Connect a voltmeter to bit 0 of the output port and verify that your program works correctly. Now modify the program so that the computer continuously outputs a square wave with a one-second period when the program is run.

b) To illustrate the use of an input port, let's program the computer to be a frequency counter. A low-frequency oscillator (<1 kHz) can easily be constructed on a breadboard using a 555 timer chip as shown in Fig. 1-22. Your job is to measure the oscillator's frequency using only the computer. This can be done easily by connecting the oscillator output to one bit of an input port and counting how many times the computer executes a timed loop during one oscillator period. To determine the length of time required to execute your timed loop, consult your Z80 technical manual and use the fact that the period of each T state is 0.5008 microseconds for a Starter System and 0.5637 microseconds for a TRS-80.

NOTE: If you're using the Starter System PIO, convert it into an input port BEFORE you hook any TTL signals to it.

c) Now we're going to play beautiful (??) music together. To do this let's build a simple circuit that connects a loudspeaker to one bit of an output port. A schematic for doing this is shown in Fig. 8-8. You can build it on one of the breadboards and connect it to your output port with clip leads. Test that everything works properly by entering a simple program that just outputs a square wave:

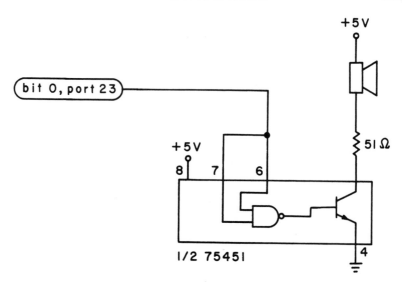

Fig. 8-8. Connecting a loudspeaker to an output port using a 75452 peripheral driver.

```
BUZZ:     XOR    A              ;output a low
          OUT    (PORT),A
          CALL   DELAY          ;leave it low for a while
          LD     A,0FF          ;output a high
          OUT    (PORT),A
          CALL   DELAY          ;delay again
          JP     BUZZ           ;repeat forever
```

You need to substitute the address of the output port you are using for PORT. Write your own DELAY subroutine, setting it up to give a delay of about 1 or 2 milliseconds.

d) Finally, write a program of your own that will let you play your keyboard like a musical instrument. When one of the number keys 0-F is pressed, a tone proportional to the key value should be produced for as long as the key is held down. No sound should be produced when no key is being pressed. To make your job a bit easier, here are a few hints:

1. If you have a Starter System, use the KPDIN subroutine given in App. F. However, the version of KPDIN given there doesn't return until a key is released, and we want it to return a value immediately. To fix this, replace the five bytes of code beginning at KEYDN5 by NOP's. This causes the computer to return from KPDIN as soon as a key is pressed. To see when a key is released, call KPDSTS after each cycle of sound is output.

2. If you have a TRS-80, you can CALL the built-in keyboard routine at

0049H. This routine hangs until a key is pressed, and then returns imme-diately with the value of the key in ASCII. To see when a key is released, we need a keyboard status routine:

```
; This routine checks to see if a key has been pressed on the TRS-80
; keyboard.  It returns A=00 and Z flag set if no key is pressed, and A
; nonzero with Z flag cleared if a key is pressed.

KYSTS:    LD      A,(387F)       ;keyboard lines memory mapped into 387F
          OR      A              ;set flags
          RET
```

In your program you should first call the keyboard routine to find which key is pressed. You then may want to convert from ASCII to hex and start outputting the appropriate tone. To see when the key is released, call KYSTS after each cycle of sound is output.

3. A good way to set the frequency is to write an inner loop that requires about 200 microseconds to complete. Execute this loop the number of times given by the keyvalue, and use the resulting delay to define one half cycle of the sound. Other choices will also work, but this one seems to make "Mary had a little lamb" sound pretty good. Have fun!

EXERCISE 9

This exercise illustrates Sec. 4-1 and requires a number of small parts that should be obtained before beginning the exercise. Photoresistors, optoisola-tors, triacs, relays, and 5-volt piezoelectric buzzers can be inexpensively obtained from Radio Shack. Solenoids should be readily available at electri-cal supply stores, and 75452's and Motorola MOC3011's should be available at any electronics distributor. In parts (c) and (d) where ac voltages are required, it is advisable to use the output of a 24-volt transformer as your ac power supply rather than the line voltage, which presents a considerable shock hazard.

NOTE: IN THESE EXPERIMENTS VOLTAGES ARE PRESENT THAT CAN RUIN THE COMPUTERS. A word to the wise is sufficient. The rest of us should proceed as follows: Before you turn on power for any experiment, double check your wiring. Then verify it by taking your voltmeter and (with power off!) attaching one lead to the high voltage source (+12V dc or 24V ac), and checking the resistance between it and every wire going to the computer to be sure it's infinite.

a) As an example of isolated input, let's build a light-activated switch for the computer using an optoisolator and a photoresistor. The photoresistor has a high resistance when it is in the dark, and a low resistance when light falls on it. Hence we can wire it in series with the LED contained in an optoisolator and turn on and off the LED by varying the light hitting the photoresistor. Light from the LED controls the conductivity of an optically coupled transistor inside the opto, and this transistor can be connected to a bit on an input port of the computer as shown in Fig. 4-3. Wire up this circuit and note how the current through the LED and the voltage at the computer input changes with the light intensity on the photoresistor. Finally write a little program that turns a 5-volt piezoelectric buzzer on or off depending on whether the room lights are off or on. The buzzer can be connected directly between an output port bit and ground.

b) Relays can be used to control many kinds of devices. Connect a relay to an output port bit as shown in Fig. 4-5, and verify that it clicks on or off, depending on the state of the computer's output bit. The diode in the circuit is there to protect the 75452 against the high-voltage spike generated when the current through the relay coil (which is an inductive load) is switched off. The main limitation of relays is their slow speed. Measure the relay's speed by hooking the relay output side back into an input port on the computer. Then write a program which measures how long it takes from the time the computer sets the output port bit until it detects a change at the input port.

c) For controlling ac-current loads, an opto-coupled triac driver such as the Motorola MOC3011 is usually the best choice. The computer drives an LED on the input side of the device and the LED output triggers a small triac on the output side of the device. This triac can then be used to control a larger triac which is in series with the load (see Section 4-1). To play with one of these devices, wire up the circuit shown in Fig. 4-10. For your load, use a light bulb, and verify that the computer can turn on and off this ac load with a simple output instruction. If you're using a 24-volt ac supply, you will need a high wattage bulb such as a clear 100W to get enough light to see out of the bulb. By using the 60 Hz real time clock circuit of Fig. 1-20, you can also make a computer controlled light dimmer. Just put the 60 Hz TTL square wave into an input port, and turn on the triac only during some variable fraction of the time the 60 Hz signal is high. Write a little program that does this.

d) As examples of other ac loads you might try a solenoid or a light bulb which is controlled by a latching solenoid (see Section 4-1 for details of how this works). A 24-volt transformer mounted next to the light bulb can be used as the ac power supply. Play with these devices and convince yourself that they can also be controlled with TTL logic levels.

8-7. Experiments With DACs and ADCs

In the two exercises below, we'll get some experience with digital-to-analog converters (DAC's), and analog-to-digital converters (ADC's). These two devices are discussed in detail in Sec. 4-2 and 4-3. In the first exercise the DAC is used in two of its most popular applications: as an analog signal generator and as a means of producing an analog display of a stored digital signal. In the second exercise the high-speed conversion capability of the ADC is used to capture an analog waveform and store it in memory, i.e., we make the computer into a transient digitizer. We then make the computer into a signal averager by digitizing a repetitive signal many times and summing the results in memory.

To do these exercises you'll need to install more sockets and bypass capacitors on the interface board so that we can add the necessary circuitry. The required sockets and their positions on the board are shown in Fig. 8-7. Review the instructions in Exercise 5 before beginning to put them on. We don't need the 8251, 74193, 74393, 1488, 1489, or cable socket for the present experiments, but now is a good time to install them. Note the three capacitors placed horizontally near the center of the board. These are used to filter the +15 and -15 volt supplies and an internal voltage reference on the DAC. Install the capacitors so that one side is connected to the ground plane (wiring side of the board), and the other side sticks thru the board leaving about one-half inch of wire protruding so that you can wire wrap connections to it. Make sure that the capacitor leads do not touch the 5-volt power plane on the component side of the board. Also note that the power and ground connections on some of the sockets you are installing are NOT in the usual corner positions.

Connect wires from pins 2 and 52 on the interface-board edge connector to two of the horizontally-mounted capacitors mentioned above. These are your filtered +15 and -15 volt supply lines. Then wire up the DAC and ADC circuits as shown in Fig. 8-6(b).

EXERCISE 10

The DAC we use in this exercise is a high quality 12 bit device (the Burr-Brown DAC80-CBI-V shown in Fig. 4-16), but only the 8 most significant bits are connected to the computer to simplify the software. Handle it with care as this DAC is more than twice as expensive as the Z80 itself! Here is what you should do:

a) BEFORE you install the DAC, plug your interface board into the computer, attach a 15-volt supply to the terminals on the Starter System or TRS-80 to S-100 bus adapter, and check that +15 and -15 volts are present on the proper pins of the DAC socket (and only those pins!). Now turn OFF both the 5 and 15-volt supplies, remove your board, and install the DAC.

b) Now check that the DAC works properly by hooking a voltmeter to pin 15 and measuring the output voltage as you use the Starter System PORT EXAM function or the OUT PORT,DATA function of TRS-80 Basic to output data to port 27H. Notice that since the DAC inverts the data and we have strapped it for a 0 to 5 volt output range, outputting 0FFH gives 0 volts and outputting 00 gives +5 volts. Next output 00H to 0FFH in steps of 10H. The DAC output should decrease smoothly from +5 to 0 volts in equally spaced steps.

c) Next look at the dynamic characteristics of the DAC by hooking the output to an oscilloscope and executing a program that causes the DAC to output a sawtooth wave to the oscilloscope. The sawtooth can be easily produced by sequentially outputting the numbers 0FF through 00 and then jumping back to repeat this sequence. Adjust the scope to get a stable display and notice how clean the waveform looks even though it consists of discrete steps. Now expand the vertical and horizontal scales so that you can see the individual steps clearly. Notice that on a fast time scale there are a lot of glitches on the output due to pickup of digital switching noise. This noise can be removed by adding a simple RC low pass filter on the DAC output consisting of a series 2.2K resistor followed by a .001 μF capacitor to ground.

d) One of the major uses of DACs is to provide a display of digitized waveforms stored in the computer's memory. Write a program which uses the DAC to display the contents of 80H memory locations on the scope. You'll find it useful to fill your memory with some simple waveform(s) so that you can tell when your program is running correctly. Notice that each memory location appears as a short line segment on the screen because the scope is always sweeping horizontally. This problem is often cured by putting in a second DAC to drive the horizontal axis of the scope, but there is a much simpler solution. Just connect one bit of another output port to the scope's Z axis. The Z axis input on a scope allows you to turn the electron beam producing the trace on or off with an external signal (usually 0 to +5 volts). The input is typically located on the rear of the scope and may be labelled something like Z-axis input, Z in, or external CRT cathode. Right after you output each location to the DAC, call a little subroutine that pulses another output port bit on for about 4 to 8 microseconds and then turns it off. With this arrangement you should see a display consisting of discrete dots instead of line segments. We need another output port for this Z axis bit and it can easily be made by connecting the output strobe for port 24H to the clock input of the unused half of the 7474 on your board. Tie preset and clear high, and connect the D input to bit 0 of the data bus. The Q output of the flip-flop is now a one-bit latched output port. With a Starter System you can also use PIO port B for your additional output port.

EXERCISE 11

The ADC used in this exercise (the National Semiconductor ADC0816 shown in Fig. 4-21) is a fairly expensive ($30) MOS chip which can be easily destroyed by static electricity. Like all MOS chips it is thus a bit of a pain to handle (especially here in the Arizona desert where the humidity is often 5% or less!). The standard drill for handling MOS IC's is as follows: When not in a socket the chip should be stored with its pins stuck in a piece of black conductive foam (not styrofoam!). Here it's safe from damage. To insert the chip, touch your hands and the foam simultaneously to a ground on such as the ground lead of your 5-volt power supply. Then, without getting up or sliding around on your seat, remove the chip from the foam and insert it in your board. If possible, keep the board on a grounded conductive foam pad when it's not in the computer. To remove the chip, make sure you've grounded yourself before you touch it, and use a tweezers or a screwdriver to gently pry the chip out and put it back in a grounded piece of foam.

a) After you've installed the ADC, you can check it out using the DAC. Make sure the DAC is putting out 0 to +5 volts full scale (negative voltages or signals greater than 5 volts will destroy the ADC), and then connect a jumper between the DAC output and the channel 0 input of the ADC. Now use the PORT EXAM function on the Starter System or the OUT PORT,DATA command on the TRS-80 to output a voltage on the DAC. To digitize and input this voltage using the ADC requires three steps. First output a 00 to port 25H. This selects channel 0 on the ADC multiplexer. Then output any number to port 26H. The port 26H strobe starts the A to D conversion. Finally input from port 26H using PORT EXAM on the Starter System or PRINT INP(PORT) on the TRS-80 to get the number. The number you get should agree roughly with the complement of the number you've output to the DAC. There will be some disparity because we have not trimmed the zero offset or gain on the DAC.

b) Next write a program that will allow you to digitize an arbitrary waveform and store it in memory. To generate a waveform, wire up a 555 on your breadboard as an oscillator which produces a square wave of frequency 100-150 Hz. Then convert the square wave into a triangle wave by adding an RC low pass filter to the output: a series 20K-50K resistor followed by a 0.1 µF capacitor to ground. When digitizing the triangle wave remember that the ADC requires 100 microseconds to make a conversion. Thus you will have to start a conversion, delay 100 microseconds, and then input the data, before you can start a new conversion. Digitize about 80H points of the triangle wave and use the display subroutine of the previous exercise to see the results.

c) Finally, write a program that digitizes a waveform and then repeats the digitization over and over, adding the result for each point in the waveform to the previous total for that point. You will then have a powerful signal averager (see Sec. 4-4) which can be used to improve the signal-to-noise ratio of an arbitrary repetitive waveform. On your breadboard construct a clean square-wave signal source and a noisy square wave derived from it as shown in Fig. 8-9. Use the clean wave as your trigger and average the noisy wave to see if you can extract a good signal. Figure 4-23 shows the kind of waveforms one should observe. Here are some hints to make your programming easier:

1. Use a 256-byte buffer to store your waveform, allocating two bytes per

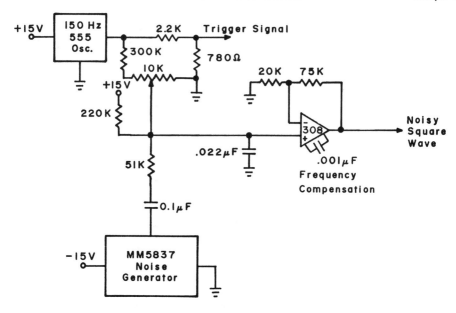

Fig. 8-9. Schematic diagram of a noisy square wave generator circuit. Filtered noise from an MM5837 noise generator chip (available from Radio Shack) is combined with a square wave by an LM308 op amp. The frequency compensation capacitor on the 308 is necessary to ensure stable operation.

point for a total of 80H points.

2. Use the 8-bit ADD instruction to add in new data. Then only the carry bit needs to be added into the high order byte of the two byte buffer for each data point.

3. Be careful when writing the code used to trigger the start of a new scan. It's not entirely trivial.

4. Modify your display routine so that it displays every other byte in your memory buffer area. Then you can use it to see the data you've taken by displaying only the low-order byte of the two bytes you've allocated for each data point. This will work when you've taken only one scan of the signal. To display the sum of many scans you should right shift (i.e., divide) your data values until the most significant bits are all in the low order byte. A subroutine to do this follows:

```
; This subroutine shifts data in a 16-bit data word right by nn
; bits.  The data word must have the form: low-order byte, high-
; order byte; i.e., the low byte must come first.  BUF is the start
; of the memory buffer area, which is assumed to be 100H bytes
; long and begin on a page boundary, i.e., at an address XX00.
```

06	nn	SHIFT:	LD	B,nn	;# of right shifts in B
21	01 XX	SHIFT1:	LD	HL,BUF+1	;hi byte of 1st word in buffer
7E		BACK:	LD	A,(HL)	;shift hi byte 1 bit right
CB	3F		SRL	A	
77			LD	(HL),A	
2B			DEC	HL	;then shift low byte
7E			LD	A,(HL)	
1F			RRA		
77			LD	(HL),A	
23			INC	HL	;point to hi byte of next
23			INC	HL	;data word
23			INC	HL	
7C			LD	A,H	;end of buffer reached?
FE	XX+1		CP	(BUF/100H)+1	
20	F0		JR	NZ,BACK	;loop back if not
10	EB		DJNZ	SHIFT1	;repeat right shift B times
C9			RET		

8-8. Stepper Motors

This exercise gives you a chance to become acquainted with the characteristics and capabilities of stepper motors. The power-supply voltages and
currents given below are for the Rapidsyn 23D-6102 stepper, but any other
4-phase stepper can be used as long as you stay within the voltage and current rating for your particular stepper. You will also need a stepper-motor

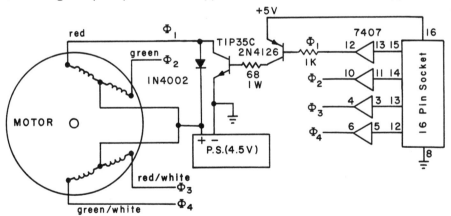

Fig. 8-10. Stepper-motor driver circuit. The complete circuit is
shown only for phase 1. The other three phases use identical circuits.

driver board such as the one shown in Fig. 8-10. The driver board can be
connected to your interface board with a ribbon cable which has 16 pin
socket connections on the ends so that it can simply be plugged into an IC
socket on both boards. The socket on the interface board should have +5

volts, ground, and four bits of output port 27H connected to it as shown in Fig. 8-6.

EXERCISE 12

a) With all power OFF, connect the stepper-motor driver board to your interface board with a ribbon cable, making sure pin 1 is connected to pin 1, etc. Next turn on the computer and output a 0FFH to port 27H using the PORT EXAM key on a Starter System or OUT PORT,DATA on a TRS-80. This should turn off all 4 phases of the stepper motor. Check to see that the outputs of the 7407 buffers on the driver board are all high. If not, you've done something wrong. Now connect a 5-volt power supply to the stepper motor driver board and measure its voltage to make sure it's between 4.5 and 5.0 volts. Do not substitute any other power supply as a voltage of over 5.1 volts can burn out the stepper motor.

b) Now you can use PORT EXAM on a Starter System or OUT PORT,DATA on a TRS-80 to check that everything is working properly. You should have bit 0 of port 27H driving phase 1 of the motor, bit 1 driving phase 2, bit 2 driving phase 3, and bit 3 driving phase 4 if everything is wired properly. Thus writing a 0EH to port 27H pulls bit 0 low and this should turn on phase 1 by bringing it low. Check that this occurs by putting a voltmeter on the phase-1 wire (the red wire on the Rapidsyn stepper) to the stepper motor. After you've verified that each motor phase is activated by the proper bit of port 27H, you're ready to run the motor. Note that you should not write a 00 to the port as this will activate all 4 phases at once and pull about 4 amps of current through the motor, causing excessive heating (not to mention the strain being put on your poor little power supply). Note also that the shaft can be turned fairly easily by hand when no windings are energized but that it is very difficult to turn when a winding is energized.

c) A program to run the motor using your keyboard is given below. The program also displays the motor position on the LED display or CRT screen. Study the program to see how it works and play with running the motor for a while. Notice that since the computer knows the motor shaft position, you can always return it to any given orientation.

To run the program on a Starter System, four external routines are needed: OUTA (given in Exercise 4), KPDIN, KPDSTS, and DISUP (all given in App. F). Make sure these routines are present in the computer at the addresses shown below. In addition, KPDIN should be modified as described in Exercise 8, so that the routine does not hang until a key is released.

```
.RADIX    16

; External addresses

OUTA      EQU    2095        ;display accumulator routine
```

```
DISMEM    EQU    2380         ;display memory origin
KPDIN     EQU    2300         ;keypad input routine
KPDSTS    EQU    2349         ;keypad status routine
DISUP     EQU    2357         ;display refresh routine
```

.COMMENT 'This program controls a stepper motor using your computer keyboard. When the "F" key is pressed the motor will step forwards (clockwise) continuously as long as the key is held down. Similarly, the "B" key will move the motor counter-clockwise. The program also keeps track of the number of steps the motor has taken (modulo 0FF) by incrementing or decrementing the location COUNT, and displays the count on the two rightmost digits of your display.'

```
STEP:     LD     HL,COUNT      ;motor position in COUNT
KYCHK:    CALL   KPDIN         ;get key value
          LD     C,A           ;save copy in C
KYCHK1:   LD     B,(HL)        ;get current position
          CP     0B            ;is key a B?
          JR     Z,CCW         ;yes, step backwards
          CP     0F            ;is key an F?
          JR     NZ,KYCHK      ;no, check keys again
          INC    B             ;increase position by 2
          INC    B
CCW:      DEC    B             ;decrease position by 1
UPDATE:   LD     (HL),B        ;store position
          LD     DE,DISMEM+4   ;put position in display
          LD     A,B           ;area
          CALL   OUTA
          CALL   STPOUT        ;step the motor
          CALL   DISUP         ;refresh the display
          CALL   KPDSTS        ;is the key still pressed?
          LD     A,C           ;restore key value and
          JR     NZ,KYCHK1     ;repeat if so
          JR     KYCHK         ;else start over

STPOUT:   LD     DE,TABLE1     ;get table address
          LD     A,B           ;get position
          AND    07            ;modulo 8
          ADD    A,E           ;index into table
          LD     E,A
          LD     A,(DE)        ;pick up motor phase
          OUT    (27),A        ;ship it out
          CALL   MSEC          ;delay a few millisec
          RET
```

; This routine delays for nn milliseconds where nn is the
; number loaded into the B register in the first instruction
; of the routine.

```
MSEC:     LD    B,08        ;set delay for nn msec
MSEC1:    LD    A,7D        ;inner loop = 1 msec
LOOP:     DEC   A
          JR    NZ,LOOP
          DJNZ  MSEC1
          RET
```

```
;table for single phase excitation
TABLE1:   DB    07,0E,0D,0B,07,0E,0D,0B
```

```
;table for dual phase excitation
TABLE2:   DB    06,0C,09,03,06,0C,09,03
```

```
;table for half-step excitation
TABLE3:   DB    09,0B,03,07,06,0E,0C,0D
```

```
;motor position stored here
COUNT:    DB    00
```

```
          END
```

For a TRS-80, load the OUTPT routine given in Exercise 4, and replace the main routine STEP above by:

```
STEP:     LD    HL,COUNT  ;motor position in COUNT
KYCHK:    CALL  002B      ;get key value
          OR    A
          JR    Z,KYCHK
          LD    C,A        ;save copy in C
KYCHK1:   LD    B,(HL)     ;get current position
          CP    42         ;is key a "B"?
          JR    Z,CCW      ;yes, step backwards
          CP    46         ;is key an "F"?
          JR    NZ,KYCHK   ;no, check keys again
          INC   B          ;increase position by 2
          INC   B
CCW:      DEC   B          ;decrease position by 1
UPDATE:   LD    (HL),B     ;store position
          LD    A,B        ;and display it
          CALL  OUTPT
          CALL  STPOUT     ;step the motor
          LD    A,(387F)   ;is the key still pressed?
          OR    A
          LD    A,C        ;restore key value and
          JR    NZ,KYCHK1 ;repeat if so
          JR    KYCHK      ;else start over
```

d) Use this program to determine the angle through which the shaft rotates per step for this motor. This is easily done by attaching a toothpick to the motor shaft with a little clay and using it as a marker to determine how many steps are required for exactly one revolution.

e) While the stepper is being run by holding a key down, look with a scope at the waveforms present at the 7407 inputs and outputs and at the stepper motor windings. Notice how the stepper motor inductance changes the clean pulses you generated at the computer.

f) The program as given runs the stepper with single-phase excitation. By changing the instruction at STPOUT to LD DE,TABLE2, the motor will run using TABLE2 which provides dual-phase excitation. Notice the difference in noise and vibration when the motor is run in this mode. Also try half stepping the motor by using TABLE3 instead of TABLE2.

g) Next see how fast you can run the motor by changing the length of the drive pulses. The length is determined by the delay routine MSEC. Shorten and/or eliminate this delay and see how fast the motor runs.

h) As a final challenging project, you might like to try making a closed loop servo system using the stepper motor. Connect two 10K potentiometers in series between your +5V power supply and ground as shown in Fig. 8-11.

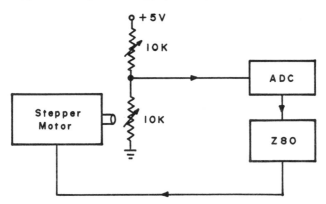

Fig. 8-11. A simple servo system. The stepper motor should adjust the lower potentiometer to maintain a constant voltage no matter how you manually turn the upper pot.

Five or ten-turn pots work best. Connect the stepper motor shaft to the shaft of one pot using a short piece of tygon or rubber tubing to couple the two. Set both pots to the middle of their range and measure the voltage obtained by your ADC. The idea is to set this voltage as your target voltage and write a program that will drive the stepper motor so that it maintains this voltage regardless of how you turn the shaft of the second pot. If you increase the resistance of the manually controlled pot, the stepper must turn its pot to increase its resistance, thereby leaving the voltage to the ADC unchanged. Once you've written your program, play with it to see if the servo loop is stable no matter how you turn the pot. Also, look at the input voltage to the ADC on a scope to see how fast the servo loop settles to its final value after a sudden change.

8-9. Serial and Computer-computer Communications

Serial communication links are used in almost all computer systems regardless of size. In the following two exercises we get a serial I/O port working which uses the 8251 USART described in Sec. 5-1, and then use this port for computer-terminal and computer-computer communications. The last two parts of Exercise 13 require either a computer terminal or a second computer with a serial port. Exercise 14, which involves computer-computer communications, requires two computers. The exercise assumes the two are a Starter System and a TRS-80, but other combinations can also be used. Two TRS-80's or a TRS-80 plus a large computer of any type can be used. It is even possible to use two Starter Systems, but because of its CRT display and full keyboard, it is preferable to have at least one of the computers be a TRS-80.

The first order of business is to wire up a serial port on your interface board. If you haven't done so already, put the necessary sockets on the board using the diagram of Fig. 8-7 as a guide. Then wire up the sockets as shown in Fig. 8-6(c). Notice that the USART clock is derived from the 2 MHz computer clock signal present at pin 49 of the edge connector. The 74193 divides this by 13 to obtain a clock which could be used directly for 9600 baud communications. Handshaking signals are a necessity at this data rate, however, so we divide the clock by another factor of 32 with a 74393 to obtain a 300 baud clock. At this data rate no handshaking is needed, keeping the programming simpler. If handshaking is desired, the appropriate hardware connections are present in Fig. 8-6(c) to implement the $\overline{DSR}$-$\overline{DTR}$ handshaking described in Sec. 5-4 (see the MODTR routine).

EXERCISE 13

a) The +V and -V pins on the 1488 should be connected to the +15 and -15 volt supplies. Make sure these connections are right and then insert all the IC's onto the board (you don't need the DAC or the ADC). The 8251 USART is a MOS chip, so handle it as you did the ADC0816. Also be sure not to interchange the 1488 and the 1489.

b) The USART must be initalized with a short software routine before it is used. A routine to do this is given at the end of Sec. 5-1. The CTRL port referred to there is port 21H on your interface board. Since this routine is just a string of output instructions, you can also do the initialization manually using PORT EXAM or OUT PORT,DATA.

c) Check that the USART is transmitting properly (after you've initialized it!) by writing a little loop that outputs a character (the data port is 20H), delays until the serial transmission is complete, and then loops backs to output it again. While running this program, look at the serial output from the 8251 and from the 1488 line driver on a scope and check to see that the output format is correct. Play with this for a while, outputting various ASCII codes and observing them on the scope. This exercise is one of the best ways to really learn about the serial communications format that there is.

d) Next put a jumper between the 1488 driver and the 1489 receiver, and write a program that outputs a character from the USART transmitter and inputs it back into the computer from the USART receiver. To do this, output a character to the USART transmitter and then poll the USART status (input from port 21H) to check the receiver ready (RxRDY) flag. When the flag goes high, input the character from the receiver (port 20H) and see that it agrees with the character you sent.

e) Now let's wire the Starter System to a terminal. The terminal's characteristics should be set up to match the way you've set up the 8251 on your interface board; namely, 300 baud, 8 bits per character, no parity bit, and 1 stop bit. The 1488 output should be connected to pin 3 on the terminal's 25 pin connector, and the 1489 input should be connected to pin 2. A special cable can be made up to do this, or the connection can be jury-rigged using wires with mini-hooks on the ends. Now write a little program that inputs a character from the computer keyboard and outputs it to the USART. With a Starter System you can use KPDIN to read the keyboard, call UBASC at 06BB in the Starter System ROM to convert the character to ASCII, and then output it to the USART. With a TRS-80 you can call the keyboard input routine as described in Exercise 8 and then simply output the contents of the accumulator to the USART since the keyboard routine returns the character in ASCII form. If you've done everything right the character should appear on the terminal's screen.

f) Finally, now that you've gotten your computer to talk to the terminal, let's get the terminal to talk to your computer. For this you need to write a little program that inputs data from the USART and outputs the value of the ASCII character on your display. You can use the OUTA or OUTAC routines given in Exercise 4 to display the character on the Starter System or TRS-80 display. Note that with a Starter System you will also need to have the routine DISUP present (see Appendix F) and that the hex value of the ASCII character will be displayed rather than the character itself.

EXERCISE 14

In the previous exercise we looked at examples of simple one way communication back and forth between a computer and a terminal. In this exercise we'll replace the terminal by a second computer and put together both directions of communication in a modem loop. Then we'll expand on this idea to make one of the computers into a smart terminal which can send or receive files as well as control another computer.

To avoid talking in generalities, we assume here that one of the computers is a TRS-80. It will be the computer we make into a smart terminal. It doesn't matter much what the other computer is (the Starter System is a good choice), as long as it's capable of running a host computer program which expects to communicate via a terminal.

a) First connect the two computers via their serial ports. Make sure the transmitter of each USART is connected to the receiver of the other. To check that the link is working, set up the host computer so that it runs a simple program which just echoes back any character it receives:

```
          CALL    INIT       ;initialize USART
LOOP:     CALL    TRMIN      ;input character from terminal
          LD      C,A
          CALL    TRMOUT     ;output it back to terminal
          JP      LOOP
```

The INIT routine is given at the end of Sec. 5-1. TRMIN is a subroutine which should look at the USART receiver-ready status bit, loop until a character is received, and then input the character, returning with it in A (see the CI routine in Sec. 2-7).   TRMOUT should loop on the USART transmitter-ready status bit until the transmitter is ready to accept a character, and then output the character contained in C (see the CO routine in Sec. 2-7).   Once you have this routine running on the host computer you should also initialize the USART on the TRS-80 and then use the Basic commands OUT PORT,DATA and PRINT INP(PORT) to see whether the link is working properly (or you can use a monitor program like TBUG on the TRS-80 and do everthing in machine language).

b) Now that the serial link is working, let's get a modem-loop program running on the TRS-80. The form of this program is discussed in detail in Sec. 5-4. One change you may want to make is to have the computer recognize the BREAK key (gives ASCII code 01) instead of ©R as the signal to return to local mode. This would seem to be a necessity since the TRS-80 has no control key, but in fact you can simulate a ©R if desired by pressing the SHIFT key and then the DOWN ARROW key followed by the R key, while continuing to hold down the SHIFT key throughout. This technique works for any other control key code as well. Enter the modem-loop program into the TRS-80 using a machine-language monitor (TBUG or an equivalent) and then test it by running the program while the echo program of part (a) above is running on the host computer. Any key you press on the TRS-80 keyboard should be sent to host and then echoed back to the TRS-80 screen.

c) Next set up the host computer to run the DEMON monitor. A listing of this program along with a detailed description of the monitor commands is given in Appendix D. Although this is a very long program if you have to type it in, it's well worth having the DEMON in your machine because it's so powerful and flexible. On a Starter System you will find it very handy to put the DEMON in an EPROM (source and machine code is available from Scroll Systems for both the TRS-80 and the Starter System). Once you have it entered into the host computer, have the computer run the program while your terminal computer is running the modem loop. If all is well, the sign-on message "Demon Monitor V1.0" should appear on your terminal. Then play with the monitor for a while learning how the various monitor commands work.

ALTERNATIVE: If your host computer is a large computer rather than a Starter System, you can just run the modem-loop program on your terminal computer and play with the operating-system commands on the large machine.

d) The big advantage of having a computer simulate a terminal is that one can ship files back and forth between the two machines. It is this feature that makes communications between two computers so much more powerful than communications between a computer and a simple terminal. TRSCOM, a program that fully implements this capability on a TRS-80, is given in App. C. Type in this program (it's available in source and machine language from Scroll Systems). You can save some effort by noting that the messages at the end of the program can be shortened to just SIGNON: DB 'TRSCOM',00. If your host computer is the Starter System, you will not be able to use the READ or WRITE routines since DEMON is not set up to handle ASCII text files. Thus these two routines can be omitted. If your host computer is a large computer, you will probably not be able to use the machine language transfer commands LOAD and SAVE. All the code between LOAD and MESSAG can then be eliminated.

Once the program is typed into the TRS-80, run it and try sending programs back and forth between the two computers. For example, if you're using a Starter System with DEMON in it as the host, try the following:

1. After TRSCOM signs on, type a (cr) (the ENTER key on the TRS-80). You can now talk to DEMON as if you were a simple terminal. Find some block of memory in the Starter System, say 2000 to 2100, that you want to send to the TRS-80 and note the memory contents at the start and end of the block. Now press BREAK to get back to TRSCOM (it will respond by signing on again).

2. Let's suppose we want to load this memory block into 4B00-4C00 in the

TRS-80. To do this type next,

LD2000,2100$4B00(cr).

The string D2000,2100 tells DEMON to display memory from 2000 to 2100. The "$" sign is typed by pressing the BREAK key (the program echoes it on the screen as a $). This gets us back to local mode, and the address 4B00 tells TRSCOM where to load the memory block in the TRS-80 when it is sent by DEMON.

3.   When the display is completed, press the BREAK key and the TRS-80 will restart TRSCOM. You can now use the J command to jump to a monitor like TBUG (or to BASIC) and examine memory in the block 4B00-4C00 to verify that the information really got transferred.

In a similar manner, one can use the S command, e.g., type

SL2000$4B00,4C00(cr)

to send a block of memory from the TRS-80 to the Starter System. Try it!

Appendix A

ASCII Table

Since the ASCII characters constitute the medium through which our print information flows, they play a particularly important role. The next page presents these characters in a table with three numeric values: the first in hexadecimal (base 16, includes letters A thru F), the second in decimal, and the third in binary. Octal values can be read from the binary. The way we have grouped the characters reveals their basic relationship to one another. In the first instance, the grouping is in 16's (hexadecimal). However a more basic grouping is in 32's, since the 26 letters of the alphabet don't fit into 16. Hence we have four columns of 32 characters. An alternative way of describing the first column, the control characters, is in the form ©c, which are generated by pressing the CTRL key and the character c at the same time. To see which character to press, just use the one in the third group of columns on the same row as the number desired in the first group of columns. For example, an alternative name for ETX is ©C, etc. The table also serves for conversion between hexadecimal, decimal and binary, up to 127_{10}.

The meanings of the control characters are: NUL, Null; SOH, Start Of Heading; STX, Start of Text; ETX, End of Text; EOT, End Of Transmission; ENQ, Enquiry; ACK, Acknowledge; BEL, Bell; BS, Backspace; HT, Horizontal Tab; LF, Linefeed; VT, Vertical Tab; FF, Formfeed; CR, Carriage Return; SO, Shift Out; SI, Shift In; DLE, Data Link Escape; DC1, Device Control 1; DC2, Device Control 2; DC3, Device Control 3; DC4, Device Control 4; NAK, Negative Acknowledge; SYN, Synchronous idle; ETB, End of Transmission Block; CAN, Cancel; EM, End of Medium; SUB, Substitute; ESC, Escape; FS, File Separator; GS, Group Separator; RS, Record Separator; US, Unit Separator; SP, Space; DEL, Delete.

Char	Hex	Dec	Binary
NUL	0	0	0000000
SOH	1	1	0000001
STX	2	2	0000010
ETX	3	3	0000011
EOT	4	4	0000100
ENQ	5	5	0000101
ACK	6	6	0000110
BEL	7	7	0000111
BS	8	8	0001000
HT	9	9	0001001
LF	0A	10	0001010
VT	0B	11	0001011
FF	0C	12	0001100
CR	0D	13	0001101
SO	0E	14	0001110
SI	0F	15	0001111
DLE	10	16	0010000
DC1	11	17	0010001
DC2	12	18	0010010
DC3	13	19	0010011
DC4	14	20	0010100
NAK	15	21	0010101
SYN	16	22	0010110
ETB	17	23	0010111
CAN	18	24	0011000
EM	19	25	0011001
SUB	1A	26	0011010
ESC	1B	27	0011011
FS	1C	28	0011100
GS	1D	29	0011101
RS	1E	30	0011110
US	1F	31	0011111

Char	Hex	Dec	Binary
SP	20	32	0100000
!	21	33	0100001
"	22	34	0100010
#	23	35	0100011
$	24	36	0100100
%	25	37	0100101
&	26	38	0100110
'	27	39	0100111
(	28	40	0101000
)	29	41	0101001
*	2A	42	0101010
+	2B	43	0101011
,	2C	44	0101100
-	2D	45	0101101
.	2E	46	0101110
/	2F	47	0101111
0	30	48	0110000
1	31	49	0110001
2	32	50	0110010
3	33	51	0110011
4	34	52	0110100
5	35	53	0110101
6	36	54	0110110
7	37	55	0110111
8	38	56	0111000
9	39	57	0111001
:	3A	58	0111010
;	3B	59	0111011
<	3C	60	0111100
=	3D	61	0111101
>	3E	62	0111110
?	3F	63	0111111

Char	Hex	Dec	Binary
@	40	64	1000000
A	41	65	1000001
B	42	66	1000010
C	43	67	1000011
D	44	68	1000100
E	45	69	1000101
F	46	70	1000110
G	47	71	1000111
H	48	72	1001000
I	49	73	1001001
J	4A	74	1001010
K	4B	75	1001011
L	4C	76	1001100
M	4D	77	1001101
N	4E	78	1001110
O	4F	79	1001111
P	50	80	1010000
Q	51	81	1010001
R	52	82	1010010
S	53	83	1010011
T	54	84	1010100
U	55	85	1010101
V	56	86	1010110
W	57	87	1010111
X	58	88	1011000
Y	59	89	1011001
Z	5A	90	1011010
[	5B	91	1011011
\	5C	92	1011100
]	5D	93	1011101
^	5E	94	1011110
_	5F	95	1011111

Char	Hex	Dec	Binary
`	60	96	1100000
a	61	97	1100001
b	62	98	1100010
c	63	99	1100011
d	64	100	1100100
e	65	101	1100101
f	66	102	1100110
g	67	103	1100111
h	68	104	1101000
i	69	105	1101001
j	6A	106	1101010
k	6B	107	1101011
l	6C	108	1101100
m	6D	109	1101101
n	6E	110	1101110
o	6F	111	1101111
p	70	112	1110000
q	71	113	1110001
r	72	114	1110010
s	73	115	1110011
t	74	116	1110100
u	75	117	1110101
v	76	118	1110110
w	77	119	1110111
x	78	120	1111000
y	79	121	1111001
z	7A	122	1111010
{	7B	123	1111011
|	7C	124	1111100
}	7D	125	1111101
~	7E	126	1111110
del	7F	127	1111111

Appendix B

Z80 Busses

This appendix summarizes the S-100 (IEEE 696), TRS-80, and Pro-Log/Mostek STD busses. To help compress the large amount of information, we use an * to indicate an active-low bus signal (overscored signals are Z80 signals defined in Sec. 3-1). Other lines are active high, or are power/clock lines. For timing diagrams and more precise definitions, see the published specifications for the individual busses. Also see Sec. 6-3.

B-1. S-100 Bus Definitions

The S-100 bus supports a 16 Megabyte address space, a CPU master, up to 16 temporary masters, e.g., for DMA operations, and numerous slaves (I/O or memory devices). To support a Z80 master and one temporary master, the only signals required are: A0-A15, DO0-DO7 and DI0-DI7 (connect both DI's and DO's to Z80 D0-D7), +8 volts, GND, ϕ, RESET* (connect to $\overline{RESET}$), INT* (to $\overline{INT}$), sINTA (to $\overline{M1}$ & $\overline{IORQ}$), NMI* (to $\overline{NMI}$), sM1 (to $\overline{M1}$), HOLD* (to $\overline{BUSRQ}$), pHLDA (to $\overline{BUSAK}$), and the four signals sOUT, sIN, sMEMR, MWRT (to $\overline{IORQ}$, $\overline{WR}$, $\overline{RD}$, $\overline{MREQ}$). Note that for traditional S-100 systems, the onboard slave data buffers should always be enabled to read the DI bus, unless the slave is actually selected for input. This gets around the timing problems associated with sOUT typically being asserted earlier than the IEEE S-100 standard states. RFSH has a de facto standard pin 66 (a NDEF pin), due to the enormous popularity of the S. D. Systems ExpandoRAM dynamic memory cards. Other NDEF pins could be used to support the Z80 daisy-chain interrupt scheme, but motherboard trace cuts would be required. Other status and control signals should be supported by a Z80 CPU card, but in principle aren't necessary for operation. Some I/O cards do make use of them, however, so beware! The extended address

231

lines are handy for banked memory operation.

Letters below in parentheses have the meanings: M - Master controlled (i.e., output) line, S - Slave controlled (i.e., input) line, OC - Open Collector to allow wired OR. A bus cycle consists of three periods: an initial period during which pSYNC and status signals are asserted, a middle period during which output data and address lines are stable and wait states can be inserted (using RDY and XRDY lines), and a final period during which actual data transfer takes place. This breakdown corresponds roughly to the Z80's timing (see Sec. 3-1), although the Z80 is substantially simpler, since it doesn't split up its status and control signals.

Pin	Signal & type	Description
1	+8 volts (B)	>7 volts, <25 volts, average <11 volts.
2	+16 volts (B)	>14.5 volts, <35 volts, average <21.5 volts
3	XRDY (S)	Bus is ready when this and pin 72 are high
4	VI0* (S, OC)	Vectored Interrupt line 0
5	VI1* (S, OC)	Vectored Interrupt line 1
6	VI2* (S, OC)	Vectored Interrupt line 2
7	VI3* (S, OC)	Vectored Interrupt line 3
8	VI4* (S, OC)	Vectored Interrupt line 4
9	VI5* (S, OC)	Vectored Interrupt line 5
10	VI6* (S, OC)	Vectored Interrupt line 6
11	VI7* (S, OC)	Vectored Interrupt line 7
12	NMI* (S, OC)	Non-maskable Interrupt
13	PWRFAIL* (B)	Power fail bus signal
14	DMA3* (M, OC)	Temporary master priority bit 3
15	A18 (M)	Extended address bit 18
16	A16 (M)	Extended address bit 16
17	A17 (M)	Extended address bit 17
18	SDSB* (M, OC)	Status DiSaBle (tristate 8 status signals)
19	CDSB* (M, OC)	Control DiSaBle (tristate 5 control signals)
20	GND (B)	Ground - common with pin 100
21	NDEF	Not to be defined
22	ADSB* (M, OC)	Address DiSaBle (tristate A0-A15)
23	DODSB* (M, OC)	Data Out DiSaBle (tristate DO0-DO7)
24	φ (B)	Master timing signal for the bus
25	pSTVAL* (M)	STatus VALid strobe
26	pHLDA (M)	Permanent master relinquishes busses
27	RFU	Reserved for Future Use
28	RFU	Reserved for Future Use
29	A5 (M)	Address bit 5
30	A4 (M)	Address bit 4
31	A3 (M)	Address bit 3
32	A15 (M)	Address bit 15
33	A12 (M)	Address bit 12
34	A9 (M)	Address bit 9
35	DO1 (M), D1 (M/S)	Data Out bit 1, or bidirectional Data bit 1

36	DO0 (M), D0 (M/S)	Data Out bit 0, or bidirectional Data bit 0
37	A10 (M)	Address bit 10
38	DO4 (M), D4 (M/S)	Data bit Out bit 4, or bidirectional Data 4
39	DO5 (M), D5 (M/S)	Data Out bit 5, or bidirectional Data bit 5
40	DO6 (M), D6 (M/S)	Data Out bit 6, or bidirectional Data bit 6
41	DI2 (S), D10 (M/S)	Data In bit 2, or bidirectional Data bit 10
42	DI3 (S), D11 (M/S)	Data In bit 3, or bidirectional Data bit 11
43	DI7 (S), D15 (M/S)	Data In bit 7, or bidirectional Data bit 15
44	sM1 (M)	signals that current cycle is op-code fetch
45	sOUT (M)	signals I/O OUTput bus cycle
46	sINP (M)	signals I/O INput bus cycle
47	sMEMR (M)	signals MEMory Read bus cycle
48	sHLTA (M)	signals that HLT instruction has been executed
49	CLOCK (B)	2 MHz square wave (40-60% duty cycle)
50	GND (B)	Common with pin 100
51	+8 volts (B)	Common with pin 1
52	-16 volts (B)	<-14.5 volts, >-35 volts, average >-21.5 volts
53	GND (B)	Common with pin 100
54	SLAVE CLR* (B, OC)	Reset bus SLAVEs (must be active with POC*)
55	DMA0* (M, OC)	Temporary master priority bit 0
56	DMA1* (M, OC)	Temporary master priority bit 1
57	DMA2* (M, OC)	Temporary master priority bit 2
58	sXTRQ* (M)	ReQuests 16-bit slaves to assert SIXTN*
59	A19 (M)	Extended address bit 19
60	SIXTN* (S, OC)	16-bit slave response to sXTRQ*
61	A20 (M)	Extended address bit 20
62	A21 (M)	Extended address bit 21
63	A22 (M)	Extended address bit 22
64	A23 (M)	Extended address bit 23
65	NDEF	Not to be DEFined
66	NDEF	Not to be DEFined
67	PHANTOM* (M/S, OC)	Disables normal slaves; enables phantom slaves
68	MWRT (M)	Memory WRiTe strobe
69	RFU	Reserved for Future Use
70	GND (B)	Common with pin 100
71	RFU	Reserved for Future Use
72	RDY (S, OC)	Bus is ready when this and pin 3 are high
73	INT* (S, OC)	Primary INTerrupt request signal
74	HOLD* (M, OC)	Requests permanent master to relinquish busses
75	RESET* (B, OC)	RESET bus masters (must be active with POC*)
76	pSYNC (M)	Signals start of new bus cycle
77	pWR* (M)	Signals valid data is being output
78	pDBIN (M)	Signals data is to be input
79	A0 (M)	Address bit 0
80	A1 (M)	Address bit 1
81	A2 (M)	Address bit 2
82	A6 (M)	Address bit 6

83	A7 (M)	Address bit 7
84	A8 (M)	Address bit 8
85	A13 (M)	Address bit 13
86	A14 (M)	Address bit 14
87	A11 (M)	Address bit 11
88	DO2 (M), D2 (M/S)	Data Out bit 2, or bidirectional Data bit 2
89	DO3 (M), D3 (M/S)	Data Out bit 3, or bidirectional Data bit 3
90	DO7 (M), D7 (M/S)	Data Out bit 7, or bidirectional Data bit 7
91	DI4 (S), D12 (M/S)	Data In bit 4, or bidirectional Data bit 12
92	DI5 (S), D13 (M/S)	Data In bit 5, or bidirectional Data bit 13
93	DI6 (S), D14 (M/S)	Data In bit 6, or bidirectional Data bit 14
94	DI1 (S), D9 (M/S)	Data In bit 1, or bidirectional Data bit 9
95	DI0 (S), D8 (M/S)	Data In bit 0, or bidirectional Data bit 8
96	sINTA (M)	INTerrupt Acknowlege (inputs data)
97	sWO* (M)	Signals data to be output this bus cycle
98	ERROR* (S, OC)	Signals bus error during present cycle
99	POC* (B)	Power On Clear (>10 msec)
100	GND (B)	System ground

B-2. TRS-80 Bus Definitions

The TRS-80 Model I has a 40-pin edge connector allowing its CPU bus to be connected to external devices. The definitions of these pins are similar to the Z80's, but differ in some important respects (egs., use of OUT* and IN* in place of $\overline{IORQ}$ combined with $\overline{WR}$ and $\overline{RD}$, respectively). The pin definitions are:

Pin	Signal	Description
1	RAS*	Row Address Strobe Output (for 4116 RAMS)
2	SYSRES*	SYStem RESet output (low for POC*/reset pushed
3	CAS*	Column Address Strobe Output (for 4116 RAMS)
4	A10	Address bit 10
5	A12	Address bit 12
6	A13	Address bit 13
7	A15	Address bit 15
8	GND	Signal ground
9	A11	Address bit 11
10	A14	Address bit 14
11	A8	Address bit 8
12	OUT*	Peripheral Write Strobe Output
13	WR*	Memory Read Strobe Output
14	INTAK*	INTerrupt AcKnowledge Signal
15	RD*	Memory ReaD Strobe Output
16	MUX	MUltipleXor Control output for 4116 RAMs
17	A9	Address bit 9
18	D4	Bidirectional data bit 4

19	IN*	Peripheral Read Strobe Output
20	D7	Bidirectional data bit 7
21	INT*	$\overline{INT}$
22	D1	Bidirectional data bit 1
23	TEST*	$\overline{BUSRQ}$
24	D6	Bidirectional data bit 6
25	A0	Address bit 0
26	D3	Bidirectional data bit 3
27	A1	Address bit 1
28	D5	Bidirectional data bit 5
29	GND	Signal ground
30	D0	Bidirectional data bit 0
31	A4	Address bit 4
32	D2	Bidirectional data bit 2
33	WAIT*	$\overline{WAIT}$
34	A3	A3 Address bit 3
35	A5	Address bit 5
36	A7	Address bit 7
37	GND	Signal Ground
38	A6	Address bit 6
39	GND	(+5 v on early models)
40	A2	Address bit 2

B-3. STD Bus Definitions

The STD bus is an ideal bus for the Z80. It has enough lines to amply support all control, address and data lines, as well as useful power lines and distributed grounds. Disadvantages, perhaps, include that it is inadequate for 16-bit CPU's and that the largest voltages on the backplane are $\pm$ 12 volts. It's definitions are:

Pin	Signal	Description
1	+5 volts	+5 v dc system power
2	+5 volts	+5 v dc system power
3	GND	System signal ground and dc return
4	GND	System signal ground and dc return
5	-5 volts	-5 v dc system power
6	-5 volts	-5 v dc system power
7	D3	D0-D7 are a bidirectional data bus
8	D7	for data exchange with memory and
9	D2	I/O devices (same as Z80's D0-D7)
10	D6	
11	D1	
12	D5	
13	D0	
14	D4	

15	A7	A0-A15 are a tristate address bus
16	A15	(same as Z80's A0-A15)
17	A6	
18	A14	
19	A5	
20	A13	
21	A4	
22	A12	
23	A3	
24	A11	
25	A2	
26	A10	
27	A1	
28	A9	
29	A0	
30	A8	
31	$\overline{\text{WR}}$	Write (same as Z80's)
32	$\overline{\text{RD}}$	Read (same as Z80's)
33	$\overline{\text{IORQ}}$	I/O Request (same as Z80's)
34	$\overline{\text{MEMRQ}}$	Memory request (same as Z80's)
35	$\overline{\text{IOEXP}}$	I/O Expansion
36	$\overline{\text{MEMEX}}$	Memory Expansion
37	$\overline{\text{RFSH}}$	Refresh (same as Z80's)
38	$\overline{\text{DEBUG}}$	Used to implement hardware single step
39	$\overline{\text{M1}}$	Machine cycle 1 (same as Z80's)
40	Status 0	
41	$\overline{\text{BUSAK}}$	Bus acknowledge (same as Z80's)
42	$\overline{\text{BUSRQ}}$	Bus request (same as Z80's)
43	$\overline{\text{INTAK}}$	Interrupt acknowledge
44	$\overline{\text{INT}}$	Maskable Interrupt request (same as Z80's)
45	$\overline{\text{WAIT}}$	Wait request (same as Z80's)
46	$\overline{\text{NMI}}$	Nonmaskable Interrupt request (same as Z80's)
47	$\overline{\text{SYSRESET}}$	System reset
48	$\overline{\text{PBRESET}}$	Push button (debounced) reset
49	$\overline{\text{CLOCK}}$	Inverted Z80 ϕ
50	$\overline{\text{CNTRL}}$	Auxiliary timing
51	PCO	Interrupt Priority daisy-Chain Output
52	PCI	Interrupt Priority daisy-Chain Input
53	AUX GND	Auxiliary ground (Bussed)
54	AUX GND	Auxiliary ground (Bussed)
55	+12 volts	+12 v dc system power
56	-12 volts	-12 v dc system power

Appendix C

Computer-Computer Communications - TRSCOM

In this appendix, we present a computer-computer communications program, called TRSCOM. Its use is discussed in Exercise 14 of Sec. 8-9, and the philosophy behind programs of this sort is discussed in Sec. 5-4. As written, the program is setup to run on a TRS-80. However, the TRS-80 dependent parts of the program have all been written as subroutines and clearly marked as hardware-dependent. By simply changing these few subroutines, TRSCOM can be run on any other computer system.

TRSCOM allows the computer system to simulate a terminal and to send files (computer programs) to, or receive files from, another computer. If the other computer is a large machine, the Read and Write commands can be used to receive and send ASCII text files or assembly-language source code. For use with small controllers TRSCOM also has Load and Save commands that receive and send machine-language programs. A detailed description of how to use the commands is contained in the program header. An appreciable number of the subroutines are taken from the DEMON monitor (App. D) and could be eliminated if the two packages are combined. This program along with the DEMON monitor is available on cassette tape or CP/M 8" single-density diskette from Scroll Systems, Inc. See the introduction to App. D for details.

The listing that follows was produced by the Microsoft macroassembler with the aid of a couple of MATE edit macros. Note that relocatable code has been produced. For the TRS-80 model I, the code should be relocated to anywhere in RAM above 4380H.

TITLE TRS-80 COMMUNICATIONS PROGRAM 7-DEC-80
.Z80
PAGE 60
0010 .RADIX 16

.comment ¶ --- TRSCOM ---

This program allows communication with a remote host computer using a TRS-80 as a CRT terminal. It also allows easy transfer of files back and forth between the two computers. The following commands are implemented:

1. **(cr)** allows transparent communication with the host computer. (cr) is the ENTER key on the TRS-80. Pressing BREAK at any time returns the user to TRSCOM.

2. **Rstring$addr(cr)** reads an ASCII file from the host computer into the TRS-80 memory. "string" indicates the command string necessary to tell the host to type out a file. The string is terminated by pressing BREAK which echoes as a $. "addr" is the starting address in the TRS-80 where you wish to load the file. After the file has been loaded into the TRS-80, pressing the BREAK key will produce a return to TRSCOM.

3. **Wstring$addr,addr(cr)** writes an ASCII file in the TRS-80 to the host computer. "string" represents the command string necessary to tell the host to copy a file from the console. "addr,addr" is the start and end address of the file in the TRS-80.

4. **Lstring$addr(cr)** loads a machine language memory image from the host into the TRS-80. "string" represents the command string necessary to tell the host to display the desired block of memory in the format of the DEMON "D" command; i.e. each byte is given as two ASCII characters, with a space character (20H) between bytes. In all other respects the "L" command works like the "R" command.

5. **Sstring$addr,addr(cr)** saves a block of TRS-80 memory by sending it to the host computer. "string" is the command string necessary to tell the host to copy data from the console. The data is sent in the format of the DEMON "D" command. "addr,addr" is the start and end address of TRS-80 memory block to be saved.

6. **Jaddr(cr)** jumps out of TRSCOM to any desired user or system program located at "addr".

After a file has been shipped to the host using the "W" command, the file should be closed by typing (cr)(eof), where (eof) is the end of file character for the host computer's operating system. ¶

; External addresses

```
0033                    DISPLY  EQU   0033    ;TRS-80 ROM display routine
002B                    KYSCAN  EQU   002B    ;keyboard ROM
```

; Symbols and I/O ports

```
000D                    CR      EQU   0D      ;carriage return
000A                    LF      EQU   0A      ;line feed
0001                    BREAK   EQU   01      ;BREAK key -> local mode
0020                    MIN     EQU   20      ;modem input port
0020                    MOUT    EQU   20      ;modem output port
0021                    MSTAT   EQU   21      ;modem status port
0002                    MDA     EQU   02      ;Receiver ready mask
0001                    MBE     EQU   01      ;Xmitter buffer empty mask
```

```
0000'  CD 009E'         TRSCOM: CALL  INIT    ;initialize screen and USART
0003'  21 0228'                 LD    HL,SIGNON ;print sign-on message
0006'  CD 021D'                 CALL. MESSAG  ;then put return
0009'  21 0000'                 LD    HL,TRSCOM ;address on stack
000C'  E5                       PUSH  HL
000D'  CD 00E2'                 CALL  CI      ;get first char typed
0010'  4F                       LD    C,A
0011'  CD 00EF'                 CALL  CO      ;echo it
0014'  FE 0D                    CP    CR      ;is it (cr)?
0016'  28 19                    JR    Z,REMOTE ;yes, go talk to host
0018'  FE 52                    CP    "R"     ;is it R?
001A'  28 32                    JR    Z,READ  ;yes, read file from host
001C'  FE 57                    CP    "W"     ;is it W?
001E'  CA 007B'                 JP    Z,WRITE ;yes, write file to host
0021'  FE 4C                    CP    "L"     ;is it L?
0023'  CA 017C'                 JP    Z,LOAD  ;yes, load file from host
0026'  FE 53                    CP    "S"     ;is it S?
0028'  CA 01CC'                 JP    Z,SAVE  ;yes, save file on host
002B'  FE 4A                    CP    "J"     ;is it J?
002D'  CA 0091'                 JP    Z,JUMP  ;yes, exit to user program
0030'  C9                       RET           ;no match, must be error
```

;Basic modem loop

```
0031'  CD 00CD'         REMOTE: CALL  MSTS    ;char waiting from host?
0034'  28 07                    JR    Z,KEYBRD ;no, go check keyboard
0036'  CD 00BE'                 CALL  MI      ;else get character
0039'  4F                       LD    C,A
003A'  CD 00EF'                 CALL  CO      ;and echo it
003D'  CD 00E8'         KEYBRD: CALL  CSTS    ;char waiting at keyboard?
0040'  28 EF                    JR    Z,REMOTE ;no, start loop over
0042'  CD 00E7'                 CALL  KI      ;yes, get the char
0045'  FE 01                    CP    BREAK   ;is it ⊙R?
0047'  C8                       RET   Z       ;yes, return to TRSCOM
0048'  4F                       LD    C,A     ;send char to host
0049'  CD 00D8'                 CALL  MO
004C'  18 E3                    JR    REMOTE  ;back to start of loop
```

;Read and write ASCII file routines

```
004E'   CD 0096'   READ:    CALL   STRING     ;send command string to host
0051'   CD 0129'            CALL   EXPR1      ;get start addr for loading
0054'   E1                  POP    HL
0055'   0E  0D              LD     C,CR       ;send a (cr) to host
0057'   CD 00D8'            CALL   MO
005A'   CD 011F'            CALL   CRLF       ;echo it
005D'   CD 00CD'   NEXT:    CALL   MSTS       ;host char waiting?
0060'   28  09              JR     Z,NOCHAR   ;no, go check keyboard
0062'   CD 00BE'            CALL   MI         ;yes, get the char
0065'   77                  LD     (HL),A     ;store the char
0066'   4F                  LD     C,A
0067'   CD 00EF'            CALL   CO         ;echo it
006A'   23                  INC    HL         ;advance pointer
006B'   CD 00E8'   NOCHAR:  CALL   CSTS       ;keyboard char waiting?
006E'   28  ED              JR     Z,NEXT     ;no, go back for next char
0070'   CD 00E7'            CALL   KI
0073'   FE  01              CP     BREAK      ;see if BREAK key
0075'   C8                  RET    Z          ;and return to TRSCOM if so
0076'   CD 0106'            CALL   MLIST      ;else send char to host
0079'   18  E2              JR     NEXT       ;and get next char

007B'   CD 0096'   WRITE:   CALL   STRING     ;send command string to host
007E'   0E  0D              LD     C,CR       ;send (cr) to host
0080'   CD 00D8'            CALL   MO
0083'   0E  02              LD     C,2        ;get start and end addresses
0085'   CD 011A'            CALL   EXLF
0088'   4E         MORE:    LD     C,(HL)     ;get a char from memory
0089'   CD 0106'            CALL   MLIST      ;send it to host
008C'   CD 0150'            CALL   HILOX      ;inc HL and exit if at end
008F'   18  F7              JR     MORE       ;else go back for next char

0091'   CD 0129'   JUMP:    CALL   EXPR1      ;get starting address
0094'   E1                  POP    HL
0095'   E9                  JP     (HL)       ;jump to it

0096'   CD 0031'   STRING:  CALL   REMOTE     ;send char string to host
0099'   0E  24              LD     C,"$"      ;echo a $ when done
009B'   C3 00EF'            JP     CO         ;output "$" and return
```

;MACHINE-DEPENDENT ROUTINES START HERE
; TRS-80 and USART initialization

```
009E'   3E  1C     INIT:    LD     A,1C       ;cursor → upper left corner
00A0'   CD 0033             CALL   DISPLY
00A3'   3E  1F              LD     A,1F       ;clear the screen
00A5'   CD 0033             CALL   DISPLY
00A8'   3E  0E              LD     A,0E       ;turn on cursor character
00AA'   CD 0033             CALL   DISPLY
00AD'   3E  BE              LD     A,0BE      ;put 8251 in command mode
00AF'   D3  21              OUT    (MSTAT),A
00B1'   3E  40              LD     A,40       ;reset it
00B3'   D3  21              OUT    (MSTAT),A
00B5'   3E  4E              LD     A,4E       ;set for 8 bits, no parity
```

```
00B7'   D3 21              OUT    (MSTAT),A
00B9'   3E 37              LD     A,37          ;enable transmit and receive
00BB'   D3 21              OUT    (MSTAT),A
00BD'   C9                 RET
```

; modem input, status, and output routines

```
00BE'   DB 21       MI:    IN     A,(MSTAT) ;is char waiting?
00C0'   E6 02              AND    MDA
00C2'   28 FA              JR     Z,MI          ;no, check again
00C4'   DB 20              IN     A,(MIN)       ;input char
00C6'   E6 7F              AND    7F            ;kill high bit
00C8'   FE 00              CP     00            ;filter out nulls
00CA'   28 F2              JR     Z,MI
00CC'   C9                 RET
```

```
00CD'   DB 21       MSTS:  IN     A,(MSTAT) ;check modem input status
00CF'   E6 02              AND    MDA
00D1'   3E 00              LD     A,00          ;return zero if no char
00D3'   28 01              JR     Z,CSRET
00D5'   2F                 CPL                  ;return 0FF otherwise
00D6'   B7          CSRET: OR     A
00D7'   C9                 RET
```

```
00D8'   DB 21       MO:    IN     A,(MSTAT) ;check modem output status
00DA'   E6 01              AND    MBE
00DC'   28 FA              JR     Z,MO          ;loop until modem ready
00DE'   79                 LD     A,C           ;then send char
00DF'   D3 20              OUT    (MOUT),A
00E1'   C9                 RET
```

; console input, status, and output routines

```
00E2'   CD 00E8'    CI:    CALL   CSTS          ;loop till a key pressed
00E5'   28 FB              JR     Z,CI
00E7'   C9          KI:    RET                  ;then return with value
```

.comment¶ On most machines, KI and CI will be identical input routines. With the TRS-80, however, the console status routine returns the value of the key, if one is pressed, and we can simply use that value when console status is called just before console input. In the places where this is done, a dummy routine KI is inserted so that the structure of the routines will be unaltered when using them on another type of computer. On the TRS-80, the sequence

```
            CALL   CSTS
            JR     Z,ELSEWHERE
            CALL   CI
```

causes problems because KYSCAN (used in CSTS and CI) is entered after a key has already been pressed.¶

```
00E8'   D5          CSTS:  PUSH   DE            ;Console status routine
00E9'   CD 002B            CALL   KYSCAN        ;use TRS-80 routine
```

```
00EC'  B7                   OR    A          ;set A=0 if no key down
00ED'  D1                   POP   DE
00EE'  C9                   RET

00EF'  79            CO:    LD    A,C        ;Console output routine
00F0'  FE 0A                CP    LF         ;don't echo line feeds
00F2'  C8                   RET   Z
00F3'  D5                   PUSH  DE
00F4'  CD 0033              CALL  DISPLY     ;use TRS-80 display routine
00F7'  D1                   POP   DE
00F8'  C9                   RET
```

;END OF MACHINE-DEPENDENT ROUTINES

```
00F9'  CD 00E2'      TI:    CALL  CI         ;get a character
00FC'  FE 0D                CP    CR         ;don't echo (cr)
00FE'  C8                   RET   Z
00FF'  C5                   PUSH  BC
0100'  4F                   LD    C,A
0101'  CD 00EF'             CALL  CO         ;echo everything else
0104'  C1                   POP   BC
0105'  C9                   RET

0106'  CD 00D8'      MLIST: CALL  MO         ;send character
0109'  CD 00BE'             CALL  MI         ;look for echo from host
010C'  4F                   LD    C,A
010D'  C3 00EF'             JP    CO         ;output character and return
```

; convert hex number in A to ASCII

```
0110'  E6 0F         CONV:  AND   0FH        ;ensure a single hex digit
0112'  C6 90                ADD   A,90       ;add 90H using BCD
0114'  27                   DAA              ; arithmetic
0115'  CE 40                ADC   A,40       ;then 40H plus CY
0117'  27                   DAA
0118'  4F                   LD    C,A        ;stick result in C
0119'  C9                   RET
```

; routines to get parameters from the keyboard

```
011A'  CD 012B'      EXLF:  CALL  EXPR       ;get 2 parameters
011D'  D1                   POP   DE         ;pop them off stack
011E'  E1                   POP   HL
011F'  0E 0D         CRLF:  LD    C,CR       ;sending (cr) to TRS-80 does
0121'  CD 00EF'             CALL  CO         ;both a (cr) and a (lf)
0124'  0E 0A                LD    C,LF
0126'  C3 00EF'             JP    CO         ;output LF and return

0129'  0E 01         EXPR1: LD    C,1        ;get one parameter
012B'  21 0000       EXPR:  LD    HL,0       ;initialize HL to zero
012E'  CD 00F9'      EX0:   CALL  TI         ;get char from console
0131'  47            EX1:   LD    B,A        ;save it
0132'  CD 0160'             CALL  NIBBLE     ;convert ASCII to hex
0135'  38 08                JR    C,..EX2    ;jump out if not hex number
0137'  29                   ADD   HL,HL      ;shift HL one nibble left
```

```
0138'   29                      ADD     HL,HL
0139'   29                      ADD     HL,HL
013A'   29                      ADD     HL,HL
013B'   B5                      OR      L           ;OR in new character
013C'   6F                      LD      L,A
013D'   18 EF                   JR      EX0         ;go back for more
013F'   E3          ..EX2:      EX      (SP),HL     ;put value on stack
0140'   E5                      PUSH    HL          ;followed by return address
0141'   78                      LD      A,B         ;see if char is a delimiter
0142'   CD 0170'                CALL    QCHK
0145'   30 02                   JR      NC,..EX3    ;jump if not (cr)
0147'   0D                      DEC     C           ;if (cr) entered & C=0
0148'   C8                      RET     Z           ; done. Else error,
0149'   C2 0000'    ..EX3:      JP      NZ,TRSCOM   ; so restart TRSCOM
014C'   0D                      DEC     C           ;got enough params yet?
014D'   20 DC                   JR      NZ,EXPR     ;no, go back for more
014F'   C9                      RET
```

; Range test: inc HL and compare to DE

```
0150'   CD 0156'    HILOX:      CALL    HILO        ;test for end of range
0153'   D0                      RET     NC          ;not reached, normal return
0154'   D1                      POP     DE          ;end of range, return one
0155'   C9                      RET                 ; level back
0156'   23          HILO:       INC     HL          ;advance pointer
0157'   7C                      LD      A,H
0158'   B5                      OR      L
0159'   37                      SCF                 ;return with CY set if HL=0
015A'   C8                      RET     Z
015B'   7B                      LD      A,E         ;compare HL with DE
015C'   95                      SUB     L
015D'   7A                      LD      A,D
015E'   9C                      SBC     A,H         ;set CY if DE<HL
015F'   C9                      RET
```

; Convert ASCII to hex. Set CY if non-hex input

```
0160'   D6 30       NIBBLE:     SUB     '0'
0162'   D8                      RET     C           ;set CY if <0
0163'   FE 17                   CP      'G'-'0'     ;set CY if >F
0165'   3F                      CCF
0166'   D8                      RET     C
0167'   FE 10                   CP      10          ;if 0-9, reset CY and return
0169'   3F                      CCF
016A'   D0                      RET     NC
016B'   D6 07                   SUB     'A'-'9'-1   ;else adjust value
016D'   FE 0A                   CP      0A          ;and set CY if : thru @
016F'   C9                      RET
```

; test for delimiters

```
0170'   FE 20       QCHK:       CP      ' '         ;set Z flag if space
0172'   C8                      RET     Z
0173'   FE 2C                   CP      ','         ;set Z flag if comma
0175'   C8                      RET     Z
```

```
0176'   FE 0D              CP    CR         ;set carry if (cr)
0178'   37                 SCF
0179'   C8                 RET   Z
017A'   3F                 CCF              ;else return Z=0 and CY=0
017B'   C9                 RET
```

;Load and save binary image routines

```
017C'   CD 0096'   LOAD:   CALL  STRING     ;send command string to host
017F'   CD 0129'           CALL  EXPR1      ;get start addr for loading
0182'   E1                 POP   HL
0183'   0E 0D              LD    C,CR       ;send (cr) to host
0185'   CD 00D8'           CALL  MO
0188'   CD 011F'           CALL  CRLF       ;echo it
018B'   06 00              LD    B,00       ;B holds count for nibbles
018D'   CD 00CD'   NXT:    CALL  MSTS       ;host char waiting?
0190'   28 0A              JR    Z,NOCHR    ;no, go check keyboard
0192'   CD 00BE'           CALL  MI         ;else get the char
0195'   4F                 LD    C,A
0196'   CD 00EF'           CALL  CO         ;echo it
0199'   CD 01AC'           CALL  STORE      ;and store it
019C'   CD 00E8'   NOCHR:  CALL  CSTS       ;keyboard char waiting?
019F'   28 EC              JR    Z,NXT      ;if not, get next modem char
01A1'   CD 00E7'           CALL  KI
01A4'   FE 01              CP    BREAK      ;see if BREAK key
01A6'   C8                 RET   Z          ;and return to TRSCOM if so
01A7'   CD 0106'           CALL  MLIST      ;else send char to host
01AA'   18 E1              JR    NXT        ;and get next char

01AC'   FE 20      STORE:  CP    " "        ;if " " initialize B to 2
01AE'   28 08              JR    Z,SETB
01B0'   05                 DEC   B          ;B=1 ==> 2nd nibble of byte
01B1'   28 12              JR    Z,NIBBL2
01B3'   05                 DEC   B          ;B=2 ==> 1st nibble of byte
01B4'   28 05              JR    Z,NIBBL1
01B6'   04                 INC   B
01B7'   C9                 RET
01B8'   06 02      SETB:   LD    B,02
01BA'   C9                 RET

01BB'   CD 0160'   NIBBL1: CALL  NIBBLE     ;convert ASCII to hex
01BE'   07                 RLCA             ;rotate into high nibble
01BF'   07                 RLCA
01C0'   07                 RLCA
01C1'   07                 RLCA
01C2'   57                 LD    D,A        ;and save in D
01C3'   04                 INC   B          ;restore B=1
01C4'   C9                 RET

01C5'   CD 0160'   NIBBL2: CALL  NIBBLE     ;convert ASCII to hex
01C8'   B2                 OR    D          ;OR in 1st nibble
01C9'   77                 LD    (HL),A     ;store in memory
01CA'   23                 INC   HL         ;and advance pointer
01CB'   C9                 RET
```

```
01CC'  CD 0096'   SAVE:   CALL  STRING    ;send command string to host
01CF'  0E 0D              LD    C,CR      ;send (cr) to host
01D1'  CD 00D8'           CALL  MO
01D4'  0E 02              LD    C,02      ;get start and end addresses
01D6'  CD 011A'           CALL  EXLF
01D9'  CD 01F7'   SV1:    CALL  LFADR     ;send (cr)(lf) and address
01DC'  CD 0204'   SV2:    CALL  BLK       ;send a blank space
01DF'  7E                 LD    A,(HL)    ;send next byte
01E0'  CD 020E'           CALL  LBYTE
01E3'  CD 0156'           CALL  HILO      ;set CY if end reached
01E6'  38 07              JR    C,EXIT
01E8'  7D                 LD    A,L       ;time for new line?
01E9'  E6 0F              AND   0F
01EB'  20 EF              JR    NZ,SV2    ;no, get another byte
01ED'  18 EA              JR    SV1       ;yes, start a new line
01EF'  CD 011F'   EXIT:   CALL  CRLF
01F2'  0E 3E              LD    C,">"     ;output end of file character
01F4'  C3 0106'           JP    MLIST     ; and return

01F7'  0E 0D      LFADR:  LD    C,CR      ;send and display (cr)
01F9'  CD 0106'           CALL  MLIST
01FC'  0E 0A              LD    C,LF      ;send (lf)
01FE'  CD 00D8'           CALL  MO
0201'  CD 0209'           CALL  LADR      ;send and display address
0204'  0E 20      BLK:    LD    C," "     ;followed by a space
0206'  C3 0106'           JP    MLIST

0209'  7C         LADR:   LD    A,H       ;send and display H
020A'  CD 020E'           CALL  LBYTE
020D'  7D                 LD    A,L       ;do same for L
020E'  F5         LBYTE:  PUSH  AF        ;save byte
020F'  0F                 RRCA            ;put high nibble into low
0210'  0F                 RRCA
0211'  0F                 RRCA
0212'  0F                 RRCA
0213'  CD 0217'           CALL  LB1       ;output it
0216'  F1                 POP   AF        ;now do low nibble
0217'  CD 0110'   LB1:    CALL  CONV      ;convert hex to ASCII
021A'  C3 0106'           JP    MLIST     ;send it and echo on console
```

; routine to display a message on console

```
021D'  7E         MESSAG: LD    A,(HL)    ;get character from memory
021E'  FE 00              CP    00        ;all done if it's a null
0220'  C8                 RET   Z
0221'  4F                 LD    C,A
0222'  CD 00EF'           CALL  CO        ;else output it and
0225'  23                 INC   HL        ; advance to next character
0226'  18 F5              JR    MESSAG

0228'  54 52 53 43  SIGNON: DB  'TRSCOM: TRS-80 Smart Terminal '
0246'  50 72 6F 67          DB  'Program',CR,CR
024F'  45 6E 74 65          DB  'Enter one of the following:',CR,CR
026C'  28 63 72 29          DB  '(cr) gives transparent communications '
0292'  77 69 74 68          DB  'with host',CR
```

```
029C'   52 73 74 72    DB    'Rstring$addr(cr) reads an ASCII file '
02C1'   69 6E 74 6F    DB    'into TRS-80',CR
02CD'   57 73 74 72    DB    'Wstring$addr,addr(cr) writes an ASCII '
02F3'   66 69 6C 65    DB    'file to host',CR
0300'   4C 73 74 72    DB    'Lstring$addr(cr) loads a memory image '
0326'   64 75 6D 70    DB    'dump into TRS-80',CR
0337'   53 73 74 72    DB    'Sstring$addr,addr(cr) writes a memory '
035D'   69 6D 61 67    DB    'image to host',CR
036B'   4A 61 64 64    DB    'Jaddr(cr) jumps out of TRSCOM',CR,CR
038A'   00             DB    0              ;end of message

                       END
```

Appendix D

The DEMON Monitor

This appendix presents the DEMON, a DEbug MONitor based on the 2K TDL Zapple monitor. Although TDL (Technical Design Labs) no longer exists, updated versions of the TDL software are available from Computer Design Labs and from Phoenix Software Associates (see pp. 184-186 for company addresses). DEMON provides facilities for examining and modifying the contents of memory locations in hex, and displaying, moving, filling, and verifying memory blocks. Input/Output ports can be read and written, and the Z80's registers can be examined and modified. Memory can be loaded from and unloaded to a remote computer. A go command is provided that allows one to jump to a user program and set up to two breakpoints. The DEMON code is ROMable, that is, it doesn't modify itself and can be put into EPROM.

DEMON works as listed here for the SD Starter System, but by changing some initial addresses and the CI, CO, CSTS, and INIT routines, it can be run on any Z80 computer. The appropriate routines for the TRS-80 are given in the TRSCOM listing in App. C. The listing is given as relocatable code. For an EPROM Starter-System version, it should be relocated to 800H.

Both source listings and machine code for expanded versions of the software listed in Appendices C thru F can be purchased from Scroll Systems (see p. 186 for address). SD Z80 Starter System versions containing DEMON and the keypad/display routines are available on cassette ($25) and in EPROM ($35). TRS-80 versions of TRSCOM and DEMON are available on TRS-80 cassette ($25). Source code and Microsoft relocatable machine code are available for all the software on CP/M 8" single-density IBM-compatible diskette ($25).

```
                            TITLE    DEMON Monitor for Z80 Starter System   27-NOV-80
                            .Z80
                            PAGE 60
0010                        .RADIX   16       ;all numbers here are hexadecimal

                            ;     DEMON MONITOR V1.0

                            ;External addresses (For a TRS-80 with 16K memory
                            ;use RST7=4012, RAM=4380, DISPO=7FF0, MEMSIZ=7FCC).

23D3                        RST7     EQU     23D3       ;RST7 instruction jumps here
2000                        RAM      EQU     2000       ;start of RAM memory
23F0                        DISPO    EQU     23F0       ;current display address ptr
23CC                        MEMSIZ   EQU     23CC       ;top of register storage area

                            ;I/O ports and predefined values STS-DIGLH can be
                            ;dropped for machines other than the Starter System).

0021                        STS      EQU     21         ;console status port
0020                        DATA     EQU     20         ;console data port
0086                        CTC2     EQU     86         ;Z80 CTC channel 2
008C                        DIGLH    EQU     8C         ;MON key intrpt enable port
000D                        CR       EQU     0D         ;carriage return char
000A                        LF       EQU     0A         ;line feed char
00EF                        PGLEN    EQU     0EF        ;page length for D command


                            ; Start the movie

0000'   21 23CC    BEGIN:   LD      HL,MEMSIZ  ;point SP at to
0003'   F9                  LD      SP,HL      ;of register storage area
0004'   EB                  EX      DE,HL      ;save stack value
0005'   01 0023             LD      BC,ENDX-EXIT ;move exit program into
0008'   21 03C1'            LD      HL,EXIT    ;RAM above register
000B'   ED B0               LDIR               ;storage
000D'   EB                  EX      DE,HL      ;restore stack value
000E'   01 FFA1             LD      BC,-5F     ;set up user's SP value
0011'   09                  ADD     HL,BC
0012'   E5                  PUSH    HL         ;and put in storage area
0013'   21 0000             LD      HL,0       ;user register values = 0
0016'   06 0A               LD      B,0A
0018'   E5         STKIT:   PUSH    HL         ;and put them in storage area
0019'   10 FD               DJNZ    STKIT      ; too
001B'   CD 02CF'            CALL    INIT       ;init keybrd interrupts, USART
001E'   21 2000    HELLO:   LD      HL,RAM     ;set display address to
0021'   22 23F0             LD      (DISPO),HL ; start of RAM
0024'   06 17               LD      B,MSGL     ;say hello to the folks
0026'   CD 0286'            CALL    TOM
0029'   11 0029'   START:   LD      DE,START   ;main loop begins here
002C'   D5                  PUSH    DE         ;set up a return to START
002D'   CD 031B'            CALL    CRLF
0030'   0E 3E               LD      C,'>'      ;output a prompt
0032'   CD 02B2'            CALL    CO
```

```
;
;
.comment¶ In small controllers where the DEMON monitor is
placed in EPROM starting at location 0, insert a jump to
RESTAR at location 0038 and a jump around locations 38-3A
at location 0035.¶
;
```

0035'	CD 02F2'	STAR0:	CALL	TI	;get a console character
0038'	D6 41		SUB	'A'	;see if its a letter
003A'	D8		RET	C	;start over if less than "A"
003B'	FE 1A		CP	'Z'-'A'+1	
003D'	D0		RET	NC	;or greater than "Z"
003E'	87		ADD	A,A	;multiply by 2
003F'	21 004B'		LD	HL,TBL	;point to command table
0042'	85		ADD	A,L	;add in offset
0043'	6F		LD	L,A	
0044'	7E		LD	A,(HL)	;get command start address
0045'	23		INC	HL	
0046'	66		LD	H,(HL)	
0047'	6F		LD	L,A	;finally have it
0048'	0E 02		LD	C,2	;set up default value for EXPR
004A'	E9		JP	(HL)	;jump to command

```
                    ; Command jump table
```

004B'	029A'	TBL:	DW	ERROR	;A -
004D'	029A'		DW	ERROR	;B -
004F'	029A'		DW	ERROR	;C -
0051'	007F'		DW	DISP	;Display memory in hex
0053'	029A'		DW	ERROR	;E -
0055'	00C0'		DW	FILL	;Fill memory with a constant
0057'	00CD'		DW	GOTO	;Go to user program
0059'	029A'		DW	ERROR	;H -
005B'	029A'		DW	ERROR	;I -
005D'	029A'		DW	ERROR	;J -
005F'	029A'		DW	ERROR	;K -
0061'	011B'		DW	LOAD	;Load memory from USART
0063'	014B'		DW	MOVE	;Move a block of memory
0065'	029A'		DW	ERROR	;N -
0067'	029A'		DW	ERROR	;O -
0069'	029A'		DW	ERROR	;P -
006B'	016F'		DW	QUERY	;Query I/O port (do I/O)
006D'	029A'		DW	ERROR	;R -
006F'	019A'		DW	SUBS	;Substitute/examine memory
0071'	029A'		DW	ERROR	;T -
0073'	029A'		DW	ERROR	;U - ("D" Unloads memory)
0075'	01C3'		DW	VERIFY	;Verify two blocks of memory
0077'	029A'		DW	ERROR	;W -
0079'	01E7'		DW	XAM	;Xamine/modify Z80 registers
007B'	029A'		DW	ERROR	;Y -
007D'	029A'		DW	ERROR	;Z -

;comment¶ **DISPLAY COMMAND** - displays the contents of memory in hex. Sixteen bytes of memory are displayed per line with the starting address of the line given as the first entry on the line. For example,

D100,200(cr) [note: (cr)=carriage return]

displays memory from address 100H to address 200H inclusive, and

D2000(cr)

displays one screenful of memory starting at address 2000H. Just typing D(cr) will display a screenful of memory starting at the last memory location displayed by a previous D command. A display in progress can be aborted by typing a ©S (control S).

In forming an address, the keyboard input routine uses only the last four most recently typed hex digits. Thus typing D12342000(cr) is equivalent to typing D2000(cr). This feature applies to all commands and is useful for correcting mistakes. Also, omitting an address is equivalent to entering 0000, e.g., entering D,2000(cr) displays memory from 0 through 2000H. Finally, any command can be aborted while it is being entered by typing a non-valid hex digit.¶

;

```
007F'   CD 032E'   DISP:    CALL   GET1          ;look for one parameter
0082'   38 11               JR     C,..D1        ;skip ahead if one entered
0084'   FE 0D               CP     CR
0086'   20 14               JR     NZ,..D2       ;skip ahead if not CR
0088'   33                  INC    SP            ;clean stack if it is CR
0089'   33                  INC    SP
008A'   ED 5B 23F0          LD     DE,(DISPO)    ;and get start from DISPO
008E'   21 00EF    ..D0:    LD     HL,PGLEN      ;get default length
0091'   19                  ADD    HL,DE         ;calc end address
0092'   EB                  EX     DE,HL
0093'   18 0F               JR     DISPIT        ;display the page
0095'   FE 0D      ..D1:    CP     CR            ;CR?
0097'   20 03               JR     NZ,..D2       ;if not, get 2nd parameter
0099'   D1                  POP    DE            ;else pop start address
009A'   18 F2               JR     ..D0          ;and use default length
009C'   CD 032E'   ..D2:    CALL   GET1          ;look for 2nd parameter
009F'   D2 029A'            JP     NC,ERROR      ;error if none entered
00A2'   D1                  POP    DE            ;pop both parameters
00A3'   E1                  POP    HL
00A4'   CD 02AA'   DISPIT:  CALL   LFADR         ;print CRLF and address
00A7'   CD 02B0'   DISP1:   CALL   BLK           ;space over
00AA'   7E                  LD     A,(HL)        ;get next memory byte
00AB'   CD 038E'            CALL   LBYTE         ;print it
00AE'   CD 037F'            CALL   HILO          ;inc pointer & see if done
00B1'   30 06               JR     NC,..D3       ;skip ahead if not done
00B3'   13                  INC    DE            ;else store end location
00B4'   ED 53 23F0          LD     (DISPO),DE    ;in DISPO
00B8'   C9                  RET                  ;and return
00B9'   7D         ..D3:    LD     A,L           ;end of line reached?
00BA'   E6 0F               AND    0F
00BC'   20 E9               JR     NZ,DISP1      ;no, print next byte
00BE'   18 E4               JR     DISPIT        ;yes, start new line
```

```
;————————————————————————————————————————
;
```

.comment¶ **FILL COMMAND** - fills a block of memory with a constant. For example,

F100,1C0,FF(cr)

fills memory locations 100H through 1C0H with 0FFH¶

```
;————————————————————————————————————————
;
```

00C0'	CD 0323'	FILL:	CALL	EXPR3	;get 3 parameters
00C3'	71	..F:	LD	(HL),C	;store the byte
00C4'	CD 037F'		CALL	HILO	;inc pointer and see if done
00C7'	30 FA		JR	NC,..F	
00C9'	D1		POP	DE	;restore stack
00CA'	C3 0029'		JP	START	;in case it got bombed

```
;————————————————————————————————————————
;
```

.comment¶   **GO COMMAND**   - allows a user to make the Z80 go to a program and start executing it. When this command is executed, the monitor takes all of the values in the register storage area (these may be displayed or modified using the X command), stuffs them in the proper registers, and then jumps to the requested program address.   For example,

G1000(cr)

causes the Z80 to jump to 1000H and start executing whatever code is there. In addition, one or two breakpoints may be set. For example,

G1000,1020,1230(cr)

transfers execution to 1000H, and IF the Z80 gets to address 1020H or 1230H, the program will stop execution and return to the monitor, printing an "@" sign followed by the address of the breakpoint that was reached (e.g. @1020H). It then prints the monitor prompt and awaits further instructions. All register contents at the time of the breakpoint are saved and may be examined using the X command. All previously set breakpoints are cancelled when any breakpoint is reached.

Breakpoints must be set only at locations corresponding to the first byte of an instruction. This is a software breakpoint system using the RST7 instruction.¶

```
;————————————————————————————————————————
;
```

00CD'	CD 03B2'	GOTO:	CALL	PCHK	;get next character
00D0'	38 40		JR	C,..G3	;go if (cr)
00D2'	28 10		JR	Z,..G0	;get breakpoint(s) if " ", ","
00D4'	CD 0372'		CALL	EXF	;else get rest of address
00D7'	D1		POP	DE	
00D8'	21 0034		LD	HL,PLOC	;find PC storage location
00DB'	39		ADD	HL,SP	;it's an offset from the SP
00DC'	72		LD	(HL),D	;store high byte of PC
00DD'	2B		DEC	HL	
00DE'	73		LD	(HL),E	;then low byte

```
00DF'  78                     LD    A,B              ;did address end with (cr)?
00E0'  FE 0D                  CP    CR
00E2'  28 2E                  JR    Z,..G3           ;yes, GO to address
00E4'  16 02      ..G0:       LD    D,2              ;2 breakpoints maximum
00E6'  21 0035                LD    HL,TLOC          ;point to trap storage
00E9'  39                     ADD   HL,SP
00EA'  E5         ..G1:       PUSH  HL               ;save the pointer
00EB'  CD 034B'               CALL  EXPR1            ;get a breakpoint address
00EE'  58                     LD    E,B              ;save delimiter
00EF'  C1                     POP   BC               ;get breakpoint in BC
00F0'  E1                     POP   HL               ;restore trap storage pointer
00F1'  78                     LD    A,B              ;look at trap address
00F2'  B1                     OR    C
00F3'  28 0A                  JR    Z,..G2           ;don't allow breakpoint at 0
00F5'  71                     LD    (HL),C           ;save bkpt addr in trap area
00F6'  23                     INC   HL
00F7'  70                     LD    (HL),B
00F8'  23                     INC   HL
00F9'  0A                     LD    A,(BC)           ;get instruction at breakpoint
00FA'  77                     LD    (HL),A           ;save that too
00FB'  23                     INC   HL
00FC'  3E FF                  LD    A,0FF            ;replace instruction with RST7
00FE'  02                     LD    (BC),A
00FF'  7B         ..G2:       LD    A,E              ;look at delimiter
0100'  FE 0D                  CP    CR
0102'  28 03                  JR    Z,..G2A          ;done if it's (cr)
0104'  15                     DEC   D                ;count # of breakpoints
0105'  20 E3                  JR    NZ,..G1          ;get one more if wanted
0107'  3E C3      ..G2A:      LD    A,0C3            ;set up jump instruction
0109'  32 23D3                LD    (RST7),A         ;at RST7 trap location
010C'  21 03FB'               LD    HL,RESTAR        ;to DEMON trap routine
010F'  22 23D4                LD    (RST7+1),HL
0112'  CD 031B'   ..G3:       CALL  CRLF
0115'  D1                     POP   DE               ;clear system return
0116'  21 0016                LD    HL,16            ;find exit routine up in stack
0119'  39                     ADD   HL,SP
011A'  E9                     JP    (HL)             ;go to it
```

;───

.comment¶   **LOAD COMMAND**   - loads machine language data into memory from a remote computer. The data must be sent by the remote computer in the format of the Demon "D" command, i.e. as two ASCII encoded hex digits per byte, preceeded by an ASCII space. The end of the data must be indicated by sending the monitor prompt character (a ">"). The load command expects only a starting address to be given. For example,

L2000(cr)

loads machine language data into memory starting at location 2000H until a ">" character is encountered. The remote computer must determine the number of bytes to be sent and insert a ">" after the last byte.¶

;───

```
011B'   CD 034B'   LOAD:    CALL   EXPR1       ;get load address in HL
011E'   E1                  POP    HL
011F'   06  00              LD     B,00        ;B=1 if previous char is space
0121'   CD 0141'   SYNC:    CALL   NYBBLE      ;get a char & convert to hex
0124'   D4 0133'            CALL   NC,BYTE     ;call BYTE if valid hex char
0127'   79                  LD     A,C         ;get back original ASCII char
0128'   FE 3E               CP     ">"         ;is it a prompt?
012A'   C8                  RET    Z           ;done if so
012B'   FE 20               CP     " "         ;check for a space
012D'   20 F2               JR     NZ,SYNC
012F'   06 01               LD     B,01        ;set B=1 if space
0131'   18 EE               JR     SYNC

0133'   05         BYTE:    DEC    B           ;do nothing if last char was
0134'   C0                  RET    NZ          ;not a space
0135'   07                  RLCA               ;rotate into high nibble
0136'   07                  RLCA
0137'   07                  RLCA
0138'   07                  RLCA
0139'   57                  LD     D,A
013A'   CD 0141'            CALL   NYBBLE      ;get 2nd hex character
013D'   B2                  OR     D           ;combine nibbles
013E'   77                  LD     (HL),A      ;store in memory
013F'   23                  INC    HL          ;advance pointer
0140'   C9                  RET

0141'   CD 02EC'   NYBBLE:  CALL   KI          ;get an ASCII character
0144'   4F                  LD     C,A         ;echo it
0145'   CD 02B2'            CALL   CO
0148'   C3 039D'            JP     NIBBLE      ;convert to hex
```

;————————————————————————————————————

.comment¶   **MOVE COMMAND** - moves a block of memory from one location to another. The command expects original start address, original end address, and destination start address as arguments. For example,

M2200,2280,1000

moves the contents of memory contained in the block 2200H through 2280H (inclusive) to 1000H through 1080H. If the original and destination memory blocks do not overlap, the original memory block is left undisturbed. However the two memory blocks can overlap with no ill effects. For example,

M2200,2275,2203

moves the contents of 2200H through 2275H up by three bytes in memory to 2203H through 2278H.¶

;————————————————————————————————————

```
014B'   CD 0323'   MOVE:    CALL   EXPR3       ;get start, end, destination
014E'   D5                  PUSH   DE          ;save end
014F'   E5                  PUSH   HL          ;save start
0150'   EB                  EX     DE,HL       ;calc. count=(end-start)
0151'   B7                  OR     A
0152'   ED 52               SBC    HL,DE
0154'   E5                  PUSH   HL          ;save count
```

```
0155'   EB                      EX      DE,HL
0156'   B7                      OR      A           ;is destination above start?
0157'   ED  42                  SBC     HL,BC       ;if so, go move
0159'   38  09                  JR      C,MOVEUP    ; end of block first
015B'   50          MOVDN:      LD      D,B         ;put destination in DE
015C'   59                      LD      E,C
015D'   C1                      POP     BC          ;count in BC
015E'   03                      INC     BC          ;include last pt in move
015F'   E1                      POP     HL          ;start in HL
0160'   ED  B0                  LDIR                ;do the move
0162'   C1                      POP     BC          ;adjust stack
0163'   C9                      RET
0164'   60          MOVEUP:     LD      H,B         ;put destination in HL
0165'   69                      LD      L,C
0166'   C1                      POP     BC          ;count in BC
0167'   09                      ADD     HL,BC       ;new end is dest.+count
0168'   EB                      EX      DE,HL       ;put new end in DE
0169'   03                      INC     BC          ;include last pt in move
016A'   E1                      POP     HL
016B'   E1                      POP     HL          ;put old end in HL
016C'   ED  B8                  LDDR                ;do the move
016E'   C9                      RET
```

;―――――――――――――――――――――――――――――

.comment¶   **QUERY I/O PORT COMMAND**   - allows one to output any value to an output port or to input a binary value from any input port. To do output, type "QO" followed by the port number and the desired value to output in hex. For example,

QO20,7F(cr)

outputs the value 7FH to output port 20H. To do input, simply type "QI" followed by the port number. Thus

QI20(cr)

inputs a byte from input port 20H. The input value is displayed in binary, i.e., if the value obtained from the input port was 45H, the display would show

QI20(cr) 01000101

    ¶
;―――――――――――――――――――――――――――――

```
016F'   CD  02F2'   QUERY:      CALL    TI          ;get next character
0172'   FE  4F                  CP      'O'
0174'   28  1C                  JR      Z,QU0       ;do output operation if "O"
0176'   FE  49                  CP      'I'         ;do input if "I"
0178'   C2  029A'               JP      NZ,ERROR    ;else it's an error
017B'   CD  034B'               CALL    EXPR1       ;get port number
017E'   C1                      POP     BC
017F'   ED  58                  IN      E,(C)       ;input from port
0181'   06  08      BITS:       LD      B,08        ;display 8 bits
0183'   CD  02B0'               CALL    BLK         ;space over
0186'   CB  23      ..Q2:       SLA     E           ;shift bit into CY
0188'   3E  18                  LD      A,'0' SHR 1 ;load "0" divided by 2
```

```
018A'   8F              ADC    A,A      ;make into "0" or "1"
018B'   4F              LD     C,A      ;print it
018C'   CD 02B2'        CALL   CO
018F'   10  F5          DJNZ   ..Q2
0191'   C9              RET
0192'   CD 034D'  QU0:  CALL   EXPR     ;get port number & value
0195'   D1              POP    DE
0196'   C1              POP    BC
0197'   ED 59           OUT    (C),E    ;output it
0199'   C9              RET
```

.comment¶   **SUBSTITUTE COMMAND**   - allows one to examine or modify memory on a byte by byte basis.   To execute the command, type "S" plus an address and then hit the space bar.   The system will respond by displaying the contents of memory at that address.   For example, typing S2000 followed by a space results in

S2000 00-

if the contents of location 2000H are 00.   Typing in a value nn at this point will change the contents of location 2000H to nnH, while hitting the space bar will leave the contents of that location alone and display the contents of the next higher location.   One can continue entering new values or hitting the space bar as long as desired.   The command is terminated by hitting carriage return.   For example,

S2000 00- 11-10 22- 33- 44-1210 55- 66-(cr)

would change locations 2001H and 2004H to 10 and leave the other locations unchanged.   Note that the keyboard input routine uses only the last two characters typed before the space bar is hit.   Thus in the above example, 12 was entered by mistake in location 2004H and then corrected by immediately typing 10 before the space bar was hit.   One 19also correct a mistake in the previous byte by pressing the backspace (©H or left arrow) key to re-display the preceeding byte.¶

```
019A'   CD 034B'  SUBS: CALL   EXPR1    ;get starting address
019D'   E1              POP    HL
019E'   7E        ..S0: LD     A,(HL)   ;get a byte from memory
019F'   CD 038E'        CALL   LBYTE    ;display it
01A2'   CD 03AD'        CALL   COPCK    ;modify it?
01A5'   D8              RET    C        ;no, all done
01A6'   28  0F          JR     Z,..S1   ;don't modify, skip ahead
01A8'   FE  08          CP     'H'-40   ;back up one byte?
01AA'   28  14          JR     Z,..S2   ;yes
01AC'   E5              PUSH   HL       ;else save pointer
01AD'   CD 0372'        CALL   EXF      ;get new value
01B0'   D1              POP    DE       ;value is in E
01B1'   E1              POP    HL       ;restore HL
01B2'   73              LD     (HL),E   ;modify memory
01B3'   78              LD     A,B      ;test for delimiter
```

```
01B4'   FE  0D                CP      CR
01B6'   C8                    RET     Z              ;done if (cr)
01B7'   23          ..S1:     INC     HL             ;next byte
01B8'   7D          ..S3:     LD      A,L            ;8 bytes on this line yet
01B9'   E6  07                AND     07
01BB'   CC  02AA'             CALL    Z,LFADR        ;yes, start new line
01BE'   18  DE                JR      ..S0
01C0'   2B          ..S2:     DEC     HL             ;decrement pointer
01C1'   18  F5                JR      ..S3           ;and print data there
```

;

.comment¶ **VERIFY COMMAND** - allows one to verify that the contents of one memory block are the same as the contents of another memory block. This is useful for checking that two copies of a program are identical and have not been changed, for example, by a crash of the system. The command expects the first block start and end addresses and the second block start address as arguments. For example,

V500,595,2000

compares the contents of memory from address 500H through 595H against the contents of memory from address 2000H through 2095H. Any differences will be shown on the display. Thus if location 527H was 00 while 2027H was FFH in the above example, the display would show

V500,595,2000
527 00 FF

assuming other locations in the two blocks were identical.¶

;

```
01C3'   CD  0323'  VERIFY:    CALL    EXPR3          ;get 3 parameters
01C6'   0A         VERIO:     LD      A,(BC)         ;compare 2 bytes
01C7'   BE                    CP      (HL)
01C8'   28  05                JR      Z,..B          ;skip ahead if they match
01CA'   C5                    PUSH    BC
01CB'   CD  01D5'             CALL    CERR           ;else print the error
01CE'   C1                    POP     BC
01CF'   03         ..B:       INC     BC             ;increment pointers
01D0'   CD  0379'             CALL    HILOX          ;and check for end
01D3'   18  F1                JR      VERIO
```

; This subroutine displays HL, (HL), and A

```
01D5'   47         CERR:      LD      B,A            ;save A
01D6'   CD  02AD'             CALL    HLSP           ;display H and L
01D9'   7E                    LD      A,(HL)         ;display (HL)
01DA'   CD  038E'             CALL    LBYTE
01DD'   CD  02B0'             CALL    BLK            ;space over
01E0'   78                    LD      A,B
01E1'   CD  038E'             CALL    LBYTE          ;display A
01E4'   C3  031B'             JP      CRLF
```

```
;
;
```

.comment¶   **EXAMINE COMMAND** - allows one to examine the contents of the Z80 registers after returning from a breakpoint or to modify the register values which will be used when the "G" command is executed. Typing

X(cr)

displays the contents of the main register set plus the "register" M=(HL), the program counter P, the stack pointer S, and the interrupt register I. Typing

X'(cr)

displays the contents of the alternate register set plus the two index registers and the refresh register R. Typing the letter X (or X') followed by a   specific register letter will display the contents of just that register. Entering a new value nn from the keyboard will enter a new value for the register. For example, entering XA when A=00 results in the display

XA 00-

If nn is now typed, A will have the new value nnH. If you do not want to modify the value, hit the space bar to display the next register or hit return to terminate the command.¶

```
;
```

```
01E7'  CD 02F2'   XAM:     CALL   TI          ;get next character
01EA'  21 046D'            LD     HL,ACTBL
01ED'  FE 0D               CP     CR          ;is it (cr)?
01EF'  28 5A               JR     Z,..X6      ;If so, display all registers
01F1'  FE 27               CP     "'"         ;is it a "'"?
01F3'  20 0A               JR     NZ,..X0
01F5'  21 0489'            LD     HL,PRMTB    ;Yep. get
01F8'  CD 02F2'            CALL   TI          ;next character
01FB'  FE 0D               CP     CR          ;If it's a (cr), go
01FD'  28 4C               JR     Z,..X6      ; display all primed registers
01FF'  BE         ..X0:    CP     (HL)        ;check register name
0200'  28 09               JR     Z,..X1      ;found it, skip ahead
0202'  CB 7E               BIT    7,(HL)      ;if end of table, no match:
0204'  C2 029A'            JP     NZ,ERROR    ; so must be error
0207'  23                  INC    HL          ;check next table entry
0208'  23                  INC    HL
0209'  18 F4               JR     ..X0
020B'  CD 02B0'   ..X1:    CALL   BLK         ;space over
020E'  23         ..X2:    INC    HL          ;get flag & bias byte
020F'  7E                  LD     A,(HL)
0210'  47                  LD     B,A         ;save copy of flags in B
0211'  E6 3F               AND    3F          ;clear flag bits to get bias
0213'  EB                  EX     DE,HL
0214'  6F                  LD     L,A         ;calculate displacement from
0215'  26 00               LD     H,0         ; SP
0217'  39                  ADD    HL,SP       ;add in SP value
0218'  EB                  EX     DE,HL
0219'  23                  INC    HL
021A'  1A                  LD     A,(DE)      ;pick up register value
```

021B'	CD 038E'		CALL	LBYTE	;print it
021E'	CB 78		BIT	7,B	;check flag bit
0220'	28 05		JR	Z,..X3	
0222'	1B		DEC	DE	;16 bit value if nonzero
0223'	1A		LD	A,(DE)	;get 2nd byte
0224'	CD 038E'		CALL	LBYTE	;print it
0227'	CD 03AD'	..X3:	CALL	COPCK	;print a "-" and get next char
022A'	D8		RET	C	;done if (cr) entered
022B'	28 19		JR	Z,..X5	;do next reg if " " or ","
022D'	E5		PUSH	HL	;else modify register value
022E'	C5		PUSH	BC	
022F'	CD 0372'		CALL	EXF	;get new value
0232'	E1		POP	HL	;put it in HL
0233'	F1		POP	AF	
0234'	C5		PUSH	BC	
0235'	F5		PUSH	AF	
0236'	7D		LD	A,L	
0237'	12		LD	(DE),A	;store new register value
0238'	C1		POP	BC	
0239'	CB 78		BIT	7,B	;is it 8 or 16 bits?
023B'	28 03		JR	Z,..X4	;skip ahead if 8 bits
023D'	13		INC	DE	;else store second byte
023E'	7C		LD	A,H	
023F'	12		LD	(DE),A	
0240'	C1	..X4:	POP	BC	
0241'	E1		POP	HL	
0242'	78		LD	A,B	;test delimiter
0243'	FE 0D		CP	CR	
0245'	C8		RET	Z	;all done if (cr)
0246'	CB 7E	..X5:	BIT	7,M	;end of table reached?
0248'	C0		RET	NZ	;return if so
0249'	18 C3		JR	..X2	
024B'	CD 031B'	..X6:	CALL	CRLF	;full register display code
024E'	CD 02B0'	..X7:	CALL	BLK	
0251'	7E		LD	A,(HL)	;get register name
0252'	23		INC	HL	
0253'	B7		OR	A	
0254'	F8		RET	M	
0255'	4F		LD	C,A	;print it
0256'	CD 02B2'		CALL	CO	
0259'	0E 3D		LD	C,"="	;print "="
025B'	CD 02B2'		CALL	CO	
025E'	7E		LD	A,(HL)	;get flag & bias byte
025F'	47		LD	B,A	;save flags
0260'	E6 3F		AND	3F	;clear flag bits to get bias
0262'	23		INC	HL	
0263'	EB		EX	DE,HL	
0264'	6F		LD	L,A	;calculate displacement
0265'	26 00		LD	H,0	
0267'	39		ADD	HL,SP	;add in SP value
0268'	EB		EX	DE,HL	
0269'	CB 70		BIT	6,B	;test for "M" register
026B'	20 0F		JR	NZ,..X9	;handle it separately
026D'	1A		LD	A,(DE)	;get register value
026E'	CD 038E'		CALL	LBYTE	;print it

```
0271'  CB 78            BIT   7,B        ;8 or 16 bit register?
0273'  28 D9            JR    Z,..X7     ;done if 8
0275'  1B               DEC   DE         ;else print second byte
0276'  1A               LD    A,(DE)
0277'  CD 038E'  ..X8:  CALL  LBYTE
027A'  18 D2            JR    ..X7
027C'  E5        ..X9:  PUSH  HL
027D'  1A               LD    A,(DE)     ;point HL at "M" register
027E'  67               LD    H,A        ; value
027F'  1B               DEC   DE
0280'  1A               LD    A,(DE)
0281'  6F               LD    L,A
0282'  7E               LD    A,(HL)     ;get the value
0283'  E1               POP   HL
0284'  18 F1            JR    ..X8       ;and print it
```

; Sign-on routine: B has length, HL points to message

```
0286'  21 03E4'  TOM:   LD    HL,SIGNON
0289'  4E        TOM1:  LD    C,(HL)     ;get a character
028A'  23               INC   HL         ;advance pointer
028B'  CD 02B2'         CALL  CO         ;output char
028E'  10 F9            DJNZ  TOM1       ;keep going till B=0
0290'  CD 02C4'         CALL  CSTS       ;see if key was pressed
0293'  C8               RET   Z
0294'  CD 02EC'         CALL  KI         ;if yes, get the char
0297'  FE 03            CP    "C"-40     ;abort if ©C
0299'  C0               RET   NZ
```

; El busto here

```
029A'  21 23CC   ERROR: LD    HL,MEMSIZ  ;get top of register
029D'  11 FFEA          LD    DE,-16     ; storage area
02A0'  19               ADD   HL,DE      ;add offset to find top of
02A1'  F9               LD    SP,HL      ;Zapple working stack
02A2'  0E 2A            LD    C,'*'      ;bungo! announce the bad
02A4'  CD 02B2'         CALL  CO         ; news
02A7'  C3 0029'         JP    START      ;and start over
```

; Miscellaneous print routines

```
02AA'  CD 031B'  LFADR: CALL  CRLF       ;print a CRLF and an address
02AD'  CD 0389'  HLSP:  CALL  LADR       ;print HL and a space
02B0'  0E 20     BLK:   LD    C,' '      ;print a space
```

;START OF SYSTEM DEPENDENT ROUTINES

;Console output, input, and status routines

```
02B2'   DB 21      CO:      IN      A,(STS)     ;is TxRDY flag high?
02B4'   CB 47               BIT     0,A
02B6'   28 FA               JR      Z,CO        ;no, check again
02B8'   79                  LD      A,C
02B9'   D3 20               OUT     (DATA),A    ;output char
02BB'   C9                  RET

02BC'   CD 02C4'   CI:      CALL    CSTS        ;is char waiting?
02BF'   28 FB               JR      Z,CI        ;no, check again
02C1'   DB 20               IN      A,(DATA)    ;input char
02C3'   C9                  RET

02C4'   DB 21      CSTS:    IN      A,(STS)     ;check modem input status
02C6'   CB 4F               BIT     1,A
02C8'   3E 00               LD      A,00        ;return zero if no char
02CA'   28 01               JR      Z,CSRET
02CC'   2F                  CPL                 ;return OFF otherwise
02CD'   B7         CSRET:   OR      A           ;set Z flag accordingly
02CE'   C9                  RET
```

; Initialize USART and keyboard interrupts

```
02CF'   3E BE      INIT:    LD      A,0BE       ;put 8251 in command mode
02D1'   D3 21               OUT     (STS),A
02D3'   3E 40               LD      A,40        ;reset it
02D5'   D3 21               OUT     (STS),A
02D7'   3E 4E               LD      A,4E        ;set 8 bits, no parity, one
02D9'   D3 21               OUT     (STS),A     ;stop bit, and 16X clock
02DB'   3E 37               LD      A,37        ;enable transmit and receive
02DD'   D3 21               OUT     (STS),A
02DF'   3E 04      INIT1:   LD      A,04        ;enable NMI int. by MON key
02E1'   D3 8C               OUT     (DIGLH),A
02E3'   3E 45               LD      A,45        ;set CTC to time out on a
02E5'   D3 86               OUT     (CTC2),A    ; -pulse into ch. 2
02E7'   3E 01               LD      A,01
02E9'   D3 86               OUT     (CTC2),A
02EB'   C9                  RET
```

;END OF SYSTEM DEPENDENT ROUTINES

; Keyboard input. TI ignores nulls, rubouts, and
;(cr)s. It also converts lower to upper case.

```
02EC'   CD 02BC'   KI:      CALL    CI          ;get a character
02EF'   E6 7F               AND     7F          ;mask off parity bit
02F1'   C9                  RET

02F2'   CD 02EC'   TI:      CALL    KI          ;get the character
02F5'   C8                  RET     Z           ;ignore nulls
02F6'   3C                  INC     A
02F7'   F8                  RET     M           ;and rubouts
```

02F8'	3D	DEC	A	
02F9'	FE 0D	CP	CR	
02FB'	C8	RET	Z	;and (cr)'s
02FC'	C5	PUSH	BC	
02FD'	4F	LD	C,A	;echo everything else
02FE'	CD 02B2'	CALL	CO	
0301'	79	LD	A,C	
0302'	C1	POP	BC	;restore BC
0303'	FE 40	CP	'A'-1	;done if char less than "A"
0305'	D8	RET	C	
0306'	FE 7B	CP	'z'+1	;or greater than "z"
0308'	D0	RET	NC	
0309'	CB AF	RES	5,A	;else convert lower case to
030B'	C9	RET		; upper case

; Convert hex to ASCII

030C'	E6 0F	CONV:	AND	0FH	;ensure a single hex digit
030E'	C6 90		ADD	A,90	;add 90H using BCD arithmetic
0310'	27		DAA		
0311'	CE 40		ADC	A,40	;then 40H plus CY
0313'	27		DAA		
0314'	4F		LD	C,A	;stick result in C
0315'	C9		RET		

; Get two parameters in DE and HL, then do (cr)(lf)

0316'	CD 034D'	EXLF:	CALL	EXPR	;get the values
0319'	D1		POP	DE	;second one goes in DE
031A'	E1		POP	HL	;first one in HL
031B'	E5	CRLF:	PUSH	HL	
031C'	06 04		LD	B,04	;output a carriage return,
031E'	CD 0286'		CALL	TOM	;a line feed, and 2 nulls
0321'	E1		POP	HL	
0322'	C9		RET		

; Get three parameters and do (cr)(lf)

0323'	0C	EXPR3:	INC	C	;set C for 3 parameters
0324'	CD 034D'		CALL	EXPR	;get 'em
0327'	CD 031B'		CALL	CRLF	
032A'	C1		POP	BC	;put last value in BC
032B'	D1		POP	DE	;second in DE
032C'	E1		POP	HL	;first one in HL
032D'	C9		RET		

; Get one parameter on the stack. Set carry clear if
; no value entered, and return delimiter in A

032E'	CD 02F2'	GET1:	CALL	TI	;get a character
0331'	FE 0D		CP	CR	;jump out if (cr)
0333'	28 10		JR	Z,ZEST	
0335'	FE 20		CP	' '	;or if space
0337'	28 0C		JR	Z,ZEST	
0339'	FE 2C		CP	','	;or if comma

```
033B'   28 08              JR      Z,ZEST
033D'   CD 0372'           CALL    EXF         ;get a parameter
0340'   E1                 POP     HL          ;pop it off stack
0341'   E3                 EX      (SP),HL     ;put back on stack
0342'   E5                 PUSH    HL          ;followed by return address
0343'   37                 SCF                 ;set CY flag
0344'   C9                 RET

0345'   21 0000    ZEST:   LD      HL,0        ;put zero on stack
0348'   E3                 EX      (SP),HL     ;followed by return address
0349'   E5                 PUSH    HL
034A'   C9                 RET

034B'   0E 01      EXPR1:  LD      C,01        ;get 1 parameter

                  ; Parameter entry handled here, only hexadecimal
                  ; allowed. Entering just a (cr) returns a 0000. C must
                  ; contain the number of parameters to enter.

034D'   21 0000    EXPR:   LD      HL,0        ;initialize HL to zero
0350'   CD 02F2'   EX0:    CALL    TI          ;get char from console
0353'   47         EX1:    LD      B,A         ;save it
0354'   CD 039D'           CALL    NIBBLE      ;convert ASCII to hex
0357'   38 08              JR      C,..EX2     ;jump out if not hex number
0359'   29                 ADD     HL,HL       ;shift HL one nibble left
035A'   29                 ADD     HL,HL
035B'   29                 ADD     HL,HL
035C'   29                 ADD     HL,HL
035D'   B5                 OR      L           ;OR in new character
035E'   6F                 LD      L,A
035F'   18 EF              JR      EX0
0361'   E3         ..EX2:  EX      (SP),HL     ;put value on stack
0362'   E5                 PUSH    HL          ;followed by return address
0363'   78                 LD      A,B         ;see if char is a delimiter
0364'   CD 03B5'           CALL    QCHK
0367'   30 02              JR      NC,..EX3    ;jump if not (cr)
0369'   0D                 DEC     C           ;if (cr) entered should have
036A'   C8                 RET     Z           ;C=0. done if so
036B'   C2 029A'   ..EX3:  JP      NZ,ERROR    ;else jump to ERROR
036E'   0D                 DEC     C           ;got enough parameters yet?
036F'   20 DC              JR      NZ,EXPR     ;no, go back for more
0371'   C9                 RET
0372'   0E 01      EXF:    LD      C,1         ;get one parameter
0374'   21 0000            LD      HL,0
0377'   18 DA              JR      EX1         ;with first char already in A

                  ; Range testing routines. CY set if range exceeded

0379'   CD 037F'   HILOX:  CALL    HILO        ;just return if no carry
037C'   D0                 RET     NC
037D'   D1                 POP     DE          ;return one level back if
037E'   C9                 RET                 ;CY set
037F'   23         HILO:   INC     HL          ;advance pointer
0380'   7C                 LD      A,H
0381'   B5                 OR      L
```

```
0382'   37              SCF                 ;return with CY set if HL=0
0383'   C8              RET     Z
0384'   7B              LD      A,E         ;compare HL with DE
0385'   95              SUB     L
0386'   7A              LD      A,D
0387'   9C              SBC     A,H         ;set CY if HL<DE
0388'   C9              RET
```

; Print routines

```
0389'   7C      LADR:   LD      A,H         ;display H and L on console
038A'   CD 038E'        CALL    LBYTE
038D'   7D              LD      A,L
038E'   F5      LBYTE:  PUSH    AF          ;print A in hex
038F'   0F              RRCA                ;put high nibble into low
0390'   0F              RRCA
0391'   0F              RRCA
0392'   0F              RRCA
0393'   CD 0397'        CALL    LB1         ;output it
0396'   F1              POP     AF          ;now do low nibble
0397'   CD 030C' LB1:   CALL    CONV        ;convert hex to ASCII
039A'   C3 02B2'        JP      CO          ;display on console
```

; Convert ASCII to hex. Set CY if non-hex input.

```
039D'   D6 30   NIBBLE: SUB     '0'
039F'   D8              RET     C           ;set CY if <0
03A0'   FE 17           CP      'G'-'0'     ;set CY if >F
03A2'   3F              CCF
03A3'   D8              RET     C
03A4'   FE 10           CP      10          ;if 0-9, reset CY and return
03A6'   3F              CCF
03A7'   D0              RET     NC
03A8'   D6 07           SUB     'A'-'9'-1   ;else adjust value
03AA'   FE 0A           CP      0A          ;set CY if : thru @
03AC'   C9              RET
```

; Check routines

```
03AD'   0E 2D   COPCK:  LD      C,'-'       ;output a "-"
03AF'   CD 02B2'        CALL    CO
03B2'   CD 02F2' PCHK:  CALL    TI          ;get a console character
03B5'   FE 20   QCHK:   CP      ' '         ;set Z flag if space
03B7'   C8              RET     Z
03B8'   FE 2C           CP      ','         ;set Z flag if comma
03BA'   C8              RET     Z
03BB'   FE 0D           CP      CR          ;set CY if (cr)
03BD'   37              SCF
03BE'   C8              RET     Z
03BF'   3F              CCF                 ;else return Z=0 and CY=0
03C0'   C9              RET
```

; This routine must run in RAM

```
03C1'   C1      EXIT:   POP     BC          ;throw out R and I reg. values
```

```
03C2'   FD E1              POP    IY            ;load index registers
03C4'   DD E1              POP    IX
03C6'   18  04             JR     SKIP
03C8'   00                 NOP                  ;SD System puts RST7 here
03C9'   00                 NOP                  ;deleting these NOP's requires
03CA'   00                 NOP                  ;changing all offsets in ACTBL
03CB'   00                 NOP
03CC'   F1        SKIP:    POP    AF            ;load alternate register set
03CD'   C1                 POP    BC
03CE'   D1                 POP    DE
03CF'   E1                 POP    HL
03D0'   08                 EX     AF,AF'        ;and then main registers
03D1'   D9                 EXX
03D2'   D1                 POP    DE
03D3'   C1                 POP    BC
03D4'   F1                 POP    AF
03D5'   E1                 POP    HL
03D6'   F9                 LD     SP,HL
03D7'   00                 NOP                  ;reserved for EI
03D8'   21  0000           LD     HL,0          ;user HL value stored here
03DB'   C3  0000           JP     0             ;user PC value stored here
03DE'   0000               DW     0000          ;storage area for 1st breakpt
03E0'   00                 DB     00            ;and instruction replaced
03E1'   0000               DW     0000          ;storage for 2nd breakpt
03E3'   00                 DB     00            ;and instruction replaced
                  ENDX:
```

; Signon message

```
03E4'   0D 0A 00 00 SIGNON: DB    CR,LF,00,00,00,"Demon Monitor V1.0"
0017              MSGL      EQU    $-SIGNON
```

; Restart. This is the breakpoint handling routine.

```
03FB'   E5        RESTAR:  PUSH   HL            ;temporarily save registers
03FC'   D5                 PUSH   DE
03FD'   C5                 PUSH   BC
03FE'   F5                 PUSH   AF
03FF'   21  23CC           LD     HL,MEMSIZ     ;set HL=top of
0402'   EB                 EX     DE,HL         ;register storage
0403'   21  000A           LD     HL,0A         ;calc. SP value at break
0406'   39                 ADD    HL,SP
0407'   06  04             LD     B,4
0409'   EB                 EX     DE,HL         ;and put in DE
040A'   2B        ..R0:    DEC    HL            ;store SP,AF,BC,DE
040B'   72                 LD     (HL),D        ;in register storage area
040C'   2B                 DEC    HL
040D'   73                 LD     (HL),E
040E'   D1                 POP    DE
040F'   10  F9             DJNZ   ..R0
0411'   C1                 POP    BC            ;get PC pushed by RST7
0412'   0B                 DEC    BC            ;adjust to value at break
0413'   F9                 LD     SP,HL         ;point SP at register storage
0414'   21  0025           LD     HL,TLOCX      ;and calc breakpt
0417'   39                 ADD    HL,SP         ; storage address
```

0418'	7E		LD	A,(HL)	;compare to PC value at break
0419'	91		SUB	C	
041A'	23		INC	HL	
041B'	20 04		JR	NZ,..R1	;jump to ..R1 if no match
041D'	7E		LD	A,(HL)	
041E'	90		SUB	B	
041F'	28 0C		JR	Z,..R3	;jump to ..R3 if match found
0421'	23	..R1:	INC	HL	;compare PC value to 2nd
0422'	23		INC	HL	; breakpoint
0423'	7E		LD	A,(HL)	
0424'	91		SUB	C	
0425'	20 05		JR	NZ,..R2	;jump to ..R2 if no match
0427'	23		INC	HL	
0428'	7E		LD	A,(HL)	
0429'	90		SUB	B	
042A'	28 01		JR	Z,..R3	;jump to ..R3 if match found
042C'	03	..R2:	INC	BC	;no match, re-adjust PC value
042D'	21 0020	..R3:	LD	HL,LLOCX	;calc HL storage
0430'	39		ADD	HL,SP	; address.
0431'	73		LD	(HL),E	;store HL value at break
0432'	23		INC	HL	;(its in DE)
0433'	72		LD	(HL),D	
0434'	23		INC	HL	
0435'	23		INC	HL	
0436'	71		LD	(HL),C	;and store PC value at break
0437'	23		INC	HL	
0438'	70		LD	(HL),B	
0439'	C5		PUSH	BC	
043A'	0E 40		LD	C,"@"	;print an "@" sign
043C'	CD 02B2'		CALL	CO	
043F'	E1		POP	HL	
0440'	CD 0389'		CALL	LADR	;followed by the break address
0443'	21 0025		LD	HL,TLOCX	;calc breakpt storage
0446'	39		ADD	HL,SP	; address
0447'	01 0200		LD	BC,200	;set C=00, B=loop counter
044A'	5E	..R4:	LD	E,(HL)	;get breakpt address in DE
044B'	71		LD	(HL),C	;and put 0000 in breakpt
044C'	23		INC	HL	; storage
044D'	56		LD	D,(HL)	
044E'	71		LD	(HL),C	
044F'	23		INC	HL	
0450'	7B		LD	A,E	;skip to ..R5 if no breakpt
0451'	B2		OR	D	;was stored
0452'	28 02		JR	Z,..R5	
0454'	7E		LD	A,(HL)	;else replace RST7 with
0455'	12		LD	(DE),A	; instruction byte
0456'	23	..R5:	INC	HL	
0457'	10 F1		DJNZ	..R4	;repeat for second breakpoint
0459'	08		EX	AF,AF'	
045A'	D9		EXX		
045B'	E5		PUSH	HL	;now save alternate register
045C'	D5		PUSH	DE	; set
045D'	C5		PUSH	BC	
045E'	F5		PUSH	AF	
045F'	DD E5		PUSH	IX	;and index registers

```
0461'   FD E5                   PUSH   IY
0463'   ED 57                   LD     A,I        ;and I and R
0465'   47                      LD     B,A
0466'   ED 5F                   LD     A,R
0468'   4F                      LD     C,A
0469'   C5                      PUSH   BC
046A'   C3 0029'                JP     START      ;all done, back to user prompt
```

```
                                ;Define register storage displacements from normal
                                ;stack location.
```

```
0034                            PLOC    EQU   34
0035                            TLOC    EQU   35
0025                            TLOCX   EQU   25
0020                            LLOCX   EQU   20
```

.comment¶ The following table is used to determine a valid register identifier and its displacement from the stack pointer. Each entry is two bytes long. The first byte is the register name. Bit 7 set indicates end of table. The second byte is an offset of the register storage location from the current storage location OR'ed with a two-bit flag:

```
                           00XXXXXX = 8 bit register
                           10XXXXXX = 16 bit register
                           11XXXXXX = special code for (HL) "register" ¶
```

```
046D'   41 15 42 13  ACTBL:   DB    "A",15,"B",13
0471'   43 12 44 11           DB    "C",12,"D",11
0475'   45 10 46 14           DB    "E",10,"F",14
0479'   48 31 4C 30           DB    "H",31,"L",30
047D'   4D F1                 DB    "M",31 OR 0C0
047F'   50 B4                 DB    "P",34 OR 80
0481'   53 97                 DB    "S",17 OR 80
0483'   49 03 80 00           DB    "I",03,80,00
0487'   00 00                 DB    00,00
0489'   41 09 42 0B  PRMTB:   DB    "A",09,"B",0B
048D'   43 0A 44 0D           DB    "C",0A,"D",0D
0491'   45 0C 46 08           DB    "E",0C,"F",08
0495'   48 0F 4C 0E           DB    "H",0F,"L",0E
0499'   4D CF                 DB    "M",0F OR 0C0
049B'   58 87                 DB    "X",07 OR 080
049D'   59 85                 DB    "Y",05 OR 080
049F'   52 02 80              DB    "R",02,80
```

```
                           END
```

Appendix E

Tiny Operating System

In this appendix a very small, but workable, operating system is given. The program provides only the bare minimum number of commands: examine memory, change memory, and jump to a user program. Nonetheless, the program illustrates in simple form some of the features that all operating systems have in common. See Sec. 2-9 for a discussion of how the tiny operating system works.

Note that the routines of App. F are required for this program to work with the Z80 Starter System. With a TRS-80, you should relocate the program to start at 4B00 and use the following external address and key values:

STKPTR	EQU	4BFF	;top of stack
MEMSTR	EQU	4C00	;start of free memory
NEXT	EQU	20	;space bar
MEMXAM	EQU	58	;X key
MON	EQU	4D	;M key
EXEC	EQU	47	;G key

Instead of KPDIN, use the TRS-80 KYBRD routine given at the end of this appendix, and instead of DISPLY given in the listing, use

```
DISPLY:  LD    A,(HL)
         JP    OUTPT
```

where the routine OUTPT is given at the end of Sec. 8-2.

```
              TITLE  TINY OPERATING SYSTEM  18-SEP-80
              .Z80
0000'         ASEG
0010          .RADIX    16          ;All constants are hexadecimal
              ORG       2200        ;Program ORiGin

              ; External addresses and key values

23A8          STKPTR  EQU   23A8    ;Top of stack location
2380          DISMEM  EQU   2380    ;Z80 Starter DISplay MEMory
2300          KPDIN   EQU   2300    ;Get next key, refresh display
2000          MEMSTR  EQU   2000    ;Memory start
0013          NEXT    EQU   13      ;Look at next location
0017          MEMXAM  EQU   17      ;Go into examine mode
0012          MON     EQU   12      ;Go into address change mode
0010          EXEC    EQU   10      ;Jump to (HL)
```

.comment ¶The tiny operating system begins here. After some initialization, a command dispatcher routine (COMMND) decodes command keystrokes and jumps to the appropriate routine. Only 4 command keys are recognized: NEXT, MEMXAM, MON, and EXEC. Any other command key produces a monitor restart.¶

```
2200  3A 23A8   TINYOS: LD    SP,STKPTR ;Set SP to top of stack
2203  21 1FFF           LD    HL,MEMSTR-1 ;Point to memory start-1
2206  3E 13             LD    A,NEXT    ;Set up to examine memory
2208  11 2208   COMMND: LD    DE,COMMND ;Push return address to
220B  D5                PUSH  DE        ;COMMND (routines RET here)
220C  FE 13             CP    NEXT      ;NEXT key?
220E  28 0D             JR    Z,NEXTX
2210  FE 17             CP    MEMXAM    ;MEMory eXAMine key?
2212  28 0D             JR    Z,MEMX
2214  FE 12             CP    MON       ;change MONitor address?
2216  28 11             JR    Z,CHGADR
2218  FE 10             CP    EXEC      ;EXECute key?
221A  20 E4             JR    NZ,TINYOS ;If not, restart monitor
221C  E9                JP    (HL)      ;Else go wherever user wants
```

; Increment memory address (pointed to by HL), display and
; modify its contents. Modification loop keeps shifting
; typed digits into right digit of memory byte until a
; command is typed.

```
221D  23        NEXTX:  INC   HL        ;Increment memory pointer
221E  CD 2238   XAM:    CALL  DISPLY    ;Display HL, (HL)
2221  CD 2300   MEMX:   CALL  KPDIN     ;Get next digit for (HL)
2224  D8                RET   C         ;Return for Commands
2225  ED 6F             RLD             ;Rotate digit into (HL)
2227  18 F5             JR    XAM       ;Loop
```

; CHanGe ADdRess routine: keeps shifting in typed digits
; from right side until command typed.

```
2229   CD 2300    CHGADR:  CALL   KPDIN      ;Get next digit for HL
222C   D8                  RET    C          ;Return for Commands
222D   29                  ADD    HL,HL      ;Shift HL left 4 bits
222E   29                  ADD    HL,HL
222F   29                  ADD    HL,HL
2230   29                  ADD    HL,HL
2231   B5                  OR     L          ;OR in new digit
2232   6F                  LD     L,A        ;Update HL
2233   CD 2238             CALL   DISPLY     ;Update display RAM
2236   18 F1               JR     CHGADR
```

; Routines to display memory address given by HL and the
; contents of that address, (HL).

```
2238   11 2380    DISPLY:  LD     DE,DISMEM  ;Point at display RAM
223B   7C                  LD     A,H        ;Display H first
223C   CD 2244             CALL   OUTA
223F   7D                  LD     A,L        ;Then L
2240   CD 2244             CALL   OUTA
2243   7E                  LD     A,(HL)     ;Finally (HL)

2244   4F         OUTA:    LD     C,A        ;Output A. Save A
2245   0F                  RRCA              ;Rotate left digit to right
2246   0F                  RRCA              ; position
2247   0F                  RRCA
2248   0F                  RRCA
2249   CD 224D             CALL   STORE      ;Store right digit
224C   79                  LD     A,C        ;Get original right digit back

224D   E6 0F      STORE:   AND    0F         ;Kill left digit
224F   12                  LD     (DE),A     ;Store digit
2250   13                  INC    DE         ;Inc. pointer for next CALL
2251   C9                  RET               ;RETurn for STORE, OUTA,
                                             ; and DISPLY
```

;TRS-80 KYBRD ROUTINE

```
                           ORG    4A50
4A50   CD 002B    KYBRD:   CALL   002B       ;use TRS-80 keyboard routine
4A53   B7                  OR     A
4A54   28 FA               JR     Z,KYBRD    ;loop till key pressed
4A56   FE 30               CP     "0"
4A58   D8                  RET    C          ;RET with CY set if <"0"
4A59   FE 47               CP     "G"
4A5B   3F                  CCF               ;or if >"F"
4A5C   D8                  RET    C
4A5D   D6 30               SUB    30         ;convert ASCII to hex
4A5F   FE 10               CP     10
4A61   3F                  CCF
4A62   D0                  RET    NC         ;RET with CY=0
4A63   D6 07               SUB    07         ;adjust if A-F
4A65   C9                  RET
```

END

Keyboard/Display Routines

This appendix provides keyboard input and seven-segment display subroutines for the SD Starter System computer. Three routines are given: KPDIN scans the keypad and returns the decoded key value, KYSTS checks whether a key has been pressed, and DISUP refreshes the seven-segment display. Sec. 3-7 discusses the hardware that these routines control. Equivalents of the subroutines are contained in the Starter System ROM, but they are not in subroutine form and hence are unavailable to user programs.

```
              TITLE    KEYPAD AND DISPLAY ROUTINES    3-DEC-80
              .Z80
0010          .RADIX   16              ;all numbers hexadecimal here
0000'         ASEG                     ;Absolute assembly starting
              ORG      2300            ; at 2300H

              ; I/O ports and external addresses

;0086         CTC2     EQU    86       ;CTC channel 2 used for MON
0088          SEGLH    EQU    88       ;7-SEGment LatcH port
008C          DIGLH    EQU    8C       ;DIGit 74LS273 LatcH
0090          KBSEL    EQU    90       ;KeyBoard column SELect port
064F          D20MS    EQU    064F     ;Delay 20 MSec routine
07A6          SEGPT    EQU    07A6     ;7-SEGment Pattern Table
07B9          KYTBL    EQU    07B9     ;KeYboard hash TaBLe
2380          DISMEM   EQU    2380     ;DISplay MEMory origin
;─────────────────────────────────────────────────────────────
;
```

comment ¶ **KEYBOARD INPUT:** gets a digit from Z80 Starter System keyboard. 0-0F are decoded as such. EXEC, SS, MON and NEXT have codes 10H thru 13H. REG', REG, PORT and MEM follow with 14H-17H. BP, PUNCH, LOAD and PROG follow with 18H-1BH. The display is refreshed using DISUP while waiting for input.

ON ENTRY: no arguments
RETURNS: keyboard digit in A. CY flag set if A>0F.¶

;───

2300	E5		KPDIN:	PUSH	HL	;Save most registers
2301	C5			PUSH	BC	;Prevent CTC from interrupt-
2302	3E	47		LD	A,47	; ing if MON, EXEC, SS, or
2304	D3	86		OUT	(CTC2),A	; NEXT are typed
2306	CD	2357	KEYDN:	CALL	DISUP	;Display digits in DISMEM.
2309	CD	2349		CALL	KPDSTS	;Check keyboard status. Z
230C	28	F8		JR	Z,KEYDN	;flag set means key pressed
230E	06	40		LD	B,40	;setup B to turn on one row
2310	CB	08	KEYDN2:	RRC	B	; of keys
2312	78			LD	A,B	
2313	D3	8C		OUT	(DIGLH),A	;turn row on
2315	DB	90		IN	A,(KBSEL)	;is a column low?
2317	E6	1F		AND	1F	
2319	FE	1F		CP	1F	;if not,
231B	28	F3		JR	Z,KEYDN2	;repeat for next row
231D	0E	00		LD	C,0	;Translate row bit position
231F	0D		KEYDN3:	DEC	C	;into a negative count
2320	CB	38		SRL	B	
2322	20	FB		JR	NZ,KEYDN3	
2324	CB	21		SLA	C	;Shift count into high nibble
2326	CB	21		SLA	C	;for KYTBL lookup. Each key
2328	CB	21		SLA	C	;gets unique value with this
232A	CB	21		SLA	C	;algorithm.
232C	81			ADD	A,C	;Add in column mask
232D	21	07B8		LD	HL,KYTBL-1	;Point at hash table - 1
2330	23		KEYDN4:	INC	HL	;Scan table for match
2331	04			INC	B	;B keeps the count
2332	BE			CP	(HL)	
2333	20	FB		JR	NZ,KEYDN4	
2335	05			DEC	B	;Now B has decoded key value
2336	CD	064F		CALL	D20MS	;Debounce keypad
2339	CD	2349	KEYDN5:	CALL	KPDSTS	;Wait till key is released
233C	20	FB		JR	NZ,KEYDN5	
233E	3E	01		LD	A,1	;Reenable MON interrupts
2340	D3	86		OUT	(CTC2),A	
2342	78			LD	A,B	
2343	C1			POP	BC	;Restore registers
2344	E1			POP	HL	
2345	FE	10		CP	10	;Command?
2347	3F			CCF		;Set CY if so
2348	C9			RET		

;───

.comment ¶**KEYBOARD STATUS**: Checks to see if a key is being pressed on the Starter System keypad.

ON ENTRY: no arguments

RETURNS: A=0 and Z flag set if no key is pressed. A≠0 and Z flag cleared if key is pressed.¶

;───

```
2349  3E  FF      KPDSTS:  LD    A,0FF         ;Turn off segment sources
234B  D3  88               OUT   (SEGLH),A
234D  3E  3F               LD    A,3F          ;See if a key is pressed
234F  D3  8C               OUT   (DIGLH),A     ;Check all rows at once
2351  DB  90               IN    A,(KBSEL)
2353  F6  E0               OR    0E0           ;Turn on noncolumn lines
2355  3C                   INC   A             ;If nothing pressed, all high
2356  C9                   RET                 ;So Z flag set if nothing
```

;

.comment ¶ **DISPLAY UPDATE** outputs the contents of locations DISMEM thru DISMEM+5 onto the Starter System's LED display. Each of the 6 digits is turned on once for 1 msec.

ON ENTRY: desired hexadecimal digits to display in DISMEM thru DISMEM+5

RETURNS: all registers unchanged

;

```
2357  E5          DISUP:   PUSH  HL            ;save all registers used
2358  D5                   PUSH  DE
2359  C5                   PUSH  BC
235A  F5                   PUSH  AF
235B  21  2380             LD    HL,DISMEM     ;Each bit on in B
235E  06  20               LD    B,20          ; turns a digit on
2360  AF          DISUP1:  XOR   A             ;first turn all digits off
2361  D3  8C               OUT   (DIGLH),A
2363  7E                   LD    A,(HL)        ;get a digit from DISMEM area
2364  11  07A6             LD    DE,SEGPT      ;DE = segment table
2367  83                   ADD   A,E           ;index into table
2368  5F                   LD    E,A
2369  1A                   LD    A,(DE)        ;get segment pattern
236A  D3  88               OUT   (SEGLH),A     ;and output it
236C  78                   LD    A,B           ;turn on the selected digit
236D  D3  8C               OUT   (DIGLH),A
236F  3E  7D               LD    A,7D          ;delay for 1 millisecond
2371  3D          DELAY:   DEC   A
2372  20  FD               JR    NZ,DELAY
2374  23                   INC   HL            ;point to next no.
2375  CB  38               SRL   B             ;shift bit to turn next digit on
2377  20  E7               JR    NZ,DISUP1     ;loop back if B not zero
2379  F1                   POP   AF            ;restore all registers
237A  C1                   POP   BC
237B  D1                   POP   DE
237C  E1                   POP   HL
237D  C9                   RET
```

END

Z80 Instruction Codes

This section presents the Z80 instruction op codes in alphabetical order along with machine codes for easy reference. Please see the Zilog Z80 CPU manual (among others) for a complete discussion of the codes. "d" below stands for a one-byte relative displacement (-80H up to 7FH), n stands for one byte (two hexadecimal digits) and nn for two bytes.

8E	ADC	A,(HL)		85	ADD	A,L
DD 8E d	ADC	A,(IX+d)		C6 n	ADD	A,n
FD 8E d	ADC	A,(IY+d)		09	ADD	HL,BC
8F	ADC	A,A		19	ADD	HL,DE
88	ADC	A,B		29	ADD	HL,HL
89	ADC	A,C		39	ADD	HL,SP
8A	ADC	A,D		DD 09	ADD	IX,BC
8B	ADC	A,E		DD 19	ADD	IX,DE
8C	ADC	A,H		DD 29	ADD	IX,IX
8D	ADC	A,L		DD 39	ADD	IX,SP
CE n	ADC	A,n		FD 09	ADD	IY,BC
ED 4A	ADC	HL,BC		FD 19	ADD	IY,DE
ED 5A	ADC	HL,DE		FD 29	ADD	IY,IY
ED 6A	ADC	HL,HL		FD 39	ADD	IY,SP
ED 7A	ADC	HL,SP		A6	AND	(HL)
86	ADD	A,(HL)		DD A6 d	AND	(IX+d)
DD 86 d	ADD	A,(IX+d)		FD A6 d	AND	(IY+d)
FD 86 d	ADD	A,(IY+d)		A7	AND	A
87	ADD	A,A		A0	AND	B
80	ADD	A,B		A1	AND	C
81	ADD	A,C		A2	AND	D
82	ADD	A,D		A3	AND	E
83	ADD	A,E		A4	AND	H
84	ADD	A,H		A5	AND	L

E6 n	AND	n		CB 6F	BIT	5,A
CB 46	BIT	0,(HL)		CB 68	BIT	5,B
DD CB d 46	BIT	0,(IX+d)		CB 69	BIT	5,C
FD CB d 46	BIT	0,(IY+d)		CB 6A	BIT	5,D
CB 47	BIT	0,A		CB 6B	BIT	5,E
CB 40	BIT	0,B		CB 6C	BIT	5,H
CB 41	BIT	0,C		CB 6D	BIT	5,L
CB 42	BIT	0,D		CB 76	BIT	6,(HL)
CB 43	BIT	0,E		DD CB d 76	BIT	6,(IX+d)
CB 44	BIT	0,H		FD CB d 76	BIT	6,(IY+d)
CB 45	BIT	0,L		CB 77	BIT	6,A
CB 4E	BIT	1,(HL)		CB 70	BIT	6,B
DD CB d 4E	BIT	1,(IX+d)		CB 71	BIT	6,C
FD CB d 4E	BIT	1,(IY+d)		CB 72	BIT	6,D
CB 4F	BIT	1,A		CB 73	BIT	6,E
CB 48	BIT	1,B		CB 74	BIT	6,H
CB 49	BIT	1,C		CB 75	BIT	6,L
CB 4A	BIT	1,D		CB 7E	BIT	7,(HL)
CB 4B	BIT	1,E		DD CB d 7E	BIT	7,(IX+d)
CB 4C	BIT	1,H		FD CB d 7E	BIT	7,(IY+d)
CB 4D	BIT	1,L		CB 7F	BIT	7,A
CB 56	BIT	2,(HL)		CB 78	BIT	7,B
DD CB d 56	BIT	2,(IX+d)		CB 79	BIT	7,C
FD CB d 56	BIT	2,(IY+d)		CB 7A	BIT	7,D
CB 57	BIT	2,A		CB 7B	BIT	7,E
CB 50	BIT	2,B		CB 7C	BIT	7,H
CB 51	BIT	2,C		CB 7D	BIT	7,L
CB 52	BIT	2,D		DC nn	CALL	C,nn
CB 53	BIT	2,E		FC nn	CALL	M,nn
CB 54	BIT	2,H		D4 nn	CALL	NC,nn
CB 55	BIT	2,L		CD nn	CALL	nn
CB 5E	BIT	3,(HL)		C4 nn	CALL	NZ,nn
DD CB d 5E	BIT	3,(IX+d)		F4 nn	CALL	P,nn
FD CB d 5E	BIT	3,(IY+d)		EC nn	CALL	PE,nn
CB 5F	BIT	3,A		E4 nn	CALL	PO,nn
CB 58	BIT	3,B		CC nn	CALL	Z,nn
CB 59	BIT	3,C		3F	CCF	
CB 5A	BIT	3,D		BE	CP	(HL)
CB 5B	BIT	3,E		DD BE d	CP	(IX+d)
CB 5C	BIT	3,H		FD BE d	CP	(IY+d)
CB 5D	BIT	3,L		BF	CP	A
CB 66	BIT	4,(HL)		B8	CP	B
DD CB d 66	BIT	4,(IX+d)		B9	CP	C
FD CB d 66	BIT	4,(IY+d)		BA	CP	D
CB 67	BIT	4,A		BB	CP	E
CB 60	BIT	4,B		BC	CP	H
CB 61	BIT	4,C		BD	CP	L
CB 62	BIT	4,D		FE n	CP	n
CB 63	BIT	4,E		ED A9	CPD	
CB 64	BIT	4,H		ED B9	CPDR	
CB 65	BIT	4,L		ED A1	CPI	
CB 6E	BIT	5,(HL)		ED B1	CPIR	
DD CB d 6E	BIT	5,(IX+d)		2F	CPL	
FD CB d 6E	BIT	5,(IY+d)		27	DAA	

35	DEC	(HL)		ED BA	INDR	
DD 35 d	DEC	(IX+d)		ED A2	INI	
FD 35 d	DEC	(IY+d)		ED B2	INIR	
3D	DEC	A		E9	JP	(HL)
05	DEC	B		DD E9	JP	(IX)
0B	DEC	BC		FD E9	JP	(IY)
0D	DEC	C		DA nn	JP	C,nn
15	DEC	D		FA nn	JP	M,nn
1B	DEC	DE		D2 nn	JP	NC,nn
1D	DEC	E		C3 nn	JP	nn
25	DEC	H		C2 nn	JP	NZ,nn
2B	DEC	HL		F2 nn	JP	P,nn
DD 2B	DEC	IX		EA nn	JP	PE,nn
FD 2B	DEC	IY		E2 nn	JP	PO,nn
2D	DEC	L		CA nn	JP	Z,nn
3B	DEC	SP		38 d	JR	C,d
F3	DI			18 d	JR	d
10 00	DJNZ	d		30 d	JR	NC,d
FB	EI			20 d	JR	NZ,d
E3	EX	(SP),HL		28 d	JR	Z,d
DD E3	EX	(SP),IX		02	LD	(BC),A
FD E3	EX	(SP),IY		12	LD	(DE),A
08	EX	AF,AF'		77	LD	(HL),A
EB	EX	DE,HL		70	LD	(HL),B
D9	EXX			71	LD	(HL),C
76	HALT			72	LD	(HL),D
ED 46	IM	0		73	LD	(HL),E
ED 56	IM	1		74	LD	(HL),H
ED 5E	IM	2		75	LD	(HL),L
ED 78	IN	A,(C)		36 n	LD	(HL),n
DB n	IN	A,(n)		DD 77 d	LD	(IX+d),A
ED 40	IN	B,(C)		DD 70 d	LD	(IX+d),B
ED 48	IN	C,(C)		DD 71 d	LD	(IX+d),C
ED 50	IN	D,(C)		DD 72 d	LD	(IX+d),D
ED 58	IN	E,(C)		DD 73 d	LD	(IX+d),E
ED 60	IN	H,(C)		DD 74 d	LD	(IX+d),H
ED 68	IN	L,(C)		DD 75 d	LD	(IX+d),L
34	INC	(HL)		DD 36 d n	LD	(IX+d),n
DD 34 d	INC	(IX+d)		FD 77 d	LD	(IY+d),A
FD 34 d	INC	(IY+d)		FD 70 d	LD	(IY+d),B
3C	INC	A		FD 71 d	LD	(IY+d),C
04	INC	B		FD 72 d	LD	(IY+d),D
03	INC	BC		FD 73 d	LD	(IY+d),E
0C	INC	C		FD 74 d	LD	(IY+d),H
14	INC	D		FD 75 d	LD	(IY+d),L
13	INC	DE		FD 36 d n	LD	(IY+d),n
1C	INC	E		32 nn	LD	(nn),A
24	INC	H		ED 43 nn	LD	(nn),BC
23	INC	HL		ED 53 nn	LD	(nn),DE
DD 23	INC	IX		22 nn	LD	(nn),HL
FD 23	INC	IY		DD 22 nn	LD	(nn),IX
2C	INC	L		FD 22 nn	LD	(nn),IY
33	INC	SP		ED 73 nn	LD	(nn),SP
ED AA	IND			0A	LD	A,(BC)

1A	LD	A,(DE)	5F	LD	E,A
7E	LD	A,(HL)	58	LD	E,B
DD 7E d	LD	A,(IX+d)	59	LD	E,C
FD 7E d	LD	A,(IY+d)	5A	LD	E,D
3A nn	LD	A,(nn)	5B	LD	E,E
7F	LD	A,A	5C	LD	E,H
78	LD	A,B	5D	LD	E,L
79	LD	A,C	1E n	LD	E,n
7A	LD	A,D	66	LD	H,(HL)
7B	LD	A,E	DD 66 d	LD	H,(IX+d)
7C	LD	A,H	FD 66 d	LD	H,(IY+d)
ED 57	LD	A,I	67	LD	H,A
7D	LD	A,L	60	LD	H,B
3E n	LD	A,n	61	LD	H,C
46	LD	B,(HL)	62	LD	H,D
DD 46 d	LD	B,(IX+d)	63	LD	H,E
FD 46 d	LD	B,(IY+d)	64	LD	H,H
47	LD	B,A	65	LD	H,L
40	LD	B,B	26 n	LD	H,n
41	LD	B,C	2A nn	LD	HL,(nn)
42	LD	B,D	21 nn	LD	HL,nn
43	LD	B,E	ED 47	LD	I,A
44	LD	B,H	DD 2A nn	LD	IX,(nn)
45	LD	B,L	DD 21 nn	LD	IX,nn
06 n	LD	B,n	FD 2A nn	LD	IY,(nn)
ED 4B nn	LD	BC,(nn)	FD 21 nn	LD	IY,nn
01 nn	LD	BC,nn	6E	LD	L,(HL)
4E	LD	C,(HL)	DD 6E d	LD	L,(IX+d)
DD 4E d	LD	C,(IX+d)	FD 6E d	LD	L,(IY+d)
FD 4E d	LD	C,(IY+d)	6F	LD	L,A
4F	LD	C,A	68	LD	L,B
48	LD	C,B	69	LD	L,C
49	LD	C,C	6A	LD	L,D
4A	LD	C,D	6B	LD	L,E
4B	LD	C,E	6C	LD	L,H
4C	LD	C,H	6D	LD	L,L
4D	LD	C,L	2E n	LD	L,n
0E n	LD	C,n	ED 7B nn	LD	SP,(nn)
56	LD	D,(HL)	F9	LD	SP,HL
DD 56 d	LD	D,(IX+d)	DD F9	LD	SP,IX
FD 56 d	LD	D,(IY+d)	FD F9	LD	SP,IY
57	LD	D,A	31 nn	LD	SP,nn
50	LD	D,B	ED A8	LDD	
51	LD	D,C	ED B8	LDDR	
52	LD	D,D	ED A0	LDI	
53	LD	D,E	ED B0	LDIR	
54	LD	D,H	ED 44	NEG	
55	LD	D,L	00	NOP	
16 n	LD	D,n	B6	OR	(HL)
ED 5B nn	LD	DE,(nn)	DD B6 d	OR	(IX+d)
11 nn	LD	DE,nn	FD B6 d	OR	(IY+d)
5E	LD	E,(HL)	B7	OR	A
DD 5E d	LD	E,(IX+d)	B0	OR	B
FD 5E d	LD	E,(IY+d)	B1	OR	C

B2	OR	D		CB 91	RES	2,C
B3	OR	E		CB 92	RES	2,D
B4	OR	H		CB 93	RES	2,E
B5	OR	L		CB 94	RES	2,H
F6 n	OR	n		CB 95	RES	2,L
ED BB	OTDR			CB 9E	RES	3,(HL)
ED B3	OTIR			DD CB d 9E	RES	3,(IX+d)
ED 79	OUT	(C),A		FD CB d 9E	RES	3,(IY+d)
ED 41	OUT	(C),B		CB 9F	RES	3,A
ED 49	OUT	(C),C		CB 98	RES	3,B
ED 51	OUT	(C),D		CB 99	RES	3,C
ED 59	OUT	(C),E		CB 9A	RES	3,D
ED 61	OUT	(C),H		CB 9B	RES	3,E
ED 69	OUT	(C),L		CB 9C	RES	3,H
D3 n	OUT	(n),A		CB 9D	RES	3,L
ED AB	OUTD			CB A6	RES	4,(HL)
ED A3	OUTI			DD CB d A6	RES	4,(IX+d)
F1	POP	AF		FD CB d A6	RES	4,(IY+d)
C1	POP	BC		CB A7	RES	4,A
D1	POP	DE		CB A0	RES	4,B
E1	POP	HL		CB A1	RES	4,C
DD E1	POP	IX		CB A2	RES	4,D
FD E1	POP	IY		CB A3	RES	4,E
F5	PUSH	AF		CB A4	RES	4,H
C5	PUSH	BC		CB A5	RES	4,L
D5	PUSH	DE		CB AE	RES	5,(HL)
E5	PUSH	HL		DD CB d AE	RES	5,(IX+d)
DD E5	PUSH	IX		FD CB d AE	RES	5,(IY+d)
FD E5	PUSH	IY		CB AF	RES	5,A
CB 86	RES	0,(HL)		CB A8	RES	5,B
DD CB d 86	RES	0,(IX+d)		CB A9	RES	5,C
FD CB d 86	RES	0,(IY+d)		CB AA	RES	5,D
CB 87	RES	0,A		CB AB	RES	5,E
CB 80	RES	0,B		CB AC	RES	5,H
CB 81	RES	0,C		CB AD	RES	5,L
CB 82	RES	0,D		CB B6	RES	6,(HL)
CB 83	RES	0,E		DD CB d B6	RES	6,(IX+d)
CB 84	RES	0,H		FD CB d B6	RES	6,(IY+d)
CB 85	RES	0,L		CB B7	RES	6,A
CB 8E	RES	1,(HL)		CB B0	RES	6,B
DD CB d 8E	RES	1,(IX+d)		CB B1	RES	6,C
FD CB d 8E	RES	1,(IY+d)		CB B2	RES	6,D
CB 8F	RES	1,A		CB B3	RES	6,E
CB 88	RES	1,B		CB B4	RES	6,H
CB 89	RES	1,C		CB B5	RES	6,L
CB 8A	RES	1,D		CB BE	RES	7,(HL)
CB 8B	RES	1,E		DD CB d BE	RES	7,(IX+d)
CB 8C	RES	1,H		FD CB d BE	RES	7,(IY+d)
CB 8D	RES	1,L		CB BF	RES	7,A
CB 96	RES	2,(HL)		CB B8	RES	7,B
DD CB d 96	RES	2,(IX+d)		CB B9	RES	7,C
FD CB d 96	RES	2,(IY+d)		CB BA	RES	7,D
CB 97	RES	2,A		CB BB	RES	7,E
CB 90	RES	2,B		CB BC	RES	7,H

CB BD	RES	7,L		CB 0C	RRC	H
C9	RET			CB 0D	RRC	L
D8	RET	C		0F	RRCA	
F8	RET	M		ED 67	RRD	
D0	RET	NC		C7	RST	0
C0	RET	NZ		D7	RST	10H
F0	RET	P		DF	RST	18H
E8	RET	PE		E7	RST	20H
E0	RET	PO		EF	RST	28H
C8	RET	Z		F7	RST	30H
ED 4D	RETI			FF	RST	38H
ED 45	RETN			CF	RST	8
CB 16	RL	(HL)		9E	SBC	A,(HL)
DD CB d 16	RL	(IX+d)		DD 9E d	SBC	A,(IX+d)
FD CB d 16	RL	(IY+d)		FD 9E d	SBC	A,(IY+d)
CB 17	RL	A		9F	SBC	A,A
CB 10	RL	B		98	SBC	A,B
CB 11	RL	C		99	SBC	A,C
CB 12	RL	D		9A	SBC	A,D
CB 13	RL	E		9B	SBC	A,E
CB 14	RL	H		9C	SBC	A,H
CB 15	RL	L		9D	SBC	A,L
17	RLA			DE n	SBC	A,n
CB 06	RLC	(HL)		ED 42	SBC	HL,BC
DD CB d 06	RLC	(IX+d)		ED 52	SBC	HL,DE
FD CB d 06	RLC	(IY+d)		ED 62	SBC	HL,HL
CB 07	RLC	A		ED 72	SBC	HL,SP
CB 00	RLC	B		37	SCF	
CB 01	RLC	C		CB C6	SET	0,(HL)
CB 02	RLC	D		DD CB d C6	SET	0,(IX+d)
CB 03	RLC	E		FD CB d C6	SET	0,(IY+d)
CB 04	RLC	H		CB C7	SET	0,A
CB 05	RLC	L		CB C0	SET	0,B
07	RLCA			CB C1	SET	0,C
ED 6F	RLD			CB C2	SET	0,D
CB 1E	RR	(HL)		CB C3	SET	0,E
DD CB d 1E	RR	(IX+d)		CB C4	SET	0,H
FD CB d 1E	RR	(IY+d)		CB C5	SET	0,L
CB 1F	RR	A		CB CE	SET	1,(HL)
CB 18	RR	B		DD CB d CE	SET	1,(IX+d)
CB 19	RR	C		FD CB d CE	SET	1,(IY+d)
CB 1A	RR	D		CB CF	SET	1,A
CB 1B	RR	E		CB C8	SET	1,B
CB 1C	RR	H		CB C9	SET	1,C
CB 1D	RR	L		CB CA	SET	1,D
1F	RRA			CB CB	SET	1,E
CB 0E	RRC	(HL)		CB CC	SET	1,H
DD CB d 0E	RRC	(IX+d)		CB CD	SET	1,L
FD CB d 0E	RRC	(IY+d)		CB D6	SET	2,(HL)
CB 0F	RRC	A		DD CB d D6	SET	2,(IX+d)
CB 08	RRC	B		FD CB d D6	SET	2,(IY+d)
CB 09	RRC	C		CB D7	SET	2,A
CB 0A	RRC	D		CB D0	SET	2,B
CB 0B	RRC	E		CB D1	SET	2,C

CB D2	SET	2,D		CB FD	SET	7,L
CB D3	SET	2,E		CB 26	SLA	(HL)
CB D4	SET	2,H		DD CB d 26	SLA	(IX+d)
CB D5	SET	2,L		FD CB d 26	SLA	(IY+d)
CB DE	SET	3,(HL)		CB 27	SLA	A
DD CB d DE	SET	3,(IX+d)		CB 20	SLA	B
FD CB d DE	SET	3,(IY+d)		CB 21	SLA	C
CB DF	SET	3,A		CB 22	SLA	D
CB D8	SET	3,B		CB 23	SLA	E
CB D9	SET	3,C		CB 24	SLA	H
CB DA	SET	3,D		CB 25	SLA	L
CB DB	SET	3,E		CB 2E	SRA	(HL)
CB DC	SET	3,H		DD CB d 2E	SRA	(IX+d)
CB DD	SET	3,L		FD CB d 2E	SRA	(IY+d)
CB E6	SET	4,(HL)		CB 2F	SRA	A
DD CB d E6	SET	4,(IX+d)		CB 28	SRA	B
FD CB d E6	SET	4,(IY+d)		CB 29	SRA	C
CB E7	SET	4,A		CB 2A	SRA	D
CB E0	SET	4,B		CB 2B	SRA	E
CB E1	SET	4,C		CB 2C	SRA	H
CB E2	SET	4,D		CB 2D	SRA	L
CB E3	SET	4,E		CB 3E	SRL	(HL)
CB E4	SET	4,H		DD CB d 3E	SRL	(IX+d)
CB E5	SET	4,L		FD CB d 3E	SRL	(IY+d)
CB EE	SET	5,(HL)		CB 3F	SRL	A
DD CB d EE	SET	5,(IX+d)		CB 38	SRL	B
FD CB d EE	SET	5,(IY+d)		CB 39	SRL	C
CB EF	SET	5,A		CB 3A	SRL	D
CB E8	SET	5,B		CB 3B	SRL	E
CB E9	SET	5,C		CB 3C	SRL	H
CB EA	SET	5,D		CB 3D	SRL	L
CB EB	SET	5,E		96	SUB	(HL)
CB EC	SET	5,H		DD 96 d	SUB	(IX+d)
CB ED	SET	5,L		FD 96 d	SUB	(IY+d)
CB F6	SET	6,(HL)		97	SUB	A
DD CB d F6	SET	6,(IX+d)		90	SUB	B
FD CB d F6	SET	6,(IY+d)		91	SUB	C
CB F7	SET	6,A		92	SUB	D
CB F0	SET	6,B		93	SUB	E
CB F1	SET	6,C		94	SUB	H
CB F2	SET	6,D		95	SUB	L
CB F3	SET	6,E		D6 n	SUB	n
CB F4	SET	6,H		AE	XOR	(HL)
CB F5	SET	6,L		DD AE d	XOR	(IX+d)
CB FE	SET	7,(HL)		FD AE d	XOR	(IY+d)
DD CB FE d	SET	7,(IX+d)		AF	XOR	A
FD CB FE d	SET	7,(IY+d)		A8	XOR	B
CB FF	SET	7,A		A9	XOR	C
CB F8	SET	7,B		AA	XOR	D
CB F9	SET	7,C		AB	XOR	E
CB FA	SET	7,D		AC	XOR	H
CB FB	SET	7,E		AD	XOR	L
CB FC	SET	7,H		EE n	XOR	n

Subject Index